Studies in the Social and Economic History of the Witwatersrand 1886–1914

Volume 1

New Babylon

By the same author

Chibaro: African Mine Labour in Southern Rhodesia, 1900–1933 (Ravan Press, Johannesburg, 1976)

Studies in the History of African Mine Labour in Colonial Zimbabwe (Mambo Press, Gwelo, 1978), with I. R. Phimister

Studies in the Social and Econmic History of the Witwatersrand, Volume 2, New Nineveh (Ravan Press, Johanesburg, 1982)

The photograph on the cover depicts the Hatherley Distillery, near Pretoria, taken shortly after its official opening in 1885. It is reproduced from S. Kemp, *Black Frontiers* (London, 1932).

Charles van Onselen

Studies in the Social and Economic History of the Witwatersrand 1886–1914

Volume 1

New Babylon

Ravan Press Johannesburg

Published by Ravan Press (Pty) Ltd.,
409–416 Dunwell, 35 Jorissen Street,
Braamfontein, Johannesburg 2001, South Africa

First impression 1982

ISBN 086975 210 3

Printed in Great Britain by
Butler & Tanner Ltd, Frome and London

We are grateful to the editors of *Review* and *History Workshop Journal* for permission to use material from earlier versions of two of the studies contained in this volume: 'The World the Mine Owners Made' (*Review*, 3, Fall 1979); and 'Randlords and Rotgut' (*History Workshop Journal*, 2, 2 Autumn 1976).

To Belinda, Gareth and Jessica

Ancient Nineveh and Babylon have been revived. Johannesburg is their twentieth century prototype. It is a city of unbridled squander and unfathomable squalor. Living is more costly than one's wildest dreams. All the necessaries of life are impudently dear. Miners of England and Australia, however poor may be your lot, however dark your present prospects, let no man tempt you to South Africa with tales of the wages that are paid upon the Rand! The wages are high indeed, but the price the workers pay for them is paid in suffering and blood.

A. Pratt, *The Real South Africa* (1913)

Contents

List of tables and illustrations ix
Abbreviations x
Preface xi
Introduction xv

An Overview

1 **The world the mine owners made: social themes in the economic transformation of the Witwatersrand, 1886–1914** 1

The foundations of economy and society on the Witwatersrand, 1886–1891 3

Deep-level economic demands for a new social order, 1892–1899 10

Reconstruction, mining hegemony and the social origins of the modern Witwatersrand, 1902–1914 24

Social Control

2 **Randlords and rotgut, 1886–1903** 44

The black worker as consumer – the rise of the liquor industry, 1881–1896 48

Stalemate – the black worker as worker and consumer. The Peruvian connection and the rise of the illicit liquor syndicates, 1897–1899 67

The black worker as worker – the spoils of a war fought for the mine owners, 1899–1903 88

3 **Prostitutes and proletarians, 1886–1914** 103

Heritage of the Cape – daughters of the old proletariat, 1886–1896 106

Gifts from the Old and New Worlds – the daughters of Europe, 1895–1899 109

Policies of pragmatism – British control of European women, 1902–1906 135

The Transvaal's own – daughters of the new proletariat, 1907–1914 143

The Geography of Class

4 **Johannesburg's Jehus, 1890–1914** 163

Urban transport under the dominance of a rural bourgeosie, 1889–1899 165

Urban transport under the hegemony of mining capitalism, 1900–1914 179

Index 204

List of tables and illustrations

Tables

1	Eerste Fabrieken Hatherley Distillery Ltd., profitability 1893–99	53
2	Imports of plain *Aguardente* through Lourenço Marques, 1894–1903	55
3	Brothels in central Johannesburg, by nationality, October 1895	112
4	Number of clients calling at the 'Sylvio Villa' brothel, 29 November 1897–12 December 1897	124
5	Johannesburg City and Suburban Tramway Co. Ltd., Financial Statement, 1891–98	168
6	Number of licensed cab drivers and cabs in Johannesburg, 1904–14	185

Maps

1	Pretoria and the Witwatersrand, c. 1905	25
2	Johannesburg's horse tramways	166

Photographs

1	Transport riders in the Market square Johannesburg, before the South African War	21
2	The staff at Hatherley Distillery Ltd., 1892	50
3	Joseph Silver at the time of his trial	127
4	Unnamed members of the American Club, Johannesburg – a court exhibit submitted during the trial of Joseph Silver, 1899	133
5	Johannesburg's horse-drawn tramway service – a Kruger concession	176
6	The electric tram introduced to Johannesburg in February 1906	194

Abbreviations

B.W.E.A.	British Women's Emigration Association
C.A.J.	Cabmen's Association of Johannesburg
C.D.U.	Cab Drivers' Union
E.D.N.L.A.	Employers' Domestic Native Labour Association
I.L.P.	Independent Labour Party
M.L.A.	Member of the Legislative Assembly
N.Z.A.S.M.	Netherlands South Africa Railway Company
R.U.I.C.	Rand Unemployed Investigation Committee
S.A.C.S.	South African Colonisation Society
S.A.E.C.	South African Expansion Committee
S. & D.N.	Standard and Diggers' News
S.L.C.	Special Liquor Committee
T.M.A.	Transvaal Miners' Association
W.L.V.A.	Witwatersrand Licensed Victuallers' Association
W.N.L.A.	Witwatersrand Native Labour Association
Y.M.C.A.	Young Men's Christian Association
Z.A.R.	Zuid Afrikaansche Republiek
Zarp	Zuid Afrikaansche Republiekeinsche Polisie

Preface

Ignorance has many virtues, amongst them the fact that it tends to produce a feeling of self-confidence which allows one to contemplate large projects with a sense of complete equanimity. In the early seventies I decided to undertake at least two studies based on the historical transformation of societies in south-central Africa engendered by the mineral discoveries of the late nineteenth century. The first of these would concentrate on the social experience of black workers at the point of production – more especially on the gold mines of Southern Rhodesia. The second would look at the experience of non-mining classes in a region which was nevertheless dominated by extractive industry – the Witwatersrand – and attempt to explore some of the wider world that the mine owners made.

In 1976 the first of these studies appeared as *Chibaro: African Mine Labour in Southern Rhodesia, 1900–1933*. The second, however, soon began to exceed the bounds of a single volume and now stands complete as *Studies in the Social and Economic History of the Witwatersrand, 1886–1914*. Unfortunately, *New Babylon* and *New Nineveh* have been some time in the making, and this can be partly accounted for by the fact that the task of writing and researching the work was undertaken over a period of six years in five different settings – Oxford, Geneva, London, New Haven and Johannesburg.

Throughout this period and at all of these places I have enjoyed the support of many colleagues and several institutions. Writing social history is both an expensive and an esoteric business and it needs a very special sort of body to fund a man who is, amongst other things, set on determining how many customers frequented a certain Johannesburg brothel during the course of a certain summer's evening in 1897. Amongst others who were willing to tolerate and even encourage such mindless enquiries, however, were the Institute of Commonwealth Studies at the University of London where I spent a happy year as a Junior Research Fellow in 1975. Even more felicitous and intellectually profitable were the three years which I spent as a Ford Foundation Research Fellow at a sister institution – the Centre of International and Area Studies at the University of London – between 1976 and 1979. In addition, I have profited from being attached as a Visiting Fellow to the South African Research Programme at Yale University during the fall term of 1978, and – since 1980 – from my research affiliation to the African Studies Institute at the University of the Witwatersrand.

Not all institutions, however, are willing to take so tolerant a view of social history or those who write it. Some, for reasons that are not always easy to understand, appear to be, if not obstructive, then at very least unduly defensive. Of such institutions which operate archival policies that are far more restrictive than those practised by most modern western governments, at least two deserve special mention – the Chamber of Mines of South Africa and Barlow Rand Ltd. Both these institutions take the view that the historical documents now in their possession constitute 'private' collections and that they are therefore at liberty to determine whom they will allow to have access to these archives. In a narrow legalistic sense there is undoubtedly considerable merit to this argument, but viewed from other perspectives it seems to be rather more open to question. Throughout the period under consideration in this study – 1890 to 1914 – the Chamber of Mines, and, to a lesser extent, Barlow Rand's predecessors, played an unashamedly public role in the making and shaping of South African society. Public actions in some measure engender public responsibilities and the mere passage of time does not transform them into private behaviour. It is all the more unfortunate therefore that serious professional researchers should, on a somewhat arbitrary or selective basis, be denied access to documents which could help to shed valuable light on a past which belongs to all South Africans.

But the world – even the world the mine owners made – has more to offer than frightened custodians of the past; it also has many helpful guides to the present who are more than willing to assist a historian who has, all too frequently, lost his way. In the course of negotiating several unfamiliar archival paths, for example, I have frequently received the generous help of specialists who either made copies of their own research material available to me, or else pointed me in the direction of more fruitful sources. I am most grateful for their assistance and I hope that they will not take it amiss if I do not list their names here. Fellow professionals will find their help acknowledged at the point where it often counts most – the footnotes.

This historian, however, is also perfectly capable of losing his way between the look-alike airports of Africa, Europe and the United States. Here again, it has been my good fortune to have many good friends who have not only lent me valuable support during the course of my research but who, through their warmth and hospitality, have given me time to recover my sense of social direction at several crucial moments. Their homes have been my homes and I am greatly indebted to Guerino and Cora Bozzoli, Peter Delius, Stanley Greenberg and Rosa DeLauro, Keith and Dixie Griffin, Bill Johnson and Anne Summers, Diana Phimister, Richard Rathbone and – especially – Barbara Trapido.

Four other people – Tim Couzens, Shula Marks, Ian Phimister and Stanley Trapido – have helped, encouraged and supported me in so many different and valuable ways that I find it difficult to thank them adequately. I consider myself to be singularly privileged to have had these model professionals not only as advisers and informed critics but as friends. If there is any merit in this work then it is largely as a result of their unstinted efforts.

All authors are aware, however, that books are never simply the product of one person's enterprise, and I am also acutely aware of the help that I have received from three other friends – Barbara Cowap, Wendy Cullinan and Georgina Relly. It is their efficiency that has enabled me to spend many more hours writing than would normally be possible, and their remarkable skill and accuracy which have provided the publishers with a superb manuscript. I would like to offer them my sincere thanks.

Writing does not come easily to me – something to which most of the people mentioned above can testify. I find it to be a slow, difficult and demanding task and the final product seldom pleases me for more than a day or two. My greatest debt of all, therefore, is to those who are closest to me and my work. Nobody could ask for more than I have asked from Belinda, Gareth and Jessica. They, more than anybody else, have shared in the making of this work and it rightly belongs to them. It comes with my deepest gratitude.

C. van Onselen
Johannesburg
July 1981

Introduction

Viewed from virtually any angle, the Witwatersrand, during the three breathless decades which separate the discovery of gold in 1886 from the outbreak of the First World War in 1914, constitutes something of an historian's dream. In a little less than thirty years, a republic founded on a modest agricultural economy was transformed into a colony boasting the world's largest and most technologically sophisticated gold-mining industry – a traumatic transition which was overseen by four different governments, punctuated by an attempted *coup*, and at one stage completely halted by a bloody conflict lasting two and a half years. Into this cauldron of capitalist development poured men, women and children drawn from all over the world, giving the Rand a cultural diversity and social texture that bubbled with excitement and vitality. And, as this new and remarkably complex industrial society was moulded, the entire process was recorded – often in a wealth of detail – in the annals of industry, government commissions of enquiry, the reports of municipal and state officials, the accounts of insiders and outsiders, and in any one of half a dozen newspapers.

Yet, for all its obvious appeal and vulnerability to imaginative attack, the social history of the Witwatersrand and that of its principal city, Johannesburg, has remained relatively intact. In the midst of an industrial revolution, timid historians – lamenting the absence of an indigenous aristocracy – have tip-toed through the tree-lined avenues of the northern suburbs, peering into the homes and lifestyles of the 'Randlords', attempting to put a romantic gloss on the ceaseless pursuit of wealth at a time when, elsewhere in the city, the dusty streets were bursting at the seams with a seething mass of struggling humanity. It is almost as if by concentrating exclusively on the exploits of a small number of ruling-class actors the people could be ignored, and the city would somehow be endowed with a mythical collective past which was more becoming to its present role as one of the major finance capitals of the world. Perhaps Herman Charles Bosman in his *A Cask of Jerepigo* had such historians in mind when he complained that:

> They are trying to make Johannesburg respectable. They are trying to make snobs out of us, making us forget who our ancestors were. They are trying to make us lose our sense of pride in the fact that our forebears were a lot of roughnecks who knew nothing about culture and who came here to look for gold.

Bosman, however, was far from pessimistic about the outcome of this process and he continued by pointing out that:

> We who are of Johannesburg, we know this spirit that is inside of us, and

> we do not resent the efforts that are being made to put a collar and tie on this city. Because we know that every so often, when things seem to be going very smoothly on the surface, something will stir in the raw depths of Johannesburg, like the awakening of an old and half-forgotten memory, and the brick-bats hurtling down Market street will be thrown with the same lack of accuracy as when the pioneers of the mining camp did the throwing.

Amongst other things, it is the social historian's duty to help stir the raw depths of the city in the hope that Market street might one day be restored to some of its former glory.

New Babylon, New Nineveh constitutes an extended and thematically linked exercise in historical materialism which seeks to set the experience of selected groups of ordinary people in Johannesburg within the wider context of the industrial revolution that engulfed the Witwatersrand at the turn of the century. By situating these groups within the emerging structures of the society and refracting their experiences through the process of class struggle, it seeks to demonstrate how, during these formative decades, the ruling classes gradually came to assert their control over the subordinate classes on the Rand and exercise a powerful influence over where they lived, how they spent their non-working hours, how domestic labour was allocated within their homes, and how they were to endure periods of unemployment. Hopefully, it represents not so much the grinding and grating of so many abstracted categories against the processes of history, as the analytically informed chronicle of the warm, vibrant and intensely human struggle of people seeking to find a place of dignity and security within a capitalist world that encroached on them all too quickly.

A large part of the course and nature of this struggle was ultimately determined by the changing economic imperatives of the mining industry, and by the mine owners' drive to accumulate capital during the series of spectacular booms and slumps which mark the period under examination. But, despite the industry's ever-growing strength, the mine owners did not always enjoy a free hand in their conflict with the subordinate classes; during the era of the Kruger Republic the state – through which this struggle was partly mediated – was, in the final analysis, dominated by an aspiring agricultural bourgeoisie. Much of *New Babylon, New Nineveh* is therefore concerned with charting the changing nature of the state between 1886 and 1914 – from one that gave preference to the accumulation of capital in the countryside before 1899, to one that came to favour the pursuit of profit by urban industrial enterprise after 1902 – and demonstrating how this, in turn, affected the lives of liquor sellers, prostitutes, cab drivers, washermen, domestic servants, transport riders, brickmakers and members of the working classes. In particular, this study attempts to pay some attention to the years immediately after the war, the so-called 'reconstruction period', during which the new governing class, largely freed from any direct electoral responsibility, replanned the Rand's principal city, and the state – during a crucial interlude – came to adopt an unashamedly instrumental role in shaping the future of an increasingly industrial society.

The resistance of the under classes to that shaping process – both at their places of employment and well beyond it – was at various times culturally informed, subtle, extensive and militant. Formal resistance, as expressed through petitions, deputations, demonstrations, marches and strikes, drew on strands as diverse as the English trade union tradition and Jewish experience of the Bund in Eastern Europe; while less formal resistance – but nonetheless well organised – as manifested in intimidatory displays, assaults or gang activities, could be influenced by aspects of Pedi youth culture, the Zulu regimental system, or the ethnic bonds uniting gangsters drawn from Manhattan's lower east side. But what was perhaps most impressive about this working class in the making was the manner in which its members borrowed, shared and adapted practices drawn from older settings and put them to work in the new environment. Cape 'Malay' cab drivers added their names in Arabic script to the petition of their Afrikaner counterparts addressed to President Kruger in the name of the 'working classes'; black washermen organised along Zulu military lines wearing turbans adopted from Asian *Dhobi* custom went on 'strike' when their livelihoods were threatened; while gangs of *Amalaita* 'houseboys' molesting white women in suburban streets took to wearing the red insignia of organised labour. In new Babylon the need to speak a common language – and to a limited extent even that came with the advent of *fanakalo* – was somewhat diminished as the social cement of class attempted to bond together the first generation of a new proletariat.

Finally, this study, in attempting to come to terms with the richness and complexity of the unfolding conflict on the Witwatersrand, and in trying to do justice to the simultaneous demands of both structure and process, has been inspired by the efforts of a remarkably talented group of scholars who have never ventured down the intellectual by-ways of Transvaal history. The influence which the works of Eugene Genovese, Herbert Gutman, Eric Hobsbawm, George Rudé, Gareth Stedman Jones and Edward Thompson have had on this author should nevertheless be very obvious to the more seasoned travellers in the fields of social history.

CHAPTER ONE

The world the mine owners made

Social themes in the economic transformation of the Witwatersrand, 1886–1914

> The struggle for wealth is at no time an edifying spectacle. Johannesburg has been a leaven in the land which has proved by no means an unmixed blessing to South Africa. The financial adventurer who has wandered to the Transvaal is not the type of man who would demonstrate the highest side of European civilisation to the Boers.
>
> Violet Markham, *Notes from a Travelling Diary*, 1899

In 1870 the first stirrings of a new giant in the area north of the Vaal river became apparent when alluvial gold was discovered in the Murchison range of the Zoutpansberg district. Three years later there were further rustlings when more alluvial gold was discovered at Pilgrim's Rest in the Lydenburg district, and a little more than a decade later still, in 1884, there was an even more significant movement when the first reef deposit was uncovered at Barberton in the eastern part of the country. A mere 24 months later, however, the giant sat up uneasily for the first time when the most substantial reef deposits yet were discovered on the Witwatersrand.

At first, few international observers took the slow-moving Transvaal mining industry particularly seriously – and why should they have? In 1886, the year that the Rand was discovered, the new industry produced only 0.16 per cent of the world's gold output and was still clearly dwarfed by its more formidable Australian and American rivals. By 1898, however, the new giant was already firmly on its feet, without serious challengers, and producing no less than 27 per cent of the world's gold. By 1913 the Witwatersrand mining colossus bestrode the economic world, producing no less than 40 per cent of the world's gold output. Highly visible from even the most far-flung of financial outposts, this imposing new profile of profit captured the attention and imagination of a whole generation of European capitalists. In 1890 the par value of capital invested in the Rand mining industry stood at 22 million pounds sterling, by 1899 it had reached 75 million pounds, and by 1914 it had climbed to a staggering 125 million pounds.[1]

This dramatic shift, as the Transvaal abruptly transferred its economic weight from its agricultural to its industrial leg over a brief period of thirty years, transformed the Witwatersrand and, in time, the whole of southern Africa. For a length of some 40 miles along the line of reef, from Springs in the east to Krugersdorp in the west, the accommodating ridges and depressions of the Witwatersrand became pock-marked with all the signs of an industrial revolution – mining headgear, ore dumps, battery stamps, reduction works, slimes dams and the frayed ends of railway lines. Besides, and in between these starker thickets of technology, the same revolution also spawned a series of urban sponges – the mining compounds and towns – that were called upon to absorb the ever-increasing numbers of black and white miners who made their way to the new goldfields at the turn of the century. And, in the midst of all of these developments, almost exactly half-way along the line of the reef outcrop, lay the social, political and economic nerve centre of the new order – Johannesburg.

Fathered by gold and mothered by money, Johannesburg's impatient and demanding parents scarcely allowed their charge time to pause in infancy or linger in adolescence before pushing it out onto the streets of the economic world. The tented diggers' camp of the eighties soon gave way to the corrugated iron structures of the mining town of the mid-nineties, and then to the more substantial brick buildings of an industrial city with suburban homes during the first decade of the twentieth century. By 1896 the 3,000 diggers of the original mining camp were lost in a town of 100,000 residents and, by 1914, these 100,000 were in turn becoming harder to find in a city with over a quarter of a million inhabitants. The inexorable pressure exerted by people, houses, shops, offices and factories pushed back the municipal boundaries from five square miles in 1898, to nine square miles in 1901, and then – more ambitiously still – to an enormous 82 square miles in 1903.

Given the company that the parents kept, it is scarcely surprising that the child lost its innocence at an early age. With white workers ranged against black, skilled miners against the mine owners and the Randlords against the state, Johannesburg was racked by class conflict during much of this period. By the outbreak of the First World War the city had been chosen as the centre of an unsuccessful attempted uprising against the government of the day, been occupied by the army of an invading Imperial power, and subjected to at least three bouts of such serious industrial unrest that troops had to be called in to help maintain order. It was these turbulent events, the city's cosmopolitan immigrant population and the all-consuming worship of wealth which, in 1910, prompted the visiting Australian journalist, Ambrose Pratt, to comment: 'Ancient Nineveh and Babylon have been revived. Johannesburg is their twentieth-century prototype. It is a city of unbridled squander and unfathomable squalor.'[2]

The new Babylon and new Nineveh which Pratt saw all too clearly in 1910, however, had already been 25 years in the making and, as in any other city, its complex economic, political and social structures had all been erected at their own distinctive pace. Indeed, what characterised much of Johannesburg's early growth was its markedly uneven development; something which in turn reflected how closely the city was pulsed by the changing profitability of the mining industry during its formative decades. Predictably, Johannesburg's periods of greatest economic growth tended to coincide with the most noticeable investment spurts in the mining industry – 1888–89, 1895 (the great 'Kaffir Boom'), 1899, 1902–03 and 1908–09. Politically, the most dramatic change in the fortunes of the Rand were undoubtedly occasioned by the South African War (1899–1902); whilst the periods of greatest social re-structuring appear to have taken place during the three major depressions that were interspersed between the booms in the mining industry – 1890–91, 1896–97, and 1906–08.[3]

But to separate out artifically the social, political and economic components to the city's historical development in this way ultimately conceals more than it reveals; since it is precisely the linkages between these strands that are of most interest to those who wish to understand how the mining industry – directly and indirectly – came to govern important aspects of life beyond the mine shafts. This chapter then, by way of an introduction, seeks to illustrate a few of the ways in which the world the mine owners made affected the lives of some of the ordinary people on the Witwatersrand between 1886 and 1914.

The foundations of economy and society on the Witwatersrand, 1886–1891

The initial discoveries of gold on the Rand were made along the length of the reef outcrop as it stretched from east to west in the series of rocky ridges which gave the region its name. Both the fact that the reef protruded at the surface along this line, and that the gold itself was held within the matrix of a more friable and weathered conglomerate in its upper reaches facilitated the first – and easiest – phase of the production process. Hundreds of small-scale, under-capitalised 'diggers' simply excavated rows of trenches from which the gold-bearing reef was relatively easily removed by pick and shovel. From there the ore was transported to the steam-driven stamps where it was crushed, after which it was amalgamated with quicksilver before being retorted to yield its gold. However, it was particularly during the two latter stages of the production process – milling and recovery – that the diggers and others were made to realise just what a mixed blessing the new goldfields constituted. For while the Rand gold deposits had the inestimable virtue of being extremely regular and reliable, they also had the vice of being of an exceptionally low grade. This meant, as one observer has noted, that: 'From its inception, mining development on the Rand was both labour and capital intensive. A large labour supply, elaborate machinery, and chemical works were required to profitably recover gold from the low grade ore.'[4]

In the very first flush of development, however, the importance of this harsh economic reality did not fully dawn on hundreds of diggers who were in any case perhaps more interested in the speculative gains that could be made from the buying and selling of small claims, than in the more rigorous demands of productive mining. But speculation of its own accord has a limited economic momentum, and within eighteen months of the fields being opened the infant industry made the first of its many demands for more substantial capital investment. The response to this cry for capital came in the boom of 1888–89 as several joint stock companies were floated – many of the more important ones drawing on the expertise and financial resources of capitalists who had earlier made their fortunes on the Kimberley diamond fields. This development, as small individual enterprises tended to give way to larger companies, heralded the decline of the digging community and in 1889 the Diggers' Committee gave way to the newly formed Chamber of Mines.

It was also during the latter stages of this first boom, and for a while thereafter, that a few of the more far-sighted mining financiers started systematically buying up land that was situated at some distance from – but parallel to – the original line of the reef outcrop. Quick to appreciate the significance of the fact that the reef dipped away steeply to the south, these astute investors realised that if shafts were sunk to the south of the existing diggings, then the gold-bearing reef would eventually be intersected at deeper levels. Thus throughout much of 1889 and 1890 larger companies such as H. Eckstein & Co. – later part of the powerful Wernher, Beit & Co. – moved to acquire that property which would in due course make deep-level mining a reality on the Rand.[5]

But no sooner had this important element in the long-term future of the industry been assured than the goldfields were struck by what seemed like a technological disaster. From mid-1889 producers discovered that gold-bearing reef drawn from below a depth of about 120 feet resisted amalgamation during the later stages of the recovery process. Whereas reef extracted from closer to the surface had had its gold freed by weathering and oxidisation, that drawn from lower down had its particles of the precious mineral firmly locked into the conglomerate by pyrite crystals:

> With no immediate solution at hand, yields of the producing mines declined sharply. This setback collapsed stock values and forced hundreds of companies to wind up. The crash ruined hundreds of small miners and promoters who sold off what assets they could. The buyers were larger operators with financial resources sufficient to ride out the fall, purchase additional mining ground cheaply, and invest in a solution to the refractory ores.[6]

This technologically triggered financial crisis might therefore have left the larger companies temporarily starved of investment capital, but it also left them poised for expansion when the first signs of economic recovery came. Those signs did not appear for at least two years, and throughout 1890 and 1891 the Witwatersrand and its principal mining town languished in a serious depression.

All of these events, the inital boom, the increasing hold of the mining companies, the purchase of the land to the south of the outcrop, and the subsequent slump, helped first to sketch, and later to fill out in bolder strokes, the outline of life in Johannesburg between 1886 and 1891; and, as might be expected, the earliest picture to emerge came almost as caricature. The discovery of gold and the boom that followed drew hundreds of diggers, miners, traders, adventurers, agents and speculators to a mining camp which, within months, gave way to a mining town loosely centred on the Market square. Throughout 1888–89 the market and its surrounding dusty streets filled with produce merchants, traders, shops, offices, banks, bars, saloons and canteens, formed the focal point for incoming transport riders as well as members of the digging community who were dependent on food and mining supplies brought into the geographically isolated South African Republic by ox waggon. The clamour set up by all of this human activity competed uneasily – and largely unsuccessfully – with the continuous din of the nearby mining machinery to produce a veritable cacophony of sound. It was only in 1890 and 1891, when many of the more vulnerable newcomers to the Rand had settled down into their less familiar roles as unemployed workers, billiard markers, barmen, skittle-alley attendants, vagrants, petty thieves and burglars during the depression, that both the tempo and volume of this noise abated somewhat.

Beyond the dust and noise of the mining town, however, there were already to be detected the outlines of a few striking features which, during the following decade and a half, did much to influence Johannesburg's social development. Of these, two are of particular importance to the more detailed studies which follow this introductory essay. First, it is worth noting how overwhelmingly male-dominated the town was throughout the period leading up to the South African War. Initially uncertain about the economic future of the goldfields, and later about their political fate as *uitlanders* under the Kruger regime, Johannesburg's immigrant miners were for many years extremely reluctant to commit their wives and children to a settled life on the Witwatersrand. This, together with the expense and difficulty of getting to the Transvaal before the rail link with the Cape was established in January 1893, meant that early Johannesburg was largely devoid of working-class family life. Thus, while a few of the wealthy mine owners and a section of the commercial middle class soon set up home on the Rand, the large majority of workers had to be content with considerably less – the skilled white miners from Cornwall, Cumberland and Lancashire taking up residence in the town's numerous 'boarding-houses', and the unskilled black workers from the Cape, the Transvaal and Mozambique being pushed into the repressive conformity of the mine compounds.[7]

Secondly, it is equally important to note the geographical distribution of these racially divided working-class institutions. The large majority of the Rand's boarding-houses were located either on the mining property itself, or in one of the town's two major working-class suburbs – Jeppe in the east and Fordsburg in the west. The mine compounds, which housed the black workers, were – without exception – situated on mining property. This meant that most working-class accommodation, like the line of reef which it followed, tended to extend along the east–west axis of the Witwatersrand. More significantly, however, it also meant that most workers – skilled and unskilled – lived close to the point of production, and that in early Johannesburg no great distance separated the place of residence from the place of work.

These clusters of workers, concentrated in the boarding-houses and mine compounds of the Witwatersrand, produced, reproduced and accentuated several elements of late-nineteenth century working-class culture – and, in the case of the white miners, elements of British male working-class culture in particular.[8] Drinking, gambling and whoring, which would probably have played an important part in the emerging working-class culture of the Rand in any case, became largely divorced from the broader mediating influences of family life, and thus assumed a central role in the lives of thousands of skilled and unskilled miners. This dependence of black and white workers on alcohol and prostitutes to lend some meaning to an otherwise alienated social existence was swiftly appreciated by the Transvaal ruling classes who, through a combination of strength and weakness, chance and design, came to operate a policy of social control which had its roots deeply embedded in the sociological realities of boarding-house and compound culture.[9] Put starkly, the Kruger government and the mine owners – sometimes acting jointly, and sometimes of their own accord – encouraged black workers to consume alcohol, and tolerated the recourse of white workers to prostitutes in order to safeguard the long-term accumulation of capital in the industrialising state.

As early as 1881, President Kruger took the first somewhat optimistic step towards industrialising the Transvaal when he granted a concession for the manufacture of alcohol from locally grown products to the Pretoria-based entrepreneur, A. H. Nellmapius. This venture, which two years later commenced production as *De Eerste Fabrieken in de Zuid Afrikaansche Republiek Ltd.*, initially experienced considerable difficulty in finding a market for the liquor manufactured from the agricultural surplus of Boer farmers. Once the Witwatersrand goldfields were discovered, however, the company's prospects were transformed overnight. In May 1889 it was noted of the distillery that, 'from a very modest beginning on a tentative scale, its success has become unprecedently rapid, and it is now developing itself into a great industry'.[10] Three years later, in 1892, De Eerste Fabrieken became a public company, and amongst the most prominent investors in the new venture were several of the Rand mine owners.

On the goldfields this growth of a 'great industry' in the countryside reflected itself in an explosion in the number of retail liquor outlets along the reef. The number of licensed canteens on the Witwatersrand rose from 147 in 1888 to 552 in 1892 – a threefold increase over a four-year period. To the delight of shareholders in what was by now the Hatherley Distillery, these canteens sold an ever-increasing quantity of cheap liquor to the Rand's thirsty miners during the following years. For some of the mine owners, however, this growth of the retail liquor trade proved to be a double delight. Mine owners with a financial interest in Hatherley could not only look forward to a handsome dividend from the distillery, but to the prospect of a more stabilised – if not more sober – black labour force since the many migrant workers who spent their wages in liquor saved less of their earnings than their more abstemious colleagues, and thus tended to labour underground for periods that were significantly longer than would otherwise have been the case. Thus, by 1892 the Randlords and the Kruger government were locked into a class alliance which, in rather different ways, was to the financial benefit of both the mine owners and Boer agricultural producers.

But if this class alliance on the question of the use and consumption of alcohol in the industrialising republic was consciously and aggressively fostered by the Randlords and the Kruger government, largely because of the direct profits which it could yield, then the same was not true of the more complex issue of prostitution. In the latter case, the official attitude of muted acceptance was gradually developed over a number of years, went largely unstated, and serviced the accumulation of capital in a more indirect way.

It was during the boom years of 1888 and 1889 that scores of prostitutes drawn from the southern African coastal regions first made their way inland to the new goldfields of the Witwatersrand. A few years later, and more particularly during 1892–93, these early arrivers were joined by a significant influx of 'coloured' prostitutes – women who had been driven north of the Vaal by the progressive implementation of the Contagious Diseases Act in several of the leading Cape Colony towns. Almost all of these pioneers of vice found themselves positions as 'barmaids' in the canteens, or else openly plied their trade from the 'rooms' to be found at the back of the more notorious drinking dens. In either case, however, their presence on the premises was welcomed by the liquor retailers who, through their powerful trade organisation, the Witwatersrand Licensed Victuallers' Association (W.L.V.A.), acknowledged the ability of these women to draw customers to their businesses. Thus, although the Johannesburg Sanitary Board had the power to initiate prosecutions, and although some government officials objected strongly to the social effects of this trade in vice, there was little – if any – official action taken against prostitutes during the late 1880s or the early 1890s. A government anxious to protect a liquor industry that benefited its most powerful constituents, and a mining industry that sought to attract and stabilise a working class on the Witwatersrand, between them had good reasons for condoning this conspicuous inactivity.

Both prostitution and drinking, therefore, partly grew out of the male culture that was rooted in the boarding-houses and the mine compounds. But the fact that most of the Rand's labouring population was collectively housed in institutions closely tied to the line of reef had effects that reached beyond these two elements of working-class culture. It also helped to shape the limited economic opportunities which existed outside the confines of the mining industry, and as such assumed some importance for those blacks and whites who were seeking ways of resisting entry into the working class as unskilled labourers. It is within the context of this wider struggle against proletarianisation that employment in the fields of domestic service, the construction industry and transport during the period 1886–91 has to be seen.

Right from the moment of its establishment, Johannesburg evinced a notable demand for domestic servants of all colours and of both sexes.[11] Much of the early demand for black male servants in particular, however, came from the relatively small number of middle and ruling-class families who considered a team of 'houseboys' to be part of their colonial birthright. This, together with the absence of white working-class households in any significant number, meant that while the demand for 'houseboys' within a certain narrow stratum of Rand society was always high, the overall size of the service sector for African males remained relatively small during these early years. While the majority of the Witwatersrand's skilled and semi-skilled white workers remained confined to the boarding-houses, the possibility of blacks seeking to avoid labour on the mines by obtaining positions as 'houseboys' remained limited.

There was one domestic service, however, which the hundreds of boarding-houses did not provide for the immigrant miners, and it was this unavoidable omission which created an alternative economic opportunity for certain blacks. Because the town lacked a major natural system of drainage which would allow for the ready removal of effluent, the Johannesburg

Sanitary Board for several years prohibited the washing of clothing in residential areas since it feared that slops tipped into the dusty streets would soon come to constitute a serious health hazard for the European community. This, and the absence of any steam laundries, meant that for some time the labouring men of the Witwatersrand were called upon to do their own laundry in one of the streams on the outskirts of the town – a tedious, time-consuming task which ate into the precious hours which the miners had set aside for their recreation.

From 1890 onwards, however, small groups of Zulu-speaking washermen – often drawn from the same rural areas in Natal which supplied the Rand with many of its 'houseboys' – established themselves on the banks of the Braamfontein *spruit* in the vicinity of Sans Souci. These hundred or two hundred turbanned men, who modelled themselves along the lines of the Hindu *Dhobi* or washermen's caste which they had seen at work on the East coast, soon dominated Johannesburg's hand-laundry business. Bound into an ethnically based organisation which in some respects resembled a medieval European craft guild, this association of *AmaWasha* quickly won formal recognition from the Sanitary Board, and its members did much to ease the domestic burden of the immigrant miners who were without recourse to the labour of their wives and daughters.

It was also largely because of this reason – the absence of the European miners' wives and children – that the demand for white working-class housing on the Rand during this period remained limited. But if the limited call for small family cottages had a marginally depressing effect on the construction industry, then it was more than compensated for by the demand for other types of structures as the mining camp started to give way to the mining town. The boom of 1888–89, in particular, saw the erection of a large number of shops, offices and workshops in addition to the many new structures of all types commissioned by the mining industry. All of this building activity occasioned a pronounced demand for bricks and it was this early need of the mining town which, as in the case of the laundry business, afforded yet another group of South Africans being pushed out of the countryside the chance of urban survival.

In late 1887 dozens of poor Afrikaner families – ex-*bywoners* who had either been driven off the land by natural disasters such as drought, or else who had become the early victims of the growing commercialisation of agriculture in the Transvaal hinterland – petitioned the State President for the right to manufacture bricks from the clay to be found on certain government land bordering the Braamfontein spruit to the south-west of the original mining camp. Kruger, aware of the difficulty which his unskilled countrymen experienced in obtaining employment of any kind in the mining industry, agreed to this request as a temporary measure which would in some way help to ease the plight of some of his most vulnerable burghers. The former bywoners, however, promptly built their homes on this property, and within months the site gave rise to a local industry of some importance as the landscape became dotted with clay diggings, puddle machines, kilns, stacks of drying bricks and scores of horses and carts. By the early 1890s, the Brickfields had started to assume an even more permanent aspect and became well known as a place of economic refuge for the Afrikaner poor.

It was during the course of this same search for a place of economic refuge that another group of burghers driven off the land found that they too could put some of their rurally acquired skills to good urban use. Shortly after the diggings were proclaimed, a few Afrikaners used what limited capital they had to acquire small hooded 'Cape carts' and horses, which they then proceeded to ply for hire in the town as cabs. Initially there was very little demand for such a cab service, not least because, as we have seen, the majority of the inhabitants lived close to their place of employment. But, as the mining town started to stretch out a little along its east–west axis, so first a modest and later a steady demand for cheap transport between the two outer suburbs and the inner business district developed. When the Johannesburg Cab Owners' Association was formed in January 1891, it attracted over eighty members – mostly Afrikaners, but also including amongst its numbers some 'Cape coloureds' and a few European immigrants.

By then, however, the long-term prospects of running a successful transport business in the promising mining town had already been thoroughly assessed by the ubiquitous A. H. Nellmapius.[12] Early in 1889, at the height of the first boom on the Rand, the Pretoria entrepreneur approached the Kruger government with a request for a concession which would entitle him to operate an animal-powered tramway service in Johannesburg for a period of thirty years. Here, as with the liquor concession, the State President and his closest advisers were much taken with the idea of an urban industrial development which could provide an important market for Boer farmers – in this case, forage, mules and horses. The government thus granted the concession, but Nellmapius, always hard-pressed for cash, almost immediately sold it to a Rand mining company owned by Sigmund Neumann, Carl Hanau and H. J. King.

A few months later, in September 1889, Neumann and his partners – all well-known men in local financial circles – floated the Johanesburg City & Suburban Tramway Co. Ltd. This venture, which its promoters believed would one day be allowed to operate a more profitable electric tramway system, attracted a considerable amount of speculative interest, and prominent investors included Porges & Co. – yet another forerunner of the powerful Wernher, Beit & Co. – and, in Europe, N.M. Rothschild & Sons. With its working capital readily secured, the company proceeded at once with the necessary survey and construction work, and in February 1891 the City & Suburban line which ran for a length of four and three-quarter miles along Commissioner street, between Jeppe in the east and Fordsburg in the west, was opened to the public.

A year marked by depression, however, 1891 was possibly not the most auspicious moment at which to commence operations, and at the end of the eleven months the shareholders in City & Suburban could look at a gross profit which amounted to very little more than £2,000. It was largely this dismal return on their capital and the inability to pay a dividend which, late in 1891, prompted the directors to approach Kruger with a request that the company be allowed to electrify its line. For reasons which Nellmapius would have understood a lot better than the subsequent concession holders, the government turned down this request – perhaps the first, but certainly not the last occasion on which Kruger thwarted the desire of Rand mining capitalists and international bankers for immediate profits in order to protect the longer-term interests of his agricultural producers.

But if the Z.A.R. government had shown its willingness to protect the interests of some of its more powerful supporters during a depression year, then it proved to be a lot less concerned about the economic fate of another – and more vulnerable – section of its constituency during the same year. The discovery of gold on the Witwatersrand had come as a major economic blessing to the country's transport riders; throughout the late eighties and the early nineties hundreds of burghers with limited capital and the requisite skills made a good, and at times even a lucrative living, by conveying mining supplies and foodstuffs between the coastal cities and the Transvaal. Indeed, so well did this business develop in the years before the railways reached the Rand that it caught the eye of the government as a potential source of revenue. Thus, in 1891, the State President persuaded a slightly reluctant *Volksraad* to impose a toll of thirty shillings on each waggon carrying loads of up to 6,000 lbs along the Republic's main roads. This measure, which would have been unpopular in the countryside at any time, must have aroused particular resentment during the depression and it was strongly resisted by the transport riders.

All of these occupations – transport rider, cab driver, brickmaker, washerman, 'houseboy', prostitute and liquor seller – point to an important sector of the rapidly emerging Rand economy which, although ultimately linked to the mining industry and its wider needs, could offer persons a living outside of the mainstream of the working class. Most of these positions, which depended on the deployment of a combination of unskilled or semi-skilled labour and a modest amount of capital, were filled by people drawn from within southern Africa, and most of the incumbents appear to have weathered the first really serious economic storm on the Witwatersrand. Admittedly, in 1890 the local press did complain about the activities of a gang of well-organised 'Zulu' burglars and it is possible that this was the first tell-tale sign of black unemployment which, a few years later, was to assume larger and even more organised proportions in the shape of *Umkosi Wezintaba* – 'The Regiment of the Hills'. But, in general, Africans and Afrikaners alike survived the depression of 1890–91 fairly well, and emerged relatively unscathed. The same, of course, was not true of those who were perhaps in the most vulnerable position of all – those who had only their labour to sell to a primary industry that was languishing in a trough of economic uncertainty: the skilled and semi-skilled immigrant miners drawn from the United Kingdom, Australia and elsewhere. It was these men who, throughout 1890, 1891 and a large part of 1892, were forced to turn to the most menial of casual labour or, where this proved to be unavailable, were made to suffer the pains of open unemployment. Above all other groups of workers on the Rand, it was the hundreds of unemployed miners who stood to gain most from a rapid recovery of the mining industry.

Deep-level economic demands for a new social order, 1892–1899

The financial crisis in the Rand mining industry brought about by the problems associated with the treatment of pyritic ore in 1889 meant that 'at a crucial time of moving into deep-level operations, the main source of funds for mining development began to dry up'.[13] From early 1890, therefore, the leading mining companies were called upon to deal with two major problems in order to secure their long-term viability – the one technical and the other financial. But, since the solutions to both of these problems were ultimately intertwined with the immediate need to restore investor confidence in the Rand, the mine owners could not afford to work on one to the neglect of the other and thus between 1890 and 1893 there was a significant re-marshalling of resources and a great burst of creative capitalist energy which ultimately helped to place the industry on a much firmer footing.

Late in 1890 sections of the mining industry started to experiment with an amalgamation and recovery technique which had first been developed and patented in Glasgow – the MacArthur-Forrest process. This technique, which relied on first dissolving the gold in a weak cyanide solution and then precipitating it with the aid of zinc metal shavings, immediately produced spectacular results. Whereas other methods of recovery retrieved between 60 and 80 per cent of the gold from crushed ore, the MacArthur-Forrest process yielded almost 90 per cent. This discovery – or at least its rediscovery and application on a larger scale in a new setting – not only ensured continued production, but provided the mines with bigger yields.[14]

Both the MacArthur-Forrest process and mining at deeper levels, however, called for new plant and equipment and thus exacerbated the mining companies' need for capital at a most unpropitious moment in the industry's history. Amongst the very first to appreciate the magnitude of this problem, and to take important steps towards its resolution, were the owners of the company that had earlier led the move to acquire deep-level properties – Wernher, Beit & Co. Between 1890 and 1892 Wernher, Beit & Co. rationalised their holding in such a manner as to allow them to make use of the immediate profits generated by their outcrop mines to provide operating subsidies for their deep-level mines which, they suspected, would in time yield even larger and more continuous profits.

The rationale underlying this highly successful tactic was further refined and extended when Wernher, Beit & Co. publicly launched Rand Mines Ltd. in 1893. This venture offered nervous investors the opportunity to buy their way into a portfolio of shares carefully spread between deep-level and outcrop mines, the chance to benefit from the advantages that would flow from the pooling of administrative resources, and the right to share in the profits that would flow from the efforts of a team of exceptionally talented mine managers. In these respects Rand Mines was 'the prototype of the group system which in the twentieth century was to become the financial mainstay of the South African mining industry'.[15] Not surprisingly, this development was soon emulated by a half-dozen or so of the other leading companies on the Rand and this in turn gave rise to a number of new mining houses – amongst them, Cecil Rhodes' and Charles Rudd's Consolidated Gold Fields of South Africa Ltd. In retrospect it can be seen that: 'The nine main gold mining groups in the 1890s all owed their origin, therefore, as much to the financial crisis associated with the collapse of the first great investment boom as to the financial exigencies of deep level mining.'[16]

Through the early nineties these two major developments – the success of the MacArthur-Forrest process on the one hand, and the emergence of the group system on the other – interacted in a mutually reinforcing way to breathe new life into the mining industry. The steadily returning confidence of 1893 gave way to a sharp upturn in share prices in late 1894, and by mid-1895 the Rand was enjoying an unparalleled boom. Several of the leading companies, including Wernher, Beit & Co. and Consolidated Gold Fields, made use of this exceptionally favourable financial climate to unload some of their less promising shares in outcrop mines onto the market, and to rationalise further their holdings. By late 1895 the major mining companies on the Rand were more committed to a future that was built around deep levels than ever before.

But despite the spectacular recovery of the stock market, many of the mine owners – and more particularly those who had staked their fortunes on the future profitability of the deep levels – had cause for growing concern by 1895. As the development of the deep levels accelerated through the mid-nineties, so it became increasingly apparent that deep-level mining entailed costs which differed significantly from those of outcrop mining. There were several reasons for this. First, deep-level mining necessitated the employment of a much larger pool of unskilled black labour – and at a cost which could only be reduced if the hard-pressed Z.A.R. administration was willing to assist the industry in the task of effectively disciplining and controlling its work force. Secondly, because of their geological nature, deep levels used far greater quantities of dynamite for rock-breaking operations than did outcrop mines. This problem was aggravated by the fact that the dynamite was supplied at a price through a company which enjoyed a monopoly – a feature which in turn could ultimately be attributed to Kruger's concessions policy. Thirdly, the cost of both coal and mining supplies was to an extent artificially inflated by another set of controversial government measures and this too tended to press harder on the deep-level mines than on the outcrops. Finally, the state's taxation policy – if not in principle, then at least in practice – tended to weigh more heavily on the deep-level than on the outcrop mines. Most of these economic grievances could in the final analysis be traced to political roots: 'The deep level capitalists and technical advisers argued that, with efficient government in the Transvaal, the cost of native labour and explosives and coal and imported supplies could be so sliced that the costs of production on the Rand could quickly fall by maybe 15 or 20 per cent.'[17]

Throughout the period 1893–95, as the leading companies continued to shift the balance of their investments from outcrop to deep-level mines, so the industry and its spokesmen – pushed by a growing sense of urgency – unsuccessfully sought to resolve these difficulties and other questions such as those surrounding the issue of the *bewaarplaatsen* by appealing to the Pretoria administration.[18] When the great 'Kaffir Boom' collapsed in September 1895, and the pioneer deep-level mine, the Geldenhuis Deep, failed to yield a profit two months later, several of the deep-level mine owners came to the conclusion that it was 'through the unkind economic environment which Kruger's policies had created' that 'the high profits which their bold investments would normally have won were being converted to losses'.[19] It was thus during the closing months of 1895 that the plans of Otto Beit, Lionel Phillips, George Farrar, John Hays Hammond and other mine owners meshed with the wider imperial ambitions of Cecil Rhodes, and the conspirators proceeded to invite Dr. Jameson to lead a military force to overthrow the Kruger government.

The Jameson Raid, which started out as a plot within the confines of smoke-filled rooms in the houses of high finance, ended as a low-level farce in the open veld near Krugersdorp. On the last day of December 1895 Jameson and his men surrendered to Boer forces and were marched to Pretoria where they and members of the instigating 'Reform Committee' were made to stand trial for the armed invasion of the Republic. The Raid, which had been meant to herald the advent of a new season of economic confidence in the mining industry and its future, had precisely the opposite effect – it rocked rather than rescued the Rand. The recession which had started in late 1895 soon deepened into a full-scale depression which lasted through 1896, 1897 and a large part of 1898.

What the Jameson Raid did manage to do, however, was to administer a severe political jolt to the Kruger government. The effect of this alone would probably have been enough to make the government reconsider its attitude towards the mining industry and its needs, but the emergence of a more compliant attitude on the part of the state was further facilitated by the ensuing depression. Between 1896 and 1898, the Kruger government made serious, consistent and determined efforts to improve the quality of its administration, and to accommodate the mine owners' steadily escalating demands for a new order which could more effectively nurture the growth of industrial capitalism. In some respects then the Jameson Raid marked an important turning point in the history of the Rand since, after that date, the Kruger state through its actions – hesitant, grudging and deeply suspicious as they were – slowly started to admit the mining industry to a more important role in the political economy of the Transvaal.

Perhaps one of the first signs of this new – albeit gradually emerging – attitude on the part of the Pretoria administration came in 1896 when the government, after discussions with the mining industry that dated back to March 1894, promulgated the Pass Regulations to facilitate the control of black workers on the Witwatersrand. Leading spokesmen for the industry were forced to concede that this was a 'good law', although they did express serious reservations about the manner in which it was being enforced.[20] More significant by far, however, was the important concession which the Kruger government made when it agreed to the appointment of an Industrial Commission of Enquiry to examine the grievances of the mining industry in 1897. This very professional team of investigators, which included representatives of the mining industry, produced a wide-ranging and penetrating report which was severely critical of the government's economic policies. Although Kruger and his colleagues could not be expected to act immediately upon all of these recommendations – some of which contained serious implications for the Republic and its allies – the government did, despite the rapidly deteriorating political situation, manage to modify certain aspects of the Gold Law, and to arrange for a 10 per cent reduction in the rates charged by the Netherlands South African Railway Company.

Moreover, it was not only the mining industry's narrower and more immediate economic demands which the state inched towards accommodating in the years leading up to the South African War. After the Jameson Raid the

Kruger government also took serious, and in some cases impressive steps, to meet the mine owners' ever-expanding demands for a social and political order that was more compatible with the wider needs of urban capitalism. From June 1898 the new State Attorney, J. C. Smuts, made vigorous efforts to reform and improve the quality of the police force on the Witwatersrand. As a result of these efforts the systematic theft of gold amalgam was partially checked, and – more importantly – the illicit sale of alcohol to black mineworkers was severely disrupted, so improving the efficiency of the industrial labour force. In August 1899 no less a person than Friedrich Eckstein, speaking on behalf of the mine owners at the monthly meeting of the Chamber of Mines, paid public tribute to the State Attorney and his Chief Detective for the success which they had enjoyed in suppressing the illicit liquor trade.[21]

Likewise, when militant unemployed white workers threatened to mount serious disturbances in Johannesburg during 1897, the government moved with 'commendable promptitude in regard to the question of relief to the indigent'.[22] Throughout late 1897 and most of 1898, the Pretoria administration – with the active and grateful assistance of the mine owners – helped to control urban unrest amongst the working classes in the principal city on the Witwatersrand. Finally, in yet another political concession, Kruger increased Johannesburg's powers of local government when he granted it municipal status in late 1897. Although still somewhat circumscribed by the requirement that half the members of the Town Council had to be burghers, this move – when set within the context of the political climate created by the mine owners and their powerful allies – can be seen as yet another gesture of reconciliation on the part of the Kruger government. When all of these actions are taken into account, it seems a little harsh to dismiss the government's policies towards the mining industry in the pre-war period as being simply those of 'neglect and obstruction'.[23]

By late 1898 a measure of confidence in the future of the Rand had been restored in public if not in private circles, and in 1899 there was a short spurt of investment in the mining industry. By then, however, the die had been cast and the Kruger government found itself ranged not only against the nervous and demanding mine owners, but against an increasingly interventionist British government which felt that its long-term imperial interests in southern Africa were seriously jeopardised by an independent Zuid Afrikaansche Republiek. In October 1899, after a political crisis which had lasted some months, Kruger's burghers found themselves pitted against the might of the British army in a conflict which, in the final analysis, hinged around gold and the future of the Republic's enormously profitable mining industry.[24]

In retrospect then, the period between 1892 and 1899 was one of crucial importance and severely fluctuating fortunes for the Witwatersrand and its inhabitants. The mining industry eased itself out of the slump of the early nineties to enjoy an unprecedented boom in 1895, only to have the deep-level mine owners overreach themselves in the Jameson Raid, and see the share market slide into a depression before speculative interest in the industry was once again briefly restored for a few months before the outbreak of the South African War.

This dramatic rise and fall in the economic tide over a period of seven years, however, constituted more than simply a cyclical movement from slump to boom and back to slump again. The depression of 1896–98, in particular, marked a structural shift of qualitative importance in the Rand's economy as a whole, and as such left a deep imprint on the lives of the ordinary people which we have been examining.

When De Eerste Fabrieken became the Hatherley Distillery in 1892 it put a partnership which had been developing between Boer agricultural producers and the mine owners ever since the opening of the goldfields onto a slightly more formal footing. Over the next three years, in particular, the Pretoria distillery produced an ever increasing quantity of cheap alcohol which the Rand's many canteen keepers readily sold to the mining industry's expanding black labour force. As the real costs of deep-level mining became increasingly apparent during the middle of the decade, however, so the mine owners started to have second thoughts about the wisdom of using alcohol as one of the primary means of attracting and stabilising their supply of cheap labour. By 1895 it was estimated that between 15 and 25 per cent of the black labour force was always unfit for work because of drunkenness and, as the Chamber of Mines pointed out in its report of that year, this meant that 'the scarcity of labour was intensified, as companies able to get them had to keep far more boys in their compounds than were required on any one day to make up for the number periodically disabled by drink'.[25]

This growing contradiction, where on the one hand the mine owners sought to use and profit directly and indirectly from the sale of alcohol to their black workers, and on the other they wished to reduce the cost and inefficiency of the labour force, became increasingly unmanageable as the deep-level mines approached the critical production stage. The leading mine owners accordingly shifted their stance from being in favour of the controlled use of alcohol in the years leading up to the 'Kaffir Boom' to the point where, shortly after the onset of the depression in 1896, they advocated the 'total prohibition' of the sale of alcohol to black mineworkers and others. When the Chamber of Mines informed the Pretoria administration of this change of policy and of its desire to have new legislation to meet it, it found members of the Volksraad to be divided over the issue. Whereas President Kruger and his closest supporters were strongly opposed to any move which would ultimately restrict the size of the market for Boer produce, others – including many of the 'progressives' who had serious reservations about the social and economic implications of the government's concessions policy – favoured the idea of 'total prohibition'. It was thus with some relief that the Chamber of Mines discovered that when Act No. 17 of 1896 was eventually passed by the Volksraad it contained a 'total prohibition' clause which would be put into effect on 1 January 1897.

The mine owners and their 'progressive' allies, however, soon found that 'total prohibition' had to contend with a formidable array of opponents which included, amongst others, the State President and his Executive Committee, the well-connected owners of Hatherley Distillery and the many members of the Witwatersrand Licensed Victuallers' Association. Throughout 1897 and the first half of 1898 these parties made vigorous but unsuccessful attempts to get the Volksraad to sanction a return to the *status quo ante*. But if 'total prohibition' continued to hold firm in theory throughout this 18-month period, in practice the law was breached on a massive scale. Large and well organised illicit liquor syndicates soon sprung up and through most of the 'prohibition' period East European immigrants – with the aid of a venal Z.A.R. police force – continued to supply black miners with enormous quantities of cheap imported potato spirits. 'Total prohibition' was 'total' in name only.

From mid-1898, however, this situation started to change and the illicit liquor dealers and their allies in uniform found themselves on the defensive. There were two related reasons for this. First, the Volksraad reaffirmed its adherence to the principle of 'total prohibition' and this time the State President appears to have accepted the majority sentiment without qualification. Secondly, in an attempt to co-opt some of his 'progressive' opposition and accommodate the desire for reform, Kruger appointed Smuts to the position of State Attorney. The new State Attorney and a young colleague, F. R. M. Cleaver, devoted their first months in office to the task of ridding Johannesburg's notorious police force of corruption. Thus, when an H. Eckstein & Co.-financed newspaper, the *Transvaal Leader*, appeared on the streets for the first time in 1899 with a well orchestrated demand for immediate action against the illicit liquor syndicates, the state was in a much better position to respond than it had been earlier. And, as we have seen, by the time that the war broke out even the mine owners were forced to acknowledge the Kruger government's achievement in this arena.

Unskilled black workers on the Witwatersrand during the 1890s therefore found themselves in the position where, before the deep-level mines went into production they were allowed – if not actually encouraged – to consume large quantities of alcohol, while after 1896 they were expected to exercise maximum restraint as the mine owners and the state sought to mould them into a more disciplined industrial labour force. The other major section of the working class, the skilled white immigrant miners, found that one of their major social outlets – recourse to prostitutes – experienced a broadly similar change in fortune over the latter half of the decade. But, for several reasons – not least of all the fact that prostitution and its associated effects cost the mining industry less than did alcohol – the Kruger government was left to tackle this task of reform on its own.

Between 1892 and 1894 Johannesburg's prostitutes were, for the most part, made up of women who hailed from the Cape Colony and who tended to ply their trade individually from the bars and canteens of the mining town. This comfortable local arrangement, however, was rudely interrupted by the explosive growth of the town during the 'Kaffir Boom' and by the rail links which the Rand developed with the east coast during the mid-nineties. In particular, the arrival of the railway line from Lourenço Marques in January 1895 did much to change this situation since it placed the Rand – via the cheap passages of the German East African Shipping Line – within convenient reach of several continental ports. Scores of French, German and Belgian prostitutes, who had previously competed for customers in the relatively stagnant northern markets of the older European cities, now turned their attention to the new and rapidly expanding towns generated by the South African industrial revolution. In addition, dozens of Russo-American women and their gangster pimps, for a rather different set of reasons, also chose to abandon New York City during the same period and make their way to the Rand. By 1896, then, the picture had changed dramatically, and

Johannesburg's prostitutes were largely 'continental women' who, with the aid of their pimps, openly solicited customers for the many brothels established in houses in the centre of town.

This burgeoning public trade in vice was to the immediate benefit of at least two parties in the town – the landlords, including 'men of repute, banking corporations and eminent firms' who derived inflated rents from letting properties to brothel-keepers, and retail liquor merchants who continued to benefit from the custom which prostitutes drew to the bars and canteens which they frequented.[26] In addition, the presence of prostitutes in such large numbers helped to make life on the Rand a little more bearable for single miners and, to the extent that it assisted in attracting and stabilising the industry's semi-skilled and skilled workers, it met with the tacit approval of the mine owners. Neither the mine owners nor any of their newspapers – neither of which were otherwise characterised by their reluctance to raise private or public questions about the moral well-being of sections of the working class – brought the issue of prostitution and its effects to the attention of the government, or embarked on any campaign to deal with organised vice in the mining town.

But not everybody in Johannesburg proved to be equally phlegmatic about these new developments. Several of Kruger's local officials, the non-propertied middle class, and more particularly the Rand's clergymen, were dismayed by the rapid spread of venereal disease, embarrassed by displays of public indecency, shocked by allegations of 'white slavery', and perfectly horrified to learn that some continental prostitutes were willing to accept black as well as white customers. From mid-1896, representatives of these groups put the Sanitary Board and the Pretoria administration under increasing pressure to draft legislation which would effectively destroy the 'social evil' on the Witwatersrand.

At first, however, neither the members of the Sanitary Board nor the State President and his Executive Committee were particularly anxious to take drastic steps against organised vice on the Rand – the former because they feared the political consequences of alienating powerful groups such as the landlords and the liquor merchants, and the latter because they were counselled about the naivety of simply attempting to legislate prostitution out of existence by some of Kruger's senior Dutch advisers who had first-hand experience of such matters in Holland. But, as the 'social evil' became more entrenched in Johannesburg and pressure on the government increased, the issue could no longer be avoided, and in 1897 as well as 1898 the Volksraad enacted new legislation to deal with the problem.

Both of these laws, however, remained a dead letter. An ambivalent attitude about the value of such legislation in the office of the Johannesburg Public Prosecutor, the systematic bribing of the Morality Police and – above all – the power and pervasive influence of the gang of former New York City pimps, ensured that organised prostitution on the Rand continued to thrive for some time after this legislation was passed. It was only after Smuts and Cleaver mounted a carefully planned counter-offensive against the leading gangsters involved in the vice trade that there was a significant improvement in the situation. By August 1899 the Kruger government had taken impressive strides towards its goal of reforming the police force and smashing the hold of organised crime on the Witwatersrand.

The continuing vitality of the trade in sex and alcohol through the largest part of the nineties, however, revealed to what extent the pre-war Rand remained characterised by the features which we cited earlier – the predominance of a male population and its accommodation in distinctive institutions situated relatively close to the points of production. While the 'Kaffir Boom' did undoubtedly help to swell the size of Johannesburg's middle class it failed to persuade most of the white migrant workers about the wisdom of bringing out their wives and children to settle on the Rand. Thus, while the boom did force the expanding white population to spill over into the suburbs immediately surrounding Jeppe and Fordsburg, the vast majority of white miners continued to be housed in boarding-houses while their black counterparts remained confined to the compounds. As before, these social realities did much to influence the size and shape of opportunities in the service sector of the local economy – and more especially so for domestic servants and the members of the washermen's guild.

The rapid expansion of Johannesburg after 1892 produced a swift and pronounced escalation in the demand for white servants – either as 'cooks-general' in middle or ruling-class homes, or as cooks or housemaids in hotels and boarding-houses. This demand which peaked during the 'Kaffir Boom', however, did not immediately fall off in the depression which followed the Raid, and by late 1896 there was still a considerable shortfall in the number of specialist servants available on the Rand. In an attempt to alleviate the labour shortage and at the same time engineer a fall in the high wages that it was forced to pay its existing employees, the 90 members affiliated to the Witwatersrand Boarding-House Keepers' Protection Association organised a campaign to import specialist servants from London during early 1897. This move, which was vigorously opposed by members of the Witwatersrand's Hotel Employees' Union, does not appear to have met with any great success.[27]

Denied the flow of imported labour which they would have preferred, the boarding-house keepers and other householders turned instead to substituting cheap unskilled black labour for more expensive semi-skilled white labour as the mid-decade depression deepened. After 1897 there was therefore an increase in the demand for 'houseboys' and, for a variety of reasons, most of these positions came to be filled by Zulu speakers drawn from neighbouring Natal. By 1899 there were several hundred 'houseboys' at work on the Rand who could look forward to an average monthly wage of eighty shillings – a sum which already contrasted sharply with the fifty shillings which black miners on average earned each month. Although the mine owners remained silent about this on the eve of war, in time it proved to be a development which met with the strong disapproval of the mining industry.

But if the prospects for the wage-earning 'houseboys' generally improved during the years between 1892 and 1899, then those of the self-employed Zulu washermen tended to fluctuate somewhat more dramatically. While the period started on a cheerful enough note for the AmaWasha as the guild's membership rose from about 500 in 1892 to over 1,200 in 1895, it ended on a distinctly gloomier one as their numbers again fell back to about 500 by 1899. This rise and decline in the fortunes of the guild, however, did more than merely reflect the dominant influence of the 'Kaffir

Boom' and the ensuing depression – it also marked an important structural change in the service sector of the local economy that could be traced back to certain developments that took place in 1895.

In 1895, at the height of the 'Kaffir Boom', the Witwatersrand's spring rains failed to materialise and during the drought that followed the Johannesburg Sanitary Board officials became alarmed at the dangerously low levels in the streams and 'pits' at the Zulu washing sites. In the interests of public health therefore, it was decided that the washermen should be removed to a new and more distant site on the farm 'Witbank' where they would be able to enjoy the use of a permanent and more abundant supply of clear water. This move, however, imposed a more taxing cost structure on the washermen's business and it was thus strongly opposed by most of the members of the guild. Eventually, after several unsuccessful appeals to the Sanitary Board and a week-long protest 'strike', the AmaWasha were forced to make the move to the new site in December 1896.

Neither the rapid growth in the number of washermen before this, nor the subsequent plan to have them permanently removed from the immediate vicinity of the town, escaped the attention of Johannesburg's leading financiers – including some of whom, like Otto Beit, had strong interests in the mining industry. In October 1895 the first of several companies to promote steam laundries was floated, and by April 1898 the town could boast a half-dozen such enterprises. Thus, by the time that the hapless Zulu washermen were eventually allowed to return to town in August 1897 – as a result of a series of lengthy legal battles fought largely on grounds of self-interest by the old site owners – they not only had to contend with the effects of the depression, but with the growing competition of the capitalist industries which had sprung up during their absence at Witbank.

In certain important respects the story of the Zulu washermen during this period was also the story of another group of the self-employed that we have been examining – Johannesburg's Afrikaner brickmakers. Between 1892 and 1895 both the brickmakers and the town's building contractors enjoyed the benefits of the upturn in the Rand's economy as the number of plans which the Sanitary Board approved for construction rose from 1,200 in 1894 to over 2,500 in 1895. By 1896 there were over 1,500 brickmakers and several thousand manual labourers of different races at work on the most important of the brickmaking sites on the banks of the Braamfontein spruit. Then, just at the moment that building activity in the town started to slacken off markedly after the Raid, the brickmakers were served with a final notice by the government to quit this central site in order to make way for a marshalling yard needed by the expanding Netherlands South Africa Railway Co. In July 1896, after a series of unsuccessful appeals to Kruger, the majority of the brickmakers reluctantly left Braamfontein and made their way to the alternative site which the government had provided them with on the farm 'Waterval', some six miles out of town.

As in the case of the washermen, this move imposed a new and more demanding cost structure on the brickmakers at a time when they were least able to defend themselves. The number of building plans approved by the Sanitary Board fell from 1,500 in 1896 to just over 1,000 in 1897, and then to a disastrously low 440 in 1898. In addition, the brickmakers – like the washermen – found that some of the mine owners were more than willing to move into the economic space which they had been forced to vacate. In 1896 H. Eckstein & Co. bought a controlling interest in the newly floated Johannesburg Brick and Potteries Co., and this highly mechanised modern industrial enterprise soon dominated the local market for bricks. Unlike the washermen, however, the small brickmakers were not allowed to re-occupy their old business sites at a later date, and this made their subsequent struggle against the developing hold of industrial capitalism even more difficult. Under the circumstances it was hardly surprising that there were hundreds of brickmakers amongst Johannesburg's unemployed between 1896 and 1898.

The fortune of many of the town's Afrikaner cab drivers during this period can be traced along the same economic graph which indicated gathering success during the early nineties followed by a sharp reversal in mid-decade. Between 1892 and 1895 most of Johannesburg's cabbies prospered as the arrival of the railways and the growth of the white population during the boom occasioned a greater demand for transport within the town. The cab owners, however, were not the only ones to detect this improvement and, in 1895, the owners of the City & Suburban Tramway Co. approached the Pretoria administration with yet another request that it be allowed to extend and electrify its lines on the Rand. The Kruger government again rejected this request – not so much because it wished to defend its urban cab-driving constituents against the advances of mining or industrial capitalism, but because it wished to protect the tramway company as an important market for the products of its more powerful rural constituents. Thwarted in its desire to electrify the system, the City & Suburban Co. decided instead to extend its horse-drawn lines by 25 per cent in 1896. As in the other cases we have been considering, this development came at a particularly bad time for the self-employed cab owners, who not only had to contend with the extended competition of a powerful company, but with the enormous rise in the prices of horses and forage after the rinderpest epidemic. Over a period of twelve months, four out of every ten cab drivers in the town were thrown out of work as the number of licensed cabbies in Johannesburg slumped from 1,200 in 1896 to 700 in 1897.

When the Afrikaner cab drivers and brickmakers made their way to the dole queues, however, they soon discovered that many of the places were already occupied by members of yet another group of formerly self-employed kinsmen – the transport riders. After the discovery of gold, the Kruger government made energetic efforts to provide the Witwatersrand with a set of rail links to the coast and by the mid-nineties several of these schemes had come to fruition. The arrival of the railway from the Cape in January 1893 was followed exactly two years later by the arrival of the line from Delagoa Bay in January 1895, and ten months later by the arrival of the line from Natal in October 1895. But, while the development of this capitalist infrastructure undoubtedly helped to fuel the spectacular growth of the 'Kaffir Boom', it spelt disaster for the geographically dispersed and badly organised transport riders who could only provide isolated instances of spontaneous resistance to the advent of steam transport north of the Vaal. It was the railway revolution of 1895, followed shortly thereafter by the rinderpest epidemic, that did most to render thousands of Afrikaner transport riders permanently unemployed and,

Transport riders in the Market square, Johannesburg, before the South African War

of these, several hundred found their way to Johannesburg's working-class suburbs of Fordsburg and Vrededorp.

Both the extent and the nature of this rapid build-up in the numbers of unemployed on the Rand took the Republic's ruling classes by complete surprise. While obviously aware of the depression and some of its social consequences, the government and the mine owners were initially of the opinion that most of the unemployment in Johannesburg was of a cyclical nature that derived from a temporary loss of financial confidence in the mining industry, and that most of those affected were thus single skilled immigrant miners who would be readily re-absorbed into the workforce once faith in the future of the Rand had been re-established. It was only after a series of menacing incidents and an unruly mass protest march in the centre of the town during the last quarter of 1897, that the Kruger administration and the mining companies became aware of the fact that much of the unemployment was structural in nature – that it derived from the first great spasm of capitalist development on the Witwatersrand and that many of the whites most badly affected were unskilled married Afrikaners who could not readily be absorbed into the working class.

Once this dimension of the problem was appreciated, however, the mine owners moved in quickly to control the situation. Within four days of the protest march during which a leading local journalist had narrowly escaped with his life, H. Eckstein & Co. announced its intention of taking on two hundred unskilled Afrikaners as surface workers on its mines. This gesture was soon followed by other mine owners, and within four weeks over five hundred Afrikaners had been found such positions in the industry. In addition, most of the large mining companies made generous cash donations to the Rand Relief Fund in an attempt to stem the rising tide of social tension within the town.

The Kruger government too, as we have seen, moved 'with commendable promptitude in regard to the question of relief to the indigent'. Within a week of the march it announced its intention of building an 'industrial school' to train the children of poor burghers, the setting up of a project to employ the workless women of Vrededorp in a public laundry, and a scheme to employ unskilled Afrikaner males on the construction of the Main Reef Road. While the first two of these schemes never came to fruition, the Pretoria administration did spend no less than £30,000 on the public works programme between early 1898 and late 1899. It was thus the employment generated by the Main Reef Road construction works that did most to ease class antagonism within the town, and the mine owners – sensing this – eased up on their contributions to Rand relief agencies after September 1898.

The economic crisis and structural unemployment of 1896–98, however, extended beyond the confines of Johannesburg's white working-class suburbs. Drought and rinderpest in the countryside pushed more blacks from neighbouring Natal onto the Rand labour market at precisely the moment that the mine owners were reducing wages and giving employment preference to the longer-working Shangaan labourers drawn from Mozambique. This, together with a marked decline in the demand for 'shop boys', 'messenger boys', *togt* workers and the collapse of employment opportunities in the washermen's guild and brickfields, meant that there was not only a general build-up in the level of black unemployment on the Rand during this period, but that much of it was 'Zulu' unemployment.

But, unlike the poor whites, unemployed blacks always found it difficult to linger in the urban areas, and this was particularly true after the pass laws had been promulgated in 1896. It was largely because of this that many of the 'Zulu' unemployed and some hardened criminals moved into the protective surroundings of the Klipriversberg to the immediate south of Johannesburg where, under the leadership of a remarkable man known as Jan Note, they were organised into a quasi-military body known as the 'Regiment of the Hills' or 'Ninevites'. This organisation, which contained within itself certain mutually contradictory elements, was partially fired by a sense of social justice while at the same time being involved in a series of profoundly anti-social activities. Its members, who saw themselves as being in a state of rebellion against the government's laws, lived largely by robbing passing migrant workers of their wages or from the proceeds of well-organised burglaries in the towns. By the outbreak of the war, when most of its members made their way back to Natal, the Regiment of the Hills had become a well-established feature of the Witwatersrand's criminal underworld.

Looking back then, it can be seen that the Witwatersrand and its inhabitants experienced a great lurch towards modern industrial society between 1892 and 1899, and that in general this was a movement which was facilitated rather than frustrated by the Kruger government. As H. J. and R. E. Simons have pointed out in a much-quoted passage:

> Few agrarian societies were so richly endowed or well equipped as the Transvaal for an industrial revolution. The republic attracted educated and professional men from Holland or the Cape, and was beginning to produce its own specialists. Left to itself it would have developed an efficient administration, a network of railways and roads, and adequate supplies of water and power. Far from being intractable, the burghers expanded production to provide foodstuffs for the Rand, built railways linking it to the ports, enacted an excellent mining code, kept order over unruly, rebellious fortune-hunters, repelled an armed imperialist invasion, and held the world's greatest military power at bay for more than two years.[28]

Neither the mine owners nor their powerful allies, however, were content either to accumulate capital at a pace that was dictated by a rural bourgeoisie, or to share more generously the proceeds of an industrial revolution with Boer agricultural producers. The war of 1899–1902 was not so much a dispute over the desirability of capitalism as a goal for the Transvaal, as a conflict between two competing bourgeoisies about the terms and paths along which it could best be sought.

Reconstruction, mining hegemony and the social origins of the modern Witwatersrand, 1902–1914

While the South African War severely disrupted the mining industry and caused indirect losses estimated at £25 million as capital lay in enforced idleness for many months, the Rand mine owners and investors had every reason to be optimistic once restrictions on mining operations were lifted in December 1901. Several administrative measures enacted by the British government, 'the most important of which were the reduction of railway rates and the adoption of a new duty on dynamite in the 1903 Customs Union Convention', initially helped to reduce the industry's average working costs.[29] This, together with a development loan of £35 million to the new Colony, did much to restore confidence in the future of the Rand and 1902–3 saw a significant spurt of investment in the mining industry.

But, as had happened at least once before in the history of the industry, Witwatersrand geology brought the European investment balloon back to earth just at the moment that it threatened to float away from economic reality. Soon after the war it became even more apparent than it had been in the late 1890s that the grade of ore recovered from the Rand mines fell off rapidly as the reef was pursued at ever greater depths.[30] At first, the effects of this were partially offset by selectively mining the higher-grade sections of the reef, but this short-term strategy did not offer any long-term solution to the problem. To make matters worse, this difficulty presented itself at a time when the industry was already being forced to contend with an acute shortage of cheap black labour.[31] This in turn tended to force up African wages and thus contributed substantially to an increase in the average working costs of the mines – a feature which became particularly noticeable after 1903.

Caught between a rapid falling off in the grade of ore being mined on the one hand and rising labour costs on the other, the post-war industry was soon confronted with a serious crisis of profitability. Normally, the way out of such a difficulty would have been for the producers to put up the price of their product and thus protect their profit margins. But, since gold was sold at a fixed price over fairly lengthy periods of time, the mine owners were denied this orthodox economic response. Instead, the mine owners countered in the only remaining way possible – they attempted to maximise output while minimising working costs.[32]

The programme to expand output took two related forms. First, the post-war industry mined gold 'at levels which increasingly approximated to the average grade of the deposits as a whole, rather than to the higher average grade of part of the deposits'.[33] This brought hitherto unexploited ground into production and widened the productive basis of the industry as a whole. Secondly, the mine owners introduced a series of technological innovations which greatly facilitated the programme of expanded production. Amongst these were the installation of tube mills, the extension of stamping capacity and the introduction of mechanised rock drills. Although some of these developments – notably the introduction of the rock drill – eroded the skills of the more highly paid white miners and thus contributed to the marked

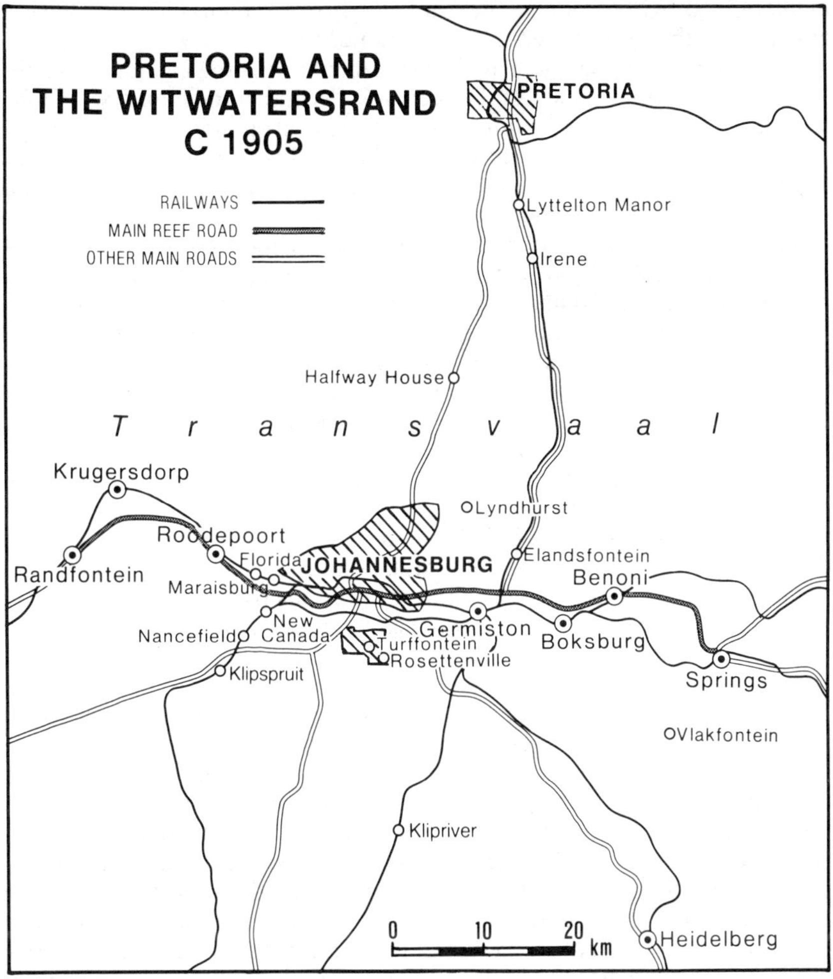

industrial conflict of this period, the programme as a whole was spectacularly successful and between 1901 and 1912 output rose at an average of 14.2 per cent per annum.

The attempt to minimise costs, however, proved to be far more difficult to manage. Apart from the few immediate post-war administrative successes noted above, and the economies of scale that flowed from a programme of expanded production, the mine owners at first had little to show for their efforts on this front. Despite the operation of the Witwatersrand Native Labour Association (W.N.L.A.), which the mine owners had specifically created to eliminate competition for unskilled labour within the industry and to hold down wages, the cost of African labour continued to rise alarmingly in the months after the signing of the Peace of Vereeniging. Early in 1903, therefore, the mine owners – with the active support of the post-war British administration – set out to explore new and radical ways of aiding the ailing industry and within twelve months the first of thousands of Chinese indentured labourers arrived on the Witwatersrand.

But not even the arrival of Chinese labourers in growing numbers after 1904 could immediately arrest the economic decline in the industry, and for several years the grade of ore mined continued to fall off more rapidly than did average working costs, thus exacerbating the industry's profitability crisis. Although the seriousness of this situation was to some extent masked by the tendency of the mine owners 'to distribute dividends in excess of figures justified by existing profit margins', most investors remained deeply sceptical and 'between 1902 and 1907 the market value of the shares of the 42 producing and dividend-paying companies on the Rand fell by over 50 per cent'.[34]

From about 1906, however, Chinese labour did help the industry to gradually recover its financial footing. The army of indentured labourers dramatically reduced the costly turnover of unskilled labour and enabled the industry to expand production at a crucial moment in its history. In addition, and at least as important, was the manner in which Chinese labour allowed the mine owners to undercut African labour, and after 1907 black wages in the industry declined in both real and monetary terms. All of this assisted the Rand in general, and the mines in particular, to recover from the serious economic depression of 1906–8, and in 1909 'almost as much foreign capital flowed into the mining industry as had come in in the previous three and a half years'.[35] After this turning point had been reached the policy of output maximisation and cost minimisation continued to gain momentum with increasingly beneficial results for the mine owners and their fellow investors. After a further round of industrial conflict in 1913–4, however, the mining industry found itself on the eve of yet another economic downturn.

While these booms and slumps in the fortunes of the mining industry did much to determine the pulse of economic life and the shape of society on the Witwatersrand between 1902 and 1914, not all of the fluctuations were of equal importance or significance. As in the pre-war era, it was the depression – this time of 1906–8 – that left the deepest imprint on the lives of those that we have been examining, and which most clearly marked the second great spasm of capitalist development on the Rand. But, unlike the Kruger era, this latter period was also characterised by radical political developments that were specifically designed to facilitate the emergence of a social infrastructure that was fully compatible with the needs of industrial capitalism.[36] And, of the three different governments that were responsible for the Transvaal between 1902 and 1914, it was the one that was free from any direct accountability to an electorate – the Milner administration – that intervened most directly to lay the foundations of modern industrial society on the Witwatersrand.[37]

When Johannesburg was fully re-opened to civilians in 1902 it immediately became the focus of attention for the Rand's working-class refugees whose financial resources had been exhausted by their prolonged and enforced stay at the coast.[38] Thousands of refugees, joined by hundreds of wartime immigrants, flooded back into the Rand's principal industrial city in a desperate scramble to find employment. The more fortunate of the skilled and semi-skilled male workers, aided by the early promise shown by the mining industry, succeeded in this search for jobs and quickly re-established themselves in their old quarters. But it was precisely this – the cautious re-entry of the majority of white workers into the Transvaal and their tendency to take up residence in boarding-houses, rather than in homes with their families – that initially caught the eye of politically sensitive observers, including one who was later to become British Prime Minister. In October 1902 James Ramsay Macdonald ventured the opinion that:

> President Kruger was perfectly right in refusing to recognise Johannesburg as a civic community which had settled into an organic part of the State. You have simply to walk through the wage-earning districts of the town to see the numerous working-class dining rooms; you have simply to try and find a workman at home in Johannesburg, to discover that his home is only a bedroom, which he generally shares with a fellow workman, and that family life – upon which the state is built – may be said hardly to exist amongst great sections of the population. Men rent beds, not houses, in the Golden City.[39]

Had this eminent working class sympathiser visited the compounds spread along the Reef he would have discovered an even more alienating and depressing absence of 'family life' amongst the black miners.[40]

Not all the white workers returning to the Rand, however, made their way to the boarding-houses or the mining companies' 'single quarters'. A significant minority of craftsmen and qualified artisans did indeed set up home in the more established working-class suburbs such as Jeppe, Troyeville, Belgravia and Fordsburg, thus contributing to a serious post-war housing crisis in a city that was already notoriously expensive to live in. At the other end of the scale, unskilled labourers and the unemployed – many of them Afrikaners – crowded into the lower end of Vrededorp or the 'Brickfields' where they contributed to a more threatening social problem. As the Commissioner of Police, E. M. Showers, reported in early 1902:

> These places are not laid out in any kind of order, and it is quite impossible to make any kind of arrangement for keeping any watch on the low class of people living in the place, or for an effective guard over the property of people living in the Town.[41]

Post-war Johannesburg thus began to re-assert two of the features which had characterised it in earlier periods – a preponderance of adult males over females, and a tendency for the working classes to be clustered close to the points of production. In the latter period, however, the 'labouring classes and the dangerous classes' were pushed into closer proximity than ever before, and nowhere was this more evident than in the poorest south-western quarter of the city where parts of Fordsburg, Vrededorp, the Brickfields and the Indian location merged into one another.

The Milner administration proved to be remarkably sensitive to these social problems and the extent to which their possible political consequences could jeopardise the long-term development of industrial capitalism on the Witwatersrand. In September 1902 the Governor of the Transvaal announced the appointment of a commission 'to enquire into and Report on the Johannesburg Insanitary Area Improvement Scheme'.[42] This scheme, piloted along the lines of the Westminster Housing of the Working Classes Act of 1890, led to the effective demolition of the Brickfields and surrounding 'slum' areas, and their replacement by the commercial centre of Newtown. This was followed in 1903, with less success, by a commission to enquire into 'the scarcity of housing accommodation in Johannesburg, as especially affecting the members of the artisan working classes and those earning small salaries'.[43] In mid-1903 the Transvaal Immigration Department, in close cooperation with the London-based South African Colonisation Society, stepped up its efforts to introduce British female domestic servants to the Witwatersrand – a move calculated, amongst other things, not only to remedy the imbalance in sex ratios in the new colony, but to help displace black male domestic servants into the mining industry.[44] And, in October 1903, the administration approved new by-laws which enabled local authorities to deal more effectively with several 'private' locations for blacks in urban areas along the Reef.[45]

All of these measures were, in differing degrees, designed to help stabilise the Rand's skilled white proletariat, secure British hegemony, and facilitate social control by separating the labouring classes from the dangerous classes. But if it was the Witwatersrand in general that was the object of the administration's interest, then it was Johannesburg in particular that was singled out for special attention. It was here, more than anywhere else, that Milner and his colleagues were concerned to prevent the eruption of open class conflict, and, to this end, the administration constantly urged the mine owners to develop a wider appreciation of the needs of industrial capitalism. This pressure was particularly evident in two areas – the question of white working-class housing, and the related issue of town planning.

Between 1896 and 1899 the cost of building white working-class homes on the Witwatersrand rose substantially as a result of the high price of machine-made bricks and cement – factors which were, to a very large extent, under the direct control of the mine owners who dominated the latter industries.[46] This gave rise to a situation where the supply of houses fell well behind demand, thus aggravating the subsequent post-war housing shortage on the Rand. By 1903 the shortfall of houses was sufficiently pronounced for the members of the Johannesburg Housing Commission to debate seriously the feasibility of working-class housing being provided by the state or local government. After careful consideration, however, the commission came to the conclusion that the situation would best be alleviated through the initiative of 'private enterprise'.

As the part of 'private enterprise' best placed to help overcome the shortage, and as the employers who stood to lose most from the crisis in working-class accommodation, the mine owners paid some attention to the commission's findings. Over a 36-month period between 1903 and 1905 the H. Eckstein & Co.-controlled Johannesburg Brick and Potteries Co. Ltd. reduced the price of machine-made bricks on the Rand by 50 per cent, and still made a handsome profit. Responding to the fall in construction costs brought about by this and other factors, several mining companies reluctantly expanded their programme to provide housing for their European employees. Between 1902 and 1905, for example, Rand Mines, Consolidated Gold Fields and East Rand Proprietary Mines collectively spent about £400,000 on providing accommodation for married employees.[47]

But the eight hundred or so houses provided by these leading companies did not bring about a marked improvement in the overall position on the Rand, and a nervous reconstruction administration continued to push the industry to make further investments in its housing programme. In January 1906 Lord Selborne – Milner's successor in the Transvaal – again broached the subject with Lionel Phillips of Wernher, Beit & Co. The mine owners, however, constrained by the continuing and deepening profitability crisis in the industry, were unwilling to countenance any further expenditure in this direction. As Phillips put it in his reply to Selborne a few days later:

> When, therefore, you ask me to lead the way in providing more married quarters so that we may see a larger British population settled in the country and, at the same time, that the ultimate interests of the mining industry be furthered, I am obliged to answer, that while I am in full sympathy with your views, the moment is not propitious to consider any large and avoidable capital outlay.[48]

It was thus only after there had been an undoubted upturn in the performance of the industry, in 1909, that the mine owners and others were willing to resume their investment in working-class housing.

In 1910 the outgoing Transvaal government, still anxious to help find ways of getting hesitant white workers to commit themselves to a future on the Rand, appointed a commission of enquiry to examine the conditions under which certain titles to property were held in some of Johannesburg's residential areas. When this commission reported, two years later, it recommended that those tenants who were willing to pay in a modest predetermined amount should be allowed to acquire property previously held on leasehold terms under freehold conditions.[49] Significantly, this process of conversion was facilitated by the powerful Township Owners' Association, a body with exceptionally strong links to mining capital. By the same year – 1912 – some of the leading mine owners, such as R. W. Schumacher of Rand Mines, were also sufficiently confident about the future of the industry to allow white miners to buy certain houses from the company regardless of whether or not they intended remaining employees of Rand Mines.[50] The arrival of the latter situation, where the mine owners were willing to relax one of the means of control which they exercised over their more highly paid workers, was a measure of the degree to which the Witwatersrand's white proletariat was becoming stabilised, as well as de-skilled, by the outbreak of the First World War.

As we have already seen, however, it was not only the quantity and quality of housing provided for white workers that was of interest to the post-war Transvaal authorities, but its distribution through the city. Here again, it was Milner's reconstruction administration, and more particularly the man whom he appointed as Town Clerk in Johannesburg, Lionel Curtis, that was most actively involved in planning a secure future for industrial capitalism. Curtis, with his Mansion House Committee on the Dwellings of the Poor experience behind him, was always acutely aware of the class antagonisms that existed between London's east and west ends, and in 1901 he suggested that:

> What we have to fear and avoid is the creation of a similar state of things in Johannesburg – where the area north of the reef would be covered by the residences of the well-to-do, and by streets of shops supplying their wants – while the area south of the reef would be inhabited solely by the poorer employees of the mines and by an inferior class of local shopkeepers. There are, therefore, strong reasons based upon the broadest political ground for securing now and for ever that the various townships shall radiate from their economic centres, that each class shall bear the political and social burdens which should fall to their lot as members of an economic whole, and that one class should not be allowed to separate its life from another class with which it is bound up by an inseparable economic tie.[51]

Thus, in addition to being one of the prime movers to rid the inner city of its 'slum' areas, Curtis was anxious to ensure a more even spread of the working classes through the city. In order to bring this about the Town Clerk and his colleagues proposed that there be a substantial increase in the size of the city's boundaries and that, in order to offset the greater distance that would separate the worker from the point of production, Johannesburg be served by a modern system of cheap public transport.

Curtis's preliminary work on the scheme to have Johannesburg's municipal boundaries extended pre-dated any form of civilian administration on the Rand. In April 1901 he and the military officer in charge of the city, Major W. O'Meara of the Royal Engineers, after reaching agreement on the broad outlines of the Acting Town Clerk's plans, arranged for the municipal boundaries to be extended to cover nine square miles. Five months later, in September 1901, Curtis won the endorsement of Milner's nominated Town Council for a far more ambitious scheme. When the outline of this latter scheme was sent to the Chamber of Mines for 'comment', however, it at first met with resistance from some of the mine owners who feared that any substantial extension of the boundaries would inevitably include mining property, and thus render the industry liable to pay rates. It was only after Percy FitzPatrick – at Milner's request – had explained the political advantages of the scheme to the less far-sighted of his colleagues, that the mine owners agreed to support the plan. In 1903 Johannesburg's municipal boundaries were extended to embrace an area of 82 square miles – a figure which differed radically from the modest five square miles which the town had covered when Kruger first granted it municipal status in 1897.

In the meantime, however, the Town Clerk's plan for an efficient public transport system to serve a greater Johannesburg had run into difficulties. The Transvaal Concessions Commission of 1901, unwilling to alienate powerful European financiers and local mining capitalists with large holdings in the City & Suburban Tramway Co., had acknowledged the legality of the concession originally granted by the Kruger government. The company's directors proceeded to put this finding to good use, and demanded substantial compensation from the Town Council before they would be willing to relinquish their right to operate a horse-drawn tramway system in the inner city. In June 1904, after several months of negotiation, an agreement was reached for the Town Council to acquire the assets and rights of the City &

Suburban Co. at a cost of £150,000; but even so it was only in February 1906 that the electric tram finally made its appearance in the streets of central Johannesburg. Shortly thereafter, the system was extended to serve the new working-class suburbs to the north-east of the city such as Kensington and Malvern.

Looking back then, it can be seen how, although it was under the immediate post-war administration that most was done to plan for the emergence of Johannesburg as a mature industrial city, it was only some years later that most of this planning started to take effect. Equally noteworthy was the manner in which the state was called upon to take the lead in designing an appropriate socio-economic infrastructure for the city between 1902 and 1906, and constantly having to spur the mine owners to greater efforts in the fields of housing, transport and town planning at a time when the mining industry was labouring under the strains of a profitability crisis.

Once the turning point of the depression had been reached, however, Johannesburg experienced an accelerated social transformation which was relatively smoothly channelled along the lines which had been laid down by the architects of reconstruction. A marked increase in the amount of working-class accommodation available in urban areas that were increasingly accessible, saw a fall in rents at a time when other factors were already producing a gradual reduction in the cost of living in the city.[52] In general, the period between 1908 and the outbreak of the war saw a marked decline in the number of single male workers based in the boarding-houses of the inner city, and a sharp increase in the number of working-class families located in the suburbs. In 1897 only 12 per cent of the Witwatersrand's European mine employees were married and had their families resident with them in the Transvaal; by 1902 this figure had crept up to 20 per cent, and in 1912 it reached 42 per cent.[53] It is thus largely against this backdrop – the emergence of the white working-class family in the suburbs of a more socially ordered colonial city – that we have to view the changing fortunes of the groups that we have been examining between 1902 and 1914.

At the outbreak of the South African War most of the Rand's 'foreign' pimps and prostitutes fled to the coastal cities where their wartime presence and subsequent behaviour attracted much adverse comment, and ultimately helped to usher in a new round of morality legislation in the various southern African colonies. As soon as Johannesburg was re-opened to civilians, however, many of these 'undesirables' promptly made their way back to the Witwatersrand, and in July 1903 the reconstruction administration – in an attempt to be seen to be coping with an old problem – passed Ordinance 46, the 'Immorality Act'.

But, if in theory the Transvaal was now well placed to restrict the growth of the *demi-monde* in its principal industrial city, then in practice the authorities did little to curtail the activities of those European women who sold sexual services to white working-class men. Aware of the social composition of the city and sensitive to the alienated existence led by most white miners, Milner and his most senior advisers were of the opinion that 'local conditions' formed an all-important consideration in determining how the policy to combat public vice was implemented. This sympathetic concern for the lot of the boarding-house residents, however, was not extended to the compound dwellers and such police action as there was, therefore, was largely directed against those white prostitutes who were willing to take black customers – a racist double-standard which helped to increase the cultural distance separating the two major ethnic components of the working class. The years between 1902 and 1905 thus saw the re-emergence of organised vice in central Johannesburg, albeit on a somewhat diminished scale, and with a clientele that was more effectively racially segregated than it had been before the war.

For an extremely intricate set of reasons, however, this situation started to change in important respects during the depression. A campaign against certain leading vice merchants by the police in 1906 was followed by a far more successful drive during 1907–8 when scores of prostitutes – for reasons that are unfortunately not clear – assisted the authorities by turning against their pimps. The state made use of this revolt by the prostitutes to obtain the evidence necessary to deport hundreds of foreign-born 'undesirables' from the Transvaal, an offensive which was continued right up to the formation of Union in 1910 by a former Kruger official who was all too familiar with the problems of prostitution on the Rand, J. C. Smuts.

On the one hand then, the period 1906 to 1914 saw a decline in the more highly organised vice of the inner city – an administratively-led achievement that was supplemented by the fall in the demand for the services of prostitutes occasioned by the surge in the number of working-class families being established in Johannesburg at the time. On the other, however, the same period saw an increase in the more loosely organised prostitution located in the older and poorer working-class quarters around the city centre. During the depression a significant number of working women in Fordsburg and Vrededorp turned to casual sexual liaisons in order to supplement their meagre wages, and in many cases this later gave way to a full-time career of prostitution. By the outbreak of the First World War, white Johannesburg's commercial sexual needs were being largely catered for by the daughters of the Rand's own proletariat – thus ending a dependency on 'continental' women that dated back all the way to the 'Kaffir Boom' of the mid-nineties.

The other major element of social control on the Witwatersrand that harked back to the mid-nineties – the use of alcohol to help stabilise black labour – also experienced a decline in the new era. When the British army occupied Pretoria, on 5 June 1900, a proclamation issued under martial law prevented any further manufacture or sale of spirituous liquor in the town. This move effectively sealed off Hatherley Distillery as the major source of cheap liquor destined for the Rand's black mineworkers, and a few months later the military authorities followed up on this action with the large-scale arrest and deportation of foreign-born illicit liquor dealers in Johannesburg.

These swift and decisive military measures won the immediate approval of the mine owners who, sensing that their allies were winning the war, at once took steps to ensure that the mining industry would not lose the peace. At precisely the moment that the Transvaal started to experience the transition from a military to a civilian administration, a new body which enjoyed the support of most of the mine owners – 'The South African Alliance for the Reform of the Liquor Traffic' – emerged to put pressure on the reconstruction government to exercise tight control over the retail liquor trade on the Witwatersrand. Milner, however, already had strong ideas of his own on the subject and needed little persuading about the virtues of 'total prohibition' for blacks. After the concessions commission had issued its report and recommended the cancellation of the Hatherley concession with generous compensation for its owners, the reconstruction government passed Ordinance 32 of 1902 which prohibited the distillation of spirits for commercial gain in the new colony.

In 1902 Milner and the mine owners therefore picked up where the Kruger government had left off and abandoned the use of alcohol as a device with which to help stabilise the mining industry's migratory labour force, although mine managers did – for some time – continue to make use of a weekly issue of 'Kaffir Beer' as one of the means of keeping control over their unskilled workers.[54] This renewed willingness to dispense with the carrot, however, was more than compensated for by an increase in the use of the stick. The reconstruction administration 'extended the pass department, created a system of courts to deal with masters and servants legislation' and 'introduced a scheme to register the fingerprints of all mining employees to help identify workers who had deserted', while the mine owners improved the capacity of their compounds to exercise physical control over the inmates.[55] In part then, the post-war ruling classes could afford to do without some of the more indirect forms of control over the Rand's black miners precisely because they exercised so much greater direct control over workers in the mining industry.

But, despite the enhanced law-enforcement capacity of the post-war state, the sale of alcohol to black miners by persons based outside the compounds did not cease to be a minor source of irritation to the mine owners between 1902 and 1914, and more especially so during periods of economic recession when 'poor whites' in areas of high unemployment turned to the illicit liquor trade to ensure their survival. Significantly, parts of Fordsburg and Vrededorp figured prominently amongst such supply areas after 1906. Within a decade, vibrant working-class communities which had once supplied the Rand with many of its transport riders, brickmakers and cab drivers, were reduced to providing the city with a disproportionate number of its illicit liquor dealers and prostitutes.

Black miners, however, were not the only group of African men on the Witwatersrand to attract official attention after the war. The shortage of cheap unskilled labour in the mining industry forced the reconstruction administration to look well beyond the usual sources of supply, and it was during the course of this search that the growing number of Zulu 'houseboys' on the Rand came to its notice. The presence of this sizeable pool of unproductive labour amidst a serious shortage of productive labour in the colony's premier industry proved to be too much of a temptation to resist, and between 1902 and 1906 Milner and the mine owners made two major attempts to dislodge the 'houseboys' from the kitchens and force them into the compounds.

First – and as we have already noted in another context – immediately after the war the reconstruction administration set about encouraging the immigration of white female domestics from the United Kingdom in the belief that Rand employers would give preference to white housemaids over black 'houseboys', and thus dispense with the services of their Zulu servants. This well-organised venture, the South African Expansion Committee and its successor, the South African Colonisation Society, enjoyed the personal support and financial assistance of several prominent mine owners and the ubiquitous Percy FitzPatrick acted as chairman of its 'advisory council'. Secondly, in 1904, E. P. Rathbone, editor of the journal *South African Mines, Commerce and Industry*, proposed to Johannesburg householders that they establish an Employers' Domestic Native Labour Association (E.D.N.L.A.), along the lines of W.N.L.A., in order to engineer a fall in the steadily rising wages of Zulu 'houseboys'. This move, which in the short run would achieve the overt objective of reducing 'houseboy' wages, would also have the long-term effect of rendering the domestic service sector of the local economy less attractive to African men and the scheme therefore received the support of 'many industrial and representative parties'.[56]

In the final analysis, however, both of these schemes failed in so far as they were designed to increase the flow of cheap labour into the mining industry. White domestic servants never came to the Rand in sufficient numbers for them to make a significant impact on the service sector of the economy, while those who did soon absorbed the values of a colonial society and refused to undertake menial, dirty or hard labour – thus leaving intact a role for the black 'houseboy'. Rathbone, for his part, discovered that while it was one thing to get a small number of mine owners to cooperate to form a monopsonistic association like W.N.L.A. within a single industry, it was quite another to get hundreds of individual employers to put their domestic labour arrangements at risk through an outside agency such as E.D.N.L.A. When 'houseboy' wages did eventually fall, between 1906 and 1908, it was as a product of the depression and an influx of black female and child labour, rather than as a result of any external attempt at manipulating the labour market.

The failure of these early attempts to alter fundamentally the structure of the service sector meant that for much of the interwar period Zulu 'houseboys' were, to an increasing extent, brought into immediate and highly personal contact with immigrant English working-class women who were either fellow servants in the homes of the affluent, or the wives of white miners in the suburbs. This great cultural collision, between black adult males who were responsible heads of household in their own right, and young white females newly exposed to colonial society, produced a highly explosive psychological mixture which gave rise to periodic outbursts of great sexual hysteria on the Witwatersrand between 1902 and 1914. It was these recurrent 'black peril' scares and, to a lesser extent, the partially organised resistance of the 'houseboys' to colonisation as expressed through *Amalaita* gangs, that contributed to the gradual but far from complete substitution of black male by black female domestic labour in the years leading up to the First World War.

The history of the other group of Zulu speakers that we have been following – the members of the washermen's guild – was even more troubled than that of the 'houseboys' in the post-war period. Between 1901 and 1905 the Milner administration sought to bring these small black businessmen under more effective control by attempting to get the AmaWasha to occupy a single segregated site under municipal supervision. Eventually these efforts succeeded in 1906 when the washermen – after a period of prolonged harassment – were expelled from the city's perimeter and made to occupy a site adjacent to the municipal sewerage farm at Klipspruit some thirteen miles from the centre of Johannesburg.

This enforced move to an economic wasteland by administrative fiat did much to hasten the demise of the guild. It imposed a new and demanding cost structure on the Zulu washermen at the worst possible moment – the start of the depression – and thus left them vulnerable to the competition of a growing number of capitalist steam laundries as well as that of Chinese and Asian laundrymen who had been allowed to stay on in the city. To add to their difficulties the AmaWasha were also the victims of the Rand's rapidly changing social structure after 1909, as wives and black servants undertook a growing volume of domestic laundry within the confines of working or middle-class homes. All of these factors contributed to a steady decline in the average number of municipal washing licences granted to the members of the guild during this period. In 1905, the last year during which the Zulu washermen were permitted to operate on the outskirts of the city, this figure stood at 262, by 1914 it was down to 93 – a reduction of more than 60 per cent over a brief nine year period.

Johannesburg's Afrikaner brickmakers, who had been forced to vacate the city centre in 1896, fared equally dismally after the turn of the century. For a brief period during 1902–3 the 'Waterfall Brickmakers' Association' prospered as its thirty to forty members and their employees took advantage of the post-war housing boom. In the more taxing years that followed, however, the brickmakers suffered greatly as a result of being located six miles out of town – something which the Kruger government had promised to offset by providing a rail link to the city centre. High transport costs and the powerful competition provided by Eckstein's Brick & Potteries Co. did much to destroy the viability of these smaller enterprises at Waterval, and by the onset of the depression in 1906 there were hundreds of Afrikaner brickmakers amongst Johannesburg's unemployed.

These brickmakers, however, did not want for familiar company in the depression dole queues. After the war many Afrikaners had successfully re-established themselves in the local cab trade while the Town Council and the City & Suburban Co. struggled to reach agreement about the fate of the horse-drawn tramway system which Johannesburg had inherited from the Kruger government. But once this compromise had been reached, the cab drivers' days were numbered, and between 1906 – when the first electric tram appeared on the city streets – and 1909, some six hundred cab drivers were thrown out of work.

This gradual build-up in the number of unemployed white workers in Johannesburg after the war, and then the more rapid increase during the depression, did not find the Transvaal's ruling classes entirely unprepared. Early in 1903 Milner and Curtis, with the support and financial assistance of the leading mine owners, had helped to launch the Rand Aid Association. This body, once again consciously modelled along the lines of a metropolitan institution – this time the Charity Organisation Society of London – was largely designed to coordinate the provision of temporary relief to those skilled and semi-skilled workers in the city who found themselves facing short periods of unemployment, and this role it filled with relative ease during the post-war recession.

From mid-1906, however, there was an enormous and sudden increase in the numbers of both skilled and unskilled workers without jobs in the city. Immigrant workers in the building and allied trades suffering the ravages of cyclical unemployment were now joined by hundreds of unskilled Afrikaner workers rendered jobless by more lasting structural changes in the local economy. This situation brought Johannesburg's unemployed English workers with their well-developed tradition of trades unionism and organisation into much closer contact – and competition – with their Afrikaner counterparts, and extended the resources of the Rand Aid Association to pose the ruling classes with a more formidable challenge.

In 1906, Selborne – under considerable pressure from concerned local government officials along the Reef – appointed the Transvaal Indigency Commission to examine the causes of widespread unemployment in the colony, and to suggest ways of overcoming it. This commission, subsequently taken over by the *Het Volk* government, did little to provide increasingly impatient men with work, however, and when English mineworkers went on strike in May 1907 the mine owners saw the possibility of combining political expediency with economic necessity by using unskilled Afrikaners as strike breakers. But, out of a complex mixture of fear and class solidarity, Johannesburg's Afrikaner unemployed hesitated before acting as scab labour and the majority of positions were thus filled by workers drawn from further afield. It was thus left to yet another body, the Rand Unemployment Investigation Committee, to supersede temporarily the politically suspect Rand Aid Association, and create a significant number of positions for militant unskilled workers on the mines and in the municipal service between March 1908 and the end of the depression.

The trauma of unemployment and the scars of the depression, however, left their unmistakeable imprint on the class consciousness of the city's Afrikaners, and this reflected itself in their continuing search for an appropriate political home. Throughout the period 1908–14 poor Afrikaners in Vrededorp searched, largely in vain, for a place in a labour movement which could accommodate their distinctive needs as unskilled white workers. But, neither the nationalists of Het Volk who attempted to win their loyalty through a labour wing of the party, *Arbeid Adelt*, nor the trade unionists of the craft-dominated Labour Party could capture and hold the allegiance of these vulnerable workers, thus exacerbating the turbulence of working-class politics in the city. As late as May 1914, the Johannesburg Town Council, during the course of its evidence to the Relief and Grants-in-Aid Commission, noted that these workers 'had overturned every political party, and would overturn any political party which might be in power unless a remedy was provided to remove their appalling poverty and degradation'.[57] A mere two months later, in July 1914, the first of several working-class leaders in Vrededorp joined the ranks of the newly established National Party.

For the unenfranchised black workers of the city, however, there was nowhere to turn to for even temporary relief from the problems of poverty and unemployment. The use of Chinese indentured labour on the mines, structural changes in the local economy during the depression, and the dislocation caused by the Bambatha Rebellion in rural Natal, all appear to have contributed to growing 'Zulu' unemployment on the Rand after 1906. Confronted by the more effective repressive capacity of the reconstruction state and its successors, these unemployed men soon found themselves either locked up in prison, or else seeking shelter in the disused mine shafts, prospect holes or abandoned houses on the city's periphery – all well-established haunts of Jan Note's lumpenproletarian army.

But, whereas before the turn of the century some of the Ninevites' activities had been inspired by a sense of social justice and the desire to cling to aspects of a peasant lifestyle in a rapidly industrialising society, after the war Note's organisation appears to have become increasingly anti-social as the mining revolution produced its first significant numbers of fully proletarianised black workers. After 1910 the Ninevites hid themselves more effectively from the endless pass raids of the police by taking refuge in the mine compounds, from where they launched criminal sorties not only against white property in neighbouring towns, but against black migrant workers. It was as a result of these essentially apolitical activities that Note's army found itself locked in a confrontation with the forces of the state during much of 1912 and 1913. Denied orthodox outlets in a repressive and racially discriminatory state, the Witwatersrand's black unemployed turned to crime rather than politics for a solution to their problem.

Conclusion

When gold was discovered on the Witwatersrand in 1886 it hurtled Kruger's slumbering Zuid Afrikaansche Republiek into the modern era of industrial capitalism. Within months, rural notables who had previously presided over a slowly developing agricultural economy were called upon to exercise control over one of the fastest growing and most technologically sophisticated mining industries in the world. And, within little more than a decade, the near bankrupt Z.A.R. was transformed into the wealthiest and most powerful state in southern Africa.

The vision of a journey from rags to riches via the path of industrialisation was not one which had entirely eluded the Z.A.R.'s overlords – indeed, Kruger's plans for the industrial development of the Transvaal pre-dated the discovery of gold on the Rand when he helped to christen the Eerste Fabrieken as *Volkshoop* in 1881. But what Kruger and his colleagues had always envisaged was the emergence of a state in which industry was the logical outgrowth of, and ultimately dependent on, the output of a dominant agricultural sector. Kruger's concessions policy was thus initially designed to foster the growth of a very particular set of enterprises – namely, those that converted the agricultural output of his Boer constituents into products which could be sold within the slowly developing markets of the Republic and its adjacent territories.

What the discovery of gold did, however, was to sweep aside the major assumptions on which the concessions policy had been predicated. Almost overnight the Z.A.R.'s rulers found themselves governing a state in which extractive industry rather than agricultural production constituted the mainstay of the economy. The concessions policy, originally designed to facilitate the accumulation of capital in the countryside by nationals, now had to be hastily extended to meet the changing demands of European capitalists in the urban centres of the Witwatersrand as the mining industry moved from outcrop diggings to deep-level production within the space of a decade.

Kruger and his colleagues' strategy for industrialisation was thus overtaken by events. Once committed to the concessions policy, however, the Z.A.R. government found it virtually impossible to stage a retreat. If, after the discovery of gold, Kruger had simply abandoned the concessions policy as originally conceived and opened the Republic to the unrestricted competition of foreign products, he would have had to sacrifice important markets – such as those of the distillery and the tramway company – at precisely the moment that these enterprises were starting to channel a significant flow of funds back into the countryside. Moreover, after 1890 the government was faced with strong domestic opposition to the concessions policy from its 'progressive' rivals, while after 1896 criticisms of those concessions which adversely affected the cost structure of the mining industry were difficult to entertain in view of the political climate generated by the Jameson Raid.

It is within this wider context and on this broader testing ground that the Z.A.R. government's strategy for industrialisation has to be reassessed. Kruger's concessions policy cannot simply be refracted through the rapidly changing demands of the mining industry and be said to have failed. If the policy was indeed a failure in so far as it did not relieve the growing pressure on the cost structure of the mining industry after the opening of the deep levels, then this 'failure' has surely to be offset against the 'success' which it enjoyed in attempting to serve agriculture. It is only once the evolving concessions policy has been situated within the political economy of the Z.A.R. as a whole, and its strengths and limitations more rigorously examined through detailed case studies, that we will be able to arrive at a more balanced judgement of Kruger's strategy for industrialisation.

If, however, Kruger's vision of a republic founded on an agricultural base with an industrial outgrowth was eclipsed by the mining revolution, then it was Milner who – with the help of the mine owners – re-aligned the social, political and economic infrastructure of the Transvaal in such a way that it became an industrial state served by agriculture. But, whereas the economic and political aspects of the reconstruction programme have been subjected to close scrutiny – and more especially as they directly affected the mining industry – the social planning which the post-war administration put into the creation of a modern industrial state has been somewhat neglected.

As noted above, much of the Milner administration's efforts in the latter field were directed towards increasing social control over the Rand's population; by separating the labouring classes from the dangerous classes in 'slums' such as the Brickfields and the 'washing locations', and by attempting to distribute and stabilise white working-class families in the suburbs of an enlarged city. These strategies for separating the residential areas of various subordinate groups – on an intra-class as well as an inter-class basis – were in some cases buttressed by further divisions introduced at the place of work. It was, for example, Johannesburg's post-war administration which initiated the distinction between 'first' and 'second class' cabs in the city, a division which exacerbated the differences of colour and class in a trade which, in times of crisis, had tended to manifest a degree of inter-racial cooperation. Likewise, one of the effects of relegating the AmaWasha to Klipspruit in 1906 was to separate the Zulu washermen from those Asian Dhobis with whom they had been labouring in great harmony for several years. These, and other examples which may be drawn from changes in policy relating to the issuing of municipal hawking and trading licences, suggest that it may be profitable to mount a more systematic examination of the manner in which the occupational and residential patterns of the subordinate classes on the Witwatersrand were brought into greater alignment during the first decade of the twentieth century.

Here again, however, the 'success' achieved by the Milner administration in the field of social planning during a period when it was largely freed of any direct electoral accountability, will have to be offset against the subsequent 'failure' of town councils more closely bound by local class interests to extend the Curtis initiative. When W. C. Scully visited Johannesburg in 1911 he was still struck by 'the sudden transition from splendour to squalor on the western side of the city', and by numerous 'slum-warrens' housing 'Europeans of various nationalities – Indians, Chinese, Arabs, Japanese, Kaffirs and miscellaneous coloured people of every hue'.[58] These inter-racial 'slum-yards', which yielded their own distinctive sub-cultures, merit closer study; not only because of their intrinsic interest, but because they will heighten our understanding of the various ways in which they helped to inform – and in turn were informed by – the emerging culture of the city's black labouring population.

In much the same way, the changes in white working-class culture that accompanied the move from the boarding-houses of the inner city to the working-class homes of the suburbs needs to be explored. In general, this shift heralded a decline in the male-centred leisure time activities of drinking, whoring and gambling in various forms, and the rise of more 'balanced' family entertainment centred around the theatre, the cinema and communally organised sport and recreation. It also, however, helped to increase the growing social distance between white and black miners. Workers, who at one time had been drawn closer together by their need for alcohol and prostitutes as an escape from the privations of boarding-house and compound life, now found themselves inhabiting different social worlds, as white miners, in growing numbers, 'settled down' to family life. Lionel Phillips was certainly aware of all these dimensions – and of the new opportunity which it afforded the mine owners when, during the course of a letter to Lord Selborne in 1906, he noted that:

> The Recreation Hall and the opportunity for social intercourse and rational entertainments which it affords can also, I think, be made a valuable instrument in raising the tone of the working man. I intend personally to go to as many entertainments at the mines as possible, as I am a great believer in the effect of personal intercourse and if those men who are at the head of mining affairs attend functions of this order, the example will no doubt be followed by those employees and their wives who have not hitherto come into much contact with the miners, artisans and men of that class. With novel labour conditions, such as we have in this country, success will depend in no small measure upon the White

> man being superior in fact, as well as in name, and setting an example to the unskilled Kaffirs or Chinamen. An increase in the class of respectable married men, with their families, would undoubtedly tend in this direction, so I am entirely with you in this connection.[59]

From this and other evidence we have, it is clear that both ruling-class initiative and subordinate-class expression will have to be carefully charted and distinguished when the history of working-class culture on the Rand comes to be written.

It is only once this latter task is completed, and we can add our knowledge of the emerging working-class culture to our greater understanding of the de-skilling of white workers over the same period, that we will be in a position to appreciate more fully the nature and significance of the European miners' struggle during the first two decades of the twentieth century.[60] After the advent of deep levels, white workers not only gave their labour to the mining industry, they committed their whole lives – and those of their wives and children – to a future based on the Witwatersrand. Given this escalating commitment it is less than surprising that they responded with growing anger and violence when their livelihoods were put at stake in 1907, 1913 and 1922; nor is it surprising that they did not win the support of the majority of their fellow workers who had been left stranded in the shadows of the compound. Had they done so, they would have succeeded in launching an even more effective challenge to the world the mine owners made.

Notes

1 See P. Richardson and J. J. Van-Helten, 'The Gold Mining Industry in the Transvaal, 1886–1899', in P. Warwick (ed.), *The South African War* (London 1980), pp. 18–19.
2 A. Pratt, *The Real South Africa* (London 1913), p. 166.
3 See R. V. Kubicek, *Economic Imperialism in Theory and Practice* (Duke University Press, Durham N.C. 1979), p. 24.
4 *Ibid.*, p. 40.
5 G. Blainey, 'Lost causes of the Jameson Raid', *Economic History Review*, 18, 1965, p. 353. See also, Richardson and Van-Helten, 'The Gold Mining Industry in the Transvaal, 1886–1899', p. 27.
6 Kubicek, *Economic Imperialism in Theory and Practice*, p. 43.
7 For an analysis of the repressive functions of the compound system see C. van Onselen, *Chibaro* (London 1976), pp. 128–86.
8 For some of the difficulties arising from the use of this concept see R. Johnson, 'Three Problematics: elements of a theory of working class activities', in J. Clarke, C. Critcher and R. Johnson (eds.), *Working Class Culture* (London 1979), pp. 201–37.
9 See also, however, G. Stedman Jones, 'Class Expression *versus* Social Control? A critique of recent trends in the social history of "Leisure"', *History Workshop*, 4, 1977, pp. 163–74.
10 'Eerste Fabrieken', *Standard and Diggers' News*, 14 May 1889.
11 For a fuller discussion of this complex topic see, Vol. 2, Chapter 1, 'The Witches of Suburbia', pp. 2–8.

12 For a schematic outline of Nellmapius' career in the Transvaal see H. Kaye, *The Tycoon and the President* (Johannesburg 1978).
13 Richardson and Van-Helten, 'The Gold Mining Industry in the Transvaal, 1886–1899', p. 28.
14 Kubicek, *Economic Imperialism in Theory and Practice*, pp. 43–4.
15 See R. Mendelsohn, 'Blainey and the Jameson Raid: The Debate Renewed', *Journal of Southern African Studies*, 6, 2, 1980, p. 162. See also Richardson and Van-Helten, 'The Gold Mining Industry in the Transvaal, 1866–1899', p. 28.
16 Richardson and Van-Helten, 'The Gold Mining Industry in the Transvaal, 1886–1899', p. 20.
17 Blainey, 'Lost causes of the Jameson Raid', p. 359.
18 For a brief discussion of the *bewaarplaatsen* problem see Mendelsohn, 'Blainey and the Jameson Raid: The Debate Renewed', pp. 161–2.
19 Blainey, 'Lost causes of the Jameson Raid', p. 359. See also, however, Mendelsohn, 'Blainey and the Jameson Raid: The Debate Renewed', p. 165.
20 D. Bransky, 'The Causes of the Boer War: Towards a Synthesis', unpublished paper delivered to the Workshop on South Africa, Oxford 1974, pp. 10–11.
21 See below, Chapter 2, 'Randlords and Rotgut', p. 86.
22 'To the Relief', *Standard and Diggers' News*, 19 August 1897. See also Vol. 2 Chapter 3, 'The Main Reef Road into the Working Class', p. 130.
23 Richardson and Van-Helten, 'The Gold Mining Industry in the Transvaal, 1886–1899', p. 34.
24 For an excellent analysis of the role of gold in the international economy at the turn of the century and some of its implications for the Transvaal see S. Marks and S. Trapido, 'Lord Milner and the South African State', *History Workshop*, 8, 1979, pp. 50–80.
25 Transvaal, *Annual Report of the Chamber of Mines 1895*, p. 75.
26 See Chapter 3 below, 'Prostitutes and Proletarians', pp. 114–5.
27 Much of this episode can be reconstructed from the following items in the *Standard and Diggers' News*: 'We'll Import Abigails', 26 December 1896; 'The Witwatersrand Boarding-House Keepers' Protection Association', 9 January 1897; 'Hotel Employees – Indignation Meeting', 27 February 1897; and Henry Percival to the Editor, 25 March 1897.
28 H. J. and R. E. Simons, *Class and Colour in South Africa, 1850–1950* (Harmondsworth 1969), p. 61.
29 This, and much of the section that follows, is heavily reliant on Peter Richardson's detailed account of the mining industry in the post-war period. See P. Richardson, 'Coolies and Randlords: The Structure of Mining Capitalism and Chinese Labour, 1902–1910', p. 5. (Unpublished seminar paper, Institute of Commonwealth Studies, University of Oxford, 1979).
30 'Between 1899 and 1910, for example, there was a sharper decrease in the average grade of ore mined on the Witwatersrand than at any other period between 1887 and 1965. The grade of ore sent to the mill declined from a ten-year annual average of 11.748 dwts per ton between 1890 and 1899, to an annual average of 6.572 dwts per ton in 1910.' Richardson, 'Coolies and Randlords', p. 1.
31 For some of the reasons behind this see D. Denoon, 'The Transvaal Labour Crisis 1901–1906', *Journal of African History*, VII, 1967, pp. 481–94.
32 The importance of the output maximisation and cost minimisation programme in the post-war period has been well illustrated in F. A. Johnstone, *Class, Race and Gold* (London 1976).
33 Richardson, 'Coolies and Randlords', p. 2.
34 *Ibid.*, p. 3.
35 *Ibid.*, p. 11.

36 For a thorough appreciation of the complex and sophisticated manner in which the mine owners set about the task of moulding a society that would meet the needs of primary industry during this period see B. Bozzoli, *The Political Nature of a Ruling Class: Capital and Ideology in South Africa 1890–1933* (London 1981). See especially chapters 1 and 2.

37 See D. Denoon, *A Grand Illusion* (London 1973).

38 For an account of the war-time plight of the Rand refugees see D. Maclaren, 'The Politics of Discontent: The Grievances of the Uitlander Refugees, 1899–1902', *Journal of Southern African Studies*, forthcoming.

39 J. Ramsay Macdonald, *What I Saw in South Africa* (London 1902), p. 103.

40 For a wider and slightly more systematic discussion of some of the elements of this problem see E. P. Rathbone, 'The Problem of Home Life in South Africa', *19th Century Review*, August 1906, pp. 245–53. For an appreciation of Rathbone's important role as an ideologist for capitalist development on the Witwatersrand during this period see B. Bozzoli, *The Political Nature of a Ruling Class*, pp. 26–35.

41 Transvaal Colony, *Report of the Commission Appointed to Enquire into and Report on the Johannesburg Insanitary Area Improvement Scheme, 1901–03*. Letter from E. M. Showers to the Town Clerk, Johannesburg, 12 February 1902, p. 10.

42 *Ibid.*

43 Transvaal Colony, *Report of the Johannesburg Housing Commission 1903*, p. 1.

44 See Vol. 2, Chapter 1, 'The Witches of Suburbia', pp. 11–13.

45 See Vol. 2, Chapter 2, 'AmaWasha', pp. 90–1.

46 See especially V. Markham, *South Africa, Past and Present* (London 1900), pp. 375–6.

47 See L. Phillips to Lord Selborne (Private), 24 January 1906, in M. Fraser and A. Jeeves, *All That Glittered* (Cape Town 1977), pp. 147–50.

48 *Ibid.*

49 *Report of the Transvaal Leasehold Townships Commission 1912* (U.G. 34–1912). A more detailed study of this neglected subject would also have to take into consideration some of the following evidence: *The Financial Relations Commission (Transvaal), 1906; The Townships Act, 1907; The Townships Amendment Act No. 34 of 1908; The Townships Amendment Act No. 30 of 1909;* Transvaal Colony, *Mining Regulations Commission 1910*, Vol. 1, pp. 63–6, 71; and *Report of the Small Holdings Commission (Transvaal)* (U.G. 51–13).

50 See especially, 'Holdings and Homes', *The Star*, 8 November 1912.

51 L. Curtis, *With Milner in Africa* (Oxford 1951), p. 260.

52 See especially, *Report of the Small Holdings Commission (Transvaal) 1912*, para. 16, pp. 8–9.

53 *Ibid*. Even this latter figure, however, was considered to be too low for a developing capitalist economy.

54 Transvaal Colony, *Final Report of the Mining Relations Commission* (Pretoria 1910), pp. 77–86.

55 P. Warwick, 'African Labour during the South African War, 1899–1902', unpublished seminar paper presented at the Institute of Commonwealth Studies, University of London, October 1975.

56 See Vol. 2, Chapter 1, 'The Witches of Suburbia', p. 14.

57 'Problem of Poverty – Inequitable Municipal Doles', *Rand Daily Mail*, 25 May 1914.

58 W. C. Scully, *The Ridge of the White Waters* (London 1912), pp. 207–14.

59 Lionel Phillips to Lord Selborne (Private), 24 January 1906, *in* M. Fraser and A. Jeeves (eds.), *All That Glittered*, p. 148. See also Phillips's suggestion at the time of founding the Johannesburg Art Gallery that fellow capitalists should give generously to the cause in order to help 'counteract those tendencies which provide an exaggerated sense of hatred in the minds of the "have nots" against the

"haves"'. *Ibid.*, L. Phillips to J. Wernher, 30 May 1910, pp. 224–5.

60 This exercise has been performed in a most skilful and suggestive manner in the English context in G. Stedman Jones, 'Working Class Culture and Working Class Politics in London 1870–1900; Notes on the Remaking of a Working Class', *Journal of Social History*, 1974, pp. 461–508.

CHAPTER TWO

Randlords and rotgut 1886–1903

The role of alcohol in the development of European imperialism and southern African capitalism, with special reference to black mineworkers in the Transvaal Republic

The presence or absence of an agricultural surplus has always played a central role in the historical transition of pre-capitalist modes of production into capitalist modes. At the very least, the inhabitants of the new towns and the emerging proletariat have to be fed by the food produced on the land. The capacity of various systems to produce such an agricultural surplus during the transformation to capitalism, however, has varied significantly, as has the ability of the emerging social formation to absorb it. In general though, it seems plausible to suggest that the development of European capitalism is as much punctuated by the absence of an agricultural surplus as by its presence. It is largely, although not solely, for this reason that rising prices, starvation and food riots occupy such an important chapter in European economic history.[1]

But having noted this broad pattern, social and economic historians should also be prepared to pay close attention to those cases in which substantial agricultural surpluses *were* generated. In Europe, as elsewhere, any one of a number of reasons could account for such surpluses and often the contributing factors were regionally specific – for example, land distribution, technological innovation or the cost of labour. It is not simply the genesis or size of the surpluses that should be noted however, but their rather specific *quality*. Here it is important to realise that in some respects agricultural commodities had almost unique properties during the historical development of capitalism in the eighteenth and nineteenth centuries. Unlike many such commodities today, fresh produce could not be stored for relatively lengthy periods, processed into tinned foods, or transported across vast distances to the more certain markets offered by affluent societies. Thus, during the European transition to capitalism, the producer was faced with a potentially substantial loss if he could not dispose of his agricultural surplus – a problem which still troubles the contemporary producer, albeit to a lesser extent. Historically, it was precisely for this reason that producers sought ways of storing the value of their commodities, or minimising the losses they were likely to sustain in the event of over-production. Through distillation, agricultural surplus was converted into spirits and not only was part of its value maintained, but in some cases the price actually increased as the commodity matured. Capital accumulated through spirit distillation thus provided one of the clearest visible links between a declining agriculturally based feudal regime, and a modern industrial capitalist order.*

In several parts of Europe such capital was initially accumulated through the creation and exploitation of local markets. During the eighteenth century in Rumania, for example, the Porte had prohibited the export of corn from any of the provinces. Faced with grain surpluses, the Rumanian landlords took to distilling spirits which they then used in paying their labourers. The remainder of the spirits they obliged villagers to buy at the public houses which they opened on their estates.[2] In Russia liquor leases were widely sold between 1712 and 1863. These leases proved to be 'a significant means of primary accumulation of capital', and 'were the origin of the later fortunes of the large industrial bourgeois families of the Yakolevs, Zlobins, Saposhnikovs, and Kokorevs'.[3] The Russian nobility were also not above the liquor trade and the princes Dolgoruki, Gagarin, Kurakin and Potemkin all earned a sizeable part of their income from the sale of spirits.

The development of such local markets, however, did not mean that producers came into direct contact with the consumers. Usually the spirits found their way to the new markets via the European publicans – the petty bourgeoisie. For this reason it was the publicans, rather than the producers, who came to figure prominently in the popular perception of the liquor trade – an understandable but unfortunate fact, given that many publicans were Jewish. In Russia and the Ukraine, for example, most of the canteens in the rural areas during the mid-nineteenth century were owned by Jewish businessmen. The *korchma* or tavern was a prominent part of peasant life and many Ukrainian folk songs of the time bemoaned the peasant's indebtedness to the local jew. In the urban areas too, Jewish traders figured prominently in the sale of alcohol to factory workers.[4] This, amongst several other factors, made Jewish tavern keepers obvious targets of local hatred and resentment, and they suffered accordingly during the disturbances and pogroms of the nineteenth century. Among the many Jewish refugees who made their way to the Transvaal Republic and elsewhere at this time, there must have been more than a few korchma keepers.

But with or without the aid of an intermediary petty bourgeoisie, there were limits to the type and quantity of spirits which producers could unload on local markets. Nowhere were these limitations more apparent than in the case of Germany. During the last three decades of the nineteenth century there was

* Unlike the pavement artist, no researcher is ever in the position where he can honestly say, 'all my own work'. This is especially true of this study, and I am indebted to many people for their help – including the editors of *History Workshop*. I would particularly like to thank Belinda Bozzoli, Martin Legassick, and Stanley Trapido for valuable discussions; also for making research material available to me. I would also like to thank Juan Esteban, Wolf Mersch and Yury Boshyk. Their excellent Portuguese, German and Ukrainian I have distorted to my own ends.

a substantial increase in the average yield of potatoes per acre in Prussia and Germany. This phenomenon was especially noticeable in the rye-and-potato economy which dominated the lighter soil areas of Prussia. The increased yield, however, was something of a mixed blessing, since it came at a time when the consumption of the potato as a vegetable was declining in the domestic households of Prussia and Germany. The Junkers, confronted with an increased potato crop amidst declining demand, turned to the time-honoured solution of distillation – a practice which, in the Prussian case, dated back at least to the seventeenth century. But this time the scale of the operation was qualitatively different, since a special steam apparatus for mashing silo potatoes had been developed in 1873, and large 'distillation domains' came into existence.[5]

The Junkers found, however, that their problems did not end with the large-scale conversion of potatoes into spirits. From 1880 onwards, the domestic markets of Prussia and Germany showed an increasing preference for the superior quality alcohols that were being distilled from grain. By the 1890s producers were finding themselves with large stocks of potato spirits which sold extremely slowly in domestic European markets. It was largely for this reason that the producers turned to the less discriminating and captive colonial markets which the imperial powers had shared out amongst themselves after the Berlin Conference of 1884. This solution was greatly facilitated in the German case by the considerable political power and influence which the largest distillers enjoyed. The spirit producers and others saw to it that rail freight charges to the port of Hamburg were reduced, and that an annual subsidy to the value of £45,000 was paid to the German East African Steamship Company.[6] With such incentives to exporters, it was possible for Africa to become an outlet for enormous quantities of potato spirits in the late nineteenth century.[7]

Not all of Africa, however, was equally vulnerable to imperial penetration. The degree to which, and the speed with which, European economic forces could conquer and capture new markets was largely dependent on the extent and nature of underdevelopment in the various parts of the continent. In Mozambique, for example, there was a relatively well established bourgeoisie which had long provided mercantile middlemen for Portuguese producers. For several decades these merchants had sold cheap Portuguese commodities – including alcohol – to Africans who constituted the local market. As middlemen rather than producers, they were willing to sell anything – not excluding German potato spirits – for a share of the profits.

What was true of Mozambique, however, was not true of the independent Boer Republics in southern Africa. These regimes had their own rural bourgeoisie in the form of white farmers who were themselves directly and actively involved in agricultural production. During the last quarter of the nineteenth century a considerable number of districts within the Republics were grain exporting, and in the villages and towns there was a sizeable market for spirits. Here too, the combination of agricultural surplus and local markets made distillation a real business possibility. Even a modest town like Harrismith, in the eastern Orange Free State, could house 'Demarillac's Distillery' which, in 1895, was worth over £4,000.[8] In the Transvaal, as early as 1870, 32 liquor licences were issued in Potchefstroom, 17 in Pretoria, 15 in

Wakkerstroom, and 5 in Heidelberg.[9] Markets such as these, located in independent states, served by a local petty bourgeoisie and supplied by national producers, were usually protected from competition by high import duties.[10] That they were relatively inaccessible geographically, and of modest size by international standards, may also have rendered them less vulnerable to initial imperial economic penetration. Indeed, had this configuration of factors remained constant, the Transvaal Republic might have experienced a more gradual 'decline of feudalism and rise of towns', like that of Europe, in which capital accumulated from distillation contributed to the subsequent development of industrial capitalism. 'Factors', however, seldom remain constant, and they certainly did not do so in the Transvaal during the late nineteenth century.

In 1886 gold was discovered on the Witwatersrand. This discovery jolted the Transvaal into an era of rapid industrial development. An influx of fortune-seeking Europeans and an ever expanding army of black mineworkers crammed themselves into mushrooming towns such as Krugersdorp, Johannesburg and Boksburg. Virtually overnight the Witwatersrand became one of the biggest, wealthiest and fastest growing markets in sub-Saharan Africa. This expanding conurbation, with its numerically preponderant black population spread along the Reef, promised new rewards to national and international entrepreneurs. The stage was set for a battle of conflicting class interests in which the participants were drawn from throughout Europe, Mozambique and the Transvaal. At the very heart of that conflict lay alcohol and the African mineworker. As a Johannesburg newspaper editorial put in in 1892:

> Today, despite his faults, the Kaffir is a distinct source of support to many hundreds here; he is acquiring the habit of clothing himself and he is becoming used to luxuries, thereby creating and increasing a trade that is a means of existence to a considerable section of the mercantile community. The covetous director, the interested temperance advocate, and the wily monopolist begin to see this, and they desire him for their own. They tell you they desire only to suppress drunkenness among natives, to secure a reliable labour supply for the mines, to regulate native passions, and to protect the public and the shareholder. Would that their motives were so noble! Unhappily there lurks behind their pretty speeches and still prettier sentiments the Policy of Grab.[11]

Clearly, there was no lack of contemporary awareness of the importance of the class conflict surrounding the issue of alcohol and black workers.

Who exactly, and what precisely, was involved in this conflict? Did these issues simply pass by a rural Afrikaner farming community that was thoroughly steeped in the conservatism of a Calvinist tradition? What were the objectives of the newly emerging industrial bourgeoisie, and what was the nature of its relationship with the temperance advocates? What was the role of the Afrikaner state? Were black workers simply passive consumers, or did they respond more actively? The remainder of this essay will seek to establish who these interested parties were, and why they advocated particular policies at certain historical junctures – in short, it will seek to expose the political economy that underlay the 'Policy of Grab'.

The black worker as consumer

The rise of the liquor industry, 1881–1896

During 1873–4 several hundred diggers and prospectors made their way to the promising goldfields discovered at the small eastern Transvaal town of Pilgrim's Rest. Amongst the new arrivals there was a young Hungarian Jew by the name of Alois Hugho Nellmapius. Making good use of his expertise as a mining engineer, Nellmapius soon established himself as one of the most successful and prosperous diggers in the area. Nellmapius, however, had an economic eye capable of scanning broader business horizons than mining – which was perhaps as well, given the rather short life of the eastern Transvaal goldfields. While at Pilgrim's Rest, Nellmapius also started, and successfully ran, a mule caravan service which traversed the tsetse-fly infested country between the town and Delagoa Bay. The central purpose of this service was to provide mail links between country and port, but it would be surprising if Nellmapius's returning caravans did not also bring with them some of the cheap contraband Portuguese liquor which played such an important part in the life of the mining camp.[12]

Nellmapius used this early success to consolidate his career and diversify his interests. He became a successful farmer, and eventually came to run a large estate near Pretoria which earned the reputation of being a 'model' agricultural enterprise. His success and abilities soon attracted the attention of notables in the Transvaal and, in particular, he became the friend and confidant of S. J. P. (Paul) Kruger. Nellmapius was the person primarily responsible for selling the idea of concession-granting to the President of the Republic.[13] Concessions, 'that is the handing out by the state to private individuals or private groups of the exclusive right to manufacture certain articles subject to certain guarantees, and in return for a substantial payment', became the corner-stone of early Transvaal industrial policy.[14]

On 3 October 1881 the *Volksraad* (Parliament) of the Zuid Afrikaansche Republiek (Z.A.R.) – the Transvaal – passed Article 44. This granted A. H. Nellmapius a concession 'for the sole right to manufacture from grain, potatoes, and other products growable in the Transvaal, excepting tree-fruits and grapes, and the right to sell in bulk and bottle free of licence' such spirits.[15] The President's friend was granted this original concession for a period of 15 years on condition that the distillery was operational by 1 July 1882. Weeks before this latter date was reached, however, on 7 June 1882, Nellmapius (in return for a 20 per cent share) ceded the concession to a partnership comprised of himself, the cousins Isaac and Barnet Lewis, and Barnet's brother-in-law, Samuel Marks.[16] It was this partnership which gave birth to *De Eerste Fabrieken in de Zuid Afrikaansche Republiek Ltd.* ('The First Factory Ltd.') and in June 1883 a proud President Kruger personally opened the new distillery and christened it *Volkshoop* – 'The People's Hope'.

A director of the distillery at a later date, Hugh Crawford, was therefore largely correct when he noted that: 'The distillery was established, and its operations commenced before the goldfields of either Barberton or the Transvaal (Witwatersrand) were discovered, and at a time when the country was poor, its population small, and business very limited.' These early business realities, however, did not prevent the Volksraad from continuing to perceive the factory as Volkshoop. As the economic climate in the Transvaal changed in the mid-1880s, so the *hoop* of the *volk* grew. When asked to modify and confirm the terms of the concession on 23 June 1885, members of the Volksraad took the opportunity to make additional demands for development. In return for extending the monopoly for a period of 30 years to 30 June 1912, they insisted on the state receiving an annual payment of £1,000 and a guarantee that a glass factory and cooperage works would be erected at the distillery.[17] In return, the company was to continue to enjoy exemption from any other form of taxation.

These additional development requirements specified by the Volksraad extended the company's resources, and none more so than the glass factory which was ultimately constructed only in 1894.[18] However, the dramatically changed economic conditions in the Transvaal after the mid-1880s assisted the company. In particular, the rapid growth and development of the Witwatersrand goldfields transformed the prospects of business success for Volkshoop from probability to certainty. In May 1889 it was noted of the distillery that, 'from a very modest beginning on a tentative scale, its success has become unprecedentedly rapid, and it is now developing itself into a great industry'.[19]

The tangible proof of the emergence of a 'great industry' was to be found on the 4,000-acre site of the distillery on the banks of the Pienaars river, some 10 miles east of Pretoria. On what was formerly Sammy Marks's Hatherley Farm, there arose a reservoir with a capacity of 170,000 gallons of water, a 30 horsepower plant for electricity generation, a four-storey central distillation plant, a boarding-house for accommodating white workers, houses for married European employees and a suitably prestigious separate house for the distillery manager. The buildings most likely to attract the attention of the Transvaal *burghers* (citizens), however, were the three large grain stores, each with a capacity of 5,000 bags. These stores, and indeed the entire factory site, could be viewed from managing director Marks's 'splendid residence' some one and a half miles away at Zwartkoppies.[20]

By 1889–90 the factory employed at least 50 white and over 100 African workers. In December 1889 the German distillation plant was working at full capacity, and producing 1,000 gallons of proof spirit per day from grain supplied exclusively by Transvaal burghers.[21] Even this output, however, was insufficient to maintain stocks, and the management embarked on a programme of expansion. New boilers, kilns, malting floors, stills and storage space were all being added to the factory when, in mid-December 1889, a fire broke out and disrupted production.

The setback caused by the fire proved to be less serious than it might have been, and the company merely lost two months' production. What concerned Marks and his colleagues more, however, was the fact that the distillery had been left uninsured and that the fire was considered to be the work of an arsonist. The owners of the factory were sufficiently convinced of this theory to offer 'a £2,000 reward for the apprehension and conviction of the person or persons implicated in this fiendish act'. In the months after the fire the reward remained unclaimed, the distillery was insured, and the owners

The staff at Hatherley Distillery Ltd., 1892

took the opportunity of making a change in the factory management. Sammy Marks raided Demarillac's Distillery in Harrismith – hailed at the time as 'one of the largest distilleries in the world' – for new managerial talent, and Thomas Strachan came to Pretoria to replace the previous manager, Stokes. Under Strachan's management a series of improvements were made and the business experienced steady expansion. The resources of the company were again stretched, however, when a second fire broke out in the four-storey distillery on 29 May 1891. But since the plant had just been insured for £6,000, and the maturing stock carefully isolated from the distillery proper, the effect of the fire was less serious than might otherwise have been the case.[22]

Nevertheless, in view of the excellent prospects of the company and the need for expansion, these setbacks left De Eerste Fabrieken in de Zuid Afrikaansche Republiek relatively starved of badly needed capital. Marks's solution to this problem was to allow the company to go public. In November 1892, in exchange for £122,000 and shares, the holders of the concession made it over to Eerste Fabrieken Hatherley Distillery Ltd.[23] With the advantage of a listing on the London Stock Exchange, Hatherley Distillery was able to attract international as well as national capital, and the company was on the threshold of a period of spectacular expansion.

Seldom, if ever, could ambitious plans for industrial expansion have been launched into a safer or more sympathetic business environment. What more could capitalists ask for than a government-granted monopoly in a rapidly expanding market? As the sole producer in the Transvaal of cheap spirits for African consumption, Hatherley Distillery found itself catering for a market of 14,000 black miners in 1890, 88,000 in 1897, and an enormous 100,000 by 1899. Privileged access to a market that expanded nearly ten times in as many years was an important part of the Hatherley success story.

It was not only the size of Hatherley's market that was important, however, but its quality. In particular, the fact that the majority of the 100,000-strong workforce was drawn from Mozambique was of the utmost importance. For at least several decades prior to the industrialisation of the Witwatersrand, the peasants and workers of Mozambique had been sold large quantities of wine and spirits – inferior quality alcohol that flowed from the vats of metropolitan Portugal. There is substantial evidence to show that the more proletarianised Africans of southern rural Mozambique, and the black workers of the urban areas along the coast, were considerably addicted to alcohol by the early 1890s.[24] In 1894, the British Consul in the territory, W. A. Churchill, noted how large quantities of spirits were sold in 'up country stores', and that black workers 'spent the greater part of their wages in alcohol, known as "Kaffir Rum"'.[25] In the following year Churchill noted in his annual report that the landing agents in the ports often experienced the greatest difficulty in finding sober black workers. Indeed, this problem became so well known that ships from South Africa brought their own dockers with them to off-load cargo in the Mozambique ports.[26]

The link between alcohol consumption in Mozambique and the recruitment of African miners for the Witwatersrand was also clear to observers in the 1890s. The syndrome of rural underdevelopment and peasant indebtedness ensured that the canteens of the countryside became good recruiting centres for Transvaal labour agents.[27] On the mines themselves the poverty and relatively advanced proletarianised status of an *isidakewa* ('drunkard' – also the African name for Charlie Chaplin), was readily apparent. 'In a store where the boy's belongings were hanging', noted one observer, 'a drunkard's sack was generally noticeable by its age, and leanness of aspect.'[28] Also, African miners returning to Mozambique were at least as likely to be carrying back gas-piping for use in domestic distilleries, as they were to be taking a gun.[29]

This link between alcohol and workers from Mozambique was of considerable importance to both Hatherley and the mining industry. The Pretoria distillery was catering not only for a rapidly expanding market, but also for one in which the potential consumers already had a well-developed predilection for the product. The mining industry, for its part, was quite content for its workers to spend their wages on Hatherley products if they so desired. For, the more money the mineworkers spent on liquor, the less they saved; and the less they saved, the longer they worked before returning to the peasant economies of their rural homelands. In other words, mine owners realised that wages spent on liquor helped lengthen the periods of migratory labour, and tended to produce a more stabilised labour force – in short, it facilitated the process of proletarianisation.

Few of these marketing realities escaped the attention of investors when the Hatherley Company went public in late 1892, and £350,000-worth of £1 shares became available.[30] As possibly the only other large-scale investment opportunity in the Transvaal, the distillery attracted local mining capital seeking to spread and diversify its holdings. A significant proportion of the shares were subscribed to by South African mining capitalists, and throughout the 1890s the depth and extent of their holdings was reflected in the directorships of the company. Besides Sammy Marks, the board of Hatherley Distillery during the 1890s included, at various stages, the following mining capitalists: J. N. De Jongh (Executive Member of the Transvaal Chamber of Mines 1897–1909, President of the Chamber 1906–7); S. Evans (mine manager, associated with the Eckstein Company after 1898 and made a full partner in 1902); L. Ehrlich (before 1894, director of the Ferreira, Modderfontein, Knights, Wolhuter, Main Reef and other Transvaal companies of the S. Neumann Group); and A. Epler (Executive Member of the Witwatersrand Chamber of Mines 1899–1909, and later managing director of Transvaal Goldfields Ltd.).[31]

Where national capital went successfully, international capital was not slow to follow. Thus, Hatherley also came to have a significant number of English, French, Austrian and German shareholders.[32] The interests of these various European investors were safeguarded by individual members of the Hatherley board who acted as the agents of international capital. Director J. H. Curle (mining correspondent of the *Economist*), held an informal brief for English shareholders, while the Bavarian, Ludwig Ehrlich, looked after the portfolio of German investors. During the 1890s the Austrian, Adolf Epler, undertook this task not only at Hatherley but in other concerns as well, and was candidly described in a publication of the time as 'a representative of Foreign Capital in South Africa'. The French investors in Eerste Fabrieken looked to yet another director for their protection – Henri Duval, who was also the manager of the *Banque Française de l'Afrique du Sud* in Johannesburg.[33]

With the benefit of some of the most astute managerial talent available in the Transvaal, and the financial muscle provided by national and international capital, Hatherley Distillery set course for a period of spectacular development. Especially during the early 1890s, Hatherley Distillery was the undisputed master of the Witwatersrand liquor market.

Table 1. Eerste Fabrieken Hatherley Distillery Ltd., profitability 1893–99

Year	Gallons sold	Net profit or loss	Dividend declared
1893	272,616	+£47,404	16%
1894	316,046	+£48,399	16%
1895	386,281	+£98,274	20%
1896	298,130	+£69,569	12%
1897	63,191	−£46,988	–
1898	153,594	+£10,490	–
1899	86,998	+ £2,737	–

Compiled from data contained in *Special Liquor Committee of the Chamber of Mines, Report, 1898*, p. 111, and *Command 624*, June 1901, p. 73.

Any industry which could yield dividends ranging from 12 per cent to 20 per cent was, however, likely to attract the envious attention of competitors, and the large new market in the Transvaal had not escaped the notice of other spirit producers. In theory, Hatherley's monopolistic position was absolutely secure. Besides being the sole producer of grain spirits in the Z.A.R., the company, through its privileged exemption from excise duty, was in a position to undercut any imported spirits. For example, 'Cape Smoke', the notorious cheap brandy produced in the western Cape, could not compete on the legal Rand markets because of high import duties.[34] Through diligent reading of the small print in inter-state treaties, however, one group of spirit producers in southern Africa *did* find a weakness through which they could attack Hatherley Distillery's dominant position. The Treaty of Commerce entered into by the Transvaal and Portugal in 1875, ratified in Pretoria in 1882, and not due to expire until 1902, made provision for the produce of Portugal to enter the Z.A.R. free of duty.[35] It was this chink in the legal armour of Kruger's Republic that producers in Mozambique exploited fully in the mid-1890s. After 1894, and especially after 1895, once the railway line from Delagoa Bay to the Witwatersrand had been opened, Hatherley's firm hold on the Transvaal market was seriously undermined by cheaper spirits originating from two very different sources.

First, rum 'which was distilled at a fraction of the cost at which grain spirit is produced', undercut Hatherley products.[36] In Mozambique, producers such as the Companhia do Assucar de Moçambique turned their attention to the profits to be derived from rum distillation. In 1894 the Companhia's distillery at Mopea produced 5,000 gallons of rum specifically for the Rand market.[37] The following year saw such an expansion of rum distillation that the Companhia exhausted its supplies of sugar. With excess distillation capacity on hand, the Companhia approached the Portuguese government for permission to import additional quantities of sugar from

Natal.[38] The fact that the president of the Companhia, Frederico Ressano Garcia, was also a minister in the Portuguese government no doubt helped ensure that this permission was granted. Since members of the Portuguese ruling elite were personally involved in the manufacture of spirits, and the Z.A.R.'s rail outlet to the sea was at stake, it is perhaps not surprising that the Transvaal government admitted this trade because of 'high political considerations'.[39] In the following years the Companhia consistently manufactured spirits from sugar drawn not only from Mozambique, but from Natal and Mauritius as well. By 1896 the Companhia was still expanding rum production and sharpening its competitive edge through price reductions – the latter being achieved by replacing European personnel at the Mopea distillery with African artisans.[40]

The pattern of expansion to be seen in the Companhia do Assucar's activities was repeated at other distilleries throughout Mozambique. In 1895 the distilleries of Portuguese East Africa exported 84,528 gallons of spirits to the Z.A.R.; in 1896 this rose to 255,157 gallons; in 1897 to 357,260 gallons; and by 1898 it had reached 456,000 gallons.[41] This business bonanza, perhaps without precedent in the economic history of Mozambique, saw the ownership of several distilleries change hands.[42] New capital was attracted to distilleries that could produce alcohol at three shillings a gallon, and command a wholesale price of eight shillings a gallon on the Witwatersrand. Profit margins of this order also warranted investment in new plant and equipment, and the large French company at Lourenço Marques, the *Societé Française de Distillerie*, expanded its activities in 1895. The Societé built a large new distillery on the banks of the Inkomati river, 100 yards from the Transvaal frontier, at the border village of Ressano Garcia.[43] This venture too received the blessing of the Portuguese government.

Second, Hatherley's grain spirits were undercut by cheaper German potato spirit. Indeed, so cheap was the German potato spirit that it undercut even the sugar-based imports from Mozambique.[44] But because of the high import duties in the Z.A.R., German potato spirits could not penetrate the market directly – like 'Cape Smoke', they would simply have ceased to be cheap if imported in the orthodox manner. Both Prussian producers and Transvaal importers therefore had to find a way round this problem if they wished to share in the profits that could be made in the Z.A.R. Well aware that this customs barrier had already proved vulnerable on the eastern border with Mozambique, international capitalists set to work, weaving the sort of legal magic by which the potatoes of Prussia became converted into the 'produce of Portugal'. It was in this latter guise that thousands of gallons of German and Prussian potato spirits flooded into the Transvaal from 1894 onwards.

During the 1890s German liners took on their cargoes of potato spirits at the port of Hamburg. From there, they would fan out into two large southward arcs that embraced the west and east coasts of Africa respectively. The liners *Thekla Boben*, *Hausa*, *Bida* and *Ilorin* worked the Atlantic, and discharged their cargoes in ports from Lagos in the north, to Luanda in the south.[45] The ships of the German East Africa Line, however, worked with a slightly different routine. After taking on their cargoes, the liners *König*, *Herzog*, *Kanzler*, *Admiral* and *Reichstag* would first make for the port of Lisbon. There, they would lie overnight with their cargo of Prussian potato spirit. Then, after a suitable number of hours had elapsed, they would receive a 'certificate of naturalisation' from a port official and, from then on, the cargo would be 'produce of Portugal'.[46] Thereafter the ships would head east through the Suez Canal, and then south into the Indian Ocean. In the 1890s the most important port of call on the southern run was Lourenço Marques. It was in this latter port that the liners discharged the bulk of their cargo of potato spirit – alcohol that was partly destined for local consumption within Mozambique, and partly for the Witwatersrand.[47] The extent of this traffic between 1894 and 1903 is clearly evident from Table 2.

Table 2. Imports of plain *aguardente* through Lourenço Marques, 1894–1903

Year	Quantity in Litres
1894	195,038
1895	182,182
1896	517,709
1897	215,297
1898	195,129
1899	123,839
1900	32,681
1901	28,771
1902	15,977
1903	108

It should be noted that large quantities of the same 'fire-water' were also off-loaded at the ports of Inhambane, Chinde and Quelimane.
Table derived from A. Freire D'Andrade, *Relatorios solne Moçambique*, Lourenço Marques 1907, p. 40.

The Transvaal liquor consumer of the 1890s was thus likely to be drinking spirits coming from one of three basic sources: Hatherley, any one of several Mozambique distilleries, or Germany. Seen another way, the consumer could also, in order of declining cost, be drinking either grain, sugar or potato spirits. He would also, however, be drinking a good deal more than plain alcohol, and, in terms of the cost to his health, he was likely to be paying a good deal more than he bargained for. Even in their 'pure' form direct from the distilleries, these spirits contained a high proportion of amylic alcohol. This latter form of alcohol, also known as fusel oil, was a poisonous by-product of the fermentation process. Samples of Hamburg potato spirit, taken in West Africa, in 1902, revealed a proportion of fusel oil by weight which varied from 1.26 per cent to 4.4 per cent. When a Transvaal chemist analysed spirit from the same source in 1895, he declared it 'unfit for internal use'.[48] Spirits that started their manufactured life unfit for human consumption in their 'pure' form, hardly improved as they passed through the hands of various other intermediaries in the Transvaal.

Most of the spirits which entered Johannesburg first found their way to the wholesalers: firms such as Meskin and Davidoff, Vogelman and Friedman, Kantor Ltd., T. Friedman Ltd., I. Herzfeld Ltd., or Blum & Co. Ltd.[49] A couple of these firms, Kantor and Blum, dealt only in bulk supplies of spirits which they sold directly to smaller bottling concerns. The majority, however, opted for the higher profits to be made through processing the raw spirits into the fiery commercial brands that apparently satisfied the tastes of black and white consumers on the Rand.

Firms involved in the processing business, such as Meskin and Davidoff, required three things in addition to raw spirits: a large supply of bottles, various chemicals and essences, and a stock of forged cork tops and brand labels. The first requisite was obtained through the endless collection of 'empties' from the canteens and back streets of Johannesburg; at a later date some were undoubtedly supplied from the glass works at Hatherley. The second was purchased from a local firm of wholesale chemists – P. J. Peterson & Co.[50] The third requisite – forged labels – came from the firm responsible for printing the *Standard and Diggers' News* – Messrs Matthew and Walker. These forgeries, frequently making use of well-known brand names, suggested that the spirits were manufactured in various European countries such as Scotland, France or Holland. Several different forgeries were printed on a single sheet, and the customer could then cut out the label which he considered appropriate to his product.[51]

Armed with these prerequisites the firms then set about manufacturing various brands of liquor according to recipes that were widely known within the trade. 'Kaffir Brandy', price 16/6d per dozen bottles in 1899, was prepared according to the following formula: 15 gals. Delagoa proof spirit, 15 gals. water, 1 gal. cayenne pepper tincture, ½ lb. mashed prunes, 1½ oz. sulphuric acid and 1 oz. nitric acid. This 'brandy' was coloured through the addition of a suitable quantity of burnt sugar. 'Kaffir Whisky', price 14/6d per dozen bottles in 1899, required the following ingredients: 100 gals. of Delagoa Bay proof spirit, 1 gal. tincture of prunes, 3 lbs glycerine, 1 pint green tea, ½ oz. acetic acid, 20 drops of creosote and 12 drops of oil of cognac. 'Dutch Gin for Kaffirs', price 15/6d per dozen bottles in 1899, required the following: 100 gals. Delagoa Bay proof spirit, 1 gal. sugar syrup, 1 lb tincture of orange peel, 4 oz. turpentine, 1 oz. juniper oil and ½ oz. of fennel. To this concoction was added bead without colouring (an additive partly composed of sulphuric acid), and then the entire quantity of 'gin' was filtered through charcoal.

For the benefit of European consumers in the working class some of the recipes were varied slightly, and the processing was made a little more sophisticated. Whisky, for example, was prepared in exactly the same way as 'Kaffir Whisky' except that it was filtered more frequently. Further, a layer of oak sawdust, when available, was added to the whisky in order to imbue it with a distinctive flavour. The *Transvaal Leader* warned its white Johannesburg readers in 1899: 'Do not be aghast at the prospect of drinking sulphate of copper and green tea, acetic acid and oil of Neroli as Martell's Five Star Liqueur Brandy; you have done it often enough.' Basically, white and black workers alike were expected to drink the same poisonous concoctions. The white workers, however, were required to pay slightly more for their 'refined' taste. Whereas 'Kaffir Ginger Brandy' sold at 16/6d per dozen bottles, the same quantity of 'White Ginger Brandy' cost 22/6d.[52]

The fact that these different types of 'liquor' were sold in vast quantities through public outlets was well known at the time. As early as April 1890, the *Standard and Diggers' News* devoted an entire editorial to the subject. It pointed out how, in a neighbouring colony (probably Mozambique), Hennessy and Martell's XXX Brandy had been analysed, and found to consist of potato spirit, fusel oil, burnt sugar, spirits of nitre and oil of cognac. The editorial continued:

> We cannot prove that what is drunk here as retailed is like these samples, but he would be a bold man who would bet on the purity of the liquor ordinarily retailed in Johannesburg. A public officer is absolutely needed to deal with such matters.[53]

This plea for a public analyst fell upon deaf ears, as did a further appeal two months later. Although subsequent legislation did make legal provision for a public analyst there was no such official in 1895, and as late at 1898 the situation was still unremedied. The government of the Z.A.R. knew only too well that if an analytical chemist started probing the composition of Rand liquor, then the finger of guilt would ultimately point not only to the wholesalers of Johannesburg, but to influential capitalists in Lisbon and Hamburg as well. That was a political price which the Transvaal government was unwilling to pay. The liquor was thus allowed to pass unchallenged from the wholesalers to the retail outlets spread across the Witwatersrand – the canteens.

There was no shortage of canteens in the industrialising republic. As early as 1888 there were 393 licensed canteens throughout the Transvaal and of these, no fewer than 147 were in the more concentrated Witwatersrand area. A mere four years later, in 1892, the number of licensed canteens on the Witwatersrand had jumped from 147 to 552. And it is estimated that at the zenith of the liquor trade in 1895, between 750 and 1,000 canteens could be found in the area between Krugersdorp in the west and Nigel in the east. Even by 1898, when the licensed retail liquor trade had declined substantially, there were 495 recognised outlets in the magisterial districts of Krugersdorp, Johannesburg and Boksburg, and in the same year the Licensing Board had to deal with 165 new applications.[54]

Numerically significant from an early date, this petty bourgeoisie was quick to recognise its class interests, and to organise accordingly. As early as 1888 the canteen keepers of the various mining districts had got together to form the Witwatersrand Licensed Victuallers' Association (W.L.V.A.). By March 1890 W.L.V.A. had 100 members, and the executive was considering applications from a further 40 prospective members.[55] The Association protected members when their licences were threatened, petitioned the state to liberalise the liquor laws in an attempt to expand the size of its legal market, and sought to limit competition by exercising control over the numbers of retailers entering the trade.[56] While the canteen keepers were without the international connections or power that the liquor producers enjoyed, they were a local and national force to be reckoned with.

While the organisational power of the retailers was undoubtedly impressive, it should not be forgotten that the liquor trade also operated within a wider context, which tended to produce its own constraints. A colonial ruling class which had established a state by conquest, and which held out hopes for an industrialising economy, was never likely to endorse a *laissez-faire* policy wholeheartedly. In theory, the right of the canteen keepers to sell unlimited quantities of spirits to the growing number of black workers was severely circumscribed. According to the regulations, the Liquor Licensing Boards strictly vetted all new applications for licences, and issued only those which were considered to be in the public interest. The liquor law of 1889 made it clear that a canteen keeper could sell alcohol to an African only on the production of a permit signed by a white master, and that the police and courts could enforce these requirements. Other less onerous constraints derived from the wrath of employers, or the hostility of 'public opinion' which objected to an unfettered trade that produced large numbers of drunken, noisy, and at times violent black workers. The barriers that these supposed constraints erected, however, were less than formidable in the harsher light of practice.

The attitudes of the Witwatersrand Liquor Licensing Boards to the scores of applications reaching them throughout the 1880s and early 1890s can euphemistically be described as 'open' or 'flexible'. During the first decade of mining development, virtually any applicant who could raise the necessary fee was granted a retail liquor licence. Strong petty-bourgeois representation on the early Licensing Boards ensured a considerable degree of overlap between what was perceived as 'business' and what passed for the 'public interest'. In July 1889 the Boards were taken to task by the local press for not balancing the number of retail outlets in Johannesburg against the 'public interest':

> In one corner of this town, within two minutes of the Exchange, there are no less than from 10 to 12 licensed drinking shops. If the whole town is looked over it will be found that purely drinking dens are out of all proportion to the requirements of the people, and outside the town the conveniences for Kaffirs in procuring drink are legion.[57]

Even after limited state representation on the Boards was provided for in late 1892, there was little change in this basically liberal attitude on the part of the local authorities.[58]

Occasionally, it is true, objections *were* made to the granting of canteen licences. The more honest of these petitions, such as that of the Braamfontein Ratepayers' Association to the Johannesburg Liquor Licensing Board in 1894, categorically spelt out the threat that canteens presented to local property values. Usually, however, this real objection was hidden beneath eloquent concern over 'social nuisance' or 'health'. Even in such cases, however, the aspirant canteen keeper stood a good chance of getting the objection overruled if he could elicit the support of a local notable.[59] The pre-1896 canteen keeper could thus look for protection to a basically sympathetic Licensing Board; at the very least, the number of retail liquor licences granted on the Rand kept abreast of the expanding population.

The canteen keepers of this era had little reason greatly to fear 'public opinion'. Certainly there was a constant stream of individual complaints to stem the volume of liquor sales, or to diminish drunkenness. Such organised public protest as there was occurred mainly during the initial period of rapid expansion in 1891–2, and was largely the work of two bodies.

Particularly in 1892, both the Labour Union and the Transvaal Temperance Alliance briefly acted as media of 'public opinion'. The geographical segregation of the races was not so marked at this time, and the Labour Union became concerned when its white members were attacked by drunken black miners. Thus, in November of that year the Union organised an 'anti-drink demonstration' which attracted about 700 whites and several local organisations – the one notable absentee was a representative from the powerful Chamber of Mines.[60] The Union, however, soon found that it had more important concerns and turned its attention to other issues. The Transvaal Temperance Alliance, for its part, appears to have had an equally transient effect on liquor policy. Several factors could account for this failure. It is possible that in the frenzied atmosphere of a money-making town, poorly endowed with middle-class moral custodians, few people were willing to devote time to such matters. By August 1892 the Alliance could muster only 70 members. However, it is equally plausible that the Alliance failed because it attracted a leadership that had other concerns besides temperance matters. Perhaps it was simply a combination of common sense and coincidence that led to the formation of the Alliance in 1892 – the same year that the Hatherley Distillery Co. went public. It would be stretching matters too far, however, to make coincidence also account for the fact that the Alliance was presided over by William Hoskin. As chairman of the local Chamber of Commerce, Hoskin's concern over canteens and African sobriety was unlikely to be totally divorced from his other interests – in black spending patterns on the Witwatersrand.[61] For obvious reasons, merchants would be pleased if African wages spent in canteens could somehow be diverted into traders' tills.

This weakness of 'public opinion', and the strength of the Licensed Victuallers' Association as an almost dominant fraction of the local petty bourgeoisie, combined to give canteen keepers on the Witwatersrand considerable room for economic manoeuvre. But, important as these factors undoubtedly were, they were perhaps ultimately less significant than yet another factor – the deep-seated ambivalence of mining capitalists towards the liquor trade at this stage.

Mine owners were aware that alcohol helped them secure and control black workers, and they were therefore most reluctant to countenance any attempt to close canteens. In fact, the mining capitalists found that they had to act as a brake on 'public opinion' which was tending to demand total prohibition for all Africans. At a large public meeting held in 1891 to discuss the liquor traffic, the capitalists and their spokesmen unsuccessfully tried to persuade the audience that total prohibition for black workers was 'premature'. Similarly, in the same year, a mining commissioner could state in court, without fear of contradiction in capitalist circles, that 'nearly everyone is agreed that total prohibition would be disastrous to the native labour position'. When there was further loose talk about 'total prohibition' in 1892, the *Standard and Diggers' News* warned its readers in an editorial that it was the liquor trade 'alone that ensures the Fields a labour supply. Constrict it, and the Rand's real troubles will begin.'[62] As late as 1895 the *Annual Report of the Chamber of Mines* made it clear that, while the capitalists wanted stricter control of the liquor traffic, they did not favour total prohibition.[63]

This apparently tolerant attitude of most mining capitalists towards the canteens was not a casual by-product of *laissez-faire* boardroom philosophy. Far from it: the mine owners took their cue from the hard school of practical experience. In particular, they were guided by their mine managers, the men in the lower echelons of the industry who had the most immediate experience of the problems involved in obtaining and controlling African labour.[64] It was these mine managers who were most aware that alcohol could 'attract' labour to the miserable compounds and that it assisted in the proletarianisation of migrant labour – all without direct cash cost to the company. In fact, a significant number of mine managers actually operated an industrial variant of the notorious *dop* system – the *tot* system, which formed part of the wages of the agricultural labourers in the Cape. When the use of alcohol in the control of black mineworkers was debated in the local press in 1891, it was noted that:

> . . .at Kimberley [diamond mines] familiarity with the glass has built moderation in the black man, while it is admitted that better work is got out of him when he sees the prospect of a cheering glass at the end of a day's labour. That is very generally admitted on these Fields also, where the permit system is largely taken advantage of by employers of coloured labour. At not a few works permits are regularly issued for supplies to the native hands, the reasonableness of the request for stimulating refreshment being amiably admitted on the grounds that the 'boy' so humoured and so refreshed is the better labourer.[65]

Chamber of Mines' policy and ideology up to 1895 were firmly rooted in practice.

The mine managers' attitude towards the canteens might have crystallised most clearly on the issue of labour control, but several of them also had a more direct and immediate interest in the success of the retail liquor trade. As early as 1889 it was reported that one could 'see the names of managers of gold companies attached to the applications for canteen licences near the claims, and in recommendation thereof'.[66] It is possible that in some cases the mine managers had little option but to make such recommendations, since they were merely responding to directorial pressure from higher up in the industrial hierarchy. At the Spes Bona, George Goch and Henry Nourse mines, for example, the canteen keepers on the mining property were all closely related to mining directors. With such powerful backing it would have been a foolish mine manager who withheld his 'recommendation' for a liquor licence. But in most cases the mine managers got involved in the canteen business of their own volition in order to supplement their incomes. While the number of canteens close to the compounds was relatively small and the competition limited, the managers could expect fairly good returns from their 'shares' in the liquor business. As the number of canteens grew, however, so competition increased, and the managers had to act more vigorously in order to ensure that 'their' canteen still got its share of the trade. By 1895 some of their methods, and those of their subordinates, the compound managers, aroused the resentment of the W.L.V.A. A deputation from the W.L.V.A. to the Chamber of Mines complained that 'on some mines natives are ordered to go to a particular canteen in which some employee of the company has a pecuniary interest. . .'.[67] Thus the mine managers were *not*, at this stage, fundamentally opposed to the consumption of alcohol by their employees.

All these factors facilitated the emergence and entrenchment of the retail liquor trade during the first decade of the Witwatersrand's development. Finally, however, it was the state which made a vital contribution to these developments. In the eyes of Kruger and his government, Hatherley Distillery occupied a position of twofold importance. First, the distillery lay at the very centre of the State President's concessions policy and his strategy for industrialisation. Kruger was proud of his Eerste Fabrieken, and also a particularly close friend of its major shareholder, Sammy Marks. The President's attachment to Marks and the distillery was at least strong enough for him to spend one Christmas holiday at Hatherley. Second and more important, the Eerste Fabrieken provided a steady and expanding market for large quantities of the burghers' grain and fruit – a point which Kruger unfailingly brought to the notice of the distillery's critics.[68] As a producer who personally supplied large quantities of citrus for Hatherley's 'Orange Wine' from his farm 'Boekenhoutfontein', the State President had first-hand experience of this fact, which would also have appealed to other members of the Afrikaner rural bourgeoisie.[69] Whilst these fundamentals of business life remained constant, the state's attitude towards the canteen keepers was hardly likely to be one of uncompromising hostility.

In the early 1890s it was not simply a question of the state being unwilling to act against the liquor retailers; often it was *unable* to do so. Johannesburg had a population of about 25,000 people in June 1899. The entire population of the magisterial district, spread over a considerable area, was served by a police force of 35 men – of which only half was on duty at any one time. Not only was this 'Zarp' force (Z.A.R. police) very small, it was also very disorganised. There were no rules, regulations, codes or laws which allowed the Commandant of the police to discipline his ill-uniformed men. Salary gradations in the lower and middle ranks were non-existent, and a sergeant with five years' experience received as much as a newly appointed constable. To make matters worse, the salaries were very poor and most irregularly paid – on one occasion in 1895 the Zarps were forced to go on 'strike' in order to obtain their earnings. All this, together with the fact that Z.A.R. nationals alone were eligible to serve in the force, meant that the police could attract only men of the most doubtful calibre. Poor illiterate Afrikaners, drawn from the most proletarianised stratum of rural society, were ill-suited to law enforcement duties in a brash mining town dominated by foreign workers, traders and capitalists. The force was 'one of the greatest scandals in the State' and, in 1894, the Commandant of Police, D. E. Schutte, wrote an open letter in which he publicly admitted:

> I acknowledge the *rottenness* of the entire police force, but decline to accept the disgrace attached thereto, having striven to reorganise the same, but failed through lack of support.[70]

Clearly, the police force hardly represented the strong arm of the state.

Commandant Schutte's problems, however, did not end with the personnel of the Zarps, since his force was also somewhat hampered by the liquor law. A decision handed down by the High Court made it very difficult to obtain a conviction against any canteen owner who sold liquor to black workers without a permit. By 1891 the Court held that only licensees could be prosecuted for this offence and, since most canteen keepers had employees who undertook the actual serving of alcohol, convictions were few and far between.[71] In the lower courts, at least one magistrate took the opportunity, in passing sentence, of severely criticising the law which made it so difficult for the police to set up successful 'traps'.[72]

The canteen keepers were not slow to exploit any of these weaknesses, nor to open up others. They approached the badly paid policemen and succeeded in bribing a large number of Zarps.[73] The 'business insurance' provided by bribery was supplemented by other more practical precautions. Most canteen keepers employed a 'gang of spies to watch the approach of the police from every possible corner and frustrate their movements'.[74] These 'spies' and 'sentries' constituted the early rudiments of a petty-bourgeois business army which was to adopt a more organised form, and assume a more aggressive posture during the class war of 1897–9.

Because of the weakness of the state, the ambivalence of the mining capitalists, the studied indifference of the Afrikaner ruling class and the sympathy of the petty-bourgeois dominated Licensing Boards, the retail liquor trade boomed before 1896. The boom, however, was not without its costs. It killed hundreds of workers – black and white – who consumed that working-class poison passing commercially as 'liquor'.[75] It was 'a common thing', noted one contemporary observer, 'to find "boys" lying dead on the veld from exposure and the effects of the vile liquids sold them by unscrupulous dealers'.[76] The Superintendent of the Johannesburg Cemetery was more than familiar with notices of interment that listed the cause of death as 'alcoholic poisoning'. He was reported to have surveyed one such corpse and remarked: 'Several of these every week – the cursed stuff burns their insides, and they never recover after a drinking bout.'[77] The same liquor also contributed to the many murders in the mining town, as well as to the large-scale 'faction fights' that broke out amongst black workers of different ethnic origin. It was also responsible for the enormous social problem of drunkenness or, in the idiom of the day, it created 'hordes of drunken Kaffirs'.

These human costs of the liquor industry left the alliance of class interests in the Z.A.R. relatively unmoved. There was, however, another cost which moved them more – the cost to capital. Thus, while no commercial or industrial leaders were willing to complain or protest about the number of working-class *deaths* caused by alcohol, they were more than ready to abhor the cost to capital in terms of inefficiency and lowered productivity. In the short term, the deaths of the workers did not matter to the capitalists; the dead miner of today was bound to be replaced by the Lancastrian, Cornishman, Zulu or Shangaan of tomorrow. What *did* matter was that those who were alive should form the core of a sober, productive and efficient labour force. Given the level of alcohol consumption, however, not even that could be guaranteed, and thus the capitalists' wage bills were unnecessarily increased.

Now, this unnecessarily high wage bill had been a feature of the mining industry since at least the late 1880s. By the mid-1890s, however, the Witwatersrand mines were experiencing the important financial and structural changes which were associated with the transition from earlier forms of mineral exploitation to deep-level mining.[78] Significantly less speculative than earlier ventures, deep-level mining offered the industry a long-term future; but in turn it demanded a more realistic cost structure. It is thus significant that during this period of readjustment, in 1895, the Chamber of Mines complained that:

> . . . drunkenness was on the increase at the mines, and that, in consequence, the scarcity of labour was intensified, as companies able to get them had to keep far more boys in their compounds than were required on any one day to make up for the number periodically disabled by drink.[79]

The percentage of the black labour force 'disabled by drink' each day was officially estimated by the mine owners to be of the order of 15 per cent, but others put it as high as 25 per cent.[80] It obviously added significantly to the item which was already the single largest mining cost on the Rand – African wages.

By 1895–6 it was becoming very clear to mine owners that a massive contradiction had found its way into the capitalist development of the Transvaal: any further expansion in a large and very profitable liquor industry would be at the expense of the very motor of capitalism, the mining industry. This contradiction was not without irony, since individual mining capitalists had themselves helped to create the Hatherley liquor machine which now jeopardised their long-term profits. Two contemporary writers, Scoble and Abercrombie, put this succinctly at the time, noting of the Pretoria distillery:

> This is the temple [Hatherley] where are distilled those nectars which goad the Kaffirs of the reef to deeds of derring-do, and it would certainly have paid the present concessionaires, who have large mining interests, far better never to have started it could they have secured instead a concession for 'total prohibition'.[81]

But although the contradiction itself may have become fully visible in 1895, there is no doubt that mining capital, as opposed to individual mining capitalists, had for some time past taken into account its longer-term profitability requirements. It was this secondary strand of thinking amongst mine owners, the recognition of the longer-term need for a sober and efficient working class, which underpinned the 'ambivalence' of mining capital noted earlier. Thus, from an early date the Chamber of Mines, while not in favour of 'total prohibition', undertook a series of actions which attempted to control the black workers' liquor consumption. At the very time that Hatherley, individual mining capitalists, mine managers and the canteen keepers were allowing a contradiction to develop whereby the black man on the Rand was primarily a liquor *consumer*, capital, as embodied in the Chamber of Mines, was establishing those footholds from which it could ultimately destroy the developing contradiction, and ensure that the African was primarily a *worker*. It is to this latter set of actions that we now turn.

Before 1896, in order to secure the cheap and sober black workforce which alone could guarantee profits, the Chamber of Mines could choose to fight on any one of three fronts. First, it could go for a head-on confrontation with the producers of alcohol – particularly Hatherley, which was the major supplier. Second, it could put pressure on the state to administer the liquor laws more efficiently. Third, it could conduct a campaign against the petty bourgeoisie which, to an increasing extent, was expanding its control of the canteen business. Of these three, the first front was obviously the most difficult to fight on. Hatherley's central role in Kruger's industrialisation strategy, the distillery's importance for the grain market and the State President's friendship with Sammy Marks, all combined to rule out that possibility. The Chamber therefore concentrated its efforts on the second and third fronts.

The Chamber of Mines sought to undermine the canteen keepers' position at the very source of petty-bourgeois power – the Liquor Licensing Boards. Using 'public opinion' which showed growing concern over the 'hordes of drunken Kaffirs', the Chamber attempted to apply the brake to the process of granting retail licences. By April 1890 the state was already on the defensive, and the government agreed that in future all licences granted by the Boards would have to be ratified in Pretoria. The large public meeting of 1891 held in order to discuss the liquor traffic (see above p. 59), generated further activity by the mining capitalists. The mine owners and their spokesmen got public support for a motion demanding that no new liquor licences be granted in mining areas, and that existing licences should not be renewed. They then arranged for this and other resolutions on the liquor question to be taken to Pretoria by a deputation under the leadership of mine owner, George Goch.[82]

Through exercising continual pressure for what it chose to term 'local representation', the Chamber also succeeded in getting its President appointed to the Johannesburg Liquor Licensing Board in 1895. Delighted with its success in Johannesburg, where it described the new system as 'working well', the Chamber tried to expand its power base to include Krugersdorp and Boksburg. The politicians of Pretoria, however, were wary of the expanding power of the mining capitalists, and the government resisted further Chamber of Mines pressure in this direction. By the mid-1890s the Liquor Licensing Boards were becoming increasingly politicised, and they were simply one of several arenas in which mining capital was pitted against the Afrikaner ruling class. This emerged with even greater clarity in the wake of the Jameson Raid in December 1895. In 1896 the government refused to allow the incoming President of the Chamber of Mines, J. Hay, to replace Lionel Phillips on the Johannesburg Board. Instead, the government pointedly allocated his seat to H. F. Pistorius, President of the Chamber of Commerce, and by so favouring the petty bourgeoisie, underlined its continued suspicion of mining capital.[83] In general, battle honours on this front were shared, since the government tended to play off the petty bourgeoisie, or fractions of it, against the advances of mining capital.

On the second front – the attempt to get more efficient state action against illicit liquor sales – the Chamber of Mines enjoyed slightly greater success. Here, away from the politics of committees and on the open ground of 'public opinion', the Chamber could harness more support. In particular, it attempted to exploit the groundswell of white annoyance at the amount of public drunkenness and violence amongst black workers. Individual members of the Chamber of Mines frequently raised these issues in the columns of the local press, and they were also active at public meetings. At the 1891 meeting they got support for motions which demanded that the government change the rules of evidence as they affected liquor cases, and that offenders should be given prison sentences in addition to fines.

This type of Johannesburg-residents-cum-Chamber-of-Mines 'public opinion' was not the stuff of which spectacular victories were made. Not only was this a subordinate strand of thinking *within* the Chamber, but what was 'public opinion' to the Chamber of Mines was not necessarily 'public opinion' to the Volksraad. Nevertheless, the ideological offensive of individual activists within the Chamber of Mines should not be underrated. Locally the effect of this 'public opinion' could be seen, and nowhere more clearly than in the court of Magistrate van den Berg.[84] Between September 1889 and June 1891 the average fine for selling liquor to a 'native' without a permit increased five times, from £10 (or one month in prison), to £50 (or three months).[85] Perhaps more important still was the long-term effect of the Chamber's campaign. This early offensive laid the foundations from which a strong attack could be launched on the canteen keepers in 1897–9. Before 1895, however, the Chamber of Mines could not claim a general success on this front, as was clearly indicated by the continuing liquor boom.

By 1891 the Chamber of Mines was also worrying at the state on another front, attempting to obtain an efficient and corruption-free police force which could deal with the large-scale theft of gold amalgam by white workers, and the enormous consumption of illicit liquor by black workers. On this issue, the tactic of the Chamber was to exploit the strains of disunity within the Afrikaner ruling class. In particular, the mine owners attempted to make use of the growing Afrikaner 'progressive' opposition to President Kruger.

The 'progressives' did not constitute a party as such, but formed rather a loosely knit Afrikaner political alliance in broad opposition to the Kruger administration. Two of the central figures in this alliance were the widely respected Lukas Meyer, and Ewald Esselen, a former judge of the High Court. Under their guidance the opposition of this group became increasingly well organised and effective between 1890 and 1892. In clear and outspoken terms they denounced corruption, maladministration, and government policies on the franchise, railways and concessions. In the 1893 election they achieved their greatest advance when their presidential candidate, General Piet Joubert, almost succeeded in defeating Kruger.[86]

Kruger responded in 1894 by devising a scheme by which he hoped to upstage his new Afrikaner political rivals. Seeking to take some of the wind out of the 'progressive' sails, he offered Ewald Esselen the post of State Attorney. Esselen accepted the offer, leaving behind him a lucrative £5,000-a-year law practice. The gamble which Kruger had taken in appointing this Scottish-trained lawyer, who was broadly opposed to his policies, was quickly spotted by the Chamber of Mines.

The Chamber noted with some approval Esselen's first act on taking office – the separation of the hitherto single post of State Attorney and Head of Police. The mine owners had long suspected that previous police commandants were personally involved in the illicit liquor traffic; Esselen's action gave them more room to manoeuvre.[87] Once the departments were separated the Chamber of Mines felt free to approach the State Attorney about the problem of the police. The mine owners suggested to Esselen that a special force of detectives be established to deal exclusively with the problems of gold thefts and illicit liquor sales. In order to overcome the old problem of low salaries and police corruption, it was proposed that the 'specials' be jointly paid by the state and the Chamber of Mines.[88] Esselen agreed to these proposals, and in order to implement the scheme he recruited Andrew Trimble from the Cape colonial service as Chief Detective. By August 1894 things seemed to be working quite well. 'Specials' such as Charles and Freddy Ueckermann, who were based in Pretoria and reported directly to the State Attorney, regularly raided illicit liquor dens in Johannesburg and received one-third of the fines imposed on canteen keepers.[89]

At this stage the Chamber of Mines had every reason to be optimistic. Its indirect incursion into Afrikaner politics seemed to be reaping dividends. Throughout September and October 1894 the 'specials' put the canteen keepers under great pressure.[90] At one stage, in a desperate attempt to come to terms with the new legal regime, the W.L.V.A. even went so far as to agree to close all 'Kaffir Bars' on Sundays. For his part, Andrew Trimble tried to extend this initiative and secure its effectiveness by policing the police. In January 1895 he arrested the senior detective in Johannesburg, Donovan, on a charge of accepting bribes from a canteen keeper named Greenstone.[91] He then persuaded State Attorney Esselen to arrange for Donovan's dismissal from the police force.

The Chamber of Mines, however, had chosen to make its indirect advance into a most sensitive area: one that involved intra-ruling class politics, and one which also ultimately affected the economic interests of the Afrikaner bourgeoisie. No sooner did Trimble's campaign get under way, than opposition groups started agitating for the Chief Detective's removal. The canteen keepers, particularly the Chairman of the W.L.V.A., Foote, and a nephew of Sammy Marks's, S. Heymann, consistently travelled to Pretoria, where they lobbied against the confirmation of Trimble's appointment. Their agitation came at a fortuitous moment. Kruger and his supporters were becoming disenchanted with their policy of *toenadering* (conciliation) towards the 'progressives'. When Trimble's appointment came up for ratification before the Volksraad and Esselen chose to make it an issue of confidence, Kruger saw his opportunity for getting rid of both men. The appointment was not confirmed, Esselen resigned, and Kruger appointed one of 'his' Hollanders, Dr H. Coster, as State Attorney. Coster's first action was to reappoint Donovan, the very man Esselen had sacked, as chief detective in Johannesburg.[92] The Chamber's first attempt to exploit cleavages within the Afrikaner ruling class was less than a complete success.

By late 1895 the Chamber of Mines was faced with this bitter disappointment and it had achieved only limited success on other fronts. The retail liquor trade boomed, and 1895 saw an all-time high in Transvaal alcohol consumption – the contradiction within capitalist development was at its most acute. Confronted with what it could only consider as a series of unsavoury realities, the Chamber realised that the time was ripe for a more radical approach to the liquor problem. On 6 July 1896 the Chamber of Mines called a special meeting to consider the 'liquor question', and from it emerged a new stance. The mine owners jettisoned their old demands for stricter and more efficient *control* of a system which allowed black workers access to alcohol through employer-issued permits. The capitalists were now willing to abandon any benefits which they might have reaped from the operation of their own industrial variant of the dop or tot system. Instead, the meeting directed the Volksraad's attention to 'the immediate necessity for legislation by which the sale of intoxicating liquors to natives in the mining districts and surrounding fields shall be totally prohibited'.[93] In calling for 'total prohibition' the Chamber of Mines had finally reached a position which a section of Johannesburg 'public opinion' had reached at least five years earlier. Slowly, reluctantly and only after numerous other courses had been tried, the Chamber of Mines had to abandon the exploitation of alcohol as a means of social and economic control over black workers.

Having achieved ideological fusion with 'public opinion' in pursuit of 'total prohibition', the Chamber of Mines was in a stronger position to challenge the Kruger government. It again sought out the discordant group within the Afrikaner ruling class – the 'progressives'. This time it used the local Volksraad member, Geldenhuis, to lobby for a 'total prohibition' clause in any new legislation on liquor. Geldenhuis in turn joined forces with another well-known Volksraad 'progressive', J. P. Steenkamp, and with Chief Justice J. G. Kotzé. These three, with the aid of other Raad members, ensured that when Act 17 of 1896 was passed it contained a 'total prohibition' clause. This time, for a variety of complex reasons, the divisions within Afrikaner politics had been capable of rapid exploitation and had yielded a handsome dividend. Hereafter, the Chamber of Mines clung tenaciously to the 'total prohibition' clause under all circumstances.

In general the Chamber of Mines could look back on the years before 1896 as something of a failure, since their black workers had been treated primarily as consumers for the benefit of the liquor industry and its allies. Equally, however, the Chamber could look forward to 1 January 1897, when the 'total prohibition' clause would become effective. As the last weeks of 1896 slipped by, the mine owners had every reason to believe that they were on the verge of a golden age in which they would have sober, efficient and cheap labour.

Stalemate – the black worker as worker and consumer

The Peruvian connection and the rise of the illicit liquor syndicates, 1897–1899

In order fully to appreciate and understand the problems of the liquor producers in this second period, it is necessary to recapitulate what had occurred in the months immediately before.

As viewed from Sammy Marks's position in the Hatherley boardroom, 1896 and especially 1897 were bad years for business. Ever since the opening of the Lourenço Marques railway line in 1895, increasing quantities of Delagoa Bay rum and German potato spirits had found their way to the Witwatersrand. The Pretoria distillery's grain spirit simply could not hold its share of the market against the cheaper imported liquor. In 1896, for the first time in its history, Hatherley found itself with falling sales, and between 1895 and 1896 net profits fell from £98,274 to £69,569. The principal producers and wholesalers in Mozambique had become increasingly well organised. In order to protect their own profit margins, the firms in Portuguese East Africa had got together to form an 'Alcohol Trust' in 1896. Members of the 'Trust' agreed to 'sell only an equal number of gallons each, in proportion to the demand', and more important, they had agreed on 'a uniform price'.[94] In effect, two giant competitors were challenging each other for the Transvaal market – a situation far removed from the cosy concession that Marks and his partners had bought nearly a decade earlier. Then, as if this picture of business-woe was not already dark enough, came the growing talk of 'total prohibition'. No sooner had the rumours of 'total prohibition' been circulated than the 1896 liquor act had been passed. When 'total prohibition' came into force on 1 January 1897 Hatherley Distillery was required to make the traumatic transition from being a squeezed competitor to being a producer with virtually no market at all. Overwhelmingly dependent on its liquor sales to black workers, Hatherley was totally unprepared for such a dramatic setback. The lowered profit margin of 1896 looked handsome beside the net loss of £46,988 sustained in 1897.

In attempting to overcome this increasingly depressing situation, Marks and his fellow directors could have adopted any one of three basic strategies. First, they could have fought a defensive battle in order to retain what had been theirs in the past – monopoly production for a black retail market unhampered by cheaper imports. In practice this would have involved getting 'total prohibition' lifted, and at the same time stopping the Delagoa Bay trade in spirits. As a supplement to this strategy, the Pretoria distillery would have to continue to supply, to the best of its ability, the illicit liquor dealers who continued to operate despite the nominal 'total prohibition'. Second, by adopting innovative and creative marketing strategies they could try to redefine 'their' market. Here the most logical move would be to try switching to the European retail liquor trade, in the hope that this would compensate for the 'lost' African market. Third, Hatherley itself could attempt to get into the rum and potato spirits business – an aggressive move that would protect the distillery from price-cutting should the African market be resuscitated to its full former strength. In practice this would mean going 'multi-national' and somehow reaching agreement with the powerful 'Alcohol Trust' in Mozambique. Given the magnitude of the problems facing Hatherley, the directors could not afford to dismiss any of these possibilities. Making full use of the business brains on his board, as well as their wide range of contacts, Marks started to work on all of these strategies.

Four months before 'total prohibition' was due to be enforced, the managing director opened his campaign to defend the Pretoria distillery. He wrote to the government on 6 August 1896, protesting about the new liquor law and pointing out that it severely damaged the concession which he and his partners had been granted. Six weeks after 'total prohibition' came into effect, on 19 February 1897, Marks again wrote to the government in similar vein. Neither of these initiatives brought any response from an unsympathetic administration, and Marks realised that he would have to approach them yet again. On 30 April 1897 he wrote his strongest letter, containing a final plea, and making new proposals. The managing director on this occasion first chose to remind the Volksraad of the capital invested in the distillery, and of the fact that the glass factory had been erected almost solely at its insistence. Marks followed up this rather stinging reminder with yet another telling point. He pointed out to the Raad that the poisonous duty-free spirits which came into the Transvaal made a mockery of its concession to him, and that it hardly qualified as the 'produce of Portugal'. Having established his case, Marks then proceeded to put forward his proposals. He suggested that the state undertake more rigorous quality control measures against the liquor sold on the Rand – a blow aimed directly at cheap potato spirits – and requested permission to import, duty-free, blending materials and essences required for his business. Finally, he asked that the distillery be compensated for the losses which it had been forced to sustain as a result of government measures.[95] Virtually all of this appeal was ignored.

The absence of a positive government response might have disappointed Marks, but it could hardly have surprised him. After all, it was only a matter of months since the Volksraad had voted for the 'progressive' measures contained in the liquor act. Marks knew as well as any man in the Transvaal that Kruger was personally sympathetic to the canteen keepers and to Hatherley, but that he could not muster sufficient support to reverse the relevant clauses in the act. If Marks was to get the Volksraad to act then he had somehow to increase the State President's and his supporters' political leverage. In order to do this Marks probably worked through his nephew, who was also the manager of Hatherley's Johannesburg branch, S. L. Heymann.

Samuel Heymann started his working life as an apothecary in a small village near Moscow before making his way to South Africa. In the 1870s, at the age of 19, he 'marched like a modern Dick Whittington from Cape Town to Kimberley, and thence to Pretoria, and presented himself to his uncle, Mr. Sam Marks'.[96] Subsequently he worked his way up from a 'subordinate position' in the Hatherley organisation to the post of Johannesburg director. Heymann was a very influential figure in local business circles, and politically ambitious. As a credit-granting wholesaler he held considerable power over canteen keepers and was a member of the Chamber of Commerce as well as being Vice-President of the W.L.V.A.[97] He was politically active as a lobbyist during the Trimble affair, and on at least one occasion stood for office in local elections. For all these reasons he was well placed to be Sammy Marks's campaign manager, and when the distillery's books subsequently showed that, during 1897 sums from £20 to £40 were paid to unnamed persons to organise petitions calling for an end to 'total prohibition', there could be little doubt that most of the organisation was undertaken by Samuel Heymann.

In order to avoid raising the suspicions of the two most hostile Volksraad members, Steenkamp and Burger, these petitions were so worded as to make no mention of 'Hatherley Distillery'.[98] Although the exact fate of these petitions is unknown, it seems probable that they entered the political currency of the time, and that they played their small part in the liquor commissions of 1898 and 1899.

At the same time that he was writing to the government and organising a petition programme, Marks was also making important changes within the distillery itself. In particular, he ensured that there was a shift in production away from cheap spirits and towards the manufacture of quality liquor more suitable for European customers. This move neatly supplemented his request to the government for tighter quality control of spirits sold on the Witwatersrand, and he underlined his seriousness in this regard by arranging for the recruitment of top-class distillers in Europe. By early 1897 these new distillers – R. van Eibergen Santhagens from the Netherlands, Le Farge from France, and H. Coffey from Scotland – were at work at Hatherley.[99]

Neither of these two broad courses outlined above, however, were in themselves sufficient to place Hatherley on a sound economic foundation. Individually these strategies were inconclusive, and collectively they had the disadvantage of being time-consuming. By mid-1897 it was abundantly clear to Marks and his colleagues that their long-term security lay in making a quick and definitive entry into the Delagoa Bay trade, which was still the major supplier of the now illicit liquor market in the Transvaal.

Sammy Marks's first move was to contact the two Lourenço Marques wholesalers at the very centre of the 'Alcohol Trust' – Hunt and Auerbach, and Joost and Gubler. It is probable that the former of these firms acted as the wholesale outlet for the Societé Française de Distillerie. The latter firm certainly acted in that capacity for the Mopea Distillery which belonged to the Companhia do Assucar. Messrs Joost and Gubler were also involved in the potato spirits business since they acted as the local representatives of the German East Africa Line and, perhaps significantly, their business premises also housed the Imperial German Consulate. Through these firms and another intermediary, Baron d'Inhaca, Marks tried to establish exactly how much capital Hatherley would require to get control of the largest liquor producer in Mozambique. By early December 1897 the board of Hatherley Distillery knew that they needed at least £50,000 to acquire a controlling interest in the French company's distilleries at Lourenço Marques and Ressano Garcia, and to protect their vulnerable Mozambique flank.[100]

Knowing how much to raise was one thing. Knowing how to raise it was another. In looking for a solution to this problem Marks and his colleagues could be confident that the Paris *Bourse* (Stock Exchange) would be interested in the prospect of a large company, especially one with a good record like Hatherley, taking over the French company. If they did not know it themselves, then Henri Duval of the Banque Française de l'Afrique du Sud in Johannesburg would certainly have told them. The directors therefore decided to raise the capital through a new share issue. It seems likely that many of the 75,000 £1 shares made available to the public were placed in Paris. At the same time the Pretoria company decided to establish a permanent 'Paris Committee' of four members – a structure which had a precedent in the form of a similar 'London Committee'. By the end of 1897 Sammy Marks was the chairman of a company with listings in Paris and London, and with an issue share capital of close on half-a-million pounds.[101]

From this stronger base, negotiations for the acquisition of the French company could continue. On 12 January 1898 the chairman of the French company, Mr Villar, and the secretary of his Ressano Garcia Distillery, Mr Paul Regnet, were both present at a meeting of the Hatherley board. By this time, the Societé de Distillerie's price had risen by £10,000 and the deal was finally concluded at £60,000. By 31 January 1898 Hatherley Distillery was in formal control of the Harmonia Distillery in Lourenço Marques and the newer distillery at Ressano Garcia.

Since 1895 Hatherley had been forced to drop its prices in an attempt to compete with the cheaper imported spirits – a factor which had no doubt made a substantial contribution to the shrinking profits in Pretoria.[102] Having bought control in the largest company in Mozambique, Marks now had access to the 'Alcohol Trust', and he could set to work on the price problem with the interests of the parent company in mind. By March 1898 the 'Alcohol Trust' had reached a new price and marketing arrangement that met with Hatherley approval. The new terms effectively limited the competition of all the Lourenço Marques distilleries bar one, and that of the Mopea Distillery to the far north. With virtually all the distilleries catering for the Witwatersrand market in line, the 'Alcohol Trust' was ready for a move into Johannesburg. By mid-1898 the 'Trust' had established a large depot in Kruis street, where its wholesale activities were managed by J. F. De Villiers.[103]

All this success in Mozambique still did not satisfy the Hatherley board who had been stung out of any possible complacency by their loss of £46,000 in 1897. In particular, they remained worried by the threat posed by one of the smaller factories in Lourenço Marques, Dyball's Distillery. It was for this remaining competitor which was still outside the 'Trust' that Sammy Marks developed a special, costless strategy. Marks instructed the firm of Hunt and Auerbach to take out an option to buy Dyball's on behalf of Hatherley Distillery. In practice, however, Marks and his colleagues did not have the slightest intention of buying the distillery. Instead, they merely made use of the option to suspend spirit production at Dyball's, and to prolong the negotiations for as long as possible. This strategy was made clear to Hunt and Auerbach in a letter from the secretary at Hatherley, J. P. H. Faure, on 2 April 1898. Although it cannot be conclusively proved, it seems possible that Marks's scheme eventually worked. Dyball's, on the strength of the option, certainly suspended production until June 1898, a sacrifice of at least three months' output. By 1899 there is no evidence of a 'Dyball's Distillery' in active production in Lourenço Marques.[104]

Capital, business acumen and ruthless determination all contributed to the relative ease with which the Pretoria financial generals had captured Mozambique. Their task, however, had also been made easier by the comparative indifference of the Portuguese capitalists – a surprising development given the latter group's interest in spirit production in the early 1890s.

The indifference of the Portuguese capitalists dated back to 1896. During that year not only had the 'total prohibition' clause been passed in the Transvaal, but the Cape farmers had experienced a particularly bad wine harvest. Prominent Portuguese capitalists and the Lisbon administration decided that this was an opportune moment to break into the wine market of southern and central Africa. A senior civil servant was sent to tour the region and to report on the business prospects. In the wake of this report a large wine depot was opened in Lourenço Marques, and a wholesale business under S. F. Belford was established in Pretoria. Belford not only sold wine reasonably successfully, but also tried to get a 'wine concession' from the Transvaal government.[105] To put it at its crudest: Pretoria's capital had succeeded in getting into Mozambique because Portuguese capital was partly intent on establishing itself in Pretoria. On the one hand, new industrial capital wished to monopolise spirit production for the African market, while on the other, older mercantile capital hoped to dominate the European wine market offered by settler societies. Whatever the cause of these developments, they suited Hatherley in the short run. In twelve months Sammy Marks steered his enterprise from a £46,000 loss to a £10,000 profit (1898).

The battle waged for the ownership of the means of production in Mozambique between 1897 and 1898 revealed several things. For one, it showed the capacity of South African based capital to move into profitable sectors of economies in adjacent countries before the South African War. More fundamentally, it demonstrated that larger capital had to consume smaller capital when the former was faced with a declining rate of profit. Most important for present purposes, however, it showed that the capitalists knew that they still had access to a market for their product – why else fight for spirit production in a period of so-called 'total prohibition'? The fact that the market remained accessible after 1897 was not primarily due to the efforts of the capitalists themselves. For that vital condition the owners of the distilleries, the capitalists, had to thank another class – the petty bourgeoisie who owned the canteens.

When 'total prohibition' came into effect on 1 January 1897 at least half the canteens in the mining areas of the Transvaal closed down.[106] The new law and the stiffer penalties it contained simply frightened the more timid half of this sector of the petty bourgeoisie out of business. Many of the other canteen keepers, however, took heart. What other Rand businessmen could point to a market in which competition had been reduced by 50 per cent at a stroke? Moreover, canteen closures had the effect of reducing supply while demand remained at least constant. In practice this pushed up prices and profit margins. In 1898 a bottle of Delagoa Bay spirits cost 6d to produce, the Transvaal importer sold it for 2/6d per bottle, and the illicit liquor dealer sold it to African consumers at 5/- or 6/- per bottle.[107] Higher profit margins, in part a by-product of prohibition itself, ensured the persistence of the illicit liquor market on the Witwatersrand.

Some of these liquor sales took place in 'kaffir eating houses' and stores in the vicinity of the mining compounds. Often the quantities sold here were relatively small, and the trade was organised on a somewhat spasmodic basis. In several cases an essentially law-abiding storekeeper would bolster his sales through occasional trading in a commodity which yielded a handsome profit. In other cases, canteen keepers would cater essentially for the legal European trade and occasionally sell the odd bottle of spirits to Africans at the back door. These outlets, however, were largely insignificant and they constituted merely the tip of the illicit iceberg. More important by far were the large and well-organised syndicates which developed in an illicit trade that could yield profits of 100 per cent to 150 per cent. These syndicates formed the very core of the illicit liquor business, and as early as March 1897 conducted a trade which the Chamber of Mines branded as 'rampant'. With the passage of time they became even more entrenched, and it was they who formed the nucleus of a petty-bourgeois army which defied the state and the mine owners between 1897 and 1899. But in order to appreciate fully who was involved in these syndicates, why they developed and how they operated, it is necessary to turn to earlier decades and another continent.

As suggested earlier, spirit production and the liquor trade had played an important role in the development of European capitalism. Within that trade Jewish communities had figured prominently – especially in the petty-bourgeois function of korchma keepers. Precisely because they were exposed in such visible class and ethnic positions, these communities were frequently persecuted, and pogroms forced thousands to emigrate to many countries during the nineteenth century. With the economic development which followed in the wake of the discovery of diamonds (1867) and gold (1886), southern Africa became an increasingly attractive refuge for such emigrants. Many of the Jewish refugees who came to Africa must have been generally aware of the role liquor could play in a developing economy, whilst yet others probably had personal experience of the trade. But, as is generally the case with immigration and developing economies, there was no simple equality of opportunity for these different waves of Jewish refugees. In general, the greatest opportunities arose for those who came earliest, in the 1860s and 1870s, at the very start of modern industrial capitalism, when the class structure was least developed. The later arrivals of the 1880s and 1890s came into a socio-economic system with a more developed class structure, had to make do with more modest possibilities, and often ended up working for their ethnic kinsmen from Germany, Poland or Russia.

Given this broad and schematic outline, we can bring at least one new, albeit speculative, dimension to our understanding of events in the Transvaal. Now it is perhaps easier to see why the Hungarian Jew, Nellmapius, would have been so quick to appreciate the value of a liquor concession. Similarly, we can appreciate why three Russian Jews – Isaac Lewis, Barnet Lewis and Sammy Marks – were willing to go into partnership with Nellmapius when the opportunity arose. These men, amongst the first immigrants of the 1870s, came to a Transvaal which was, if not 'feudal', then at least pre-capitalist. As entrepreneurs present from the very outset of industrial development in the area, they rapidly established themselves as respected members of the emerging capitalist class. Nellmapius was one of the most prominent and powerful businessmen of his day, and at his death in 1893 President Kruger complimented him as 'a true patriot of the Transvaal'.[108] Like several of his Russian predecessors Sammy Marks accumulated considerable capital from the liquor business and came to head an 'industrial bourgeois family'.

This small and in part highly successful first wave of Jewish immigrants to the Transvaal was followed by a second wave of Europeans when gold was discovered in the mid-1880s. The men of this latter period saw their opportunities in the mushrooming towns of the Witwatersrand. Without the means, and without the personal access to the Afrikaner ruling class that would have enabled them to become capitalists, these men sought to accumulate their initial capital as a petty bourgeoisie. In particular, it was they who opened canteens and, as the korchma keepers of the pre-prohibition era, they sold spirits to black peasants who had come to the towns for a spell of wage labour. These immigrants, men like Herschfield, chairman of the Licensed Victuallers' Association (W.L.V.A.), might not have been 'respected' in the way that liquor capitalists like Sammy Marks were 'respected', but they were certainly a force to be reckoned with by the state and the mine owners.

The third wave of Jewish immigrants who entered the Z.A.R. in the mid-1890s, however, were much less fortunate than their countrymen who had arrived earlier. For these poorest of East Europeans, not even the petty-bourgeois path to capital accumulation remained open. By 1895 the Chamber of Mines and W.L.V.A. had, for very different reasons, both agreed that no more canteen licences should be issued, and the 'total prohibition' law had followed in 1896. Poor and with every prospect of remaining penniless, these unfortunate immigrants were pushed into the life of the lumpenproletariat. As perhaps the most visible, dispossessed and unsuccessful group of whites on the Witwatersrand, they were the unhappy recipients of the most vicious class and race prejudice that society could muster:

> The stranger in Johannesburg cannot but ponder on the spectacle of a Kaffir respectably arrayed in good European clothing walking in the middle of the street, with a brass ticket strapped on his arm, while on the neighbouring footway may be seen, and even smelt, some representative of European civilization, perhaps a 'Peruvian' from Poland or Russia, who has apparently not found it convenient to change his clothing or indulge in unnecessary ablutions since his entry into the country.[109]

For most of these 'very low class of Russian and Polish Jews, "Peruvians"', life in Johannesburg might have been totally miserable, but it certainly was not lonely. In 1899 it was estimated that there were over 7,000 'Russian Jews' on the Witwatersrand.[110]

After 1897 there developed amongst these different classes of Jewish immigrants various more or less explicit marriages of economic convenience depending ultimately on the liquor trade with black workers. The capitalist liquor producers, Marks and the Lewis brothers, remained in business largely because of the activities of the petty-bourgeois canteen keepers. The converse was, of course, equally true. In practice the producers and the retailers seldom met face to face, since both parties operated through another group, the merchant capitalists who acted as wholesalers. The most explicit marriage of convenience, however, took place between the petty bourgeoisie and the 'Peruvians' of the lumpenproletariat. Members of the former group had no desire to jeopardize their liquor licences through being caught personally selling alcohol to Africans, whilst the latter were so poor that any opportunity to earn money came as an offer which they could not refuse. The canteen keepers therefore:

> . . . engaged newly arrived young Russian Jews, at what might appear to them princely remuneration, agreeing in the event of the latter being trapped and prosecuted, to pay the fines, or, if they were sent to prison, to pay them a lump sum on release as compensation.[111]

It was this latter arrangement, often reinforced by kinship ties, and here termed the 'Peruvian Connection', that formed the white base line of a pyramid of business exploitation.

The size of the illicit liquor syndicates and their exact mode of organisation varied considerably. A small minority of these businesses were entirely dependent on the driving force, skill and organisational ability of one man. H. Max, for example, kept on the move continually, and never sold liquor from the same spot for more than a day or two. In some cases this type of 'mobile canteen' on a waggon had to be drawn by as many as ten oxen. Other canteen keepers, such as Tiversky of the 'Old Grahamstown Bar' or H. Joffe of the 'Old Kentish Tavern', operated from a single business base and such men would employ three or four 'Peruvian' assistants at most.[112]

The majority of medium-to-large businesses were syndicates in the more real sense that they constituted a partnership in which two, three, or four 'big men' were involved. The partnership of Judelsohn, Nathan and Cohen, for example, owned the Californian Hotel, the 'Station Bar', and the 'Ferreira's Gate Bar'. Similarly, the partnership of Friedman, Pastolsky and Katzen owned the 'Old Park', 'Jumpers' and 'Wolhuter' Bars.[113] Syndicates of this size had several 'Peruvians' and dozens of black liquor 'touts' on their pay-roll.

The largest of this type of syndicate in the late 1890s was that of Finestone, Lediker, Sacke and Schlossberg. As was often the case, some of the members of the syndicate were related (Finestone and Sacke), and the social cement of kinship contributed to the cohesiveness of the partnership. By April 1899 this syndicate was reported as having no fewer than ten illicit liquor outlets on the Rand, with a collective monthly turnover of about £46,000. Out of this, the syndicate had to pay a monthly bill for police bribes of £2,000, and this left the partners with a monthly profit of the order of £8,000. This syndicate, and another reputed to have made £18,000 during three months' trading in 1898, would probably have employed at least a score of 'Peruvians' as front men.[114] Although its size was vital, the Finestone syndicate had additional features which made it important in the financial life of Johannesburg. Like many other criminal organisations in capitalist systems, the syndicate controlled a financial empire spanning both legal and illegal business activities. Finestone was 'a prominent member of the Stock Exchange', and together with his other partners held a share in five hotels, described as 'some of the most adequately and expensively equipped establishments on the whole line of the Reef'.[115]

The biggest syndicates of all, however, revealed some of the classic hallmarks of organised crime. In the finest tradition of the criminal underground, the most powerful syndicates were 'family businesses' which dominated particular territories. Anybody who wished to open an illicit liquor canteen in the Boksburg–Benoni district, for example, would have had to come to terms with one such powerful family syndicate. But, as was explained in 1899:

> The rules are somewhat onerous. Firstly, the consent of the syndicate has to be obtained, without which the new business would not flourish for a week. Then the new-comer has to purchase his liquor at a certain wholesale store in Johannesburg [probably Friedman's]. Finally, the syndicate takes a large share of the profits. So that to start a liquor syndicate is sowing seed on the hard and unfertile rock of the Syndicate Monopoly.[116]

Just as the notorious Nathansons ruled Boksburg, so the Joffes ruled Krugersdorp and Randfontein, while the mighty Friedmans controlled central Johannesburg.

At the head of a family syndicate stood the 'Liquor King', and if like Sam Nathanson he had sons, then he would be assisted by the 'Princes'. Immediately below this 'royal family', and within the syndicate proper, there followed a hierarchy of 'Peruvians' who constituted the King's 'loyal men'. It was this business army of 'Peruvians' who organised most of the day-to-day operations in the drinking dens – men such as Sol Pastolsky who was described as 'General Commanding Officer' of the area around the New Heriot Mine. Similarly, the 'Peruvian' in control at the Nourse Deep Mine was known as 'Commandant Schutte', a humorous title which his namesake at the head of the Zarps might have found a little less amusing.[117]

Outside this immediate corps of loyal 'Peruvian' troops, the King could also place some reliance on the vast number of state officials whom he had bribed. The task of these venal officials was twofold. First, they had to ensure that no action was taken against the King's syndicate. Secondly, they had to harass the business operations of unwelcome competitors or enemies who managed to muscle their way into the King's territory. The degree of control which the King had over 'his' state officials was a matter of considerable prestige, since it accurately reflected the extent of his real power. Thus, in Johannesburg, King Friedman could claim, with considerable justification, that he was 'the real boss' of the Zarp 'Liquor Department'.[118]

But Friedman's control over the local state apparatus paled into insignificance when compared with that of 'King Nathanson' in Boksburg. Sam, or Smooel Nathanson as he preferred to call himself, was the original big gangster and racketeer on the Witwatersrand. Leaving behind a record of arson and fraudulent bankruptcies, Nathanson moved from the Cape Colony town of Prince Albert in the late 1880s in order to capitalise on the fresh possibilities in Johannesburg. On the Rand he found new respectability. At one stage he was President of the Johannesburg Old Hebrew Congregation, and as late as 1894 the names of 'Mr and Mrs S. Nathanson' figured proudly in the local press as the donors of a prestigious gift at a society wedding. The money for the gift probably came from Sam's expanding criminal operations, and it was these activities which ultimately led to Sam's fall from social grace. But predictably enough Smooel Nathanson's biggest opportunities arose when 'total prohibition' was introduced in the mid-1890s. It was then that he developed into a fully-fledged slum landlord and racketeer in the illicit liquor business.[119]

The hold which Nathanson developed on the East Rand first became apparent in 1893–4, when a motley crew of unsuccessful canteen keepers and a venal ex-Zarp detective appeared in court, accused of criminally libelling state officials. This group, comprising Messrs Globus, Shapiro, Cooper and van der Hoepen, wrote anonymous letters to Chief Magistrate van den Berg in Johannesburg and to the Volksraad, in which they pointed out some of the ways in which Nathanson corrupted and controlled Boksburg officials. When these charges were investigated they were found to be substantially correct. Embarrassed by his findings, the Johannesburg Public Prosecutor finally withdrew his charges. But the damage had been done. The Mining Commissioner, the Public Prosecutor, and the local Magistrate at Boksburg had all admitted to receiving a considerable amount of money and 'presents' from Smooel Nathanson.[120] The government's response to these disclosures was to take no action against the officials concerned or Sam Nathanson: it slowly formulated new penalties for those found guilty of bribing state officials.[121] In consequence of this leisurely approach Nathanson's control of the district became increasingly entrenched, and by 1899 the local press was confident enough to report that:

> You need no concealment in the Boksburg district; the place is a patch of the blackest villainy in the Republic. There is not one single official connected with the supervision, licensing, and control of liquor selling, from the highest magistrate to the lowest constable, who does not deserve to be cashiered.[122]

Little wonder then that Smooel could walk around his district and call himself '*Landdrost* of the Detectives of Boksburg' or, quite simply and accurately, 'The Boss of Boksburg'.

Nathanson and the other Liquor Kings of the late 1890s used their armies constantly, both to defend and to expand their empires. Like Sammy Marks, they worked on 'public opinion' by paying 'Peruvians' and other poor whites to put their signatures to petitions calling for an end to 'total prohibition'. Their political activities ensured constant movement between their districts and Pretoria, and by 1898 State Attorney J. C. Smuts described them as 'becoming a power at all elections'.[123] More important and equally sinister was the impressive way in which they could wield power when things went wrong for the syndicate. Any 'Peruvian' finally trapped by the police and brought to court was likely to benefit from strange developments which frequently took place. On at least one occasion a bottle of gin which was to be used in evidence, as if 'by some miracle . . . turned to water when brought to Court'.[124] If the material exhibits in the case did not change, then the 'Peruvian' could always look forward to unscheduled disappearances among the African witnesses for the prosecution. By late 1899 the police had to protect their 'trap boys' from pre-trial syndicate approaches by imprisoning them until the case was heard. Of course not all witnesses could, or would, come to an agreement with the syndicates. In such cases the witnesses stood the risk of less profitable and more permanent 'disappearance'. On several occasions the syndicates were suspected of organised killings on the Witwatersrand.[125]

But there were also limits to syndicate power, and the actual organisation of the drinking dens revealed this most clearly. The King would always make certain that he took out wholesale liquor licences only for those stands from which the syndicate could have guaranteed access to adjacent properties. He would also take the precaution of warning the 'Peruvians' that only *legal* sales of alcohol should take place from the licensed property. Failure to ensure this would place the licence itself in jeopardy, and in the event of successful prosecution would ultimately kill the goose that laid the golden egg.

Once the above concession to the law had been made, however, the King could set about organising the rest of his defensive strategy on the 'adjacent stand' to the licensed property. First the 'adjacent stand' – be it house or vacant property – would be linked to the licensed property by means of an underground tunnel. Thereafter the entrances to these tunnels would be hidden with the aid of elaborate false partitions and trapdoors. The carpenters and electricians would then be called in to arrange for the final protection of the unlicensed property: on vacant stands high fences would be erected along the perimeter of the property, with strategic 'look-out' posts at each of the corners; from these posts 'Peruvian sentries' would keep constant watch for the approach of the Zarps.

The dens, with an irony that the mine owners would not have appreciated, were often called 'compounds'. Many such 'compounds' and houses were further protected through the installation of a system of electric bells on the unlicensed property. This technologically sophisticated system, pioneered by one 'Fred Poplar' Cohen and widely used during prohibition, gave swift warning of the approach of any unsympathetic Zarp. In several instances final precautions were taken at the actual point of sale itself. 'Peruvian' Silverman, for example, seated himself inside a specially constructed wooden compartment into which had been cut peep-holes and the smallest of serving hatches. This arrangement enabled him to see the customer, receive the cash and dispense a bottle of spirits while remaining hidden. With such elaborate precuations it is hardly surprising that many of the illicit liquor dens were called 'forts', and that they had to be 'rushed' by the police.[126] In a very literal sense it was the *army* of the petty bourgeoisie that held the state and the mine owners at bay between 1897 and 1899.

This rapid and solid entrenchment of the liquor syndicates after 1897 did not escape the attention of the state. The Volksraad realised to its embarrassment that 'total prohibition' was 'total' in name only. Even if the state *had* wanted to turn a blind eye to the massive illicit liquor trade it would not have been allowed to do so. Sammy Marks constantly reminded members of the Raad of their obligations under his concession, while the retailers exercised their own particular brands of coercion and persuasion. The mine owners for their part made their bitter complaints well known in evidence to the Industrial Commission of Enquiry in 1897.[127] By the end of that year such insistent pressures could no longer be ignored, and the administration felt compelled to act. Early in 1898 the State President appointed the Acting State Attorney, Schagen van Leeuwen, and the Inspector General of Customs to a special Liquor Commission. The appointment of this commission must have removed some of the immediate pressure on the hard-pressed administration.

The Volksraad, however, was not the State President, and the members of the Raad certainly did not feel or respond to exactly the same pressure as Kruger. The appointment of the Liquor Commission, therefore, offered different opportunities to these two branches of the government. As far as the Raad was concerned the task of the commission was clear – it had to find ways of defeating the illicit liquor syndicates, and to suggest ways of enforcing the Liquor Act of 1896. For Kruger, personally sympathetic to the liquor industry, the commission offered an opportunity to renew his battle with a Volksraad which basically favoured 'total prohibition'. If the Liquor Commission produced suitable findings, then the State President would have valuable ammunition in his fight against the 'progressives', and a chance to protect the fortunes of his Eerste Fabrieken. With a two-man commission, one of whom was a 'loyal' Hollander, Kruger had every reason to be confident about the findings of the enquiry.

By mid-March 1898 the confidential report of the commission had been completed. Basically its findings represented a compromise between the views of the Volksraad and those of the State President. As the report put it: 'The commission is of the opinion that a moderate use of drink by the natives, under the control of or on behalf of the Government and the mine managers must in every way effect an improvement.' In order to achieve this 'moderate use', the commission proposed the adoption of a modified Gothenburg system – a type of state monopoly which seemed to work successfully in Sweden. It suggested that liquor should be sold to 'natives' in the Transvaal, but that:

> This should not take place by means of money, but by cards, or tickets, which would have been purchased by the companies from the Government, and which after being stamped with the authority of the mine managers, would again be sold to the coloured people; the latter could then, as it were, themselves exercise control over the use of drink by natives.[128]

This scheme was to be supplemented by increased quality controls, better law enforcement, and a chain of state canteens which would be the sole retail liquor outlets on the Witwatersrand. The commisioners must have hoped that this degree of 'control' would satisfy the mine owners, that the 'progressives' would be pacified by the proposed onslaught on 'abuses', and that Kruger and Marks would feel content about the prospects for Hatherley Distillery. On paper at least, the perfect compromise had been reached and the contradiction which had so plagued the development of capitalism in the Transvaal would be shortly resolved.

On 31 March 1898 the Rand mine owners were then startled to read in the *Johannesburg Times* 'that the establishment of a State monopoly in liquor was under consideration'.[129] After this press leak the state felt obliged to let the mine owners know the hitherto confidential findings of the Liquor Commission, and on 14 April Dr van Leeuwen detailed the government's proposals in a letter to the Chamber of Mines.

The mine owners were most dissatisfied with these proposals. In particular, the Chamber of Mines held two strong objections. First, it felt that there was insufficient 'local control' in the scheme – the mine owners would not have enough power to determine how many canteens there were to be, or where they were to be sited. Second and more important, it doubted the capacity of the state to administer the scheme successfully. The bribery and corruption of the police force were already clearly evident; what would happen when the officials of the Z.A.R. were directly in charge of the canteens? In fact, the mine owners were so frightened by the prospect of uncontrolled *legal* sales of alcohol to black workers that they were willing to settle for the unsatisfactory *status quo*. On 20 April 1898 the Chamber wrote back to the State Attorney reiterating its support for 'total prohibition', and calling for the effective enforcement of Act 17 of 1896.

The mine owners followed this letter with a petition along the same lines addressed to the Volksraad. This was a move calculated to exploit the divisions within the Afrikaner ruling class on the liquor question. The Chamber's uncompromising opposition to the principal recommendations of the liquor commission, as well as the mine owners' direct appeal to a Volksraad so recently committed to 'total prohibition', drastically reduced the State President's room to manoeuvre. When the amended liquor law was debated in the Volksraad later in 1898 the 'total prohibition' clause was retained by 18 votes to 8.[130] The recommendations of the 1898 Liquor Commission were never implemented.

These events, however, made it clear to the mine owners – if they needed reminding – that the State President and his closest allies were deeply committed to Eerste Fabrieken and the liquor trade. The Chamber could therefore expect another move in the same direction in the not too distant future. The mine owners were also distressed by these developments because they did not offer the industry any immediate relief from the activities of the illicit liquor syndicates. Black miners would continue to be good alcohol consumers and bad workers. Faced with this dismal prospect the mining capitalists decided on a radical initiative to shape the future in their favour. Early in May 1898 the Chamber of Mines approached van Leeuwen and asked the government whether it had any objection to the mine owners coming to a direct settlement with Eerste Fabrieken. Such a settlement, it was suggested, would meet the interests of the mine owners, the government and the distillery. The State Attorney, no doubt with Kruger's full approval, indicated his support for a new move to circumvent the impasse on the 'liquor question'. The Chamber of Mines at once set about establishing a 'Special Liquor Committee' – the mine owners' belated equivalent of the ill-fated government Liquor Commission.

The Special Liquor Committee (S.L.C.) had every reason to be optimistic about its direct approach to the Pretoria distillery. The S.L.C. was fully aware that many of the most powerful capitalists in the liquor industry were also deeply involved in the mining industry. As the Committee later put it in their report to the full Executive Committee of the Chamber of Mines:

> Your committee recognise the value of the fact that the Directors of the Hatherley Company are gentlemen who are also largely interested in the Mining Industry, and believe that if some reasonable return could be assured to the Company in lieu of that trade which, however unjustifiably, its shareholders had come to reckon upon as their due, the Chamber could count upon their loyal support in the direction indicated.[131]

Clearly, in this limited respect the contradiction within the capitalist development of the Transvaal was a strength rather than a weakness.

In an effort to exploit these interlocking interests, the S.L.C. first tried to establish what price the Hatherley Board would want for the outright sale of the liquor concession. The distillery directors made it clear that the sale of the factory would involve 'a very large sum indeed', since the company had every prospect of monopoly profits until at least 1912. Denied this most desirable solution of all, the S.L.C. tried another approach. It offered to pay the distillery an annual sum of £10,000 not 'to manufacture the spirit now used in the native trade'. This proposal, whereby one set of capitalists envisaged paying another set of capitalists *not* to produce, revealed in stark outline the contradiction besetting economic development in the Transvaal. In fact it was a contradiction of such magnitude, and it would cost so much to resolve, that the mine owners saw no reason why capital should pay for it. Instead, they proposed that the black working class should pay for its resolution! In their report back to the Executive Committee of the Chamber of Mines, the S.L.C. suggested that the fee that Africans paid for passes should be raised from one shilling to two shillings. The state, after collecting this additional revenue from the workers, would then pass on the annual compensation of £10,000 to Hatherley.[132]

When it had completed its preliminary enquiries and deliberations, the S.L.C. passed on the above recommendation, as well as others for the reform of the liquor trade, to the state. This time it was the turn of the government and Sammy Marks to be unenthusiastic. The major proposals of the S.L.C., like those of its predecessor (the government Liquor Commission), met a quick death. The state, the liquor producers and the mining capitalists simply could not reach an agreement satisfying all parties, and by June 1898 it was still a case of 'business as usual' in the liquor industry.

While 'business as usual' had an obvious appeal for the Liquor Kings, the Volksraad was less than pleased. Members of the Raad were dismayed at Zarp corruption, and embarrassed by the flagrant violations of the liquor law on the Witwatersrand. Although it was somewhat frustrated, the Volksraad continued searching for a solution to these problems. When the Raad debated the amended liquor law in 1898 it took the opportunity of calling in Commandant Schutte, and severely reprimanding him over the poor performance of the police. But perhaps the most important step towards solving these problems came when Kruger replaced State Attorney Dr van Leeuwen with J. C. Smuts. From mid-1898 onwards Smuts applied himself to the problem of stamping out corruption amongst the Zarps. His immediate efforts were concentrated at the most senior levels of the police force. When Chief Detective Robert Ferguson was caught buying gold amalgam and passing it on to Count Sarigny in November 1898, Smuts arranged for his immediate dismissal.[133] Shortly after this the officer in charge of the Z.A.R.P. Illicit Liquor Department – Inspector Donovan, of Trimble affair fame – was also replaced. These and other changes in personnel followed, until by mid-1899 Smuts was satisfied that he had reliable, efficient and uncorrupt officers in control of the Z.A.R.P. Under the Smuts regime the post of Chief Detective was occupied by officer De Villiers, and the illicit liquor section was headed by Detective Thomas Menton.[134]

These reforms, while welcome in themselves, did not go far to remove the fears and anxieties of the mine owners. The changes in Zarp personnel were largely confined to the most senior levels, and in the lower ranks, where the salaries were least adequate, police corruption remained a pervasive problem. Moreover the mining capitalists feared the possibility of yet another Kruger initiative to get 'total prohibition' lifted. Most serious of all, of course, was the fact that the Liquor Kings continued to undermine the productivity of black workers through the large-scale sale of spirits. These factors, as well as the rapidly escalating political tensions in the Transvaal during 1899, left the mining capitalists decidedly nervous and insecure. Believing that the best form of defence was attack, they decided to launch a new ideological offensive. In April 1899 the first copies of an Eckstein & Co.-financed newspaper, the

Transvaal Leader, were sold on the streets of Johannesburg. It was this newspaper which became the primary cudgel of the mining capitalists in the open class conflict which formed a prelude to the South African War.

Almost from its very first issue the *Transvaal Leader* set out on a 'Liquor Crusade' against the business armies of the petty bourgeoisie. Virtually every issue during May, June and July of 1899 contained some sensationalist exposure or other of the illicit liquor trade. No effort was spared in disclosing the names of those involved in the syndicates, and no attempt was made to conceal the hatred and contempt felt for their 'Peruvian' employees. The activities of the firms at the heart of the wholesale trade were well publicised, as were the practices of those who bottled various concoctions under the seal of forged labels. Newspaper readers were treated to detailed descriptions of defensive arrangements inside 'Peruvian Forts', and told the exact nature of the links with the adjacent stands. On several occasions even the activities of mine and compound managers who were implicated in the illicit trade were reported. The *Transvaal Leader* also took it upon itself publicly to lecture Emmanuel Mendelssohn, editor of the rival *Standard and Diggers' News*, on his 'responsibilities' to the 'public'.

On the face of it, the *Transvaal Leader*'s campaign had every appearance of a no-holds-barred, full-scale exposé for the benefit of the new court of 'public opinion'. Yet amidst all these revelations about the liquor trade and the inefficiency of the state there *was* one significant omission. Not once during all the months of the campaign did the *Leader* devote so much as a single line to the activities of the liquor producers – the capitalists. At least one shrewd reader, W. S. Cohn, spotted the deliberate omission in the mine owners' game and pointedly asked the Editor:

> But how is it that you have never shaped your enquiries in the direction of the 'Big' syndicate here [Hatherley and the Alcohol Trust], as they are the people who are supplying all these illicit dealers with the liquor?[135]

Clearly the mine owners and their agents were at war with the petty bourgeoisie and not with the capitalists; there happened to be such an embarrassing overlap between liquor capitalists and mining capitalists. Eckstein & Co. would have understood the problem, as would their Editor of the *Leader*, Samuel Evans. Evans was a manager in the Company *and* on the board of Hatherley Distillery.

But this class war of 1899 was not confined to an exchange of ideological ammunition in the editorial columns of the *Transvaal Leader*. Certainly the Editor and his principals had reasons for whipping 'public opinion' into a frenzy on the 'liquor question', but they also wanted *action*. To this latter end the Editor engaged the services of an ex-detective named Baxter.[136] Making full use of Baxter's expertise, the editorial staff of the *Leader* embarked on a programme of violence directed at the Liquor Kings and their 'Peruvians'. On Sunday mornings they would set out on carefully planned expeditions, and 'rush' the illicit liquor dens. They succeeded in smashing thousands of bottles of spirits; they tore down false partitions inside the 'forts' and ripped out trap-doors. This pioneering example of violence for the capitalists' cause was soon followed by the mine managers themselves, who also hired private detectives for the same purposes.[137] All this destruction and disruption placed the Liquor Kings on the defensive, assisted the mine owners in their quest for a productive black labour force, and made excellent copy for the Monday morning edition of the *Leader*.

Most of the justification offered for this open confrontation derived from a single incident which, fortunately enough for the *Transvaal Leader*, came very early on in its 'Liquor Crusade'. On 29 April 1899, Mrs Applebe, wife of the Wesleyan minister in Fordsburg, and a companion by the name of Wilson, were viciously attacked by a gang of men while on their way to choir practice at the local church. The woman's condition remained critical during the following days, and rumour had it that the Liquor Kings had paid gangsters to attack her because she had supplied information on their activities.[138] On 2 May, when her condition had further deteriorated, the *Leader* ran a sensational editorial entitled 'Blood upon their hands!', in which it openly accused the Kantor syndicate of Fordsburg of being behind the assault. The sense of moral indignation which this aroused in the white public was complete when the minister's unfortunate wife died on the following day.

Despite the offer of a £500 reward by State Attorney Smuts for information leading to the prosecution of Mrs Applebe's assailants, no substantial evidence was ever offered to the police, and the criminals remained undetected.[139] The whole affair, however, helped stampede 'public opinion' in the direction suggested by the *Leader*. Within days of the death there occurred a rash of public meetings. Local church congregations passed resolutions supporting the *Transvaal Leader's* campaign, and on 10 May a great public meeting was held in Johannesburg at which the illicit trade was roundly condemned.[140] At the same meeting ministers of religion sat astride their highest moral horses, striking out blindly at the enemy; in the wake of the gathering at least one of them was sued for criminal libel by Emmanuel Mendelssohn. The most important meeting of all took place at Potchefstroom on 17 May. There the members of the Dutch Reformed Church met in formal session and decided to send a deputation to Pretoria to discuss the illicit liquor trade with the State President.[141]

Amid all this pure-white moral outrage, however, there were also significant signs of black activity. African leaders, more concerned with the health and welfare of their black kinsmen than with Mrs Applebe, took the opportunity to mobilise their followers. Among these leaders were some who became prominent in the African political struggle of later decades. Saul Msane (compound manager at the Jubilee Mine) and Sebastian Msimang were among those who addressed an 800-strong working-class gathering in the Wesleyan Native Church, Albert street, on 16 May 1899. Resolutions calling for 'total prohibition' and strict enforcement of the liquor law were passed, and according to the *Leader*: 'It was remarkable that, although the boys working on the mines were largely represented, there was not a single vote against the resolutions.' On the following evening Msane was again active, this time as chairman of a meeting of 'educated natives', held at the Independent Presbyterian Church in the Braamfontein location. Here a similar set of resolutions was proposed by the Rev. Tsewu and accepted by the meeting.[142] The *Transvaal Leader* gleefully reported on these resolutions which so accurately mirrored the official Chamber of Mines' policy on the liquor trade.

With 'public opinion' at fever pitch in a community already deeply anxious about the possibilities of war with Great Britain, there was always the danger that the 'Liquor Crusade' would get completely out of hand, produce witch-hunting and lead to indiscriminate violence. Since the attention of the 'public' was so ruthlessly fixed on the problem of the 'Peruvians', the Jewish community became particularly anxious. Jews knew and understood the syndrome at work all too well. In his letter to the Editor of the *Leader* on 5 May 1899, William Cohn warned the newspaperman of some of the possible consequences of his 'Crusade':

> In your efforts to diminish this deplorable traffic there is a grave danger of creating a large amount of anti-semitic feeling, a feeling, which I may safely say, is already beginning to show signs of existence. The mischief caused by articles appearing in the Berlin *Kreuz Zeitung* and the St Petersburg *Novoe Vremia* and *Grazdanin* is well within my memory. Surely there are sufficient existing troubles and disputes in this State without introducing another, which would bid fair to eclipse all others in the intensity of its race hatred.

Within ten days the Chief Rabbi, Dr Hertz, was in the midst of a controversy about Jewish involvement in the liquor trade, and desperately trying to pour oil on increasingly troubled waters.[143]

In several cases the warnings and cautions came too late. At the Rietfontein Mine the manager took it upon himself to administer a thrashing to a liquor seller, and was promptly discharged when the case was brought to court. Egged on by the shrill cries of the *Transvaal Leader*, other self-appointed vigilantes set about prosecuting the war of the mine owners and attacked 'Peruvian Forts'. On Sunday 21 May, for example, the Wesleyan minister in Johannesburg, the Rev. Scholefield, led his congregation in an attack on a neighbouring shebeen.[144] More serious and destructive were the series of not-so-mysterious fires which happened to break out in the illicit liquor dens and hotels during May and June 1899.[145] Caught by the wave of popular hatred, African workers also took the opportunity to settle their debts with their nearest and most visible exploiters – the petty bourgeoisie:

> . . .at one of the mines 600 boys destroyed the illicit liquor store, together with all the elaborate equipment of electric alarms and signals with which the store and adjoining premises were fitted. The reason given by the natives for this action was that the store was too much of a temptation to them, so that all their money was spent on drink.[146]

Again, the mine owners and the *Leader* must have been pleased with this working-class action which tackled the 'forts' of the illicit liquor syndicates rather than the spirit factory of the mining-cum-liquor capitalists.

With 'public opinion' in high dudgeon Smuts also saw the opportunity to push more strongly against the illicit trade. Knowing that Kruger would be on the defensive, the State Attorney gave his support to the *Leader*'s 'Liquor Crusade'. In Johannesburg two of Smuts's Public Prosecutors, Cornelis Broeksma and Mostyn Cleaver, both identified themselves with the newspaper campaign. During the weeks which followed the State Attorney spent much of his time and energy in combating the syndicates, and senior members of his new department set a personal example. When there were no prosecutions forthcoming from the Fordsburg district, the State Prosecutor, Dr F. E. T. Krause, cycled around the area in an attempt to establish what was happening on the streets.[147]

Much of the State Attorney's effort, however, was frustrated by the high level of corruption among low-ranking Zarps. To circumvent this problem, Smuts adopted a suggestion which had been aired most recently by the Chamber of Mines at a large public meeting on 15 May 1899. Within Chief Detective de Villiers's department he set up a special task force under the direction of Tjaart Kruger. Men from the 'specials', such as Detective Goldberg, were selected for their particular knowledge of the liquor traffic. It became the sole objective of this nucleus of uncorruptibles to smash the big syndicates.

The initial response of the syndicates to the 'Liquor Crusade' had been one of reasonably self-confident indifference. During the early days of the campaign the Lediker syndicate had even attempted a confidence trick: it took the representatives of the *Transvaal Leader* on a public relations tour of its legitimate business fronts.[148] After the Applebe murder, however, the syndicates were forced into a more aggressive stance, and they resorted to their trusted methods of threats, bribes and corruption. Just when these methods seemed to be holding their own, the syndicates were confronted with the new and substantial challenge presented by the 'specials'.

Early in June 1899 Tjaart Kruger received two threats in anonymous letters which warned him to take the greatest care if he were to be so unwise as to extend his activities to Boksburg. The leader of the 'specials' read these letters as coming from King Nathanson himself, and decided to take up the challenge. On Saturday 3 June Kruger sent two of his Pretoria-based detectives, Heysteck and Pelser, to Johannesburg in the utmost secrecy. At Park Station they were met by Detective Goldberg, a man with personal knowledge of the Nathanson family's business methods. From there the three detectives made their way to the South Rose Deep Mine where the manager supplied them with three compound 'boys' for trapping purposes. From the mine the detectives and 'boys' set out for Smooel Nathanson's biggest 'fort' – the one behind the Railway Hotel at Germiston known to African workers as 'Pudding'.

At the 'fort' the detectives supplied the compound 'boys' with marked coins, and then sent them in as 'traps' to buy liquor. As soon as the 'boys' re-emerged with the alcohol, the detectives 'rushed' the 'fort'. They made progress without hindrance until they reached a final door, and then they were confronted not by Smooel himself, but by Prince George Nathanson accompanied by no fewer than twenty 'Peruvians'. At this point the Prince warned the detectives that, dead or alive, they would not be allowed into the heart of the 'fort'. A vigorous fight ensued. Unable to get at the marked coins, the detectives decided instead to arrest the Prince and two of the 'Peruvians' on a charge of obstructing the course of justice. The Prince was dragged off to the local charge office shouting, 'Look here you special bastards from Pretoria, I have more money than you think, I can cover you with money, and I shall go to

Pretoria and you will all have to work for me at half-a-crown a day.'

The detectives had missed the King, but George Nathanson and two employees subsequently appeared at the Boksburg Police Court, where they were each sentenced to a fine of £20 or three months' hard labour. In late June it was rumoured that King Sam Nathanson was so annoyed by the 'treacherous' behaviour of Detective Goldberg in the case that he was willing to pay £2,000 to get this 'special into trouble'.[149]

The Kings were put on the defensive by this new rigid arm of the state, and they were wary of the heavier sentences which seemed to form part of the Smuts campaign.[150] On 4 July 1899 the entire syndicate network was shocked by the news of the latest state success in the battle against the illicit liquor trade. The sharpest operator of all on the Witwatersrand, the King of the Liquor Kings, Nathan Friedman, had been arrested by Chief Detective de Villiers, following a raid on the Wiltshire Bar. Despite several attempts to pervert the course of justice, Friedman ultimately appeared in court, and in August was sentenced to ten months' imprisonment without the option of a fine.[151] This unprecedentedly harsh sentence left the syndicates sorry, the detectives delighted, and the Chamber of Mines reasonably content. At the August monthly meeting of the Chamber, Eckstein, on behalf of the mine owners, paid public tribute to the ceaseless energy and recent success of the State Attorney and his Chief Detective.[152]

The purr of content from the Chamber of Mines, however, proved to be somewhat premature. The syndicates might have lost some important battles but they had certainly not lost the war. Their hidden allies, Kruger and the liquor producers, had been left relatively unscathed. The deep divisions within the Afrikaner ruling class on the liquor question always left the syndicates with the hope of rescue by government forces fighting behind the lines. From June 1899 onwards the syndicates placed increasing faith in those allies. Pretoria might have been the seat of the State Attorney and the hated 'specials', but it was also the home of the State President.

In the wake of the Applebe murder and the public meetings to which it gave rise, several deputations made their way to Pretoria. Of these the most important was one headed by the Dutch Reformed Church in mid-May. On Thursday 25 May 1899 the Rev. Louw and three hundred members of the church assembled in Pretoria to petition the State President about the liquor traffic. At the state buildings the deputation was met by the noted enemy of Hatherley Distillery, the Chairman of the Second Volksraad, H. P. Steenkamp. Steenkamp thanked the church for the work that it had done in fighting the liquor evil. He also informed the deputation that the Raad had decided to establish yet another commission to examine the whole problem, and that the State President would hear them personally. At this point the Commandant-General of the Z.A.R., General Piet Joubert, arrived to offer the State President's apologies – Kruger's health did not allow him to meet the churchmen on such a cold morning!

The churchmen, however, were not to be shrugged off so easily, and that evening they regrouped, together with several representatives of the mining industry. At 7.00 p.m. the enlarged deputation marched down Church street towards the State President's home. Unable to avoid the burghers any longer, Kruger met their spokesmen and curtly informed them that he was entirely opposed to the present liquor laws, and that the best way round the whole problem was to create a state monopoly along the lines of the Gothenburg system. These answers did not satisfy the churchmen, who then asked to meet the President separately from the mining industry representatives.

Kruger met the churchmen again at the Executive Council chambers at 9.00 p.m. He told members of the deputation that he sympathised with their good intentions, but that he was still of the opinion that a state liquor monopoly was the best solution to the problem. Somewhat wearied by the whole day's anti-liquor agitation, he then proceeded to express his considerable annoyance to the Rev. Louw. He complained bitterly that the deputation had hampered certain approaches that he planned to make to the Raad, and that the *Uitlanders* (foreigners) in the Transvaal would make great political capital out of the fact that they undertook their agitations on the Queen's birthday![153]

As soon as news of the Raad's new Liquor Commission got out, the syndicates switched their attention from Johannesburg to Pretoria. Knowing that Kruger and the liquor capitalists favoured a state monopoly in which Hatherley was to be the sole producer, they lobbied anew for the removal of the 'total prohibition' clause. A mere two weeks after Nathan Friedman had been sentenced, the Liquor Kings succeeded in getting the information they longed for. On 26 August 1899 a disgusted *Transvaal Leader* told its readers:

> The syndicates are boasting of approaching changes in the Law as if they were as good as accomplished already, and they seem to know the mind of the Raad Liquor Commission before even that body has reported to the Raad. Prohibition, it is said, is to go by the board.[154]

A week later the commission reported to the Raad. It suggested that prohibition be lifted, that Africans be entitled to two drinks a day – one in the morning and one in the evening – but that nobody should be allowed to sell a black man a bottle of liquor.[155] These findings no doubt delighted the syndicates: if the proposals for what amounted to a new industrial dop system ever came into being, they would be able to expand their empires through the loopholes which they were bound to find in the new legislation.

At the same time, and for the same reasons, these findings must have been bitterly disappointing to the mine owners. As the clouds of war threatened to break, and the mining capitalists scurried for the protection of Cape Town, they could look back not on three years of 'total prohibition', but on three years of total frustration. What the Volksraad and the law had so faithfully promised them in 1896, the Liquor Kings, the 'Peruvians' and the Zarps had denied them over the succeeding years. Economic roots dating back at least to the 1880s had given rise to a political plant whose foliage had become hopelessly entangled. Every time that the stem of the alliance between the Chamber of Mines and the Volksraad was pulled in one direction, that of the State President and the liquor capitalists moved in another, and all the time the parasitic liquor syndicates continued to bloom. The mine owners knew that as long as Kruger and Hatherley Distillery survived, they would be confronted by a stalemate in which Witwatersrand Africans would be both liquor consumers *and* unproductive workers. They also knew that while there was war, there was hope.

The black worker as worker

The spoils of a war fought for the mine owners, 1899–1903

Prohibition, the 'specials' and the 'Liquor Crusade' of the *Transvaal Leader* all helped to make 1899 one of the less successful years for Hatherley Distillery. Yet, despite the outbreak of war with Great Britain in October, which further undermined business, the Pretoria factory continued to manufacture spirits, and at the end of the year managed to show a profit of £2,737. *South Africa*, financial journal and capitalist mouthpiece in the City of London, assured its readers that, given the circumstances, 'this result cannot be regarded as other than satisfactory'.[156]

Under Sammy Marks's skilful financial tutelage the trading year for Hatherley in 1900 was no less satisfactory – again, given the circumstances. Catering for the climate of insecurity, Marks arranged for a sum of £25,000 to be taken out of the distillery's funds and secured as a special investment. Even after this had been done, the distillery showed a gross profit of over £16,000 for the twelve months; although the shareholders were not paid a dividend they had every reason to be content with an enterprise which could point to a net profit of over £9,000 in such trying times.[157]

A trading year, however, was not the same as twelve months of war, and viewed in other perspectives 1900 was not a good one for the Pretoria company. Early in the year there had been a considerable amount of fighting in the vicinity of the factory, and the company was fortunate that very little permanent damage was done to plant and equipment. However, once Pretoria fell to the British forces on 5 June 1900, damage of a more lasting type was done to the distillery. Under martial law the Military Governor issued a proclamation prohibiting the manufacture and sale of all spirituous liquors.[158] Under the same order, Sammy Marks was forced to close the glass factory at Hatherley, and this meant dismissing all employees. This latter action involved the company in additional expense, since all the skilled workers were on contract and demanded compensation for their enforced redundancy. The Hatherley directors sharply contested these decisions, but their combination of threat and plea left the Military Governor totally unmoved. This early proclamation gave the first indication of how the Imperial authorities were to view the liquor industry in their newly acquired mining colony.

Initially the liquor capitalists were not greatly perturbed about the long-term consequences of this closure. Their ultimate confidence was reflected in the press release which the London Committee issued to English shareholders:

> The cessation of business, however, is only of a temporary nature, and when things have settled down there is every reason to anticipate that under the British Flag the Company will have a bright and prosperous future.[159]

Six, sixteen and twenty-six months later the distillery, and the glass factory, were still closed 'in obedience to proclamations issued by military authorities'.[160] In the end Hatherley Distillery never did re-open – a fate which the Transvaal gold mines certainly did not share. At some point between June

1900 and February 1903 British and other shareholders made the rather painful discovery that the Imperial army had fought a war for the mine- and not the distillery-owners.

The closure of Hatherley did not dramatically disrupt the liquor trade on the Witwatersrand during the first nine or ten months of the war. Existing stocks and a much reduced but continuing supply of liquor from the Pretoria distillery were sufficient to keep the syndicates in business. Black workers continued to buy, at new and even more exorbitant prices, the only 'cheap' liquor they could afford – Hatherley spirits or 'Nellmapius' as it was more commonly known. Both the syndicates and the black workers, however, got a foretaste of the imminent new dispensation when the Z.A.R. government took over the running of five mines in April 1900. The wages of the 12,000 black workers were unilaterally reduced from 60 to 20 shillings per month, and the Z.A.R. war administration further illustrated its no-nonsense capitalist approach by cancelling all liquor licences in the vicinity of the mines.[161]

More glimmerings in the new capitalist dawn were to be seen soon after the British forces occupied Johannesburg on 1 May 1900. Martial law was declared; within a month an important syndicate leader was arrested, and made an example of:

> . . . a certain Joffe [Barry from Krugersdorp] known on the Rand as the Liquor King, was sentenced to a heavy fine and several years' imprisonment, with the result that the whole trade was paralysed.[162]

In fact the whole trade was not 'paralysed', but the Kings had received a near-fatal blow. Further problems arose for the syndicates as the army swept through Johannesburg, rounding up what the British administration called 'undesirable immigrants'. These lumpenproletarians from Russia, Austria, Germany, Italy, Spain and France were unceremoniously bundled onto trains, and despatched to Cape Town. There, at least one party 150-strong was put aboard the *Hawarden Castle* and sent to Europe.[163] Amongst these 'undesirable immigrants' of July/August there were several 'Peruvians', and this further undermined the illicit liquor business. By September it was reported that the shebeens had 'been pretty well stamped out by the heavy penalties imposed'. The illicit liquor trade, however, was never totally eradicated – not even under the harsh regime of martial law. In February 1901, Colonel Davis, the Military Commissioner of Police, still had to devote a part of his day to it.[164] In general, however, there was no doubt that the Witwatersrand was becoming a better place for mining companies.

From their wartime base in Cape Town the mine owners watched the achievements of the Imperial army with undisguised admiration. The closure of Hatherley, the trial of Joffe and the deportation of the 'undesirables' were gifts that only a war could bestow so swiftly and generously. In less than three months the Military Governor had succeeded in achieving what the Chamber of Mines and the Volksraad had failed to accomplish in three years.[165] The joy of the mine owners, however, was the joy of caution. They knew that the Transvaal would not always be under martial law, and that the British army would not always be there to do the work of the state. What they had to do, therefore, was to ensure that the gains of war did not become the losses of peace. To this end they spent their seaside days lobbying the Imperial administration, and building up an ideological offensive against any future legislation which might allow alcohol to be sold to black men in the Transvaal. The ghost of the Volksraad's 1899 Liquor Commission continued to haunt the Chamber of Mines in its wartime home.

In July 1900, a mere four weeks after Johannesburg had been occupied, a large deputation of mine owners and commercial men approached the then Governor of the Cape, Sir Alfred Milner. The mining men described their pre-war liquor problem on the Witwatersrand in some detail to Milner, and expressed their wish that 'total prohibition' be maintained and effectively enforced. Milner gave the deputation a most sympathetic hearing and assured the businessmen that whoever took over the Transvaal's affairs after the war would probably be capable of clearing up the entire liquor question to their satisfaction within six months.[166]

A nod and a wink from a Governor – even a British Governor – did not completely satisfy mining capitalists. What would Sammy Marks and the producers of 'Cape Smoke' do once business was resuscitated and they got access to the markets of a united South Africa? For this, and other reasons, the men of the Chamber of Mines threw their weight behind a new organisation which emerged exactly as the Transvaal was making the transition from a military to a civilian administration. 'The South African Alliance for the Reform of the Liquor Traffic' united men 'keenly interested in the moral and material welfare of South Africa, mine owners, mine managers, merchants, ministers of religion and private citizens'.[167] It would appear that within the Alliance the men interested in the 'material welfare of South Africa' made considerable use of those interested in the 'moral welfare' of the country. It was the ministers of religion who undertook most of the agitation and public relations for the 'Alliance' – men like the Rev. Andrew Brown and the Rev. J. T. Darragh, the founder of St John's College in Johannesburg. During June and July of 1901 they wrote articles at home and abroad outlining the aims and objectives of the movement.[168]

First, the Alliance wished to seize the moment and secure the victories of the Military Governor. As the good Rev. Darragh put it to his English audience:

> Reforms which it would be well-nigh impossible to introduce into an old and complex civilisation can now and here be attempted with the minimum of opposition and friction. We are making a fresh start, and it will be some compensation for the sufferings of the last two years if the start is made on sane, well-considered lines. We have perfect confidence in the ability, integrity and honesty of purpose of the Administration, but amid the multiplicity of claims which will be clamouring for attention, it is just possible that this golden opportunity for settling the liquor problem may be overlooked till it is too late.[169]

Second, and more fundamental, the Alliance sought a state monopoly for the production and sale of liquor.

The idea of a state monopoly of this sort was not new to the mine owners – indeed it was very similar to the Kruger proposals of 1898–9. This time, however, the mining capitalists knew that the monopoly would be run by a state in which they had greater power, and that it would be backed by an administration which would more effectively guarantee the productivity of their black workers. In fact, the mine owners had such confidence in the competence of the incoming administration that many hankered after the old industrial dop system of pre-1897. With British backing, the use of alcohol as a means of socio-economic control again became a real possibility. Significantly, therefore, the Alliance did *not* favour 'total prohibition', and again the capitalists left it to the churchmen to explain. The Rev. Darragh told an English audience which was perhaps not fully familiar with the realities and history of the industry, what exactly it was that the mine owners contemplated:

> Many thoughtful persons feel that the mining native should be specially considered. His work, especially underground, is disagreeable, monotonous and exhausting. The East Coast natives in particular [Mozambicans] who furnish the largest number of underground workers, are used to stimulants from boyhood, and it seems unfair to deprive them altogether of what they regard as a solace. . .[170]

Like other clergymen in the Alliance, the Rev. Darragh was capable of doing a more than passable imitation of a Minister of Mines.

As the Transvaal moved from military administration to Imperial government, the mine owners had placed their money on a win/win combination which guaranteed dividends. Either they could get 'total prohibition', which would ensure them a productive labour force, or they could retain the right to use alcohol as a lever of socio-economic control in a regime backed by an efficient administration. All that remained was the 'anxious' wait to see whether the approach through Milner or the deployment of the South African Alliance ultimately triumphed. In practice the wait turned out to be less than nerve-racking.

In April 1901, within weeks of his arrival in Pretoria as High Commissioner, Alfred Milner was petitioned by the South African Alliance on the liquor question. The Alliance again underlined the benefits that had come with martial law, and urged strong government control. For his part, Milner expressed sympathy with the new movement, and suggested that they also approach Joseph Chamberlain. Additional pressure brought to bear on the Secretary of State for the Colonies would neatly supplement the Alliance's well-advanced public agitation in England. Having yet again expressed his understanding of the mining capitalists' problems, Milner set to work on his task of reconstruction.

In October 1901 Milner set up the Liquor Licensing Commission in Johannesburg to administer the resumption of the retail liquor trade.[171] As chairman of the commission he appointed a Yeomanry officer, Major Macpherson, and to assist him, a committee of Johannesburg businessmen. This military-cum-civilian licensing board was designed to produce exactly the type of conservative change that Milner and the mine owners envisaged. Initially, it kept all bars, canteens, and bottle stores closed, and only allowed liquor to be sold in hotels and restaurants between 12 noon and 9 p.m.

Milner made this exceedingly modest revival of the liquor trade even safer when, on 10 December 1901, he used his powers of proclamation as High Commissioner to gazette new liquor laws for the Transvaal.[172] His proclamation embodied the principle of 'total prohibition' for Africans, and laid down stiffer penalties for the contravention of the law than had existed under the old Z.A.R. government. Milner saw this law as a gift benefiting *all* the classes most closely involved in the reconstruction of capitalism on the Rand. With the fervour so characteristic of Imperial ideology, he wrote to Chamberlain:

> . . .undoubtedly the greatest benefit which it is in the power of the Government to confer, alike upon mine owner and native, is the suppression of the illicit drink traffic.[173]

And to put the issue beyond any doubt at all, this proclamation was followed by Ordinance 32 of 1902 which prevented the distillation of any spirits for commercial gain within the Transvaal.

Between them these measures ensured an orderly transition to liquor retailing, and limited the opportunities for illicit dealers. When the bars re-opened in Johannesburg in January 1902 they had to operate within restricted hours and provide a meal of some sort with any alcohol they served. Liquor licences came under the control of the Imperial Liquor Commissioner, and except for a brief period of public drunkenness when the bottle stores re-opened in mid-1902, there were no major disruptions on the Witwatersrand. In December 1901 Milner noted with pleasure the mine owners' claim that only one per cent of their black workforce was now absent owing to liquor consumption on any one day, as against the ten to fifteen per cent average during the pre-war years.[174] This increase in productivity, coupled with the newly reduced wage rates for African workers, left the mine owners comparatively happy. The Transvaal was becoming a safer place for mining capitalism.

The happiness of the mining capitalists was also the sorrow of the liquor capitalists. The thoroughness of the British 'reforms' and the closure of Hatherley Distillery left Sammy Marks and his colleagues far from satisfied. Marks's financial acumen, the concession, and the large number of British shareholders in the distillery all meant that Milner could not simply brush the liquor capitalists aside. In mid-1901 *South Africa* warned Milner not to see the Pretoria business as simply another Kruger concession, like the railways or dynamite:

> The Hatherley Distillery has all along been an honest concern, with an honourable management, and as such is entitled to the highest consideration at the hands of the new Transvaal authorities.[175]

To make the new revolution of the mining capitalists secure, the British administration had to eliminate the Pretoria distillery at the same time that it was 'reforming' the Rand.

Within twelve months of the outbreak of war, in October 1900, the Imperial government appointed the Transvaal Concessions Commission to examine the monopolies granted by the Z.A.R. Sammy Marks and his partners gave evidence before this commission in Pretoria, stressing that the concession had been legally granted, and that the company had kept to all the conditions attached to the grant. When the commission reported in June 1901 it found accordingly, and recommended that if the concession were cancelled the owners should be compensated.[176]

As soon as the commission reported, Sammy Marks authorised Isaac Lewis to undertake the detailed negotiations for compensation. As a figure less closely associated with Kruger than Marks, Lewis proved a wise choice. Between June 1901 and early 1903 he worked ceaselessly to extract the best possible settlement for the Hatherley shareholders. In particular, Lewis had to pursue two related objectives: first, he aimed to get a settlement as soon as possible, an objective which was basic to the shareholders' interest; second, he was intent on getting a settlement with the Milner regime rather than the Legislative Council which would succeed it – the British were likely to be more generous towards international shareholders than the local bourgeoisie who were bound to follow them.

By the end of 1902 Lewis had wrapped up his negotiations with the Milner administration, and in February 1902 details of the settlement were printed in the Hatherley Directors' Report for 1902. From the distillery's point of view the settlement appeared to be a relatively generous one. The shareholders were to be paid a cash settlement of over a quarter of a million pounds for the cancellation of the concession. In addition, stocks on hand could be sold, exempt from excise duty, and some of the liquor at Ressano Garcia and Lourenço Marques was also to be imported duty-free. In London, *South Africa* told British investors in the distillery that 'shareholders are to be congratulated on the result of the negotiations'.[177]

When these basic conditions were confirmed in the Legislative Council in July 1903 not everybody was pleased: 'Several members severely criticised the bargain, which passed only because the Government was already committed to the terms.' The resolution of the contradiction within the capitalist development of the Transvaal had to be paid for, and not all were happy with the asking price. In this case, however, the mining capitalists' and tax-payers' sorrow was the distillers' delight. Why exactly Marks and his partners were so satisfied emerged from the detailed analysis of the settlement which *South Africa* offered its readers:

> According to the balance-sheet made up to 31 December, 1902, the total assets stood at £600,000, against liabilities amounting to £475,000. At this time, the concession and goodwill stood in the accounts as representing £117,319 7s 5d which must now, in consequence of the amount the Government has agreed to pay, be increased by £180,555 12s 7d or a little over £1 12s 6d per share. In addition to this, the company will, considering the very favourable conditions granted them, undoubtedly make a large profit on the sale of the 320,000 gallons of liquor they have in stock, so that when the affairs of the company come to be finally liquidated, the return made to holders of shares should be an extremely good one. To the fact that they are to-day in this very satisfactory position shareholders are to a very great extent indebted to Mr Isaac Lewis. . .

No wonder that the financial journal could take a broad perspective and conclude, 'At this result, holders of shares in this the first industrial company formed in the Transvaal have nothing of which to complain.'[178] The owners of Hatherley Distillery went out of business with a smile, if not a chuckle.

Conclusion

The paths that states tread on their way to economic development often have local distinguishing characteristics, but they are seldom unique. The direction which the Transvaal took from the mid-nineteenth century onwards was certainly not unique – at least not in the initial period. Indeed, its quasi-feudal mode of production gave rise to certain patterns which can readily be traced in European economic history. One of the clearest of these patterns relates to the production of agricultural surplus and its consumption. By the late 1870s, and certainly by the early 1880s, the Boer farmers who had conquered the area north of the Orange river were producing sizeable grain surpluses. Like some of their European predecessors, this rural bourgeoisie sought to accumulate capital through the process of distillation, and by selling alcohol spirits to the town and villages which formed the modest local market.

But the Transvaal was not destined to remain a modest local market. Once gold was discovered on the Witwatersrand in the mid-1880s, there was a rapid and sustained increase of population within a relatively concentrated area. African and European miners, many of them with a developed taste for alcohol, poured into the towns spread along the line of the Reef – towns such as Krugersdorp, Johannesburg and Boksburg. This massive new market transformed the economic prospects of Hatherley Distillery and those of the grain producers who supplied it. From a modest 'first factory' in the Transvaal there emerged a large modern industrial enterprise enjoying the support and protection of a significant section of the Afrikaner ruling class.

Afrikaner farmers and distillery owners, however, were not the only parties interested in alcohol consumption on the Witwatersrand. Alcohol was also a matter of central concern to the new industrial bourgeoisie who owned the mines, particularly in so far as it affected their cheap black labour force. To their delight, the mining capitalists discovered that the black Mozambicans who formed the majority of the African labour force had an especially well-developed liking for alcohol. It was this liking, or partial addiction to alcohol that mine owners exploited to procure a labouring population from basically peasant economies. In 1906 F. Perry, one-time chairman of the Witwatersrand Native Labour Association (the mine owners' labour recruitment agency), noted that Mozambicans 'have always been fond of strong drink', and he continued:

> They brew themselves many kinds of native spirits, and the potent liquors of European manufacture threw open to them new vistas of enjoyment. A few of them had found their way to the diamond fields. To the Witwatersrand goldfields, which were nearer to them they came in great numbers, especially after the construction of the Delagoa Bay

> Railway. *Their earnings were spent, not on cattle but on whisky and gin.* Thus, a period of work, instead of supplying them with the means of settling down, only gave them a period of drink and idleness. *Afterwards they had to return to work in order to earn the coin wherewith to gratify their cultivated taste. In this way they have come nearer than any of the other South African races to supplying the material of an industrial, as distinguished from an agricultural population.*[179]

In short, alcohol was a distinct aid in proletarianising African peasants. Not surprisingly, therefore, there was an economic marriage of convenience – a class alliance – which bound the Afrikaner rural bourgeoisie and the mining capitalists between 1886 and 1896.

From the earliest years of the industry, however, the mine owners were also aware that alcohol was not an unqualified blessing. Spirits might have assisted the capitalists in procuring a cheap labour force, but the resulting drunkenness seriously undermined the productivity of the workers. By 1896, that is at about the same time that the mine owners were making the transition to deep-level mining which would ensure the long-term future and profitability of the industry, this problem of drunkenness had reached enormous proportions. Not only were the workers consuming vast quantities of locally produced spirits; they were also drinking so many gallons of cheaper imported potato spirits from Germany that their productivity was seriously impaired. The cost and inefficiency that resulted from this extensive drinking, at a vital transitional stage in the gold-mining industry's history, forced the new industrial bourgeoisie to take remedial action. It was at this point that the mine owners started exploiting divisions within the Afrikaner ruling class, and successfully advocating a policy of 'total prohibition' for African workers. When this policy was adopted it brought to an end the formal class alliance which had existed between the Afrikaner rural bourgeoisie and the mining capitalists.

Both the distillery owners and an important part of the Afrikaner ruling class stood to lose much through 'total prohibition', which denied them legal access to what had formerly been their most important market. Thus, between 1897 and 1899, the liquor producers and powerful elements of the Afrikaner bourgeoisie made several attempts to have the policy of 'total prohibition' reversed – in effect they made constant attempts to resurrect the old class alliance in explicit legal form. These attempts, however, had little chance of succeeding since the interests of the mining capitalists had undergone a fundamental change. Unofficially and illegally some of the essential features of the old order remained intact. In the towns the petty-bourgeois army of canteen owners, dominated by Russian Jewish immigrants and aided by the corrupt arm of the state in the form of the police, continued to supply African workers with vast quantities of spirits. *De jure* the old order might have ended on 1 January 1897 when 'total prohibition' came into effect; *de facto* it persisted well into 1899.

This stubborn persistence of elements of the old order remained a constant source of irritation, frustration and unnecessary cost to the mine owners between 1897 and 1899. But this new industrial bourgeoisie took heart when war broke out between Britain and the Z.A.R. in October 1899. The mine owners knew that the imperialists would use an efficient British administration to secure the interests of foreign capital, and to make gold mining the undisputed economic master of the Transvaal – indeed that was the very purpose of the war. And their hopes proved to be fully justified. Within 36 months the army and the British administration had closed Hatherley Distillery and compensated its owners, passed legislation to prevent any further distilling, deported 'undesirable immigrants', smashed the illicit liquor syndicates, and then rendered the entire black workforce on the Witwatersrand more productive and efficient on newly reduced wages. Gone were the remnants of the *ancien régime* – the last remaining links of the old class alliance. From the end of the war, an economically and politically subject Afrikaner bourgeoisie could construct no further form of class alliance. With the aid of imperial intervention mining capitalism had been installed as the dominant mode of production in southern Africa. In all systems of capitalism – but perhaps especially in colonial regimes – alcohol has more to do with profits than with priests and is concerned with money rather than morality.

Notes

1 See, for example, George Rudé, *Paris and London in the 18th Century* (London 1969).
2 D. Mitrany, *The Land and the Peasant in Rumania* (Oxford 1930), p. 490.
3 P. I. Lyaschenko, *History of the National Economy of Russia to the 1917 Revolution* (New York 1949), p. 411. See also W. L. Blackwell, *The Beginnings of Russian Industrialization 1800–1860* (Princeton 1968), p. 56.
4 *Novi Ukrainski Pisni Pro Hromadsku Spravu, 1764–1880* (Geneva 1881), pp. 111–12; S. Podolynsky, *Fabryki i remesla na Ukraine* (Geneva 1881), p. 130.
5 See H. Bechtel, *Wirtschaftsgeschichte Deutschlands* (Munich 1956), pp. 25–6; G. Stolper, *The German Economy 1870–1940* (New York 1940), p. 37. Also, H. Rosenberg, *Probleme der Deutschen Sozialgeschichte* (Frankfurt 1969), p. 68; H. W. Graf Finckenstein, *Die Entwicklung der Landwirtschaft in Preussen und Deutschland* (Würzburg 1960), pp. 144–5.
6 *South Africa* (London) 90, 510, 1 October 1898, p. 28.
7 By 1899 this dumping of spirits in Africa had reached such proportions, and produced such cut-throat competition, that the major European powers were forced to seek an agreement. See *Correspondence respecting the African Liquor Traffic Convention, signed at Brussels, 8 June 1899* (H.M.S.O., Command 9335, July 1899, Africa No. 7.)
8 *Standard and Diggers' News* (hereafter: *S. and D. N.*), 10 May 1895.
9 See F. J. Potgieter, 'Die Vestigting van die Blanke in Transvaal 1837–1886', *Archives Year Book for South African History*, 2, 1958, p. 94.
10 In part these import duties simply encouraged smuggling – particularly of the cheap Cape Colony brandy known as 'Cape Smoke'. See, for example, the activities of J. D. Bosman of the Paarl Wine and Brandy Company, as reported in *S. and D.N.*, 24 January 1891. Also, the Goldberg case in *S. and D. N.*, 15 July 1891. See also note 34 below.
11 Editorial, *S. and D.N.*, 29 October 1892.
12 See Miss Annie Russell's account of 'Early Transvaal Towns', republished in *S. and D.N.*, 20 April 1894.
13 *S. and D.N.*, 31 July 1893.

14 C. T. Gordon, *The Growth of Boer Opposition to Kruger 1890–95* (London 1970), p. 36.
15 'Report of Special Liquor Committee' in *Chamber of Mines of the South African Republic Tenth Annual Report for the year ending 31 December 1898*, p. 110. (This report runs from pp. 108–15, and is hereafter cited as '*S.L.C. Report 1898*'.)
16 *Report of the Transvaal Concessions Commission*, Part II, Minutes of Evidence, p. 71. (H.M.S.O., Command 624 of 1901. Hereafter: *Command 624*.)
17 *Command 624*, p. 717. See also, *Report of the Transvaal Concessions Commission*, Part I, p. 99. (H.M.S.O., Command 623 of 1901. Hereafter: *Command 623*.)
18 *Command 624*, June 1901, p. 75. From 1894 to 1898 the glass factory ran at a diminishing loss each year. By 1898 the loss was down to £2,356 for the year, and the directors expressed every hope that it would produce a profit during 1899. See the report on the Hatherley Company in *South Africa*, 42, 544, 27 May 1899, p. 482.
19 *S. and D.N.*, 14 May 1899.
20 For detailed descriptions of Hatherley see *S. and D.N.*, 14 December 1899, and 5 May 1890.
21 *Command 624*, June 1901, p. 74.
22 *S. and D.N.*, 14 and 24 December 1889; 5 May 1890; 30 May 1891.
23 *Command 623*, June 1901, p. 99.
24 See for example, J. N. Bovill, *Natives under the Transvaal Flag* (London 1900), p. 47. Also R. C. F. Maugham, *Portuguese East Africa* (London 1906), p. 283. Perhaps the most valuable evidence, however, is contained in 'Extracts from the Report of Dr Serrao De Azevedo on the Health Services of the Province of Mozambique', in Transvaal, *Report of the Liquor Commission 1908*, annexure 4, pp. 116–17.
25 *Report for the year 1894 on the Trade of the Consular District of Mozambique* (F.O. Series No. 1537) p. 4.
26 *Report for the year 1895 on the Trade of the Consular District of Mozambique* (F.O. Series No. 1760) p. 4.
27 Bovill, *Natives under the Transvaal Flag*, p. 47.
28 A. Davis, *The Native Problem* (London 1903), p. 186.
29 W. C. A. Shepherd, 'Recruiting in Portuguese East Africa of Natives for the Mines', *Journal of the African Society*, 33, July 1934, p. 254.
30 See *Command 624*, June 1901, p. 72. For issued share capital see C. S. Goldmann, *South African Mining and Finance* (Johannesburg 1895), vol. 2, p. 206; also, *S. and D.N.*, 14 November 1892.
31 *South African Who's Who 1909*, pp. 107, 147, 139 and 144.
32 Registrar of Companies, Zanza House, Pretoria, File T669, 'The Eerste Fabrieken Hatherley Distillery Ltd., List of Shareholders and their respective holdings as at 31 December 1901'. See also *Command 624*, June 1901, p. 72. See also, J. Ploeger, 'Die Maatskappy "Eerste Fabrieken in die Zuid Afrikaansche Republiek"', *Historia*, Jaargang 2, 1957, 123. (Hereafter: 'Die Maatskappy'.)
33 *South African Who's Who 1909*, p. 144; *Transvaal Leader*, 24 August 1899.
34 'Cape Smoke' was so called partly because rolls of crude tobacco were actually used in its preparation. See, for example, Fisher Vane, *Back to the Mines* (London 1903), p. 169; also note 10 above.
35 *Command 624*, June 1901, p. 73. Also, *S.L.C. Report 1898*, pp. 109–10.
36 *S.L.C. Report 1898*, p. 110.
37 *Report for the year 1894 on the Trade of the Consular District of Mozambique* (F.O. Series No. 1537) p. 15.
38 Companhia do Assucar de Moçambique, *Relatorios e Contas das Gerencias de 1895 e 1896*, p. 8.

39 *S.L.C. Report 1898*, p. 110 and p. 115. See also, J. Ploeger, 'Die Maatskappy', p. 124.
40 Companhia do Assucar de Moçambique, *Relatorios. . . 1895*, p. 24.
41 See *S. and D. N.*, 30 August 1894; *S.L.C. Report 1898*, p. 110.
42 Compare the list of distilleries in *Report for the year 1894 on the Trade of the Consular District of Mozambique* (F.O. Series No. 1537) p. 36, with that in *The Delagoa Directory for 1899* (Lourenço Marques 1899), p. 34.
43 *Report for the year 1895 on the Trade of the Consular District of Mozambique* (F.O. Series No. 1760), p. 12.
44 *S.L.C. Report 1898*, pp. 110–11.
45 For ships and cargoes to Lagos see T. Welsh, 'Contrasts in African Legislation', *Journal of the African Society*, 6 January 1903, p. 199.
46 *S.L.C. Report 1898*, p. 111.
47 Initially, of course, these cheap imports of potato spirits also hampered local distilleries within Lourenço Marques. See, for example, *S. and D.N.*, 20 October 1892. For the consumption of German potato spirits within Mozambique see *Report for the year 1894 on the Trade of the Consular District of Mozambique* (F.O. Series No. 1537), p. 36. For the role of potato spirits on the Witwatersrand see L. S. Amery (ed.), *The Times History of the War in South Africa 1899–1900*, vol. 1, p. 121.
48 Welsh, 'Contrasts in African Legislation', p. 199; *Report for the year 1895 on the Trade of the Consular District of Mozambique* (F.O. Series No. 1760), p. 11.
49 *Transvaal Leader*, 29 May 1899.
50 *Transvaal Leader*, 23 May 1899.
51 Apparently the first prosecution under the Z.A.R. Trade Marks Act occurred in 1893 when the local agents for Spenglers Gin (Rotterdam, Holland) instituted legal proceedings against S. Feinberg. The findings of the court in this case are unknown. See *S. and D.N.*, 16 September 1893; *Transvaal Leader*, 23 May 1899.
52 For these recipes see *Transvaal Leader*, 23, 24 and 25 May 1899.
53 *S. and D.N.*, 29 April 1890.
54 Figures from the following sources: F. Jeppe (ed.), *Jeppe's Transvaal Almanac for 1899*, p. 46; *S. and D.N.*, 12 October 1892; and *Report of the Chamber of Mines for 1898*, p. 134.
55 *S. and D.N.*, 30 April 1889, 6 March 1890.
56 For examples of these activities see: *S. and D.N.*, 19 December 1889; 20 April 1891; 12 October 1892; *Report of the Chamber of Mines for 1895*, p. 76.
57 *S. and D.N.*, 23 July 1889.
58 In the case of Johannesburg see *S. and D.N.*, 1892.
59 *S. and D.N.*, 27 June 1894; 9 April 1889.
60 *S. and D.N.*, 26 September and 28 November 1892.
61 For the Transvaal Temperance Alliance see *S. and D.N.*, 27 July and 26 August 1892.
62 *S. and D.N.*, 11 June and 24 August 1891; 28 November 1892.
63 'It is not, however, contended by the Chamber that there should be total prohibition': *Report of the Chamber of Mines for 1895*, p. 77.
64 In this analysis I have drawn on the extensive and detailed interpretation offered by Belinda Bozzoli in her study, 'The Roots of Hegemony; Ideologies, Interests, and the Legitimation of South African Capitalism, 1890–1940', D. Phil. thesis, University of Sussex, 1975, esp. pp. 26–84.
65 *S. and D.N.*, 20 April 1891.
66 *S. and D.N.*, 12 September 1889.
67 *Report of the Chamber of Mines for 1895*, p. 76. See also, *S. and D.N.*, 13 February 1894.
68 Gordon, *The Growth of Boer Opposition*, pp. 196, 31. See also J. Fisher, *Paul*

Kruger (London 1974), p. 161.

69 For an example of Kruger's sales to Hatherley see *S. and D.N.*, 30 April 1890; and 'Orange Wine' advert, *S. and D.N.*, 31 May 1894.

70 D. E. Schutte to the Editor, *S. and D.N.*, 11 October 1894. For further background information on the Zarps see *S. and D.N.*, 17 December 1892; 10 February 1894; 14 May 1895.

71 See the report of the Chamber of Mines' deputation to the Minister of Mines on this point, *S. and D.N.*, 5 March 1891.

72 See Montagu White's remarks in *S. and D.N.*, 24 August 1891.

73 *S. and D.N.*, 11 June 1891; L. S. Amery (ed.), *The Times History of the War in South Africa 1899–1900*, vol. 1, p. 121. For specific names and cases see, for example, *Transvaal Leader*, 8 June 1899 and 11 July 1899.

74 E. P. Rathbone to the Editor, *S. and D.N.*, 23 May 1891.

75 For an example of a European death in Pretoria, allegedly caused by the consumption of Hatherley products, see 'R.N.' to the Editor, *S. and D.N.*, 10 November 1891. After noting that a white corpse had been dragged away by the police, 'R.N.' observed: 'Is it not time this poison was officially recognised in the British Pharmacopoeia? I would suggest first, that the name remain as it is, that the active principal of the drug be known as Nellmapatine, and that the person under its influence be described as being Nellmapnatised'.

76 Fisher Vane, *Back to the Mines*, p. 179.

77 Bovill, *Natives under the Transvaal Flag*, pp. 36–7.

78 See especially G. Blainey, 'Lost causes of the Jameson Raid', *Economic History Review*, 1965 pp. 350–66.

79 *Report of the Chamber of Mines for 1895*, p. 75.

80 For the official estimates see *Report of the Chamber of Mines for 1896*, p. 117, and *Papers relating to Legislation affecting Natives in the Transvaal* (H.M.S.O., Command 904, January 1902), p. 26. For unofficial estimates see, for example, *South Africa*, 90, 516, 12 November 1898.

81 J. Scoble and H. R. Abercrombie, *The Rise and Fall of Krugerism* (London 1900), p. 95.

82 See *S. and D.N.*, 28 April 1890; 11 June 1891.

83 See *Report of the Chamber of Mines for 1895*, pp. 74, 78, and *Report for 1896* pp. 136–7.

84 Landdrost van den Berg consistently fought the illicit liquor dealers and for this he earned the support of the mine owners and J. C. Smuts. See J. van der Poel and W. K. Hancock (eds.), *Selections from the Smuts Papers*, vol. 1 (Cambridge 1965), pp. 194–5. (Hereafter *Smuts Papers*.) It is interesting to note that van den Berg was the only Republican civil servant to continue in service with the Milner administration after the South African War; see D. Denoon, *A Grand Illusion* (London 1973), p. 45.

85 See *S. and D.N.*, 3 September 1889; 6 May 1890; 14 July 1891.

86 See Gordon, *The Growth of Boer Opposition*.

87 For the mine owners' case see J. P. FitzPatrick, *The Transvaal from Within* (London 1899), p. 235.

88 Gordon, *The Growth of Boer Opposition*, p. 235.

89 See *S. and D.N.*, 8, 9 and 21 August 1894.

90 See *S. and D.N.*, 11 and 19 September, 4 October 1894.

91 For events surrounding the Trimble and Donovan affair see *S. and D.N.*, 12 and 29 January, 1 February and 8 May 1895.

92 See *S. and D.N.*, 11 and 19 September, 4 October 1894. Also FitzPatrick, *The Transvaal from Within*, p. 98.

93 *Report of the Chamber of Mines for 1896*, p. 117.

94 W. S. Cohn to the Editor, *S. and D.N.*, 5 May 1899.

95 Ploeger, 'Die Maatskappy', p. 125. More generally see *Command 624*, June 1901, p. 73.
96 *S. and D.N.*, 21 March 1894.
97 This dominance of a petty-bourgeois organisation by mercantile capital eventually led to substantial conflict and to Heymann's resignation. See *S. and D.N.*, 5, 19 and 22 January, 30 March and 6 April 1895.
98 Ploeger, 'Die Maatskappy', p. 124.
99 Ploeger, 'Die Maatskappy', p. 125; *Command 624*, June 1901, p. 73.
100 Ploeger, 'Die Maatskappy', pp. 125–6. Also, *S. and D.N.*, 6 November 1894.
101 For the placement of the shares on the Bourse see Ploeger, 'Die Maatskappy', p. 126. For the names of those on the Paris and London Committees, see 'Annual Report on Hatherley Distillery' in *South Africa*, 497, 614, 29 September 1900, p. 612.
102 Ploeger, 'Die Maatskappy', pp. 125–6; *Command 624*, June 1901, p. 73.
103 W. S. Cohn to the Editor, *Transvaal Leader*, 5 May 1899; Ploeger, 'Die Maatskappy', p. 126.
104 Ploeger, 'Die Maatskappy'; *The Delagoa Directory for 1899* (Lourenço Marques), p. 34.
105 Joaquim Mouzinho de Albuquerque, *Moçambique 1896–98* (Lisbon 1899), pp. 132–3.
106 Ploeger, 'Die Maatskappy', p. 124.
107 Report of J. E. Evans, British Vice Consul at Johannesburg, as noted in *South Africa*, 40, 518, 26 November 1898, p. 434.
108 *S. and D.N.*, 31 July 1893.
109 W. F. Bailey, 'The Native Problem in South Africa', *National Review*, 28, 1896, p. 546.
110 See E. B. Rose, *The Truth about the Transvaal* (London 1902), p. 48; *Transvaal Leader*, 30 June 1899.
111 Rose, *The Truth about the Transvaal*, p. 49.
112 Examples from *Transvaal Leader*, 19 June 1899; *South Africa*, 42, 544, 27 May 1899, p. 476.
113 *Transvaal Leader*, 19 June 1899.
114 See *Transvaal Leader*, 29 April 1899, and *South Africa*, 37, 478, 17 February 1898, p. 350.
115 *Transvaal Leader*, 8 May 1899.
116 *Transvaal Leader*, 30 June 1899.
117 For Pastolsky and 'Schutte' see *Transvaal Leader*, 1 and 2 May 1899.
118 *Transvaal Leader*, 8 June 1899.
119 For snippets of information on Nathanson see *S. and D.N.*, 23 June, 11 and 17 August and 13 October 1894, and 7 May 1895.
120 Reports on the Globus and Shapiro trial are contained in the following editions of the *S. and D.N.*: 16, 17, 23 and 28 October, and 1 and 30 November 1893.
121 *S. and D.N.*, 10 February 1894.
122 *Transvaal Leader*, 8 May 1899. See also the State Attorney's strongly worded letter to the Boksburg Public Prosecutor in van der Poel and Hancock (eds.), *Smuts Papers*, vol. 1, p. 192.
123 *Smuts Papers*, vol. 1, p. 195.
124 *Transvaal Leader*, 5 June 1899.
125 See, for example, *South Africa*, 40, 522, 27 December 1898, p. 624, and 42, 545, 3 June 1899, p. 560.
126 For this and other organisational features of the 'compounds' see the following: *Transvaal Leader*, 1 May 1899 and 5 June 1899; *South Africa*, 40, 517, 19 November 1898, p. 356, and 42, 546, 10 June 1899, p. 629; Rose, *The Truth about the Transvaal*, p. 48.

127 See H. Fox Bourne, *The Native Labour Question in the Transvaal* (London 1901), pp. 29–30.
128 *Report of the Chamber of Mines for 1898*, p. 103.
129 *Ibid.*, p. 102.
130 For a detailed outline of these events and correspondence see *Report of the Chamber of Mines for 1898*, pp. 103–7, 124.
131 *S.L.C. Report 1898*, p. 112.
132 *Ibid.*, pp. 109, 112.
133 *Smuts Papers*, vol. 1, p. 191.
134 See *Transvaal Leader*, 23 June, 4 and 15 July 1899.
135 W. S. Cohn to the Editor, *Transvaal Leader*, 5 May 1899.
136 *Transvaal Leader*, 1 May 1899.
137 See *Transvaal Leader*, 8 May 1899; Rose, *The Truth about the Transvaal*, pp. 49–50. For events at the Jumpers Mine see *Transvaal Leader*, 5 June 1899. And State Attorney Smuts instructed his Boksburg Public Prosecutor: 'If the private detective bureau traps a liquor shop, you must do your utmost to assist it.' See *Smuts Papers*, vol. 1, p. 192.
138 See *Transvaal Leader*, 29 April 1899; *South Africa*, 42, 545, 3 June 1899, p. 560.
139 *South Africa*, 42, 548, 24 June 1899, p. 743.
140 For church support see, for example, *Transvaal Leader*, 10 May 1899; *South Africa*, 42, 546, 10 June 1899, p. 588.
141 *Transvaal Leader*, 17 May 1899.
142 *Transvaal Leader*, 16, 17 May 1899.
143 *Transvaal Leader*, 15 May 1899.
144 *Transvaal Leader*, 22, 24 May 1899.
145 At the premises of Joffe and Abelheim: see *Transvaal Leader*, 18 May 1899. At Friedman, Tiverski, Pastolsky and Katzen's 'Grahamstown Bar', and at the Queen's Hotel: *Transvaal Leader*, 10 June 1899.
146 *South Africa*, 42, 546, 1 June 1899, p. 629.
147 See *Transvaal Leader*, 1, 16 May and 8 June 1899.
148 *Transvaal Leader*, 8 May 1899.
149 The above narrative is based on *Transvaal Leader*, 5 and 15 June 1899.
150 For example, Eli Rabinovitz and A. Kantor were sentenced to a fine of £100 or eight months' imprisonment with hard labour: *Transvaal Leader*, 29 April 1899.
151 See *Transvaal Leader*, 4 July 1899; *South Africa*, 43, 558, 2 September 1899, p. 508.
152 *South Africa*, 42, 556, 19 August 1899, p. 396; Rose, *The Truth about the Transvaal*, p. 50.
153 Sources for the above four paragraphs: *Transvaal Leader*, 17 and 25 May 1899; *South Africa*, 42, 548, 24 June 1899, p. 708.
154 *Transvaal Leader*, 26 August 1899.
155 *South Africa*, 44, 563, 7 October 1899, p. 8.
156 *Ibid.*
157 *South Africa*, 50, 647, 18 May 1901, p. 391.
158 *South Africa*, 47, 614, 29 September 1900. See also *South Africa*, 50, 647, 18 May 1901, p. 390.
159 *South Africa*, 47, 614, 29 September 1900, p. 620.
160 *South Africa*, 55, 712, 16 August 1902, p. 476.
161 *South Africa*, 46, 591, 21 April 1900, p. 125.
162 Amery (ed.), *The Times History of the War in South Africa*, vol. 1, p. 122.
163 These 'undesirables' disembarked in London where the Metropolitan Police initially refused to allow them entry rights. Thomas Cook and Son were instructed to give them each a one-way ticket to their country of origin, and £1 for food for the journey. Only 50 accepted this offer, and the remaining 100 were ultimately

allowed to enter London. *South Africa*, 48, 609, 25 August 1900, p. 398.
164 *South Africa*, 47, 614, 29 September 1900, p. 627, and 49, 635, 23 February 1901, p. 433.
165 This 'achievement', however, was not solely due to the Military Governor. The Governor was, on at least one occasion, pressured on this issue by Alfred Milner. See Bodleian Library, Oxford, Milner Papers, vol. 47, Diary, 11 June 1900, p. 40.
166 *South Africa*, 47, 605, 28 July 1900, p. 201.
167 J. T. Darragh, 'The Liquor Problem in the Transvaal', *Contemporary Review*, July 1901, p. 126.
168 Darragh, 'The Liquor Problem', p. 126; *South Africa*, 50, 649, 1 June 1901, p. 457.
169 Darragh, 'The Liquor Problem', p. 125.
170 *Ibid*., p. 133. This theme died hard in the Transvaal, and was resuscitated when Chinese labour supplies were no longer assured. See Transvaal, *Report of the Liquor Commission 1908*, p. 103 (particularly the 'reservations' of T. N. de Villiers and G. G. Munnik).
171 *South Africa*, 52, 667, 5 October 1901.
172 Welsh, 'Contrasts in African Legislation', p. 199.
173 *Command 904*, January 1902, p. 25.
174 *Ibid*., p. 26.
175 *South Africa*, 50, 651, 15 June 1901, p. 583.
176 *Command 623*, June 1901, p. 99.
177 *South Africa*, 57, 739, 21 February 1903, p. 610.
178 All quotations from *South Africa*, 59, 761, 25 July 1903, p. 260.
179 Speech read by F. Perry to the Fortnightly Club, 1 November 1906, on 'The Transvaal Labour Problem'. (My emphasis.)

CHAPTER THREE

Prostitutes and proletarians 1886–1914

Commercialised sex in the changing social formations engendered by rapid capitalist development in the Transvaal during the era of imperialism

'Prostitution', so the folk wisdom has it, 'is the oldest profession in the world.' Unfortunately this commonsense maxim does not constitute a particularly solid foundation on which to build a more scholarly examination of commercialised sex. By implication it suggests that in any society there would always be a certain number of women who would seek to earn their living by selling their bodies – a view akin to that which holds that while there is alcohol there will always be alcoholics. For social scientists the problem with using these home-spun wisdoms is, that while they may contain a residual element of truth, they ultimately force any systematic enquiry to centre around the pathology of the individuals concerned. While such approaches may be helpful and even profitable within certain disciplines, they are of extremely limited use to the social historian since they persistently beg the all-important questions about the nature and structure of societies in which prostitution manifests itself to any significant degree.

It is precisely with this concern for social structures in mind that most students of Victorian society have conducted their enquiries into vice, and arrived at the general conclusion that 'large-scale, conspicuous prostitution was a by-product of the first, explosive stage in the growth of the industrial city'. 'Prostitution', writes Richard Evans in a recent study, can be seen as a 'functional consequence of the rise of the urban society created by early industrial capitalism'.[1] Viewed from this latter vantage point, the social historian can scan the historical horizons of the early Transvaal with greater ease since it was here, more than anywhere else in the country, that South Africa's most explosive capitalist development took place between 1886 and 1914. Moreover, since the central thrust of this local development came *after* that of the major industrial nations elsewhere, it meant that the flesh markets of southern Africa were opening up for prostitutes at precisely the moment when those in Europe were starting to experience a decline.[2] It is only once these broad structural signposts are recognised that it becomes easier to chart and follow the historical paths of vice in Johannesburg.

If it was the glitter of gold and the pursuit of profit that first attracted hundreds of diggers to the Witwatersrand in the mid-1880s, then it was the sustained and changing demands of a fully-fledged mining industry over the next two and a half decades which continually transformed that society. As the original diggers' camp gave way to a miners' town, and then to a more settled working-class city, so – amongst many other distinctive developments – the sexual composition of Johannesburg underwent a fundamental change. The almost exclusively male digging community of the 1880s gave way, by the mid-1890s, to a town which – although still overwhelmingly dominated by migrant miners of all colours – had a more notable female component; and then, from the turn of the century onwards, to an established city with an increasingly well-balanced sex ratio.

But this sexual revolution was not achieved without its own set of social costs and concomitant traumas. When the Johannesburg Sanitary Board first conducted a census, in July 1896, the results revealed that 25,282 white males and 14,172 white females resided within a radius of three miles of the Market square – a ratio of 1.78 men to every woman in the most developed part of the city. An even more marked imbalance was found to exist amongst the black inhabitants of the city. In this case, the 12,961 black males in inner Johannesburg outnumbered the 1,234 black females producing a ratio of 10.50 men to every woman. Even this ratio paled into insignificance, however, when the African miners housed in the compounds within a three-mile radius were also taken into consideration. On the latter basis, black males outnumbered black females by 40,855 to 1,678, producing a ratio of 24.34 men to every woman.[3]

Given this fundamentally warped social fabric, it is less than surprising that Johannesburg, especially during the mid-1890s, offered substantial opportunities for prostitution. During the 1896 census, 114 'continental women' openly returned their profession as that of 'prostitute'. This honest or brazen contingent, however, merely constituted the core of a body of full-time professional prostitutes that was reliably estimated to be in excess of 1,000 women – the vast majority of these comprising recent immigrants from Europe. While a figure of this order might not appear as being intolerably high for a young mining town when viewed from the comfort of a retrospective historical glance, it constituted a more visible and urgent problem to the Victorian contemporaries of the Witwatersrand. The presence of 'women of ill-fame' in these numbers meant that there was one whore for every 50 white inhabitants of the city, or, expressed more dramatically, 10 per cent of all white women over the age of fifteen in Johannesburg were prostitutes.[4]

Furthermore, this trade in sexual favours also developed other features which tended to evoke public concern. Perhaps inevitably, prostitutes and brothels attracted a fringe element of petty criminals, thieves and gamblers to the city centre where they constituted something of a social nuisance. Even more threatening to the middle and upper classes, however, were the 200–300 pimps, 'white slavers' and professional gangsters who controlled Johannesburg's prostitution business by the mid-1890s. It was largely as a result of the efforts of this latter group that commercialised sex and police corruption came to assume a highly organised form in the city. When J. A. Hobson later looked back on some of the factors which had indirectly contributed to the making of the South African War, he noted that a system of bribery and blackmail 'was practised by the Johannesburg police in dealing with illicit bars and disorderly houses, resembling that which Tammany police established in New York'.[5] Whether or not he intended it to be so, Hobson's choice of analogy was singularly apt since, behind much of the local corruption, there were indeed American gangsters who had had first-hand experience of Tammany Hall.

Public soliciting by prostitutes, pervasive police corruption and rampant racketeering did not settle easily on the shoulders of those in authority in the Transvaal. When President S. J. P. Kruger granted the Johannesburg Sanitary Board powers of local government in 1887, the constitution, in two separate articles, made specific provision for the 'punishment of prostitutes' and the suppression of 'houses of ill-fame'. But, by the middle of the following decade, it had already become clear to members of the Pretoria government that these local by-laws were, in themselves, totally inadequate for dealing with the problem of large-scale prostitution as it now manifested itself in the principal city of the Republic. In three successive years, through three successive pieces of legislation – Law No. 2 of 1897, Law No. 22 of 1898 and Law No. 11 of 1899 – the Kruger government attempted to arm itself with the necessary statutory weapons with which to fight organised vice in Johannesburg. Not even this battery of laws, however, succeeded in ridding the Rand of its 'social evil' problem.

Immediately after the war, the incoming British administration under Lord Milner found it necessary to promulgate the Immorality Ordinance of 1903 in a renewed attempt to combat prostitution, and this was followed by the Crimes Prevention Ordinance of 1905, a measure which was at least partially used to restrict the activities of pimps. Two years later, when General Botha's *Het Volk* government first took office, it too recognised the need to take further action against offenders of the public morals and passed the Immigrants' Restriction Act of 1907. Although admittedly framed with other intentions in mind, it was this law that was widely used by the Transvaal police to deport pimps, prostitutes and other 'undesirables' from the Witwatersrand.

This barrage of legislation over a ten-year period indicated just how serious a problem prostitution was considered to be in the early years on the goldfields. The continuous need for new measures, however, also showed how deeply the 'social evil' had embedded itself within the social structure, and how difficult it was to dislodge. Indeed, it was precisely because the problem proved to be so persistent that many men in high office at the turn of the century were of the opinion that it was both futile, and inadvisable, to seek the total eradication of prostitution from society. Believing that 'the virtue of the *monde* is assured by the *demi-monde*', they and the police argued instead for the 'regulation' and 'control' of the traffic in commercialised sex.[6] Thus it was that while all the morality legislation in the Transvaal sought in principle to eliminate prostitution from the state, in practice the authorities for the most part operated a policy of selective enforcement – a policy of social control.

This essay, then, will attempt to analyse the dynamic and diverse functions of commercialised sex over the initial two-and-a-half formative decades of the Witwatersrand's capitalist development. Through a detailed case study, which explores the origin and development of large-scale prostitution during the early years of an industrial revolution, it is hoped to illustrate the limits of a policy of repression on the one hand, and that of social control on the other. In short, this essay will seek to show how various intermediaries sought to manipulate and profit from the relationship that existed between prostitutes and proletarians in the period prior to the development of a fully stabilised working class on the Witwatersrand.

Heritage of the Cape – daughters of the old proletariat, 1886–1896

When the township of Johannesburg was first proclaimed on the Witwatersrand, in October 1886, it sparked first a national and then an international scramble for the goldfields. Amongst the very first parties to reach the new Promised Land of Profit were diggers drawn from the Zuid Afrikaansche Republiek's neighbouring states on the subcontinent – Natal, the Orange Free State and the Cape Colony. It was also amongst these early arrivals that the town's first ladies of fortune were to be found, and they soon attracted the disapproving attention of President Kruger's local officials. Within months of the mining camp's establishment, Special Landdrost Carl von Brandis appealed to Pretoria for assistance in his struggle against these women who had already succeeded in spreading venereal disease through much of the town. A year later, in 1889, his appeal was echoed by a fellow magistrate when Landdrost de Beer requested the government to pass legislation which would enable them to deal with the 'hundreds' of prostitutes at the diggings. The Kruger government's view of the matter, however, was presumably that the powers conferred on the local Sanitary Board in 1887 were sufficient for dealing with the problem since no additional legislation was forthcoming from Pretoria.[7]

It is possible that in later years Kruger and his colleagues came to regret this early legislative inactivity for, while the *Volksraad* pondered over these appeals from Johannesburg, legislation was being promulgated elsewhere in southern Africa – legislation which ensured that prostitutes would not only continue to be 'pulled' towards the goldfields, but that they would also be 'pushed' northwards.

In 1885 the Cape parliament passed the Contagious Diseases Act, a mere twelve months before its British equivalent was repealed in London under pressure from the women's movement led by Josephine Butler. This controversial piece of legislation, like the Westminster statute on which it was modelled, made provision for the proclamation of scheduled towns, the registration of prostitutes and their compulsory medical examination; and by the early 1890s both Cape Town and Port Elizabeth had been proclaimed as scheduled areas in terms of the Act. The enforcement of 'C.D.' regulations at these coastal towns was understandably unpopular amongst women, and in consequence many prostitutes migrated to various inland centres, including the mining town of Kimberley which was blessed with a considerable number of bachelors. This comparatively minor influx of prostitutes to the diamond fields, however, simply succeeded in raising the wrath of the local middle classes who thought that the town had long since seen the last of its 'rough and ready' days.[8] Thus, in late 1891, partly out of a genuine desire to curb the further spread of venereal disease, and partly out of other more class-bound reasons, the city's medical practitioners agitated to have Kimberley declared a scheduled area in terms of the C.D. Act.[9] This renewed threat to the 'women of ill-fame', together with the extension of the railway to Johannesburg in late 1892, ensured that several prostitutes yet again chose to move northwards.

In Johannesburg these relatively late arrivers from the Cape joined the ranks of the true pioneers of prostitution, and by 1893 these two streams – the 'earlier' and the 'later' – were converging to produce a growing ethnic diversity amongst the prostitutes on the goldfields. While a small number of these women were black, the largest contingent by far was composed of 'Cape coloured' and white women. Despite the presence in Fordsburg of a small number of Japanese ladies of questionable virtue,[10] this meant that most of the town's prostitutes of the early 1890s shared one important feature – the overwhelming majority of them were drawn from within southern Africa. The Rand's first hawkers of vice were thus in large measure the residual product of Cape commercial capitalist development in the nineteenth century. In short, they were the daughters of South Africa's old proletariat.

But regardless of whether they were young or old, black or white, these prostitutes tended to develop a new link with commercial capital when they moved to the Witwatersrand. Most of the prostitutes in Johannesburg in the early 1890s chose to attach themselves to any one of the hundreds of canteens or hotels which abounded in the mining town. Not only did such places offer 'rooms' in a town where accommodation was always at a premium, but they also constituted a centre to which hard-drinking miners gravitated and therefore tended to provide the 'women of ill-fame' with a steady stream of customers. While the hardened full-time professional whores entrenched themselves in the premises to be found at the rear of the canteens, those part-time prostitutes on their way up or down the social scale often gained employment as barmaids within the establishment itself.[11] This close linkage between an emerging retail liquor trade and prostitution was not, of course, without historical precedent, and on the Rand this relationship was encouraged by canteen keepers for exactly the same reasons as elsewhere – namely, that the presence of barmaids and prostitutes tended to attract male customers to the establishment and increase liquor consumption.[12]

The local canteen keepers were not slow to organise themselves into a protective professional association. Indeed, by 1888 they had already bound themselves into the Witwatersrand Licensed Victuallers' Association (W.L.V.A.), and this formidable body soon wielded considerable economic and political power within the local community. Through their mouthpiece, the *Licensed Victuallers' Gazette*, members of W.L.V.A. made it clear that canteen keepers were by no means opposed to prostitution, and that if the state were to take any action against the 'social evil', it should do so through means of a Contagious Diseases Act which would give rise to a system of controlled brothels.[13]

It was this strong overt and covert support for prostitution that came from the canteen keepers and other interested groups – such as landlords who benefited from high brothel rents – which discouraged the Sanitary Board from taking legal action against any of the 'women of ill-fame' in early

Johannesburg. From the quarterly police returns in 1891, for example, it is evident that there was not a single conviction for prostitution in the town, and as late as 1893 Landdrost N. J. van den Berg was still unsuccessfully urging the Sanitary Board to use the powers it had at its disposal in order to initiate prosecutions.[14] But if Pretoria proved to be hard of hearing when it came to the problem of prostitution on the Rand in the early 1890s, then Johannesburg was positively deaf and nothing came of such appeals.

While such administrative deafness held a clear appeal for canteen keepers and others, it obviously also conferred a great boon on the people most directly threatened – the prostitutes themselves. For as long as prostitution was more or less openly tolerated in the town and unrestrained by legal action, so long prostitutes could command most of their earnings and be free of the insatiable demands of blackmailing policemen or parasitic pimps who posed as their 'protectors'. What is striking about prostitution in Johannesburg during this early period, therefore, is not only the linkage between the trades in sexual favours and alcohol, but the relative absence of large-scale *organised* prostitution. Most of the daughters of South Africa's old proletariat who turned to prostitution on the Rand before the mid-1890s were individual operators who found that they could conduct their trade largely on their own initiative, and certainly without the professional assistance of pimps and madams. This, however, was a situation which was to change rapidly and dramatically from 1895 onwards.

Gifts from the Old and New Worlds – the daughters of Europe, 1895–1899

From about 1892, when the first deep-level mines were established along the line of reef, it became increasingly clear to many outside of southern Africa that the Witwatersrand goldfields were going to prove to be not only a substantial, but a lasting proposition. As the price of tin fell in Cornwall, and as some Australian goldfields faltered and failed, so many of the 'hard rock men' set their sights on new targets and made their way to the Rand mines which, by then, had been expanding for more than half a decade. While this flow of skilled workers to the mines gained momentum through much of 1893 and 1894, it was really in 1895 that the greatest influx of all occurred.[15]

Men, mines and money all combined to produce an explosive growth mixture, but it was the added spark provided by the arrival of the railway line from the east coast which really helped to make 1895 one of the truly memorable boom years on the Rand. The advent of the rail linkage between Delagoa Bay and the Transvaal, however, did much more than merely assist in the economic transformation of the principal town on the goldfields. By providing a more immediate link between the Rand and Lourenço Marques, the railway also succeeded in placing Johannesburg – via the cheap fares of the German East African Shipping Line – in more direct contact with the ports and prostitutes of Europe. Thus it was that Johannesburg, from the mid-1890s onwards, was opened not only to the Old World's cheap liquor but also to many of its cheap women who were slowly being denied a role in the maturing industrial states of Europe.[16]

Many, if not most, of the women who chose to avail themselves of a passage on the East African Line were drawn from within Germany itself. Here, a policy which concentrated on the expansion of heavy industry tended to exclude female workers from the labour market, and consequently increased the number of structurally dislocated women who sought economic refuge in prostitution. To at least some of these women, more often than not drawn from working-class or artisan families, emigration to the Transvaal must have presented itself as an increasingly attractive proposition as their numbers grew towards the turn of the century. But, as always, there was no democracy of poverty and a policy of selective repression partly directed against 'foreign' prostitutes in Hamburg in 1894–5 ensured that many Austro-Hungarian women undertook the walk to the docks even more readily than their German sisters.[17]

The Great Depression of 1873–96, however, was no respecter of European boundaries, and elsewhere on the continent, too, problems of unemployment and under-employment made themselves felt as large-scale enterprises consolidated their operations at the expense of small craft industries. In some of the wine-producing areas of southern Europe the effect of the depression was further exacerbated when phylloxera attacked the grape vines during the early 1890s. Inevitably, this, too, contributed to the syndrome of rural female unemployment, growing poverty and a drift towards urban prostitution. The net result of these developments was to ensure that German prostitutes making the journey to southern Africa were not short of French and Belgian companions.

But not even Belgium, France and Germany exhausted the northern supply areas from which the Witwatersrand's 'women of ill-fame' were drawn since, in the 1890s, Johannesburg also boasted a contingent of 'Russian' prostitutes. Somewhat surprisingly, however, this latter group did not reach the goldfields via Hamburg and Delagoa Bay, as might be expected, but from New York via London, Southampton and the Cape ports. Although Johannesburg's 'Russian' whores had Old World origins, they were, in a more immediate sense, the product of developments in the New World.

After 1881, in particular, Jews in parts of the western Russian empire such as Poland, and in the neighbouring Hapsburg provinces of Galicia and Bukovina, experienced hardship and persecution which, by way of comparison, dwarfed the torments of industrial Europe. Poverty, to the point of endemic starvation, combined with a new round of Russian pogroms to take an awesome toll of lives in Jewish communities. Faced with this truly appalling situation, thousands of men and women from within these regions decided to emigrate to the United States of America. Here, as elsewhere, however, there were the quick-witted and the unscrupulous who were willing to feed on the ignorance and desperation of others, and many of these female emigrants found themselves tricked, recruited or forced into the trade in vice. But, irrespective of the exact route by which they entered the trade in commercialised sex, the result was often the same – the hard life of a prostitute in New York's immigrant quarter on the lower east side.[18]

While it is true that prostitution in New York pre-dated these European mass migrations, there can be no doubt that organised vice developed particularly rapidly during the late nineteenth century, and that few things did more to facilitate its emergence than pervasive municipal corruption. After 1868 the Tammany Society tightened its grip on the machinery of local government and ground out a succession of spectacularly corrupt mayors for New York City – 'Boss' Tweed, 'Honest John' Kelly and Richard Croker. These men, with the enthusiastic aid of an equally venal police force, parcelled out various of the city's wards in accordance with their ability to yield 'protection' money, and by so doing succeeded in turning public office into a series of private financial domains. Since there was nothing inherently incompatible between the rule of Tammany Hall and the existence of organised vice which was willing to pay its way, brothel and saloon keepers found that they could conduct their businesses openly and confidently – right up to 1891 that was.[19]

In 1891 a 'Massachusetts minister of Puritan ancestry', Dr Charles Parkhurst, was elected as President of the Society for the Prevention of Crime in New York. With the assistance of a private detective and a specially recruited set of 'agents', Parkhurst at once set about investigating and exposing police corruption within the city. These revelations about the connections between organised vice and a venal police force embarrassed even Tammany Hall, and soon produced a logical sequel in a thoroughly corrupt system when, in 1892, Parkhurst was summoned to stand trial on a charge of malicious slander. So convincing was the evidence which Parkhurst and his associates led, however, that the Grand Jury was forced to acquit the President of the Society for the Prevention of Crime, and tacitly concede to the existence of massive police corruption. With this victory behind him, Parkhurst found new influential allies who were willing to push for a full-scale enquiry into Tammany Hall and ultimately these agitations bore fruit when, in 1894, the state appointed the Lexow Commission to investigate police corruption in New York City. When the Commission finally issued its report, the findings more than justified Dr Parkhurst's allegations and resulted in the radical re-organisation of the city's police force. As far as Tammany Hall itself was concerned, however, the major blow really fell even earlier when its candidate in the November 1894 municipal elections, Richard Croker, was defeated by Judge van Wyck.[20]

But it was not only politicians and policemen who fell before the Parkhurst/Lexow onslaught. Pimps and prostitutes too felt the sting in the tail of the new van Wyck administration, and the years between 1892 and 1895 were not the happiest ones for those involved in organised vice on the lower east side. Indeed, from late 1894 hundreds of 'undesirables' – including scores of Jewish pimps and prostitutes – chose to abandon New York and make their way to England. London, however, proved to be something of a disappointment. Not only did the British capital possess its own well-developed trade in vice which made for serious competition, but it also failed to live up to some of the other expectations of the volatile immigrants from the Bowery. Thus, when these well-travelled Russians and Poles heard of the exciting new opportunities developing in the southern hemisphere, they did not hesitate to move yet again. While some of their colleagues in the trade opted for South America, many of the former New York pimps and prostitutes decided to make their way to the goldfields in Kruger's republic.[21]

The advance guard of this American contingent was already actively involved in prostitution on the Witwatersrand by late 1895. Over the following two years, however, their numbers were substantially augmented by the arrival of dozens of the more professional 'white slavers' and their entourages from London. When this group first became highly visible to the public in 1898, even the worldly-wise court reporter of the local *Standard and Diggers' News* was left somewhat bemused:

> There are more things in Johannesburg than are dreamt of in the ordinary man's philosophy. For instance, there is here a large and thriving colony of Americanised Russian women engaged in the immoral traffic, who are controlled by an association of *macquereaus* of pronounced Russian pedigree embellished by a twangy flashy embroidery of style and speech acquired in the Bowery of New York City, where most of them, with frequent excursions to London, have graduated in the noble profession.[22]

Clearly, the composition of the mining town's underworld was capable of leaving at least one observer surprised.

If the 'ordinary man' was somewhat amazed by the cosmopolitan nature of the local underworld, however, then there was at least one man in town who was not – Sanitary Superintendent A. H. Bleksley. As a former Sanitary Inspector in Kimberley, Bleksley had been actively involved in the attempts to get that city declared a 'scheduled area' in terms of the Contagious Diseases Act in 1891. When he later came to Johannesburg on promotion, the new Sanitary Superintendent could not have failed to notice how the town was attracting not only some of the former Cape prostitutes with whom he was familiar, but also new arrivals drawn from Europe and elsewhere. This, together with his hope that the Kruger government would eventually implement a C.D. Act of its own, led Bleksley to conduct a rough census of the town's brothels in October 1895.

Bleksley's survey, although it hardly yielded accurate numbers, did reveal that, at the most conservative estimate, there were 97 brothels in the town, and that these were occupied by some 195 prostitutes.[23] While this did show a move away from the former situation, where individual prostitutes tended to operate from single rooms in canteens or hotels, it still meant that on average there were only two to three prostitutes in each brothel. Further information about the brothels was yielded when some of Bleksley's subordinates took the trouble to indicate the 'nationality' of the 'ladies of pleasure' in each establishment. This latter set of observations indicated just how cosmopolitan Johannesburg's *demi-monde* had become and is reproduced in Table 3.

A year later, in October 1896, Bleksley repeated the exercise and when he once again conducted an impressionistic numerical survey of immorality in Johannesburg, the Sanitary Superintendent found that the town had at least 133 brothels, which were said to be occupied by some 392 prostitutes.[24] On this occasion, however, Bleksley's inspectors did not attempt to provide a breakdown of the brothels by 'nationality'. Instead, the town's officials chose to include the 'location' in their census and provide details about the ethnic

Table 3. Brothels in central Johannesburg, by nationality, October 1895

Number of brothels	'Nationality'
36	French
26	Unknown
20	German
5	Russian
2	Austrian
2	Belgian
2	American
2	Cape Coloured
1	English
1	Australian
97	Total

composition of Johannesburg's prostitutes. According to the Sanitary Superintendent's tabulations there were 91 white, 83 coloured and 48 black women involved in full-time prostitution in October 1896. It is likely, however, that these figures – like those for the previous year – hopelessly under-estimated the real number of women involved in the town's trade in vice.

But whatever the true number of prostitutes in town was, what concerned some of Johannesburg's citizens more was the fact that their number was increasing and that their existence was becoming painfully manifest. Like their Victorian counterparts in Europe, the local middle classes were not so much outraged by the existence of vice, as by the *public* existence of vice. Thus, as the number of European prostitutes in the town became increasingly visible after 1895, so sections of the public and press became more vocal in their expressions of concern. During the trades carnival in November 1896, for example, 'a carriage load of gaudily dressed women' joined the 'industrial procession' and, much to the disgust of the *Standard and Diggers' News*, 'was cheered all along the line'. Such behaviour spoke 'poorly for the good taste of the populace', warned the newspaper, since 'the demi-monde was there for gaiety, and not for advertisement'. The 'ladies of pleasure', however, excelled themselves a few months later when several of their number accosted members of Kruger's Volksraad who were visiting the mining town, and the *Diggers' News* was forced to write of the 'Public Shame'.[25] The feelings of the *Raadsleden* were not recorded.

These more spectacular forays by the town's prostitutes were conducted from their bases in that part of central Johannesburg which the more daring of the popular performers at the Empire Theatre referred to as 'Frenchfontein'. It was in this area, between Bree street in the north and Anderson street in the south, and Kruis street in the east and Sauer street in the west, that the vast majority of the town's brothels were located in the mid-1890s. In Frenchfontein, 'at the sinking of the sun, and sometimes in the full glare of the noon-day', there were daily scenes which the middle classes found even more abhorrent. From the doors, windows and verandahs of brightly painted houses with large distinctive numbers on their gate posts, women – in various stages of undress – called out endearments and invitations to passing men. Other equally unambiguous offers came from the ladies employed in the large number of 'cigar shops' in that quarter of town.[26]

But, depending on the circumstances in which they found themselves, the 'ladies of pleasure' were also capable of making more subtle approaches to potential customers. Printed cards bearing the name of the prostitute as well as that of her brothel – 'Monte Christo', 'Phoenix', 'Spire House', etc. – were often handed out at places where there were large gatherings of men, such as the railway station or race meetings. During periods of sporadic police repression, such as in late 1898, more urgent ways had to be found of communicating a change of address to customers. Under a 'Notice of Removal' in the morning paper, 'Senorita Gabriella' informed her 'pupils' of her new address, and assured them that when classes recommenced on 1 November it would be at 'moderate terms'. So confident were the former New York pimps about the permanence of some of their brothels, however, that they allowed their advertising for the 'Green House' at number 20 Sauer street to take on a slightly more lasting form. The Bowery gangsters had special 'false coins' struck and these tokens – which also circulated freely in the gambling dens which they controlled – 'bore a décolleté bust on the obverse and the name of the house on the reverse side'.[27]

As always, however, much of the gossip about the delights of the demi-monde was circulated not by coin or card, but by word of mouth amongst the male population at barber shops, canteens and race meetings. In addition, cab drivers and rickshaw-pullers were another ready source of information about the pleasures and pitfalls of Frenchfontein and, for a suitable sum, these public transporters were more than willing to act as guides.[28] The single greatest source of information about the painted ladies and their prices, however, came from the proprietors of the painted houses – the professional pimps.

Johannesburg's pre-war pimps, given the collective appellation of *macquereaux* by the local press, were in fact a far more cosmopolitan lot than this designation implied. While there certainly were Frenchmen within the ranks of this large parasitic army, there were also many pimps drawn from the other national groups represented on the Witwatersrand. Characterised by their bitter internal feuding, rivalry, treachery and violence, the 250–300 strong macquereaux were dominated by the 100 or so East European pimps, and within them, in turn, by the hard core of 50–70 'Bowery Boys' who preferred to refer to themselves as 'speculators'.[29] In the pecking order of pimpdom, the tough New Yorkers were followed firstly by the 50–60 French *souteneurs* who frequented the '*Ne Plus Ultra*' and 'Golden Lion' bars in the city.[30] Thereafter came the 20–40 German pimps who, more often than not, bore the name 'Louis', after the continental fashion.[31] The rear guard of the macquereaux was constituted from a miscellaneous collection of continental, English and Australian pimps, and possibly even one Afrikaner merchant of vice.[32]

Impressive as this list of pimps may have been, however, it still did not exhaust all the possibilities which the early Witwatersrand had to offer. After 1895 there were, at the very least, a dozen or more black touts and pimps who worked in close cooperation with some of Johannesburg's newly arrived

French prostitutes. Most of these African men, of whom we know little more than their unrevealing christian names such as John, Tom and Moses, acted as language brokers for these continental women and by so doing ensured that the cheaper non-racial brothels in town received their share of custom from black miners. Working on a straightforward commission basis, the touts received a sixpenny share out of the ten-shilling fee which the French prostitutes charged each of their black clients.[33] While most of these dealings between black middlemen and the continental whores remained largely impersonal and of a contractual nature, there is also evidence to suggest that on occasion they matured into the fuller and more complex love-hate relationships which characterise interactions between pimps and prostitutes.[34]

In addition to the black macquereaux and the scandalous sights of Frenchfontein, there were also other less visible – but more serious – signs which pointed to the explosion in commercialised vice in the mid-nineties. Whilst the presence of venereal disease amongst the town's population had been a cause for official concern as early as 1888, its spread appears to have been especially rapid after the first prostitutes fleeing the Contagious Diseases Act in the Cape established themselves on the Witwatersrand in 1893–4.[35] The fact that the subsequent influx of continental women in 1895–6 was accompanied by an increase in the number of European medical practitioners who offered 'special treatment with guaranteed success in all kinds of syphilitic diseases' did little to check the spread of V.D. Since the presence of syphilis often went undetected until the development of the Wasserman test in 1907, limited value could be attached to the medical certificates which Dr Alfred Liebaert of Belgium or Dr Roberto Villetti of Rome issued to prostitutes in the larger brothels on a fortnightly basis.[36] As a result of all these developments, both syphilis and gonorrhoea became firmly established in sections of the black and white working class after 1895.[37]

It was not only the workers' health which suffered when the daughters of Europe came to town in large numbers – there were also other prices to pay. By late 1896 a significant portion of central Johannesburg was devoted exclusively to organised vice and, as one of the morning newspapers lamented at the time, 'our best residential streets and our most important thoroughfares are dedicated to it'.[38] But if the *Standard and Diggers' News* was saddened by this use of urban housing, then the same was hardly true of landlords and property owners. These latter parties soon made the joyous discovery that brothel keepers were willing to pay substantial cash rentals for such houses in order to avoid embarrassing questions or unnecessary legal complications. As a direct consequence of this development, rents in the central part of the town climbed beyond the reach of those who earned more modest incomes, and to their considerable annoyance, working-class and lower-middle-class families found themselves being pushed out to Johannesburg's more peripheral suburbs.[39]

The proprietors of Frenchfontein, however, the men who were in large measure responsible for this working-class exodus, were no mere slum landlords. Indeed, another local newspaper, *The Critic*, claimed in October 1896 that the properties on which 'houses of ill-fame' were located were often 'registered in the names of persons of repute, of banking corporations and eminent firms'.[40] When these allegations are more closely examined, by setting the addresses of known brothels against the property registers of the time, *The Critic*'s claims are largely vindicated. C. D. Rudd, mining magnate and intimate business associate of Cecil Rhodes, appears to have been the owner of at least three such properties; the *Banque Française de l'Afrique du Sud*, a Wernher-Beit associated enterprise, owned several such houses, as did the Rand Investment Co., the Real Estate Corporation of South Africa and African Cities Properties Trust Ltd.[41] Given this interest which commercial capital developed in organised vice, it is not difficult to see why landlords figured amongst those who supported a petition in favour of the *status quo* when, in 1897, the Volksraad first indicated its intention to promulgate legislation against those owners of property who allowed their premises to be used as brothels.[42]

Nobody – least of all those in official positions – could have failed to notice the dramatic transformation which took place in the heart of the town once the 'gay ladies' of Paris and their associates established themselves in the mining capital of Kruger's Republic. Thus, when Landdrost van den Berg was again approached with a set of complaints by some of the residents of Ferreirastown, in April 1895, he took the opportunity to draft personally a set of regulations for the control of prostitution in Johannesburg. The Criminal Landdrost then forwarded his proposed by-laws to State Attorney Esselen in Pretoria, only to have them returned with the suggestion that they be first approved by the local Sanitary Board.[43]

Members of the Johannesburg Sanitary Board turned, in the first instance, to their Chief Inspector, A. H. Bleksley, who immediately conducted the first of his two surveys of local immorality. It was partly Bleksley's influence, as well as the members' own awareness of their canteen-keeping and property-owning constituency which helped to shape the Board's policy on prostitution. While drafting its own regulations in August 1895 then, the Sanitary Board took the view that it was the object of local government to *control*, rather than eradicate sexual vice – a line of reasoning not dissimilar to that which underlay most nineteenth-century C.D. Acts. When during the following month the Board took the precaution of sending a copy of its draft regulations to the Johannesburg Protestant Ministers' Association for its comment, however, it ran straight into another strand of late nineteenth-century thinking – that of Christian feminism. The local clergy, schooled in the reasoning of Josephine Butler and her feminist colleagues in Britain, objected vigorously to the enshrining of a legal 'double standard' which sought to deal with prostitutes whilst ignoring their male customers. Moreover, the ministers were particularly appalled by the customary provision which allowed for the compulsory medical examination of women who were suspected of suffering from venereal disease.[44] The Sanitary Board, however, chose to overlook these objections when it forwarded the draft regulations to the new State Attorney in December 1895.

The new State Attorney in Pretoria, Dr Herman Coster, was not immediately taken with the Johannesburg Sanitary Board's regulations for controlling brothels. A recent immigrant from Holland, Coster doubted strongly whether there was any value at all in attempting to legislate on questions of morals. The State Attorney's first inclination, therefore, was to do nothing about the suggested by-laws which he was confronted with. Such was the influx of prostitutes into Johannesburg over the following months, however, that Coster soon found this to be an unviable strategy.

In April 1896 the Landdrosts and the Commissioner of Police in Johannesburg were signatories to a letter pointing out the by now 'urgent' need for legislation to cope with the problem of immorality in the mining town. At this point the State Attorney's attitude started to waver, and the turning point came when both Dr Alfred Liebaert and the Transvaal Medical Association submitted supporting memoranda which pointed out the advantages of a system of state-controlled prostitution. Thus, when President Kruger and his Executive Committee met on 18 July 1896, the members – largely at the prompting of Dr Coster – agreed that, in principle, Johannesburg's demi-monde should be governed by a system of 'controlled brothels'. The Executive Committee concluded its deliberations on the question by referring the draft regulations back to Johannesburg for a series of relatively minor amendments.[45]

But just as this game of legal shuttlecock between Pretoria and Johannesburg threatened to come to a close, a new set of complications arose which further prolonged the mining town's administrative agony. Dr Herman Coster resigned from his position as State Attorney to be replaced by a new man – Dr Schagen van Leeuwen. As the third man to hold this office within a matter of months, the Acting State Attorney was as capable as any of his predecessors of having his own ideas of how Johannesburg's moral life should be governed. While it is unclear what exactly van Leeuwen's reservations about the Sanitary Board's regulations were, he, too, delayed ratification of the by-laws. This procrastination in Pretoria simply perpetuated the legal impasse on the Rand where local prosecutors tried in vain to convict offenders of the public's morals under a 300-year old Roman Dutch statute.[46]

Amidst this rising tide of confusion, the church now rose to add its voice. Witwatersrand clergymen of all denominations had, for some time, been deeply distressed by the prospect of the Kruger government recognising and controlling brothels rather than choosing to eradicate them. When, during the last quarter of 1896, the editor of the pro-government *De Volkstem*, Dr F. V. Engelenburg, chose to give the system of regulated vice support in the columns of his newspaper, it acted as a catalyst for a debate within clerical circles on the Rand. In particular, the Johannesburg Protestant Ministers' Association and the Young Men's Christian Association – the Y.M.C.A. – felt that the church should take a more active role in the debate on these moral issues. It was largely for this reason that the churchmen agreed that an inter-denominational deputation should seek a meeting with the State President and his Executive Committee as a matter of urgency.[47]

This deputation, under the leadership of the Rev. P. J. Meiring of the Dutch Reformed Church and Mr Norman McCulloch of the Y.M.C.A., met with Kruger and his colleagues on 6 October 1896. Also present at his meeting – possibly at the invitation of the government – were A. H. Bleksley and two colleagues representing the interests of the Johannesburg Sanitary Board. During the discussion which followed, however, it was the arguments of the clergymen rather than those of the town officials which did most to convince the State President. In essence, Meiring and McCulloch persuaded Kruger of the desirability of following a policy of 'total prohibition' in relation to brothels. Furthermore, the clergymen impressed upon the State President the need for truly urgent action on the question of immorality which by now had remained unresolved for a period of eighteen months.[48]

But if Kruger was by now totally convinced of the need to eradicate all brothels on the Rand, then the same was not true of all of his executive. In particular, it was again a Hollander – this time the State Secretary, Dr Leyds – who counselled caution and advocated a system of 'state regulation modelled on European lines'. After an 'animated discussion' within the Executive Committee, however, it was decided to refer the regulations back to Johannesburg yet again, this time with the instruction that they should be made more stringent – quickly.[49]

The Johannesburg Sanitary Board's canteen-keeping and property-owning constituency had not changed in the interim. Moreover, Bleksley and the rest of his deputation must have reported back to their colleagues on the continuing divisions amongst members of the Executive Committee on the issue of how best to cope with the town's problem of prostitution. For all of these reasons, the Sanitary Board again chose not to advocate a policy of total suppression when it once more submitted its revised draft regulations on brothels to Pretoria, on 13 October 1896. This time, Kruger was galvanised into action. Casting aside the advice of the Hollanders which had so long restrained him, the State President now demanded that the Sanitary Board immediately furnish his government with a set of regulations which aimed at the total eradication of prostitution in Johannesburg.[50]

News of Kruger's radical and uncompromising response to the Sanitary Board's latest attempts simply to 'control' vice came as a welcome revelation to Johannesburg's hitherto beleaguered clergymen. In particular, it was the members of the Protestant Ministers' Association who immediately took steps to create a suitably supportive local climate in which to sustain the State President's initiative. Within days of Kruger's move, the Rev. Meiring and Norman McCulloch of the Y.M.C.A. wrote to the State President, both to congratulate him and to inform him that they had helped to launch the 'Transvaal White Cross Purity League' – in essence a local branch of the more famous chastity league founded in Britain in 1882 by the feminist Ellice Hopkins.[51] Although the clergymen succeeded in getting only about 200 young men to take the 'purity pledge', the League did make some headway in other directions. It was, for example, the White Cross Purity League which arranged for the publication, in English, of the Rev. C. Spoelstra's 'open letter' to the Editor of the *Volkstem*, Dr F. V. Engelenburg, originally entitled '*Teedere Zaken: Een Debat over het Prostitutievraagstuk in die Zuid Afrikaansche Republiek*'. Under its new title, 'Delicate Matters', the little booklet soon sold 2,000 copies and must have reached a reasonably wide audience in the rough mining town.[52]

When the Volksraad did meet early in the following year, it did not bother to wait for the Johannesburg Sanitary Board's submission and lost no time at all in passing legislation which met with Kruger's requirements. As the *Standard and Diggers' News* put it: 'Every line of the law exhibits the stern and uncompromising attitude of His Honour the President, who, Elijah-like will hear of no half measures, and characteristically takes the shortest route to the end he has in view.'[53] In addition, the Commissioner of Police set up a special

'Morality Squad' under Detective J. J. Donovan in order to ensure that Law No. 2 of 1897 would be enforced once it had been properly gazetted.

This flurry of activity and the new sense of purpose in the administration did not go unnoticed in some of the more timid circles of Frenchfontein. When many of the prostitutes chose to leave town on the night of 8 March 1897, however, they received anything but a cheerful send-off at Park Station. A mob composed of white workers, unemployed miners and petty criminals jostled and jeered the ladies of the night, looted their luggage for liquor, and were only prevented from doing more serious damage when the station master instructed the police to draw their batons and prepare to charge the crowd. By the following morning – when the new law came into force – over three hundred prostitutes and their associates had fled Johannesburg for the Cape or Natal, 'resulting in an abundant supply of empty domiciles in and about town'. In Cape Town, to where the majority of these women had made their way, the Premier, Sir Gordon Sprigg, greeted their arrival with some distaste, and warned the Transvaal authorities that the lot of virtuous women in Johannesburg would not be made any easier now that the prostitutes who catered for the miners' baser needs had departed from the Rand.[54]

Sprigg need not have worried. For while it was true that hundreds of 'gay ladies' had deserted the Reef, many hundreds more who were made of sterner stuff had chosen to remain behind and ply their trade. Working on the assumption that even in Kruger's Republic past behaviour was often the best guide to future action, these remaining pimps and prostitutes were willing to take their chances under the new dispensation. As business people, these merchants of vice took the view that Law No. 2 of 1897 simply increased unavoidable occupational hazards, and raised necessary overhead expenditure on police bribes. The more hardened professionals of the demi-monde felt therefore that the answer to the Volksraad's legislation lay not in escape or submission, but in even more rigorous planning and organisation. Thus, while the inhabitants of Frenchfontein could hardly be accused of being disorganised in earlier years, their activities assumed new dimensions of precision in the period between 1897 and 1899.

In the underworld, organisation came most readily and most naturally to those who had previous experience of it – in this case, the former immigrant gangsters of New York City. The 'Bowery Boys', who ever since 1895 had always constituted something of a distinctive grouping within the town, soon organised themselves into a more structured gang which served to protect their gambling and vice interests in the south-western quarter of Frenchfontein. By mid-1897 these 'slouch-hatted bullies', who dominated the cafés and canteens of western Commissioner street, and who whisked out their six-shooters 'for no provocation at all', were said to have established a thorough-going 'reign of terror' in that part of the town. Given the readiness with which these American pimps produced their revolvers and the fact that the local police were unarmed, it comes as less than a surprise to learn that the Zarps seldom troubled the 'Bowery Boys', and that throughout 1897 and 1898 members of the Morality Squad tended studiously to avoid the larger brothels in their search for offenders of the *Ontucht Wet* – Law No. 2 of 1897.[55]

The Americans, however, were also experienced enough to know that it was probably unwise to rely on fire-power alone as the exclusive means with which to protect their bagnios. For this reason the 'Bowery Boys' embarked on a programme of blackmail, bribery and corruption which, in the first instance, was directed at the most obvious and vulnerable target – the badly paid members of the Morality Squad.[56] This counter-offensive by the pimps proved to be so effective that, within months of the passage of the Ontucht Wet, the former New York gangsters had succeeded not only in getting most members of the Morality Squad on their payroll, but also part of the staff attached to the Public Prosecutor's office. This meant that throughout the best part of 1897–8 the 'Bowery Boys' found themselves in the privileged position of having their own brothels protected by the legal arm of the state, while – at the same time – they could call upon the self-same officers of the law to harass or close down the operations of rival vice merchants.[57]

Although the 'Bowery Boys' grew in strength throughout this period, there can be little doubt that their organisation made its greatest strides from mid-1898 onwards when it came under the most professional criminal management possible. In late August 1898, Joe Silver, a Polish-American pimp, and his prostitute/wife, Lizzie Josephs, arrived on the Witwatersrand from London. During the early 1890s, as a young Jewish immigrant on the lower east side, Silver had led a successful double life in New York City by acting as an 'agent' for the Rev. Charles Parkhurst's Society for the Prevention of Crime, while, at the same time, being deeply involved in the Bowery underworld. After the set-back to Tammany Hall in 1894, Silver had made his way to London where he had become an important figure in the 'white slave' traffic – assisting in the recruiting and seduction of young women in the East End and then 'exporting' them to various countries, including South Africa, as prostitutes. A cunning, ruthless and violent man, Silver was soon the undisputed leader of the former New York gangsters, and earned for himself the unofficial title of 'King of the Pimps' in Johannesburg.[58]

With his undisputed talent for organising, however, Silver was anxious to push the 'Bowery Boys' to new professional heights and for this reason he was instrumental in the formation, in late 1898, of the 'American Club'. While the official name purposely did not distinguish it from the many other immigrant clubs in the town, the 'American Club' in practice constituted something rather different – an association of Polish-American Jewish pimps which, in the local demi-monde, was more simply and accurately known as the 'Pimps Club'. Amongst the names of the fifty founding members of the 'American Club' there were several, in addition to that of Joe Silver, which were to become notorious on the Witwatersrand over the next decade – Salus Budner, Joseph Epstein, Abraham Goldstein, David Krakower, Louis Shivinsky and Sam Stein.[59]

Predictably enough, the members of the club elected Joe Silver as the first 'president' of the pimps' association, and then went on to choose one of his closest henchmen, Salus Budner, as 'secretary' of the organisation.[60] In the latter case, the pimps allowed themselves the luxury of a display of Yiddish-cum-underworld humour by promptly allocating Budner the new alias of 'Joe Gold'. Perhaps the 'Bowery Boys' would have been less amused, however, if they had known that 'Silver and Gold' immediately proceeded to set up a 'secret committee' within the executive of the 'American Club', and that it was from within this latter group that the affairs of the pimps' association were really controlled.[61]

Most of Silver's personal as well as his brother pimps' business was conducted from the hired premises of the 'American Club' in Frenchfontein. It was here, at the club house, that the 'Bowery Boys' most frequently met to discuss the daily vicissitudes and requirements of Johannesburg's competitive vice trade – the hiring of suitable houses, problems with landlords, boundary disputes between rival pimps and the need to bribe different policemen. Since a good deal of this business directly and indirectly revolved around the venal Zarps, it was not an uncommon sight to see detectives entering or leaving the club premises in Frenchfontein. Indeed, so close was Special Morality Constable Hendrik Cuyler's association with the pimps, that he even consented to having his picture taken with some of them whilst standing outside the club.[62] It was also from within these premises, however, that the most secret plans of the 'American Club' emanated, and these schemes invariably centred around the question of where and how to procure new 'girls' for the brothels under the control of the Polish pimps.

During the mid-1890s the demand for prostitutes on the Rand escalated rapidly as the male population of the goldfields mushroomed with the development of deep-level mining. The pimps of Johannesburg, however, soon made the discovery that this increase in the demand for sexual services in the community did not simply parallel any demographic increases in the town. Clients of larger brothels looked forward to a regular change in the personnel of their favourite establishments and this alone occasioned the need for a regular turnover of prostitutes. In addition, the ranks of the prostitutes were also thinned out by the normal processes of attrition associated with the trade – age, disease or death. For these reasons the 'Bowery Boys' and other groups of pimps within the town found that they had to pay constant attention to the problem of providing their brothels with an adequate supply of new young 'girls'.

It is certain that some attempts were made to recruit local women into the trade in vice – a procedure which appealed to the *souteneurs* because it had the virtue of being relatively cheap. In such cases the pimps would usually send out the oldest and most trusted of their prostitutes – the madams of their houses – to the town parks and recreation areas where seemingly attractive propositions would be put to badly paid white domestic servants or other young white women.[63] Given the chronic shortage of mature women on the Rand at this time, however, this practice hardly produced a solution to the pimps' problem, and for this reason they were forced to look further afield in their search for new recruits. In the course of this latter search the pimps found that the older social formation of the Cape Colony tended to yield a slightly readier supply of poor, vulnerable or marginalised women. Small numbers of coloured domestic servants who had already been seduced by white men could occasionally be recruited from Cape 'boarding-houses', while job adverts placed in the Colony's newspapers – via bogus 'employment agencies' – sometimes succeeded in luring naive European women into the Transvaal's 'houses of ill-fame'.[64]

Not even these forays to the south, however, could keep pace with the Rand's demand for sexual services during the mid-1890s, and for this reason the 'Bowery Boys' and other groups of local pimps were forced to turn to the older societies of Europe for the bulk of their supplies of prostitutes. At least some of these European recruiting operations worked along the same lines as those employed in the Cape. Advertisements placed in British or continental newspapers offered young women an assisted passage to South Africa in order to take up well-paid positions as 'barmaids' or 'domestic servants' in Johannesburg.[65] Needless to say, once these women had been 'escorted' to the Rand by the madams of brothels posing as 'agents', the vulnerable job aspirants were pressed into an entirely different line of service to that which they had perhaps imagined when they first set out on their journey.

In other cases the 'Bowery Boys' extended the area of their direct recruiting operations by pushing the boundaries back into the heartland of eastern Europe. In mid-1898, for example, 'Bessie Levin', acting on behalf of David Levinsohn of the 'American Club', was sent on a long trip which took her well to the north-east of her and her pimp's native Poland. In the small Lithuanian village of Vilna Krevo the procuress met and offered a fifteen year old girl named Fanny Kreslo employment in London as a shop assistant at a salary of 100 Roubles a year. When the same proposition was subsequently put to the Kreslo parents they readily agreed to the 'employment' of their daughter on these terms and the two women then set off for England.

On their arrival in London Miss Kreslo was informed by Levin that her 'employer' had suddenly departed for South Africa, and that the two of them should follow him to the Rand. Isolated, vulnerable, penniless and speaking only Russian, the Lithuanian girl agreed to accompany the older and more experienced woman on the further journey south. Once in Johannesburg, Levinsohn and Levin placed the girl in a brothel in 35 Anderson street and informed her that if she wished to make her way back to Russia it would be necessary for her to earn the money for her passage by prostituting herself. After allowing Miss Kreslo the luxury of having a Polish-speaker as her first sexual partner, the pimp and his madam then proceeded to provide the young Russian woman with a wider variety of Asian, black and white customers. It was only after several months – and after the backbone of the 'American Club' had been broken – that the young woman was released from her position as a 'white slave'. In mid-1899 the police, after learning of Fanny Kreslo's age, rescued her from the house in Anderson street and arranged for the prosecution of Levinsohn and Levin.[66]

The same terrifying combination of cynical deceit and violence characterised many of the other 'white slavery' operations of the 'Bowery Boys'. During 1897–8, while still in London and living under the alias of 'James Smith', a 'draper', Joe Silver and his Polish associates conducted their business from the 'American Hotel' in Stamford road, Waterloo. Working from there, Silver, Joseph Anker, Beile Feirerstein, Jacob Shrednicki and others would undertake excursions into the East End, where the men would pose as eligible bachelors amongst immigrant Jewish girls employed in the rag trade. Such meetings would be followed by a preliminary amount of 'courting' during which the procuress, Beile Feirerstein, would present herself as adviser and confidante of the young East European women. Thereafter, the pimps would attempt to administer as much alcohol as possible to their 'fiancées' before seducing or raping them. After a further set of psychological and physical assaults, the victims would be forced on to the local streets to gain experience as whores prior to being 'exported' under escort to countries such as the Argentine or South Africa.[67]

Although the 'Bowery Boys' were, by far, the largest and best organised syndicate of 'white slavers' operating on the Rand between 1897 and 1899, they were by no means the only pimps trafficking in prostitutes on a substantial scale. Following closely in the footsteps of the Polish vice merchants were the scores of French pimps to be found in Johannesburg during this period. Within this latter group, however, it was once again a set of immigrant gangsters with first-hand experience of New York under Tammany Hall who provided the souteneurs with their most able leaders. Amongst the most noteworthy of these Franco-Americans were Paul Durenmatt, Leon Lemaire, Auguste Roger, François Saubert and – perhaps most notorious of all – a woman who had once called herself Mrs Bertha Hermann but who now chose to refer to herself as Mathilda Bertha.[68]

Mrs Bertha Hermann was first drawn to the attention of the western world when, in the mid-1890s, the famous muck-raking journalist, W. T. Stead, outlined the importance of this 'French Madam' in his book entitled *Satan's Invisible World Displayed* – an account of corruption in New York City based on the findings of the Lexow Commission. While in New York Mrs Hermann had run four brothels which, over a seven-year period between the late 1880s and the early 1890s, had required the handing over of 30,000 dollars in bribes to the Tammany police in order to remain in business. This alone made Mrs Hermann a valuable witness in the criminal proceedings which followed the eclipse of Tammany Hall. Indeed, so vital did Bertha Hermann's testimony become, that the New York police arranged for her to be kidnapped and railroaded around Canada and the western United States in an unsuccessful attempt to avoid the prosecution of certain senior officers. After this somewhat harrowing experience, the by now famous 'French Madam' developed an understandable urge to travel the world more widely under another name. In Johannesburg, Mathilda Bertha and François Saubert ran, amongst others, a large brothel at number 19 Sauer street – a house adjoining a similar establishment managed by Joseph Silver.[69]

Given their earlier shared experience of the New York underworld and the over-arching imperatives of the vice trade, it was always likely that the Franco-Americans would run the 'white slavery' part of their business in a way which closely resembled that of the 'Bowery Boys'. Young servant girls from Brussels or Paris would be lured to the Rand with bogus offers of lucrative employment and, once removed from their more familiar environment, would be seduced or raped before being turned out into the streets in order to make a living. In other cases, however, the souteneurs and their female agents would recruit young girls from professional 'white slavers' – the Parisian counterparts of Joe Silver and his associates.[70] These specialists no doubt managed to generate their own 'supplies' by exercising the familiar combination of deceit and violence over those rendered vulnerable through poverty and ignorance.

The parallels between the business operations of the Franco-Americans and the 'Bowery Boys', however, transcended any similarities which might have existed in their basic recruiting operations. The well organised and efficient manner in which they ran their larger brothels after the passage of the Ontucht Wet in 1897 also bears comparison, and perhaps one of the more revealing illustrations of this is offered by an institution which fell under French management – 'Sylvio Villa'.

Situated on the corner of de Villiers and Rissik streets, 'Sylvio Villa' undoubtedly constituted early Johannesburg's most famous brothel. For well over a decade, from 1895 when it was first opened until 1906 when it was finally closed down by the British authorities, this bagnio held the pre-eminent position in the local demi-monde. During its heyday, between 1897 and 1899, 'Sylvio Villa' operated with a staff of no less than fifteen persons – five men and ten women. At the head of the house stood the owner and managing pimp, the 'speculator' Auguste Roger. Below Roger, and assisting him, were a team of four full-time pimps who did the rounds drumming up business for the Villa, and a 'madam', Alice Muller, who in her various court appearances preferred to refer to herself as a 'modiste'. Between them, these touts in turn exercised varying degrees of control over the nine working women of the establishment – Evette Verwey, Suzanne Dubois, A. Dumas, Blanche Dumont, Marie Buffaut, Jeanne Dubois, Marie André, Jeanne Durett and Georgette Carpentier. For the sake of convenience, these latter-named ladies chose to see themselves as 'housekeepers', 'milliners', 'musicians' and 'florists' in their legal affairs.[71]

The services of these nine women, who may more accurately be referred to as being French-speaking rather than 'French', proved to be in considerable demand during the 'naughty nineties'. As level-headed business women, however, the inhabitants of 'Sylvio Villa' were willing to offer their customers more than the erotic mystique of the foreigner – they were also able to produce certificates which testified to the fact that they had recently been medically examined and found to be free of contagious disease. The pleasure of their company could be purchased at the rate of £1 'short time', or £5 per night. While these competitive prices obviously assured the nine ladies of the night a measure of cash income, it would appear that the bulk of their earnings accrued to the 'management'. All the working women of the house were called upon to pay Alice Muller the sum of £4 per month for the provision of food and accommodation, a fee which excluded the additional costs they were called upon to bear for clothing, washing and ironing and medical expenses. The levying of the £4 'board and lodging' fee alone would have yielded the 'madam' and her 'speculator' a gross income of £1,728 per annum.[72]

In addition to this, however, each of the prostitutes in 'Sylvio Villa' had a separate verbal contract with the 'management' which specified what percentage of her income had to be handed over to the 'madam'. While we unfortunately do not know exactly what this figure was in each individual case in the de Villiers street bagnio, we do know that Suzanne Dubois was called upon to hand over in excess of a quarter of all her earnings to Alice Muller. But, whatever this proportion was, it is sure to have produced Roger and his associates a handsome collective income during the course of the year since this popular brothel was hardly ever short of business. In this latter respect we are more fortunate since, from the observations of two detectives who were sent to observe the comings and goings at the French house during its prime, we know more or less precisely how many customers were entertained at 'Sylvio Villa' during the evenings over a two-week period in late 1897.[73] This information is reproduced in Table 4.

Table 4. Number of clients calling at the 'Sylvio Villa' brothel, 29 November 1897–12 December 1897

Day of the week	Date	Hours premises observed	Number of customers
Monday	29 Nov. 1897	8.30 p.m. – 1.35 a.m.	21
Tuesday	30 Nov. 1897	8.30 p.m. – 1.55 a.m.	41
Wednesday	1 Dec. 1897	7.45 p.m. – 2.40 a.m.	52
Thursday	2 Dec. 1897	7.45 p.m. – 1.53 a.m.	38
Friday	3 Dec. 1897	7.35 p.m. – 2.05 a.m.	62
Saturday	4 Dec. 1897	8.05 p.m. – 1.30 a.m.	96
Sunday	5 Dec. 1897	7.20 p.m. – 1.10 a.m.	8
Monday	6 Dec. 1897	7.25 p.m. –10.35 p.m.	18
Tuesday	7 Dec. 1897	7.25 p.m. – 1.10 a.m.	21
Wednesday	8 Dec. 1897	7.30 p.m. – 9.50 p.m.	11
Thursday	9 Dec. 1897	7.25 p.m. – 1.25 a.m.	20
Friday	10 Dec. 1897	7.15 p.m. –12.11 a.m.	26
Saturday	11 Dec. 1897	7.40 p.m. – 1.10 a.m.	54
Sunday	12 Dec. 1897	7.35 p.m. – 9.50 p.m.	7

From this it is clear that the nine women of 'Sylvio Villa' may have been 'ladies of pleasure' in name, but that in practice there must have been much hard work and little pleasure in their activities – and at no time more so than during the period which followed the month-end pay-day for mine labourers and other workers. From the same set of police observations we also know that most of these customers came to the brothel in parties of three, and that the average visit of a client to 'Sylvio Villa' took between 20 and 45 minutes to complete. Commercial sex could be obtained at a price which included a measure of fear and haste.

At least some of the fear – and certainly much of the haste – which accompanied this alienated sexual activity derived from the harassing tactics which many of the pimps of the larger brothels adopted. Since it was in the pimps' interests to ensure as large a turnover as possible, they constantly 'encouraged' customers to complete their business in a hurry. For essentially the same reason, many pimps urged the women under their control to accept black clients, since Africans, largely new to the need for this type of service and its strange cultural setting, seldom lingered on the premises. As one pimp put it: 'Kaffirs were better to encourage than white men' since 'they paid their money and did not want to stop drinking and smoking in the house'.[74]

In addition to having this time constraint placed upon them by the pimps, clients at bagnios were also apprehensive about the possibility of being relieved of their valuables while visiting the premises. Although such robberies did undoubtedly occur, it was fear of the resident pimp's violence, as well as the humiliation of a subsequent court appearance, that did most to ensure that the majority of such thefts remained unreported.[75] All of these factors contributed to the development of tensions between brothel patrons drawn largely from England and pimps who, in the main, hailed from the continent and Eastern Europe. It is therefore not very difficult to see why it was that on at least one occasion, in April 1898, a crowd of white miners and unemployed workers chose to attack a group of 'foreign' pimps whom they had managed to trap on the more public terrain of Park Station.[76]

Of course, neither these manifestations of highly organised vice, nor the scandalous scenes to which they occasionally gave rise, escaped the notice of those state officials who had been entrusted with the task of scrutinising the public's morals after the passage of the Ontucht Wet of 1897. Pretoria's problem was, however, that local government officials saw in the flagrant violations of the Morals Law only what they wanted to see. For some, such as the Commandant of Police, G. M. J. van Dam, the continued flauntings of Frenchfontein pointed to the need for more rigid enforcement of the Ontucht Wet. For others, including some of the state's most senior officers, the persistence of prostitution underlined the futility of morals legislation and emphasised the need to follow more pragmatic policies. In practice these conflicting views were obviously extremely difficult, if not impossible, to reconcile, and nowhere was this problem more apparent than in the office of Johannesburg's Senior Public Prosecutor – Dr F. E. T. Krause.

Frederick Krause, in later life a Member of Parliament for Het Volk and subsequently Judge President of the Orange Free State, was a member of one of South Africa's most distinguished and talented families. After an initial university training at Victoria College in Stellenbosch, F. E. T. Krause proceeded to the University of Amsterdam where he obtained his doctorate in jurisprudence in 1893. On his return home, Krause made his way to the South African Republic where, as part of Dr Herman Coster's legal team, he assisted in the prosecution of the Jameson Raid 'reformers'. It was immediately after this assignment, in May 1897, and a matter of eight weeks after the controversial Ontucht Wet first came into operation, that he was appointed to the position of principal public prosecutor in Johannesburg.

Krause, who married late, at the age of nearly 40, spent a good part of his life as a bachelor and perhaps this, together with his experience on the Continent, helped shape his attitudes on the problems of prostitution in society. Certainly the influential Hollanders with whom he spent much time on the Rand, notably Herman Coster and Schagen van Leeuwen, were strongly opposed to President Kruger's attempts to legislate on questions affecting public morals. In any event, Krause took the decided view that prostitution was 'a necessary evil' in society and it was this outlook which came to govern his official actions on questions of immorality.[77]

The first indication of the Senior Public Prosecutor's attitude came within weeks of his assuming office when Commandant van Dam, after lengthy consultations with Krause, issued new instructions to Detective J. J. Donovan, the man in charge of the Morality Squad. As Krause later recalled:

> The instructions received by Donovan with my knowledge and consent were . . . that where houses suspected by the police to be brothels were found, they must only take the initiative against such a house when a *bona fide* charge was made against the house, or if it was discovered to be a disorderly house; in other words, where they found that excessive drinking was going on, or where there were frequent rows.[78]

In effect this policy meant that, contrary to the spirit and letter of the Ontucht

Wet, official efforts throughout much of 1897 and 1898 were directed towards 'controlling' rather than eliminating sexual vice in Johannesburg.

As we have seen, the idea that prostitution was a 'necessary evil' and that it probably helped exercise a measure of social control over the mining population of the Witwatersrand, was not a new one.[79] What *was* new was the presence in Johannesburg of a senior state official who thought along these lines, and who was only willing to act within this prescription. F. E. T. Krause, however, soon found out that he was not alone in offering resistance to the full-scale implementation of the Morals Law. In October 1897, the first important case to be heard under the new act came before Mr Justice Jorissen in the Circuit Court, when a French prostitute named Louise Roger was charged with having unlawful sexual intercourse with a black man. In his summing up, the Judge offered such a powerful criticism of the Ontucht Wet and its consequences for the many Africans who were confronted with a life of enforced celibacy on the Rand, that members of the jury – perhaps mistakenly – came to the conclusion that they could only find the accused 'not guilty'.[80] This decision, together with Krause's own predisposition about the functioning of the Morals Act, further confounded Kruger and the church's efforts to eradicate vice from Johannesburg in the period leading up to the South African War.

This hesitancy on the part of the state and the judiciary had swift and largely beneficial consequences for the real rulers of Frenchfontein – the well-organised pimps. Predictably, it enhanced the need for, and the possibility of, bribing the poorly paid members of the Morality Squad who now enjoyed greater discretionary power in determining what exactly it was that made for a 'disorderly' house. This situation, in which a good measure of arbitrary power devolved upon those in most immediate contact with prostitutes and pimps, proved to be the ideal host culture for massive corruption. While the police continued to arrest the more vulnerable small-scale vice merchants in order to create a smoke-screen of activity and produce a steady flow of bread-and-butter convictions under the Ontucht Wet, the really large gangs which could afford to pay the necessary bribes – such as the 'Bowery Boys' – remained marvellously immune from prosecution. Not even these diversionary tactics, however, could succeed in concealing the magnitude of police venality, and over a twenty-month period, between mid-1897 and late 1898, the Morality Squad experienced a change of leadership on no less than five occasions as officers and men alike fell under the suspicion of accepting bribes and acting corruptly. Not all of these officers chose to fall from power with grace and silence, and at least one of them – J. J. Donovan – made such serious allegations about F. E. T. Krause' administration of the Morals Act that by mid-1898 even the Senior Public Prosecutor fell under the Pretoria government's suspicion.[81]

The State President and his closest colleagues, who from June 1898 onwards included a new young State Attorney by the name of Jan Christian Smuts, could not have failed to have noticed these distressing developments. Within weeks of the passage of the Ontucht Wet in early 1897, the *Standard and Diggers' News* ran an editorial pointing out that the Morals Act was, to all intents and purposes, a 'Dead Letter'. Thereafter, and for the next eighteen months, the newspaper, under the guidance of its Editor, Emmanuel

Mendelssohn, consistently drew attention to the prevalence of prostitution, 'white slavery', police corruption and the hold which the 'Bowery Boys' exercised over the local underworld.[82]

But, if the Presidential eye perhaps did not scan the editorial columns of the Rand's English press, then there can be no doubt that the Presidential ear heard the articulate voices of Afrikaner and other clergymen during the same period. In late September 1898, almost two years after they had first gone to Pretoria as part of an inter-denominational delegation to complain about Johannesburg's immorality, the Rev. P. J. Meiring and Norman McCulloch of the Y.M.C.A. again called a public meeting to discuss the continuing evils of Frenchfontein. Amongst the many public-spirited citizens and committed Christians who attended this gathering at the Y.M.C.A. to contribute to what the press termed 'a lively discussion', a reporter from the *Standard and Diggers' News* noted the presence of one 'Joseph Silver' who introduced himself to the meeting as a 'citizen of the United States'. Displaying a degree of chutzpah which probably left even his 'American Club' colleagues bemused, the 'King of the Pimps' proceeded to tell the unsuspecting audience that it would be futile to attempt to rid the town of prostitutes, and that it would be more practical if 'this class of unfortunates' were confined to one part of Johannesburg. The majority of those present, however, apparently disagreed with this view and at the end of the evening the good citizens elected yet another inter-denominational delegation to wait upon the State President, and urge upon him the need to clean up the town.[83] With uncharacteristic humility, Silver did not make himself eligible for election.

When the Rev. Meiring and the members of his delegation met the

Joseph Silver at the time of his trial

State President and his Executive Committee in the Transvaal capital on 13 October 1898, their renewed pleas met with an immediate and positive response. Kruger, with the enthusiastic support of his new State Attorney, J. C. Smuts, was now more willing than ever to contemplate decisive action against the vice syndicates of the Witwatersrand and at once undertook to have a more stringent Ontucht Wet drafted. When this new legislation – in the form of Act No. 23 of 1898 – became law in mid-December 1898, it not only contained clauses designed to cope with the problem of 'white slavery', it also made provision for the possible banishment of moral offenders from the South African Republic.[84]

The members of the delegation, however, were more painfully aware than most that the proposed new legislation would in itself, offer no real solution to the problems posed by Frenchfontein – what *was* needed, above all else, was strong, fearless and effective administration of the laws. It was for precisely this latter reason that the clergymen were pleased to have been afforded the opportunity of having a further set of private discussions with the State Attorney after their initial hearing. The delegates seized this chance to offer Smuts a detailed account of the pervasive police corruption in Johannesburg. Smuts, for his part, promised to undertake a detailed examination of the Morals Law on the Rand, and, if need be, to radically re-organise the police and the office of the Public Prosecutor.[85] Armed with this pledge and a new sense of optimism, the clergymen withdrew from Pretoria.

Smuts, true to his word, immediately set about examining the manner in which the Ontucht Wet was being implemented in Johannesburg and, within 48 hours of his meeting the clergymen, J. J. Donovan was dismissed from the police force. Over the course of the next three weeks, however, the State Attorney's investigations into corruption took him through such an incredible maze of charges and countercharges that he came to the conclusion that none of the police – or indeed the First Public Prosecutor for that matter – were above suspicion. As a result of this probing, Smuts was made to realise that, if the amended Morals Act was to stand a chance of being successfully employed against the vice syndicates, then the state would require a new and independent team of law-enforcement officers on the Rand. With this latter requirement in mind, the State Attorney started to look around for a suitable candidate to lead a new legal team in Johannesburg. The person he chose for this daunting task was a determined and talented young South African by the name of Mostyn Cleaver.[86]

When F. R. M. Cleaver was appointed to the position of Second Public Prosecutor in Johannesburg during the first week of December 1898, Smuts made it clear that the new man was to be relatively independent of the existing structures within the Public Prosecutor's office as regards the implementation of the Ontucht Wet, and that for these purposes he would report direct to the State Attorney in Pretoria. This arrangement was met with obvious resentment in the Public Prosecutor's office – and not least of all by F. E. T. Krause and his closest assistant, Cornelis Broeksma. Krause, in an apparent attempt to be deliberately provocative, continually referred to Cleaver as 'my assistant' while somebody else in the office – probably Broeksma – reported him to Pretoria 'as having spoken unprofessionally of his

Superiors in the Department'. When these efforts to humiliate and isolate Cleaver failed, a further attempt to neutralise his effectiveness on morals cases was made by burdening him with an excessive load of the department's more mundane work.[87]

The Second Public Prosecutor's problems with his fellow officials, however, were not confined to his closest colleagues – they soon spread beyond Krause's office. Members of the police force, who had even more reason to be threatened by Cleaver's presence than Krause, proved so hostile that the young Second Prosecutor felt that he was 'surrounded by enemies and spies'. Commandant van Dam in particular was deeply offended by Cleaver's suggestion that virtually all of the members of his Morality Squad were corrupt and untrustworthy. Confronted with this active resistance on all sides, the Second Public Prosecutor was forced into developing his own supportive staff structure. With Smuts's support and encouragement, therefore, Cleaver employed a trusted former school-friend, L. B. Skirving, to assist him with the prosecution work, while he hired a private detective, Arendt Burchardt of the Rand Detective Agency, to undertake the necessary police work.[88]

Quite fortuitously, the establishment of the Burchardt-Cleaver-Skirving legal team came at an important moment in the history of Johannesburg's demi-monde. In late October 1898 one of the leading 'Bowery Boys', David Krakower, and two of his fellow gangsters, Henry Rosenchild and Morris Rosenberg, decided that their membership of the 'American Club' was proving to be unduly restrictive of their business activities. The three pimps therefore decided to break with the 'Bowery Boys' and to operate as an independent team within Frenchfontein. This decision did little to endear the new group to their erstwhile colleagues in the 'American Club'. Krakower himself, however, was clearly willing to live even more dangerously. Shortly after the break with the 'Bowery Boys', he absorbed the President of the 'American Club's' wife/prostitute – Lizzie Josephs – into his vice network by offering her police 'protection' at the rate of £6 per month.[89]

These provocative actions presented an unmistakable challenge to the authority of Joe Silver and his colleagues – and the 'Bowery Boys' were not slow in formulating a reply. Within days of these developments the 'President' set plans in motion for the punishment of Krakower, whom he had known since their days together in New York City eight years earlier. First, Silver tracked down Lizzie Josephs and then he re-established his personal control over her by assaulting her severely. Thereafter he and his colleagues 'persuaded' Lizzie and other women to testify to Krakower's extortionary proclivities before constables of the Morality Squad who were already on the 'American Club' payroll. On the basis of these sworn affidavits the constables then proceeded to the public prosecutor's office where, avoiding Cleaver and the strictures of the Ontucht Wet, they succeeded in getting a warrant for the arrest of Krakower and his associates on a charge of 'theft by means of fraud'.[90]

Krakower, however, was far from being defeated, and when his case was heard in Johannesburg's Second Criminal Court, on 6 December 1898, it caused a minor sensation. Working through the medium of his exceedingly able lawyer, L. E. van Diggelen, Krakower succeeded in offering, for the first time, a detailed public account of the inner workings of the 'American Club'. In addition, van Diggelen – through the skilful cross-examination of the police and other witnesses – made certain that the court's eyes never lost sight of the hand of Joe Silver in the events that were recounted before it. Largely as a result of these efforts by van Diggelen, Krakower and his co-accused were found not guilty and discharged – to the embarrassment and anger of the 'Bowery Boys', members of the Morality Squad and the man who had led the state's case, Public Prosecutor Cornelis Broeksma.[91]

The boss of the 'Bowery Boys', of course, had more reason than most to be angered by this decision. Besides having had to suffer the humiliation of a defeat at the hands of his enemy, his own vulnerability to prosecution had been increased by the exposure of his role as President of the 'American Club'. With a characteristic combination of flair and cheek, Silver now attempted to retrieve the situation by writing a letter to the Editor of the *Standard and Diggers' News* in which he outlined his proposed course of action:

> My name having been freely mentioned as one belonging to the pimping fraternity, so that I can only express my desire to hold a mass meeting during the next few days, with the object of discussing the desirability of having these shameless ruffians driven out of our midst.
>
> Johannesburg has of late become the refuge of the above mentioned class, and the unrivalled home in South Africa of people who trade on prostitution, and unless we take some further steps to remove them, they will before long eat themselves into the community so deeply that the cure will be an impossibility.[92]

The proposed mass meeting never materialised, and if this letter fooled anybody, it certainly did not fool Mostyn Cleaver.

The Second Public Prosecutor had, in fact, observed the Krakower trial and its outcome with mounting optimism. Cleaver saw in the growing bitterness of the Krakower-Silver division an unparalleled opportunity for the state to strike a powerful blow against organised vice on the Witwatersrand. If Krakower and others could only somehow be persuaded to give direct testimony against Silver and some of his closest aides, then the 'American Club' would lose much of its organisational strength. But, while it was one thing to get those confronted with charges to give evidence against the 'Bowery Boys' when they were already in difficulty with the law, it was quite another to get them, voluntarily, to give evidence against the President of the 'American Club' when they were free men. In short, getting Krakower to defend himself against Silver was not the same as getting him to attack the 'King of the Pimps'. Cleaver therefore saw his first task as that of having to find a way in which to place Krakower, Rosenberg and Rosenchild under renewed pressure, and the best way of doing this was to have them re-arrested on new charges under the modified Morality Act.

On 29 December 1898 the three Polish-American pimps duly reappeared in Johannesburg's Second Criminal Court charged with procuration. While L. E. van Diggelen again appeared for the defence, Cleaver chose to lead the state's case personally on this occasion and, at the end of the first day's proceedings, Landdrost Dietzch adjourned the hearing to 6 January 1899. Even this restricted court appearance, however, was sufficient to convince van Diggelen and his clients that the prosecution's case had been prepared with unusual thoroughness and that it was almost inevitable that the accused would be found guilty. For his part, Cleaver now used the intervening period to place Krakower and his fellow accused under even greater pressure, and to encourage them to do a deal – namely, that in return for their willingness to give evidence against Silver and his associates in the future, the state would consider dropping the charges they were now confronted with. At some point during the first week of January 1899 David Krakower agreed to these terms.[93] This was the opening that Cleaver had been waiting for.

The Second Public Prosecutor, with the assistance of L. E. van Diggelen, now questioned Krakower about the workings of the 'American Club' in order to establish who, besides Silver, were the moving forces behind the 'white slave' traffic on the Witwatersrand. After obtaining this information, Cleaver drove home his advantage to discover that Lieutenant Murphy – the man whom Smuts had had replace J. J. Donovan as head of the Morality Squad – was in the pay of the 'Bowery Boys'. It was also in the course of this latter revelation that Cleaver discovered that, between them, Silver and Murphy had 'framed' two uncooperative Morality Squad constables named Maritz and van Vuren, resulting in their suspension from duty.[94]

Cleaver then moved swiftly and with surgical precision. Deliberately by-passing the local office, he approached Smuts for the warrants necessary to arrest his suspects and for permission to select his own force of police with which to execute the orders. Then, at nine o'clock in the evening on Monday 9 January 1899, he, and a special posse of armed and mounted police under the direction of Morality Constable S. G. Maritz, raided 45 Anderson street and other addresses in the city's vice quarter. By midnight, the four leading 'white slave' traffickers on the Witwatersrand, Joe Silver, Sam Stein, Lizzie Josephs and Jenny Stein, were all in custody in the local police cells. So too were four other leading 'madams' employed by the Silver syndicate – Lillie Bloom, Florence Maud de Lacey, Annie Schwartz and Bessie Weinberg.[95]

The following day, after obtaining an additional set of warrants from the State Attorney by telegraph, Cleaver rounded off his operation by searching the premises of the 'American Club' and Sam Stein's safety deposit box for further evidence. Thereafter, with both suspects and evidence secure, he succeeded in sealing off the two gangsters' most obvious escape-route by persuading Smuts to issue instructions which would ensure that the 'Bowery Boys' would be denied bail when they appeared in court. Thus, when Silver and Stein did appear in court briefly on the morning of 10 January 1899, they were duly refused bail, and informed that their case had been remanded until 2 February. Not even this achievement, however, was enough to satisfy the relentless and careful planning of the Second Public Prosecutor. Fearing that the remaining 'Bowery Boys' would succeed in bribing the poorer burghers who would inevitably form part of a local jury, Cleaver then arranged that while the preliminary examination of Silver and Stein would take place in Johannesburg, the trial itself would be held in Pretoria.[96]

This unusually swift and thorough offensive by the state left the members of the 'American Club' stunned – but only briefly. Within 48 hours of their President's arrest, Secretary 'Joe Gold' and two other 'Bowery Boys', Wolf Witkofsky and Harris Stadtman, decided to pay a call upon at least one person who was likely to be an important witness in any Silver trial – David

Krakower's 'wife', Sadie Woolf. When the initial offer of a bribe failed to secure that reluctant lady's cooperation, the three 'Bowery Boys' attempted to concentrate the madam's mind by suggesting that she take an extended trip out of town if she wished to continue enjoying good health and a long life. While this suggestion went some way towards intimidating the former New York City prostitute, the proposition had precisely the opposite effect on her pimp/'husband' when it was subsequently relayed to him. Knowing that he now enjoyed the protection of the state, Krakower simply assaulted the Secretary of the 'American Club' on the first occasion which presented itself.[97]

The 'Bowery Boys'' attempt at a counter-offensive, however, was soon made to extend beyond the immediate confines of David Krakower. During the latter half of January 1899, 'Joe Gold' and selected henchmen systematically worked their way through Frenchfontein alternately encouraging and threatening witnesses to give only evidence favourable to Silver in the forthcoming hearings. But their task of finding suitably compliant and credible witnesses was made virtually impossible by the efforts of the indefatigable Cleaver. During the same period the Second Public Prosecutor was equally hard at work protecting witnesses, engaging in plea-bargaining, and methodically eliminating perjurers from within the ranks of the Morality Squad. Largely as a result of this, the 'Bowery Boys' were forced into paying an increasing amount of attention to Cleaver himself and, shortly before Silver's trial, the Second Public Prosecutor started receiving offers of substantial bribes. When this failed to elicit the required response, Cleaver's mail commenced to yield a predictable blend of blackmailing letters and notes containing death threats.[98]

Neither these crude strong-arm tactics indulged in by the 'Bowery Boys', nor the more subtle and skilful letter of appeal which Silver and Stein later directed to Landdrost Dietzch from their cell in the Johannesburg prison, brought any relief to the beleaguered 'President' and his colleague. On 6 February – after almost a month's imprisonment – the preliminary examination got under way in the Third Criminal Court, and when the hearing ended eight days later, on 14 February, the two prisoners were committed for trial at the next session of the Pretoria assizes.[99] But even this news offered Silver and Stein little consolation since the precise date on which the assizes were to convene had yet to be determined by the State Attorney. Thus, while Smuts and Cleaver used the remainder of February, all of March and the first week of April to complete outstanding prosecutions against former members of the Morality Squad on charges of perjury and corruption, the two gangsters grew increasingly despondent waiting to hear the exact date set for their trial.[100]

Silver and Stein eventually appeared before Justice Esser in the Pretoria High Court on 18 April 1899, charged on several counts under the Morality Act of 1898. By that time, however, Mostyn Cleaver had succeeded in completely cutting off any access which the 'Bowery Boys' had to police witnesses who might formerly have enjoyed some credibility. But the Second Public Prosecutor had used the time put at his disposal by the State Attorney to do more than simply erode the possible case for the defence. He had also managed to build up an enormously convincing case for the prosecution. By making use of the old combination of pressure and plea-bargaining, Cleaver

Unnamed members of the American Club, Johannesburg – a court exhibit submitted during the trial of Joseph Silver, 1899

got many of Silver's intimates – including Wolf Witkofsky, Lillie Bloom and Bessie Weinberg – to give evidence on the state's behalf. Perhaps most impressive of all was the manner in which the Second Public Prosecutor and his team tracked down one of the Presidents of the 'American Club's' former partners at the London end of the 'white slavery' operations, Jacob Shrednicki, and 'persuaded' him to give evidence about the leader of syndicate's activities in the vice business. Thus, despite the fact that the two 'Bowery Boys' were ably defended by ex-Chief Justice J. G. Kotzé, Silver was found guilty after a trial lasting five days. While Sam Stein was fortunate enough to be discharged, Silver was sentenced to two years' imprisonment with hard labour, and subsequent banishment from the South African Republic.[101]

The last legal hope of the leader of the 'Bowery Boys' now lay in an appeal to the State President and his Executive Committee, but when representations were made on his behalf in early June, Kruger and his colleagues took the opportunity to endorse emphatically Mr Justice Esser's decision. Not even this, however, ended Joe Silver's problems with the Transvaal law. Early in August, while serving his sentence in the Johannesburg gaol, Silver caught hold of an African cleaner, 'Jim', and sodomised him. While this assault, together with his previous reputation as a procurer, earned Silver's name a permanent place in South Africa's black prison gangs, it did him little good when he subsequently appeared before Mr Dietzch in the Third Criminal Court charged with committing 'an unnatural offence'. The 'Bowery Boy' was convicted and sentenced to a further period of six months' imprisonment which was to take effect after the completion of his first sentence of two years' imprisonment.[102]

Within days of this distressing development, however, the 'King of the Pimps' saw the first glimmerings of new hope for his release. The Kruger government, knowing the outbreak of war with Britain to be imminent, took the precaution of moving some of its long-term and more dangerous prisoners from Johannesburg to smaller Transvaal towns whose Republican loyalties were beyond doubt. On 26 September 1899 Joe Silver, in the company of 25 other prisoners, was moved to Potchefstroom in the western Transvaal where he promptly made an unsuccessful attempt to escape from prison.[103] But, as later transpired, this escape bid proved to be unnecessary since shortly thereafter the Boer authorities – hard pressed for all available manpower – were forced into releasing all the prisoners under their control. Silver seized the war's gift of freedom and made his way to the safety of the south where, over the next five years, he proceeded to leave his own particularly indelible mark on the criminal underworlds of Kimberley, Cape Town, Bloemfontein and Windhoek.

Cleaver's well-orchestrated attack on organised vice and police corruption during late 1898 and early 1899 had nevertheless met with at least some success. Through his efforts the most important principals behind the 'white slave' traffic had been exposed and dealt with, and at the time of the Pretoria High Court trial, 'train-loads of Silver's victims were sent over the border to Cape Town'. In August this action was followed by the further amendment of the Morality Law and the expulsion of dozens of 'foreign' pimps from the Rand. Moreover, Cleaver made sure that in the months leading up to the South African War Johannesburg was served, for the first time, by a relatively honest and efficient police force.[104]

But, while the state had certainly launched a powerful attack on the forces of Frenchfontein, it had by no means defeated the army of vice. Despite the expulsion of scores of prostitutes and pimps, hundreds more remained in Johannesburg and only departed for the coastal cities when the general exodus of refugees took place later in the year. Even then, however, some left more willingly than others. On 2 November 1899 the *Standard and Diggers' News* – vigilant to the end – drew the authorities' attention 'to a gang of Bowery "hautboys" of American nationality still in town'.[105] If some of the New York City gangsters left the Rand reluctantly, they certainly did not do so under a cloud of pessimism. After all, in the prostitution business soldiers and miners were equally welcome as customers.

Policies of pragmatism – British control of European women, 1902–1906

During mid-1899, at precisely the moment when Mostyn Cleaver was rounding-off his operations against the major prostitution networks on the Witwatersrand, the Cape Colony was engaged in a debate of its own about the role of the Contagious Diseases Act of 1885 and the control of sexual vice. There, certain feminists, clergymen and Members of Parliament who had long been opposed to the 'double standard' enshrined in Cape legislation had forced a select committee to re-examine the functioning of the C.D. Act in early 1899. When this parliamentary committee issued its report it found that not only did the act not play any material role in diminishing the spread of venereal disease, but that it continued to provide – via the notorious 'compulsory examination' clause – the means by which women could be humiliated. Largely as a result of this report a measure for the repeal of the C.D. Act was introduced into the Cape Parliament in August 1899, and it was only as a result of the strong personal intervention of the Premier, W. P. Schreiner, that the bill was eventually withdrawn.[106]

Schreiner must have felt that his conservatism was vindicated when, over the following four months, the Colony, and Cape Town in particular, was inundated with pimps, prostitutes and gangsters who had either been expelled from the South African Republic or who, along with thousands of others from the Transvaal, had chosen to seek refuge at the coast when war was declared in October 1899. In addition to this influx of 'undesirables' which derived from up-country, however, the port itself continued to disgorge its own share of newly arrived criminal elements from Europe who, instead of proceeding to the Transvaal as in the pre-war period, now tended to stay on in Cape Town.[107]

Briefly invisible, these denizens of the demi-monde, who included amongst their number former members of the 'American Club', soon became more apparent as large brothels, betting houses and gaming houses started to proliferate in wartime Cape Town. While this development was readily accommodated by several unprincipled landlords in search of higher rents – such as H. J. Dempers, an Afrikaner Bond Member of Parliament who let his city property as a brothel – it received a more hostile reception from others in the local community. In October 1901, after a series of public meetings at which grave reservations were expressed about the adequacy of a local by-law which the City Council had passed earlier in the year in an attempt to cope with the 'social evil', a group of concerned clergymen approached the Attorney General, T. L. Graham, with a request that new state legislation be promulgated to combat the growth of organised prostitution in Cape Town.[108]

When Graham took the precautionary step of cross-checking the clergymen's claims with the local police he was somewhat taken aback by his findings. In addition to discovering that sexual vice was more widespread than he had anticipated, he was also distressed by the revelation that 'a considerable traffic was being carried on in Cape Town between aboriginal natives and white European women'.[109] On the strength of this rather 'disturbing' evidence the Attorney General readily persuaded the government to introduce the 'Betting Houses, Gaming Houses and Brothels Suppression Bill' to parliament in October 1902. This bill, which was more frequently known by its short title, 'The Morality Bill', was largely modelled along the lines of the former Zuid Afrikaansche Republiek's Ontucht Wet. In addition to making sexual intercourse between black males and white prostitutes an offence, it also made provision for the punishment of pimps by periods of imprisonment of up to two years, or for the inflicting of up to 25 lashes on the offenders. These latter clauses, as John X. Merriman put it while guiding the bill through parliament, were specifically designed in order to get 'at these wretches through their skin'.[110]

Understandably, these harsh provisions held little appeal for the 'wretches' concerned, and when the Morality Act came into force on 1 December 1902 it sent several Cape-based pimps and prostitutes scurrying to other corners of southern Africa in search of more congenial business climes. Joseph Silver and his associates, for example, left Kimberley for Bloemfontein where their professional activities precipitated such a social upheaval that – within four months of their arrival, in March 1903 – the Orange River Colony was forced into passing its own ordinance to provide for the 'Suppression of Brothels and Immorality'.[111] Other vice merchants, again including former members of the 'American Club', decided that the time had come for them to chance a return to the Transvaal which was preoccupied with more pressing problems. Yet others, however, decided to head for the territory which was now most vulnerable of all – Natal.

Such an influx of pimps and prostitutes from elsewhere in southern Africa into Natal was not a novel experience for the British colony. Indeed, as far back as March 1897, when Kruger had first introduced the Ontucht Wet into the Transvaal, a significant number of the departing prostitutes had made their way east and established themselves in Pietermaritzburg and Durban. This initial wave of 'undesirables', however, was soon followed by an even larger and more disturbing wave of lumpen-refugees when the war broke out in late 1899. On this latter occasion, R. C. Alexander, the Durban Superintendent of Police who kept a close watch on such developments, put the number of newly arrived prostitutes from the Rand in his city at 231. In addition to this, Alexander noted how, on average, five or six prostitutes disembarked from each German ship calling at the port during the war. This meant that in the relatively brief period between 1899 and 1902 over 300 'continental' women joined the ranks of those prostitutes who had previously been established in Durban.[112]

As in wartime Cape Town, and Johannesburg before that, this influx of vice merchants transformed the rent structure for housing in parts of central Durban. In this case the majority of premises hired to serve as brothels appear to have been owned by comparatively wealthy Asian landlords, and by one 'Latif Osman Rich' in particular.[113] But, as in the Cape and Transvaal before, it was not simply the question of housing which distressed the local authorities but the manner in which these 'continental' business women were willing to accept all paying customers on a non-racial basis. Natal settlers, along with most other white South African males, believed that such sex across the colour line permanently debauched African men, and that these erotic experiences subsequently triggered-off 'black peril' assaults on other European women. It was largely for this reason that Natal joined the elaborate post-war round of legislative musical chairs when it introduced its own Immorality Act in mid-1903.[114] Predictably enough, this law once again set in motion a cycle of movement in the flesh markets as several pimps and prostitutes chose to move to the Transvaal and other centres where they were perhaps less well known to the local police.

When the members of this latest and relatively minor influx of coastal vice merchants reached the Witwatersrand in 1903 they found that although the substantial part of Johannesburg's demi-monde had long since reconstituted itself, the prospects for selling sexual services nevertheless remained as promising as ever. In 1904 the large numbers of black and white miners in town without their wives were joined by an industrial army of Chinese indentured labourers, and all these 'unattached' males provided the 'ladies of pleasure' with a steady stream of customers. In addition to this, the war itself had of course brought with it the added 'bonus' of thousands of British troops and, in the wake of their departure, the residual force of the men of the South African Constabulary.[115] Clearly, in a town where there was such an overwhelming preponderance of males over females, the continuing economic viability of Frenchfontein was beyond question.

As in the pre-war period, however, this powerful demand for the services of prostitutes could not simply be met from local 'supplies', and thus it again called forth a highly organised response from the pimps and gangsters of Frenchfontein. Within weeks of Johannesburg being re-opened to civilians in early 1901, the old 'white slavery' lines of supply – which during the war had temporarily terminated at the coastal cities – had been extended back into the Transvaal. Under the leadership of an old friend of Joe Silver's – Louis Shivinsky – former members of the 'American Club', including Abraham Goldstein, Joe Josephs and Robert Schoub, established a new pimps' association, the so-called 'Immorality Trust'.[116] With its leadership largely drawn from the ranks of the former 'Bowery Boys', the members of the 'Trust' now looked to the well-organised 'white slave' dealers on the eastern American seaboard for many of their prostitutes.[117] In this they were largely assisted by the members of the New York Independent Benevolent Association, a notorious group of Jewish gangsters who preyed upon the women of the vulnerable East European immigrant communities on Manhattan's lower east side.[118]

But it was the older and more established supply routes which stretched directly from Europe to southern Africa which continued to yield the greatest number of the Rand's 'white slaves' in the immediate post-war period. While Hamburg and the German East African Shipping Line still played a significant part in this traffic, it was Paris – above all other cities – which dominated the 'export trade' in women, sending prostitutes drawn from a dozen different continental countries to the Transvaal and other flesh markets spread across the world.[119] Although it is difficult to determine the names of all the intermediaries connected with the southern traffic in women, it is clear that at least one of those involved was the notorious George le Cuirassier.

During the first decade of the twentieth century George le Cuirassier, his mother and their associates were amongst the foremost 'white slave' dealers in Paris – indeed, in Europe. Reported as being 'the general financier and boss of pimps and procurers' by an American Immigration Officer investigating the trade in women in 1909, le Cuirassier was also said to have 'interests in dozens of Houses of Prostitution all over the globe, including France, Manchuria, Argentine, Mexico and the United States'.[120] Certainly, when the South African market expanded particularly rapidly after the outbreak of the Anglo-Boer War, le Cuirassier had switched his business to Cape Town for several months, and it was while he was there that he was closely involved with Joseph Silver and other former members of the 'American Club'. In addition to managing a District Six brothel under the names of 'George Hyman'/'Dacheau', le Cuirassier personally supervised the movement of prostitutes between various southern African colonies.[121] If there was anybody who knew who it was that put the 'French' into 'Frenchfontein', then it was likely to have been George le Cuirassier.

With his well-developed Far Eastern interests, however, it is also possible that le Cuirassier would have known which of his colleagues in the trade it was who had helped Johannesburg to acquire a modest contingent of Japanese prostitutes in the post-war period.[122] Here again, it would appear that some of the former members of the 'American Club' were involved since G. K. Turner, a well informed observer of the international 'white slave' traffic at the time, noted how, 'After South Africa the New York dealers went by their hundreds to the East', and that 'they followed the Russian army through the Russo-Japanese war'.[123] Thus, at the very moment that the agents of the Chamber of Mines were at work in China recruiting indentured labour for the Rand mines, the agents of organised vice were also at work in the Far East, recruiting some of the Japanese prostitutes who would be used to provide sexual services for the new workers. It was these latter female recruits, the so-called *Karayuki-San*, who, during the course of 1904–5, made their way to Fordsburg and joined up with the small number of Japanese prostitutes who had been established in that quarter of the town since at least 1894.[124]

This dramatic resurgence of the organised trade in prostitution did not escape the attention of some of Johannesburg's more experienced and vigilant observers of the demi-monde – such as Joseph Hertz. As leader of the Witwatersrand Old Hebrew Congregation, Hertz had been deeply shocked by the 'American Club' revelations in early 1899 when the extent of Jewish involvement in the 'white slave' traffic had first become apparent, and had subsequently taken vigorous intra-communal measures to oppose it.[125] It was thus with some alarm that Rabbi Hertz saw familiar elements of the 'social evil' manifesting themselves again within the community, and he therefore readily agreed to participate in a private meeting which fellow clergymen and concerned citizens called to discuss the problem on 14 January 1902.

At this meeting, which drew together about twenty-five of the Rand's leading clerical, commercial and legal personalities, it was decided that the new Administrator of the Transvaal, Lord Milner, should be approached with a formal request that the police be instructed to enforce Kruger's old Ontucht Wet – Law No. 11 of 1899. Hertz, who was elected as secretary to this committee of notables, accordingly drafted a petition outlining this request, taking the opportunity to point out that many vice merchants were already back in town while 'hundreds' of pimps and 'thousands' of prostitutes were at the coastal cities awaiting their first chance to return to Johannesburg. This document – whose signatories included, amongst others, St John Carr, Hugh Crawford (of Lewis & Marks), the Rev. J. T. Darragh, Canon F. H. Fisher, The Rev. J. T. Lloyd, Advocate Manfred Nathan, the Rev. O. Owens, H. F. Pistorius (Chamber of Commerce), E. P. Solomon and Harry Solomon – was dispatched for Milner's consideration in the third week of January.[126]

The Imperial overlord took his time. On the final day of February 1902 Milner got his Assistant Private Secretary to send the petitioners a twelve-line reply acknowledging receipt of their communication, and informing them that it was 'within the competence of the Municipalities of Johannesburg and Pretoria to make by-laws for the suppression of houses of ill-fame'. In addition, however, the Secretary was instructed to point out to Hertz and his colleagues that 'no permits to return to the Transvaal' would be granted to 'persons of known bad character'.[127] But the Administrator, either through neglect or deliberate oversight, failed to instruct the Permit Department to liaise with the Criminal Investigation Department on this matter, with the result that there was a continuing influx of 'undesirables' into Johannesburg during the following months.[128]

If, however, Milner silently cherished the hope that his inaction would dispose of the matter for the foreseeable future then he was mistaken, for before the year was out the issue was raised again and this time from a more powerful quarter. By mid-1902, with the 'social evil' much in evidence locally, senior officials in the Natal administration were becoming deeply distressed by tales of how black men engaged in migrant labour on the Witwatersrand were getting sexual access to 'continental women'. On 5 September the Governor of Natal, Sir Henry McCullum, wrote to the Administrator of the Transvaal expressing his concern about the matter, and asking Milner about the possibility of the British authorities undertaking co-ordinated action to expel all 'foreign born' prostitutes from the territories under their control. In addition, McCullum suggested that the moment had probably arrived when all the southern African colonies could share uniform legislation for the control of vice. This time Milner, ever anxious to observe protocol, deflected the query to the Lieutenant-Governor of the Transvaal, Sir Arthur Lawley.[129]

Lawley, of course, was fully aware of the fact that if there was to be any action along the lines suggested, it would have to be initiated by the Administrator and his reconstruction 'cabinet'. The Lieutenant-Governor therefore simply passed the problem back to the government by asking the Attorney General, Richard Solomon, to draft his reply to McCullum. Solomon's reply no doubt reflected Milner's thinking on the subject at least as much as his own since it produced a familiar refrain. 'I see no reason for having a uniform law in South Africa for dealing generally with prostitutes', noted the Transvaal Attorney General, 'it is purely a municipal matter and must be dealt with by each State with due regard to local conditions.'[130] Lawley reproduced this line of reasoning in word-perfect fashion when he replied to McCullum on 24 October 1902.[131]

Within four months of this successful evasion, however, Milner's policy on prostitution was again under scrutiny – and this time the questions came from a quarter that was less easily dismissed. Early in February 1903 Lord Onslow, Under-Secretary of State for the Colonies, wrote to Milner, drawing his attention to the manner in which the 'white slave' traffic from Europe to southern Africa had somehow re-established itself, and enquiring what the 'permit system' was doing to disrupt this 'disgraceful' trade in women. Onslow concluded his letter with the suggestion that Milner might, via suitable 'religious or charitable associations', initiate rescue work amongst 'fallen women' in the Transvaal.[132]

This whisper from Whitehall concentrated the Imperial overlord's mind wonderfully. Within weeks of the receipt of Onslow's letter, Milner's administration was actively seeking new submissions from the very Rand petitioners whom it had earlier sent away with a flea in the ear. The members of this 'Morality Committee' had, in the interim, been working on a revised version of the Cape Betting Houses, Gaming Houses and Brothels Suppression Act which – in line with the Administrator's earlier curt suggestion – they hoped to get the Johannesburg municipality to adopt. By the second week of March this draft legislation was being studied in the Attorney General's office, and in July the Transvaal administration promulgated Ordinance 46 of 1903, the 'Immorality Act'.[133]

Although chiefly concerned to outlaw *all* sexual intercourse between African males and European women – not simply that between black men and white prostitutes – Ordinance 46 was also designed to allow for the disruption of the organised trade in vice.[134] It thus contained measures specifically aimed at those owners of property who habitually allowed their houses to be let for purposes of prostitution. Moreover, clause 21 of the new act made provision for the infliction of lashes on all males found guilty of living on the proceeds of prostitution. In legal terms at least, the Milner administration had demonstrated its intention of dealing with the 'white slave' traffic and some of its attendant evils.

But, as always, the news of imminent and harsher repressive measures for the control of vice was greeted with a twofold response by the inhabitants of the demi-monde. On the one hand there were those veteran vice merchants who saw in the new act the need to improve their professional organisation, and this they promptly did. From mid-1903 onwards, those brothels catering for African workers developed elaborate systems of lookouts, electric alarm bells and secret entrances to afford them better protection from sudden police raids.[135] On the other hand, however, there were those meeker brothers and sisters who had no taste at all for the harsher penalties contained in Ordinance

46. While many in the latter category made the familiar short journey to Cape Town, a few of the 'Bowery Boys' came to the conclusion that the time had come to move even further afield, and made their way back to New York City via Buenos Aires.[136]

The remaining East European and other pimps, however, were quick to appreciate that such trans-Atlantic trips were premature. With the exception of the clause prohibiting sex across the colour line, the Milner administration made little effort to implement the more stringent provisions of Ordinance 46. From early 1902 to late 1905, Milner and Richard Solomon's view, that policies on prostitution had to be determined 'with due regard to local conditions', held sway. Thc Commissioner of Police, E. H. Showers, correctly interpreted this guideline to mean that in a place like Johannesburg – where there existed a high proportion of single or unaccompanied white workers – prostitution should be controlled but not eradicated.[137]

In practice this meant that for some time before and after the passing of the Immorality Act, Frenchfontein was allowed to flower in a manner which had last been seen between 1895 and 1897. While public exposure and soliciting by prostitutes was prohibited, brothels with up to ten and more women were allowed to operate openly provided that their business was conducted in a suitably restrained and discreet fashion. Amongst the two to three dozen brothels located in Anderson, Rissik, de Villiers, Loveday, Bree and other streets, there were two, however, that were particularly noteworthy. 'Sylvio Villa', still operating under its old trade name but now owned by George Ducoin, alias 'Canada', retained much of its pre-war popularity, while a new establishment managed by Theodore Hovent, at 1 Jeppe street, was renowned for the variety of services it offered – the patrons being able to choose from a selection of no fewer than seventeen 'girls'. Under these flourishing business conditions, members of the 'Immorality Trust', as well as other pimps, accumulated considerable sums of capital which, in the case of the 'Bowery Boys', they eventually repatriated to New York City.[138]

Milner, however, had not forgotten the suggestion from Whitehall by Onslow that he might consider encouraging religious or charitable institutions to undertake reclamation work amongst the 'fallen women' of the Witwatersrand. Thus, shortly after the promulgation of Ordinance 46, he approached some of the clergymen on the 'Morality Committee' with offers of limited state aid for such work, and by late 1904 there were two 'rescue homes' operating in the Transvaal – the one Protestant and the other Catholic. At Irene, near Pretoria, a grant from the Beit Trust helped establish the 'House of Mercy', while at Norwood, in Johannesburg, Thomas Cullinan's generosity, aided by Milner's personal involvement in fund-raising activities, helped support a similar institution run by a French order, 'The Sisters of the Good Shepherd'. With a characteristically tough Victorian combination of Christian love and strenuous laundry work, however, neither of these institutions held great attractions for the former 'women of pleasure', and these reclamation efforts appear to have met with only modest success.[139]

This Milner marvel – whereby the authorities could on the one hand allow large brothels to operate in undisturbed fashion, and on the other encourage the reclamation of 'fallen women' – persisted throughout the period of his administration, and for several months thereafter. Then, in late 1905, the quiet comfort of this position was rudely shattered when the man in charge of the C.I.D. on the Witwatersrand, Major T. E. Mavrogordato, happened to outline the 'local conditions' policy to Milner's successor, Lord Selborne. The Governor, shocked by the discovery that wealthy vice merchants were allowed to operate relatively openly in Johannesburg, immediately wrote a pointed letter to the Attorney General, Richard Solomon, enquiring as to why it was that pimps were not being prosecuted under the provisions of Ordinance 46. The Attorney General, embarrassed by these questions, deftly passed them down the line to the Commissioner of Police, E. H. Showers. As co-authors – with Milner – of the 'local conditions' policy, both Solomon and Showers, of course, knew the answers to Selborne's questions perfectly well. But, either unable or unwilling to spell out these answers to a new Governor, the Attorney General and Commissioner of Police chose instead to assure Selborne that they would at once launch a drive against the pimps on the Rand. Then, in order to demonstrate their irritation at being pushed into this predicament by a relatively junior officer, Solomon and Showers promptly 'deputed Mr Mavrogordato to deal with the pimps'.[140]

Mavrogordato responded as well as he could to this petulant challenge from above. Within a week of receiving his directive from the Commissioner of Police on 23 January 1906, Mavrogordato's men arrested the veteran vice merchant Louis Shivinsky, now a member of the 'Immorality Trust', on charges framed under Ordinance 46. No sooner had this notorious 'Bowery Boy' been let out on bail of £1,000, however, than he fled the country. This arrest and its expensive sequel, 'which caused considerable commotion in the camp of the pimps' was followed by further vigorous C.I.D. activity during February, March and April. By May 1906 Mavrogordato could report to Showers that, besides Shivinsky and George Ducoin of 'Sylvio Villa' fame, fifteen other important pimps had fled the Transvaal, that nine of Frenchfontein's largest and best regulated brothels had been closed down, and – a bit hopefully – that 'the organisation of pimps hitherto complained of in Johannesburg has ceased to exist'.[141]

The Commissioner of Police, a little ungenerously, found these results from the C.I.D. to be 'disappointing'. Showers felt that although the established brothels had been closed down, few of the pimps involved had been successfully prosecuted, and that the results that had been achieved could as readily have been obtained by the uniformed branch of the police.[142] The Attorney General, suitably briefed by Showers, shared this opinion, with the result that over the following months the members of the Criminal Investigation Department remained under constant pressure to produce a stream of convictions under the Immorality Act.

Eventually, after nearly a year and a half of intra-departmental rivalry and tension – and only after Solomon and Showers had moved out of office – the Head of the C.I.D. made the admission which the former Milner men so dearly would have liked to have extracted from him. In May 1907 Mavrogordato wrote to the Acting Commissioner of Police, Colonel A. O'Brien, pointing out that:

> The position with regard to Public Immorality has greatly improved within the last two years; formerly large brothels containing 10 or more

> women each were allowed to exist. These institutions are not in existence now and most of the prostitutes are single women who are living by themselves or in a house. Soliciting in the streets has been reduced to a minimum and I do not think that the streets could be cleaner in Johannesburg in any other part of the world [*sic*].[143]

When O'Brien passed on this message to the new Attorney General, Jacob de Villiers, it was accepted, bringing some relief to the hitherto beleaguered chief of the C.I.D. In retrospect, however, Mavrogordato would probably have agreed that this judgement was perhaps a little naive, and certainly a bit premature. Prostitution had been a feature of the mining town ever since it was founded, and for over a decade much of Johannesburg's vice trade had shown all the hallmarks of careful organisation. These features, which ultimately derived from the deeper social structures engendered by capitalist development on the Witwatersrand and in Eastern Europe on the one hand, and from the cunning career management of professional gangsters spread across the world on the other, were unlikely to be simply blown away by a police campaign over an eighteen-month period.

The Transvaal's own – daughters of the new proletariat, 1907–1914

In May 1907, only a few months after the Transvaal attained self-governing status, members of Mavrogordato's staff compiled a return giving the names and addresses of all known pimps and brothels in Johannesburg. Possibly as a result of genuine ignorance, but more likely as a result of the bribery of some of the members of the C.I.D. concerned, this list of sixty 'houses of ill-fame' proved to be conspicuously thin on information relating to the inner city's vice district. In particular, this return managed to miss the names and business addresses of several veterans of vice still active in Frenchfontein, such as Harry Epstein, Abraham Goldstein, Joe Josephs and others; as well as those of dozens of younger Russo-American pimps who had made their way to the Rand in the immediate post-war period to become members of the 'Immorality Trust' – men such as Meyer Arenow, Isaac 'Itchky' Favours, Leon Rosenblatt and 'Chicago Jack' Linderstein.[144]

This unusual silence from and about the activities of the town's oldest and best-organised vice district persisted for several months. Then, from December 1907 to May 1908, as the Rand's post-war recession deepened into a full-scale depression, the foundations of the demi monde were rocked by tremors which emanated from the most unexpected quarter. Either because they found the financial demands of some of the members of the 'Immorality Trust' too demanding during such hard times, or for some equally cogent but hidden reason, certain prostitutes 'made up their minds to throw off the yokes of their pimps'.[145] One of the first and most important pimps to be subjected to this startling attack from below was Harry Epstein, a founder member of the 'American Club'.

As a result of information passed to the police by certain prostitutes formerly under his control, Harry Epstein was arrested by members of the C.I.D. on 14 February 1908. A seasoned professional, Epstein's immediate response was to look for the best defence lawyer in town who had first-hand experience of morality cases. To the delight of the former 'Bowery Boy', he found that sufficient money could retain the services of a lawyer who not only had an outstanding knowledge of the Transvaal legal system, but one who felt – as a matter of principle – that the law should have as little as possible to do with questions of public morality. First as Public Prosecutor in Johannesburg under the Kruger regime, and later as lawyer and Member of Parliament for the Het Volk government, F. E. T. Krause proved himself to be a friend of Frenchfontein.[146]

Right from the outset Krause distinguished himself in his defence of his pimp client. By constantly seeking remands – and being granted at least eight such requests – he managed to drag out the preparatory examination from mid-February to early April 1908. Then, when Epstein's trial finally commenced in the Witwatersrand 'C' Court on 21 May, Krause managed to employ successfully the same delaying tactic on a further six occasions. While these adjournments gave members of the 'Immorality Trust' ample opportunity to work on prosecution witnesses outside the courtroom, Krause supplemented their efforts inside the court by suggesting that all evidence which emanated from prostitutes was by its nature suspect and therefore inconclusive. An able barrister under any circumstances, Krause found that his eloquent pleadings echoed particularly loudly in the ears of a presiding magistrate who, ten years earlier, had been one of his juniors in the Johannesburg Public Prosecutor's office – W. G. Schuurman. The result of all this was that Epstein was eventually found not guilty on 17 June 1908, discharged, and refunded the £750 which he had been made to deposit with the court as bail.[147]

Epstein celebrated his victory at law in a manner which his colleagues in the pimping fraternity could only thoroughly approve of. On the evening of his release from custody, he and the chief witness for the defence at his trial, Mrs Max Kaplan, hired a cab and then drove to the various houses of the prostitutes who had dared to give evidence against him. Here, after jeering and taunting the crown witnesses, they proceeded to smash several windows before moving on to a celebratory dinner held for 'Trust' members and their 'madams' at 42 Polly street. On the following morning Epstein called at Krause's office where he stole all the papers pertaining to his case before shaving off his moustache and fleeing the country.[148]

But if Mavrogordato's men failed in the case of Epstein, then they more than compensated with the successes which they managed to achieve during the six-month long pimp/prostitute war which engulfed Frenchfontein between December 1907 and May 1908. Largely because of evidence made available to the C.I.D. by rebellious prostitutes, seventeen of the most important pimps in the local demi-monde were arrested during this period. The ensuing court cases necessitated the calling of 150 witnesses, of whom over 100 were prostitutes. 'The result', noted the newly-promoted Deputy Commissioner of Police, 'was that 10 well-known professional pimps were convicted and sentenced to terms of imprisonment varying from 6 to 12 months with lashes.'[149]

Even this onslaught did not succeed in finally destroying the 'Immorality Trust' and the remaining vestiges of the 'white slave' traffic. In October 1908 Mavrogordato could still draw the Attorney General's attention to the presence of dozens of Russo-American and other pimps on the Rand:

> The pimps referred to make no secret of their calling. Some of them live together, and there are such places in Johannesburg as pimps' boarding-houses and pimps' clubs. Some of them take houses in the country where they are supposed to live privately and where prostitutes who are imported or those who are sick take refuge till they are fit to be put on the market.[150]

It was precisely because of such remaining supportive structures that Mavrogordato now appealed to the Colonial Secretary to agree to the deportation of all foreign-born pimps and prostitutes convicted under the Immorality Act.

The Colonial Secretary had little difficulty in understanding Mavrogordato's problem or in acceding to his request. As the former State Attorney in Kruger's government who had been responsible for sending Mostyn Cleaver to Johannesburg to do battle with the 'American Club' ten years earlier, J. C. Smuts probably had a better idea than most of his colleagues in the cabinet what the C.I.D. was up against. Thus, between early 1909 and mid-1910, in a period of frenetic activity before Union, Smuts and Mavrogordato made widespread use of the Transvaal's Crimes Prevention Ordinance of 1905 and the Immigrants' Restriction Acts of 1907 and 1908 to deport hundreds of foreign-born pimps and prostitutes to Mozambique and the neighbouring colonies. From there many of these 'undesirable aliens' made the long journey home to the ports and backstreets of Europe.[151]

This campaign, and the scores of 'voluntary' departures which occurred during the same period, did much to break the dominant hold which immigrant vice merchants had exercised over Johannesburg's demi-monde ever since the mid-1890s. By July 1910, when the C.I.D. again conducted one of its periodic surveys of Frenchfontein, it could only find 17 pimps and 48 prostitutes who qualified for the category 'foreign-born'. Of the pimps, 7 were listed as being 'Jewish', 4 French, 4 German and 2 Portuguese, while the prostitutes included 20 'Russian and Polish Jewesses', 9 German, 8 French and 3 other women. Although no doubt suffering from some of the same deficiencies as earlier police reports in this regard, it seems possible that the survey did reflect some of the broader trends at work in the demi-monde since it also noted how, for the first time, South African-born women constituted the majority of white prostitutes in the town.[152]

Johannesburg's western working-class suburbs of Fordsburg and Vrededorp had always known poverty. Indeed, Vrededorp had been especially set aside by the Kruger government in 1893 for those poverty-stricken burghers who had been pushed out of the Transvaal countryside during the accelerated capitalist development of the late nineteenth century. Before the South African War many of these Afrikaners had made a living from transport riding, brickmaking or cab driving. The arrival of the railways in the mid-1890s, the destruction caused by the war itself, the mechanisation of brickmaking and the introduction of the electric tramway in 1906, however, had all contributed to growing Afrikaner male unemployment in the post-war period. Then, as if these problems were somehow not enough for the poor to bear, the recession of 1904–5 deepened into the depression of 1906–8.

Many Afrikaner families attempted to compensate for this loss of male earnings by sending out their daughters to seek such work as was available in a town dominated by the mining industry. Avoiding the lonely and humiliating experience of having to enter domestic service in the affluent homes of their English overlords in the northern suburbs, these young women turned instead to the work to be found in the small factories, dress-making concerns, bottling plants and hand-laundries closer to their homes. These menial jobs, however, hardly offered a grand solution to the grinding poverty and bitter distress confronting these communities. Besides being badly paid – yielding cash wages of between 8 and 20 shillings per week – such employment also had the disadvantage of pushing young women into the company of older and more experienced male labourers. This contact in the work place in turn gave rise to a certain degree of promiscuous behaviour and casual prostitution which, in the hardest years of the depression, more readily gave way to a full-time career in vice.[153]

This entry of the daughters of the new proletariat into the vice market was reflected in the Criminal Investigation Department's immorality return for 1907 which, for the first time, noted the addresses of a large number of brothels in Fordsburg and Vrededorp. What some members of the police found even more distressing however, was the presence of a number of teenage prostitutes in the latter suburb who readily sold their services to the local Chinese storekeepers.[154] While the sexual exploits of Maggie van Niekerk, 'Trickey' Beukes and the two Potgieter sisters were certainly known to members of the local community, the English press made certain that the more sensational cases – such as that of the prostitute Susan Broderick who became Mrs Ho King of Vrededorp – were more widely proclaimed as illustrations of the 'yellow peril' in Johannesburg.[155]

But the depression did not confine itself to the white suburbs in the cities. It had an equally devastating effect on black homesteads in the country. Here the prevailing economic climate, drought, a rebellion in Natal and a new round of cattle disease combined to force a significant number of African women to abandon the rural areas in their search for a livelihood between 1906 and 1908. Many of those women who made their way to the Witwatersrand, however, soon discovered that the one segment of the labour market which they could possibly penetrate – domestic service – was already dominated by African men who had been forced out into migratory labour by poll tax a decade earlier. It was thus largely as a result of the lack of job opportunities that a number of these women either took to beer selling or drifted into casual prostitution.

Predictably, much of this new vice was to be found in Johannesburg's black working-class areas – the town and mine locations – and by 1910 the police estimated that there were between 200 and 300 black women who could be categorised as full-time prostitutes. While these women gained most of their customers from the compounds which housed the black miners on the outskirts of the town, a small number managed to establish themselves in the old inner vice district where they drew customers of all colours. In this latter case, as with Mrs Ho King in Vrededorp, the solvent of poverty and the colour blindness of the demi-monde occasionally gave rise to its own distinctive chemistry – as when 'Black Annie Miller' forged her relationship with the Jewish pimp Reuben Waltmann.[156]

In retrospect, then, it becomes clear that Johannesburg's underworld of sexual vice was transformed by two sets of supplementary forces between 1907 and 1910. First, the police seized the opportunity offered them by rebellious prostitutes in 1907–8 to embark on an extensive campaign of deportations which, over the following years, rid the town of the majority of its so-called 'foreign-born' pimps and prostitutes. This move not only broke the decade-old dominance of *organised* vice, it also contributed to the marked decline in importance of the inner city's 'traditional' red light district – 'Frenchfontein'. Secondly, a set of economic and social forces stemming from the increased tempo in the proletarianisation of local black and white women produced a growing contingent of South African-born prostitutes in the city after 1906. In effect this meant that as visible organised vice gave way in the city centre, it tended to be replaced by the less obtrusive activities of individual prostitutes working in the poorer working-class suburbs or ghettos of Johannesburg.

The interaction of these two sets of forces, however, did not bring about a state of equilibrium in the supply of prostitutes on the Witwatersrand since the deportation of 'undesirable aliens', and the 'voluntary' exodus which accompanied it, appear to have exceeded the number of native-born women entering the profession during this period. In addition, another more deeply rooted factor made an equally important contribution to the marked decline in white prostitution in Johannesburg in the years leading up to the First World War – a slackening in the demand for commercialised sexual services occasioned by the changing social structure of a maturing industrial capitalist system. Whereas in 1897 only 12 per cent of the employees on the Rand gold mines were married and had their families resident with them in the Transvaal, by 1902 this figure had risen to 20 per cent, and by 1912 it was up to 42 per cent.[157]

These quantitative and qualitative changes in the demi-monde produced reasonably predictable responses from the other parties usually most concerned about prostitution in the city – the police, the churches and the local middle classes. The police, content with having destroyed most of the organised vice in Johannesburg, were unwilling to countenance a further 'wholesale crusade' against prostitution and thus allowed individual prostitutes to ply their trade provided that they did not openly solicit business or knowingly spread venereal disease. The churches, for their part, tended not to grieve about what they did not see. With such remaining sexual vice as there was in the city neatly tucked away in the locations or the working-class suburbs, the clergymen and concerned citizens who had earlier been so vocal in their condemnation of Frenchfontein fell strangely silent. In the remaining years before the First World War one of the few things which the Witwatersrand Church Council could find to complain about in the field of public morality was 'the exhibition in shop windows of pictures of semi-nude women' – the faintest possible echo of the naughty nineties in Nugget street.[158]

By 1914, therefore, Johannesburg had reached the point where, after nearly a quarter of a century, the relationship between prostitutes and proletarians no longer yielded a significant profit margin for organised elements of the lumpenproletariat or their petty-bourgeois partners – the landlords and the liquor merchants. But if the gangsters and small businessmen lost money as a result of this decline, then the state and the ruling classes lost something less tangible – one of the means by which they had been able to attract, stabilise and control labour during the Rand's earliest phase of industrial development.

The role which prostitution plays in a developing capitalist system is thus a complex one, and one which spans the class spectrum of society at different historical moments. In the Transvaal this role was made even more complex by the fact that most of this development occurred during the era of imperialism – that is, at a time when the world capitalist system's boundaries were being extended particularly rapidly. This meant that in one small quarter of the Witwatersrand's principal mining town there were, at the turn of the century, the social deposits of economic waves which had washed not only the shores of Africa, but of North America, South America, Europe and Asia as well. 'There are more things in Johannesburg', warned the man from the *Standard and Diggers' News*, 'than are dreamt of in the ordinary man's philosophy'.

Conclusion

If prostitution is largely a function of 'fallen women', then it is interesting to note in what sequence and in what numbers women 'happened to fall' in the Transvaal between 1886 and 1914. For nearly eight years, from 1886 to 1894, prostitution in Johannesburg was dominated by hundreds of 'coloured' women drawn from the larger commercial centres of the Cape Colony. The presence of these women – which was encouraged by the local canteen keepers – could be attributed to their advanced proletarian status, repressive legislation to control prostitution in the Cape Colony and their geographical proximity to a new area of capitalist expansion in the subcontinent.

The more permanent developments which accompanied the establishment of the deep-level mines, and the arrival on the Witwatersrand of the railway from Lourenço Marques on the east coast, however, radically transformed this situation. The presence of a large proletarian army of mineworkers combined with the low cost of steamship travel from European ports to attract thousands of continental prostitutes to the Rand from 1895 onwards. These women were soon joined by hundreds of Russo-American pimps and prostitutes from New York City who had been equally quick to spot the business potential of the new Transvaal goldfields. Between 1895 and 1899 these highly professionalised vice merchants, in alliance with local landlords and property companies, transformed much of inner Johannesburg into the red light district of Frenchfontein.

This public explosion of sexual vice in the mining town soon earned the strong moral condemnation of parts of the salaried middle class in Johannesburg – in particular, sections of the press and the church. The agitation of these latter groups to have prostitution suppressed, however, did not meet with great success initially for at least two reasons. First, Johannesburg's capital-accumulating small businessmen, the canteen keepers and the landlords, exercised a powerful influence over local government with the result that the Sanitary Board sought ways to 'regulate' rather than eliminate sexual vice in the town. Secondly, senior members of Kruger's administration, drawing on the experience of government in Holland, were unconvinced that a policy of outright suppression would succeed in ridding the town of prostitution. It was thus only after the State President personally chose to sweep aside elements of opposition and hesitancy, and appoint a determined State Attorney, that serious attempts were made to eliminate public immorality on the Rand. From December 1898 until October 1899 J. C. Smuts and F. R. M. Cleaver made vigorous, and at least partly successful efforts to smash organised prostitution in Johannesburg.

These efforts by the state to erode Frenchfontein were soon supplemented by a more powerful 'voluntary' exodus when war broke out in late 1899, and thousands of pimps and prostitutes from Johannesburg joined the throng of refugees who made their way to the coastal cities. There, the former Transvaal vice merchants were soon joined by new arrivals from Europe who were equally keen to exploit the wartime business opportunities offered by the presence of thousands of British troops. It was thus largely as a result of this influx of up-country pimps and prostitutes that the Cape, Natal, and to a lesser extent the Orange River Colony, all found it necessary to promulgate new and more repressive immorality legislation between 1902 and 1903.

This battery of racist legislation – the forerunner of the modern South African Immorality Act – caused a considerable amount of movement between the various flesh markets of the subcontinent as vice merchants sought the most congenial socio-legal environment in which to conduct their business. It was during the course of this search that many pimps and prostitutes found their way back to the Transvaal where, to their delight, they discovered that the post-war authorities were marvellously understanding of Frenchfontein. Milner, anxious to re-attract white workers back to the reconstruction state as swiftly as possible and then stabilise and control the mining proletariat, deliberately ignored the vocal objections of the local middle class and turned a blind eye to the problem of prostitution. It was only after the direct and pointed intervention of Whitehall that the reconstruction government introduced its own post-war legislation to suppress prostitution, and even then the provisions of Ordinance 46 of 1903 were only selectively enforced.

Milner's successors, however, were more concerned about prostitution, and in particular about the problem of organised vice in Johannesburg. First under Selborne, and then under Het Volk, the state made vigorous and determined efforts to break the hold which Russo-Americans and European immigrants exercised over the demi-monde. From late 1907 onwards the more prominent pimps of Frenchfontein were forced to beat a constant retreat before a police attack which, during its initial stages at least, enjoyed the support of rebellious prostitutes. The successes of the state between 1907 and

1908 were further consolidated between 1909 and 1910 when the police – actively supported by the Colonial Secretary, J. C. Smuts – managed to deport hundreds of convicted pimps and prostitutes from the Transvaal under the Immigrants' Restriction Acts of 1907 and 1908.

If these post-reconstruction campaigns effectively destroyed the dominance of organised vice in Frenchfontein, they hardly eliminated prostitution from the streets of Johannesburg. For at the very moment that the notorious continental women were being forced to leave the country in large numbers, the Transvaal was starting to yield its own corps of white and black prostitutes drawn from the ranks of the emerging indigenous proletariat. As the inner city was freed of organised vice, so the peripheral working-class suburbs and ghettos started to produce their own problems of small-scale prostitution. The latter manifestations of vice, however, did not draw the same amount of attention that prostitution had done in earlier periods in the city's history.

The changing social structure of the Witwatersrand meant that the relationship between the inhabitants of the demi-monde and the mineworkers had declined to the point where it neither yielded significant profits for the petty bourgeoisie, nor presented the ruling class with an instrument of social control over the working class. Under capitalism, the marriage of prostitutes and proletarians is not without its own interested brokers.

Notes

1 R. J. Evans, 'Prostitution, State and Society in Imperial Germany', *Past and Present*, 70, February 1976, p. 106. Nowhere is this argument more clearly stated, however, than in the writings of Alexandra Kollontai. See, especially, 'Prostitution and Ways of Fighting It', in A. Kollontai, *Selected Writings* (London 1978), pp. 261–75.

2 *Ibid.*, pp. 114, 128. See also E. J. Bristow, *Vice and Vigilance* (London 1977), pp. 154–5.

3 Calculations derived from Johannesburg Sanitary Board, *Johannesburg Census 1896*, Part 1, 'Population in Detail'.

4 *Ibid*. See also, however, M. S. Appelgryn, 'Prostitusie in die Zuid Afrikaansche Republiek', *Codicillus*, 13, 1, May 1972, pp. 26–9; and L. Freed, *The Problem of European Prostitution in Johannesburg* (Johannesburg 1949), pp. 6–7.

5 J. A. Hobson, *The War in South Africa* (London 1900), pp. 9–10.

6 Editorial, *Standard and Diggers' News* (Hereafter: *S. & D.N.*), 15 February 1897.

7 Para. based on: M. S. Appelgryn, 'Prostitusie in die Zuid Afrikaansche Republiek', p. 26; G. N. van den Berg, 'Die Polisiediens in die Zuid Afrikaansche Republiek', Potchefstroomse Universiteit vir Christelike Hoër Onderwys (P.U.C.H.O.), D. Litt. thesis 1972, p. 660; and Johannesburg Public Library (J.P.L.), Johannesburg City Archive Collection (J.C.A.), Box 214, 'Constitution of the Johannesburg Sanitary Board', Articles 40 and 56.

8 Kimberley had, of course, experienced its greatest influx of prostitutes in the 1870s. For a fictionalised account, see, for example, J. R. Couper, *Mixed Humanity* (London, no date). Also note 9 below.

9 J.P.L., J.C.A., Box 200 A., *Reports and Extracts from Reports of Medical Practitioners, Kimberley, on the Necessity of Proclaiming the Contagious Diseases Act,*

No. 39 of 1885, in the District of Kimberley, as submitted to the Kimberley Borough Council, (1891), pp. 1–6. On the functioning of the C.D. Act in the Cape see also, for example, 'A Question of Health', *S. & D.N.*, 9 August 1899.

10 The presence of these Japanese prostitutes was noted in the *S. & D.N.* of 15 February 1894. It seems possible that these Japanese women were drawn to South Africa by the diamond boom in Kimberley – see K. Miyaoka, *Shofu-Kaigai Ryuroki* (Tokyo 1968), pp. 181–2. (This reference was very kindly made available to me by Dr D. C. S. Sissons of the Australian National University.) There were certainly still Japanese prostitutes active in Kimberley in the early twentieth century. See 'Japanese Interpreter Wanted', *The Star*, 20 March 1903.

11 For this reason there were frequent complaints about prostitutes living behind so-called 'coffee shops' and canteens. Usually, it was the black or coloured prostitutes who drew white criticism. See, for example, J.P.L., J.C.A., Box 209, F. van Bardelelien to Chairman and Members of the Sanitary Board, 28 September 1893; or the cases of coloured prostitutes Lizzie Abrahams and Emily Brewis who lived behind the 'Newcastle Bar' as reported in the *S. & D.N.* of 28 December 1894. Perhaps the best description of early bars and barmaids, however, is to be found in 'Johannesburg by Night', *S. & D.N.*, 24 July 1893.

12 For some of the linkages that developed between pubs and prostitutes in England see, for example, J. J. Tobias, *Crime and Industrial Society in the Nineteenth Century* (London 1972). For a list of some of the local bars at which prostitutes were most in evidence see the meeting of the Liquor Licensing Board as reported in *S. & D.N.*, 20 March 1895.

13 For an account of the early rise and influence of the W.L.V.A. see Chapter 2 above, 'Randlords and Rotgut', p. 57. For the canteen keepers' view of prostitution see editorials in the *Licensed Victuallers' Gazette* of 17 October 1896 and 20 February 1897. See also, 'An Impudent Petition', *S. & D.N.*, 5 March 1897.

14 See *S. & D.N.*, 14 July 1891, and J.C.A., Box 216A, Asst. Landdrost N. van den Berg to Sec. and Members of the Sanitary Board on 6 and 9 September 1893.

15 As one index of Australian immigration see the figures on the increase in the volume of mail between the two countries as reproduced in *S. & D.N.*, 18 May 1895. On Cornish miners and the impact of a declining price of tin, see, for example, *S. & D.N.*, 14 June 1895.

16 For an analysis of the impact of the German East African Shipping Line on the Transvaal liquor trade see Chapter 2 above, 'Randlords and Rotgut', especially pp. 54–5.

17 See R. Evans, 'Prostitution, State and Society in Imperial Germany', pp. 106–16.

18 See M. Gilbert, 'The Jews of Austria-Hungary, 1867–1914', in his *Jewish History Atlas* (London 1969), p. 77; E. Bristow, *Vice and Vigilance* (London 1977), pp. 177–81; and Irving Howe, *The Immigrant Jews of New York* (London 1976), pp. 96–101.

19 See W. T. Stead's *Satan's Invisible World Displayed – A Study of Greater New York* (London 1898). This work, in fact, constituted the 1898 edition of Stead's *Review of Reviews Annual*.

20 See Stead, *Satan's Invisible World*, pp. 37–42.

21 For the South American connection see Bristow, *Vice and Vigilance* (London 1977), pp. 181–6. There were, of course, also a small number of pimps and prostitutes who moved between South America and southern Africa. See, for example, the case of Robert and Esther Schoub in 'A Gambling Affair', *Johannesburg Times*, 18 August 1896.

22 'A Pimpsverein', *S. & D.N.*, 7 December 1898.

23 J.C.A., Box 244, 'List of Brothels in Johannesburg, 1895', and related correspondence.

24 J.C.A., Box 244, Bleksley to Docey, undated and related rough returns dated September and October 1896.

25 This para. based on the following items drawn from the *S. & D.N.*: Editorial, 3 July 1896; 'The Social Sore', 24 September 1896; 'Trades Carnival', 12 November 1896; and 'The Public Shame', 22 July 1897.

26 This para. based on the following items drawn from the *S. & D.N.*: Editorial, 3 July 1896; 'The Social Sore', 24 September 1896; 'Public Indecency', 15 October 1896; and 'Disgusted' to the Editor, 11 December 1896. See also 'The Social Evil', 1 October 1898.

27 Para. based on: 'A Little Private "Hell"', *S. & D.N.*, 18 August 1896; 'The Social Evil', *The Critic*, 23 October 1896; and 'Notice of Removal' and 'A Relief' in *S. & D.N.* of 21 October 1898. For some continuities in this regard see also, L. Freed, *The Problem of European Prostitution in Johannesburg*, p. 9.

28 See 'The Public Shame', *S. & D.N.*, 22 July 1897. Also, interview with Mr S. R. Naidoo at Lenasia on 19 March 1977, and interview with Mr Mchwaneki Sibiya at Eshowe, 27 April 1977. For a similar rickshaw linkage operating in Natal see *South African Native Affairs Commission 1903–5*, Vol. 3, para. 21,938, p. 292, evidence of C. W. B. Scott.

29 See 'A Reign of Terror' and 'A Pimpsverein' in the *S. & D.N.* of 13 July 1897 and 7 December 1898. See also the report in the *S. & D.N.* of 2 November 1899. The term 'speculator' for pimps and other criminals appears to originate in New York gangland activity. See Jacob A. Riis, *How the Other Half Lives* (New York 1971), p. 180. At least some of the Bowery gangsters who came to Johannesburg brought the appellation 'speculator' with them. See, for example, the 'profession' of David Krakower as cited in Transvaal Archives Depot (T.A.D.), Pretoria, Z.A.R. Criminal Cases, ZTPD 3/115, State *vs* Joe Silver, Sam Stein and others.

30 See, amongst other references in the *S. & D.N.*, the following items: 'The Case of Lemaire', 8 October 1897; 'A Gambling Raid', 24 February 1898; 'Guardians of Girls', 6 October 1898; and 'Satan's World', 5 November 1898. Also, T.A.D., Jhb. Criminal Landdrost's Papers, Vol. 1940, Leon Lemaire to Messrs Schutte, van den Berg and Dr Krause, 5 October 1899.

31 See, for example, 'A Gambling Raid', *S. & D.N.*, 24 February 1898. For the origin and use of the name 'Louis' for German pimps see R. J. Evans, 'The Women's Movement in Germany', D. Phil. thesis, University of Oxford, 1972, p. 41.

32 See, for example, the case of Johan Janssen as recounted in the *S. & D.N.* of 16 July 1898.

33 For a selection of such cases see the following items drawn from the *S. & D.N.*: 'A Wanton's Bully', 28 September 1896; 'Our Demi-Monde', 7 October 1896; 'A Dusky Don Juan', 21 October 1896; 'A Score of Them', 17 November 1896; and 'The Nigger as "Macquerot"' (*sic*), 17 November 1896.

34 See, for example, the relationship between 'Jacob' and Louise Roger, a 47 year old prostitute from Burgundy as recounted in the following items drawn from the *S. & D.N.*: 'The Purity Crusade', 10 September 1897; 'Under the Ontucht Law', 11 September 1897; 'Black and White', 20 October 1897; and 'A Judge's Crusade', 20 October 1897.

35 J.P.L., J.C.A., Box 216, Medical Officer of Health, 'Report on Smallpox Inspection', 1 January 1893; and J.C.A., Box 218, District Surgeon's Report to Chairman and Members of the Sanitary Board, October 1894.

36 In 1895, Dr Liebaert was involved in attempts to legalise prostitution on the Witwatersrand. See, T.A.D., Z.A.R., S.S. Vol. 5141 (1895). For his work amongst local prostitutes see, for example, the account in the *S. & D.N.* of 15 September 1896. For an example of Dr Villettis' work, see the certificate issued to 'Miss Lily' of 'Silvio Villa' in T.A.D., Z.A.R., Jhb. Landdrost, Vol. 1852 (1898), the State *vs* Auguste Roger.

37 See, for example, J.P.L., J.C.A., Box 200A, A. H. Bleksley, Sanitary Superintendent, to Chairman and Committee, Sanitary Board, 31 January 1895; and J.C.A., Box 221, Health Inspector's Annual Report for 1895.

38 'The Social Sore', *S. & D.N.*, 24 September 1896.

39 In 1897 a three-bedroomed house used as a brothel in central Johannesburg could fetch a rent of up to £40 per calendar month – a sum well in excess of a white miner's wages. See, R. W. Hodges to Editor, *S. & D.N.*, 12 May 1897. This process of expulsion appears to have been particularly marked in late 1896. For a selection of complaints see: 'Householder' to Editor, *Johannesburg Times*, 10 August 1896; and 'An Englishman' to Editor, *S. & D.N.*, 26 September 1896.

40 *The Critic*, 23 October 1896. See also the comment of the Chief of Police in *S. & D.N.*, 1 October 1898.

41 Most of this evidence derives from Bleksley's censuses of 1895 and 1896 (see notes 23 and 24 above), and then tracing these addresses through the property registers in the Rand Registrar of Townships Office, Johannesburg. On the *Banque Française*, however, see also 'Great Ontucht Plot', *S. & D.N.*, 15 February 1899, and on the Rand Investment Co. see T.A.D., Z.A.R., Jhb. Landdrost's Collection. Vol. 1940, W. A. Miller (Sec.) to Public Prosecutor, Johannesburg, 22 March 1899.

42 See 'An Impudent Petition', *S. & D.N.*, 5 March 1897. The Volksraad in turn took great care when it debated this legislation. See 'The Public Shame', *S. & D.N.*, 1 July 1897. The first landlord to be prosecuted, one Charles Rittmann, appeared in court in early 1899, see 'The Morality Law', *S. & D.N.*, 10 January 1899.

43 Para. based on: T.A.D., S.S., Vol. 5141, File 3541/95. See also, J.P.L., J.C.A., Box 244, 'Notes Re. Regulations on Houses of Ill-Fame'.

44 This para. based on: J.P.L., J.C.A., Box 224, 'Notes Re. Houses of Ill-Fame'; and J.P.L., J.C.A., Box 221, Protestant Ministers' Assoc. of Johannesburg to Members of the Jhb. Sanitary Committee, 18 September 1895. For some of the background to Josephine Butler and her thinking see Bristow, *Vice and Vigilance*, pp. 4–6, 75–93.

45 Para. based on: J.P.L., J.C.A., Box 222, Carl von Brandis and others to Chairman and Members of the Jhb. Sanitary Committee, 8 April 1896; and T.A.D., S.S., Vol 5141, File 12731/95. See also, M. S. Appelgryn, 'Prostitusie in die Zuid Afrikaansche Republiek', pp. 26–7.

46 Para. based on the following items drawn from the *S. & D.N.*: 'Four Sinful Sisters', 2 October 1895; 'The Social Sore', 24 September 1896; and 'The Social Crusade', 19 November 1896.

47 J.P.L., J.C.A., Box 244, Members of the Deputation to Chairman and Members of the Jhb. Sanitary Committee, 7 October 1896.

48 *Ibid.* See also, 'The Social Sore', *S. & D.N.*, 8 October 1896.

49 *Ibid.*

50 Para. based on the two following items which appeared in the *S. & D.N.*, 'The Social Sore', 10 October 1896; and 'The Social Sore – Regulations Not Approved', 14 October 1896. It is significant that on this occasion too it was not Bleksley – but senior politicians on the Sanitary Board – who got involved in the re-drafting process. See J.P.L., J.C.A., Box 244, E. Hancock and others to Chairman and Members of the Sanitary Committee, 14 October 1896.

51 See T.A.D., S.S., Vol. 5141 (1895), P.J.G. Meiring (Chairman) and N. McCulloch (Sec.) to His Honour and the Executive Committee, 24 October 1896. On the origin of the White Cross League see Bristow, *Vice and Vigilance*, pp. 94–101. It was also no doubt the old but largely informal linkages between the White Cross movement and the Y.M.C.A. which partly accounted for McCulloch's interest, involvement and inspiration. See Bristow, *Vice and*

Vigilance, p. 136.

52 The Rev. C. Spoelstra, *Delicate Matters – Open Letter addressed to Dr F. V. Engelenberg* (Johannesburg, December 1896).

53 'The Public Morals', *S. & D.N.*, 15 February 1897.

54 This para. based on items in *S. & D.N.*, 9 March 1897, *Johannesburg Weekly Times*, 13 March 1897, and the *Cape Times*, 19 March 1897. The arrival of these women in Cape Town – and to a lesser extent in Durban – naturally aroused some anxiety in the coastal cities. See, for example, 'Migrated Maidens' or 'In Adderley Street', in *S. & D.N.*, 17 and 20 March 1897.

55 Para. based on the following items drawn from the *S. & D.N.*: 'Fun in Fox Street', 18 August 1896; 'A Reign of Terror', 13 July 1897; 'Police and Morals', 21 September 1897; 'The Social Ulcer', 20 November 1897; 'In Commissioner Street – Brave Show of Revolvers', 8 February 1898; and 'Blackguard Syndicates', 30 September 1898.

56 Crime reporters found it noteworthy that whenever members of the Morality Squad appeared in court they invariably entered the box 'in collarless and generally unkempt condition suggestive of slovenliness', *Johannesburg Times*, 11 June 1898. Since the majority of these policemen earned only £14 per month in a notoriously expensive city this condition was more likely to be a function of poverty than lack of self-respect. See especially Landdrost van den Berg's remarks in 'The Ontucht Plot', *S. & D.N.*, 17 February 1899.

57 See, for example, the case of Sarah Segal in 'A Pimpsverein', in *S. & D.N.*, 7 December 1898.

58 Joseph Silver is the subject of a forthcoming biography which the author is currently researching. An idea of the man and some of his Johannesburg activities, however, can be gained from some of the following items drawn from the *S. & D.N.*: 'A Pimpsverein', 7 December 1898; 'Ontucht Raid', 10 January 1899; 'The Seamy Side', 11 January 1899; 'The Great Ontucht Plot', 2 February 1899; 'Ontucht Freemasonry', 9 February 1899; and 'When Police Fall Out', 16 February 1899.

59 See especially in the *S. & D.N.*: 'A Pimpsverein', 7 December 1898, and 'Ontucht Freemasonry', 7 February 1899.

60 On Salus Budner alias Julius Budner alias Joe Gold, see, amongst others, the following items drawn from the *S. & D.N.*: 'A Pimpsverein', 7 December 1898; 'Great Ontucht Plot', 7 February 1899; 'Ontucht Freemasonry', 7 February 1899; and 'The Morality Law', 22 February 1899.

61 *Ibid*.

62 See, in *S. & D.N.*, 'A Pimpsverein', 7 December 1898; and 'Great Ontucht Plot', 15 February 1899.

63 See, for example, the Editorial in the *S. & D.N.*, 15 October 1896: 'It is a notorious fact that women make the public parks a hunting ground to supply houses of ill-fame, and young girls of tender age are continually approached by procuresses who hold out tempting visions of an immoral life'. See also, Vol. 2, Chapter 1, 'The Witches of Suburbia', pp. 24–5.

64 See, for example, the following items drawn from the *S. & D.N.*: 'Most Moral Cape Town', 10 November 1896; 'Rand Women Traps', 12 July 1897; and 'Saintly Stellenbosch', 18 November 1897.

65 Amongst others, see for example, the following items drawn from the *S. & D.N.*: 'An Infamous Traffic', 27 April 1897; 'Rand Women Traps', 12 July 1897; 'A Horrible Trade', 1 October 1897; 'Decoyed to the Rand', 17 November 1897; and 'The Police Service', 12 November 1898.

66 The entire Kreslo story was recounted, in some detail, in 'Decoyed into Sin' in the *S. & D.N.*, 7 June 1899. Unfortunately the court records pertaining to the Levin/Levinsohn trial have thus far proved to be most elusive.

67 The details surrounding these events will, hopefully, eventually be recounted in Silver's biography. Some of the relevant information, however, can be gained from the following entries which appeared in the 'Police' column of the London *Times*: 8 February 1898, 17 February 1898, 25 February 1898, and 18 March 1898. See also, however, the entry under the 'Central Criminal Court', *The Times*, 2 April 1898.

68 For some sources on French pimps in Johannesburg, see note 30.

69 On Bertha Hermann's role in New York City see W. T. Stead, *Satan's Invisible World Displayed*, pp. 126–9. In Johannesburg see: T.A.D., Z.A.R., Staatsprokureur, Gehieme Minutes. Vol. 193, File 1197/98, Statement by F. E. T. Krause, 5 November 1898. See also, in *S. & D.N.*, '"Satan's World"', 5 November 1898, and 'The Ontucht Law', 24 November 1898.

70 On French 'white slavery' activities on the Rand see: T.A.D., Z.A.R., Staatsprokureur, Gehieme Minutes, Vol. 193, File 1197/98, Statement by Detective J. J. Donovan, 4 November 1898. The clearest and most detailed example which we have of this type of French operation, however, comes from the Cape in 1901. See the Preliminary Examination of Joseph Davis (Russian 'Artist') and Marguerite de Thiesse ('modiste'), appearing on a charge of procuring Antoinette and Julienne Jacqmin for immoral purposes. Cape Archives Depot, Attorney General's Papers, Vol. 3118, Proceedings of the Supreme Court.

71 Para. based on: 'Our Erring Sisters', *S. & D.N.*, 27 September 1895; 'The Public Morals', *S. & D.N.*, 31 January 1898; T.A.D., Jhb. Landdrost, Vol. 1939, Det. A. Burchardt to Chief Detective P. de Villiers, 17 August 1899; and T.A.D., Law Dept., Attorney General File 172/06, Chief Det. Inspector T. E. Mavrogordato to the Commissioner of Police, 12 February 1906.

72 See the statements of Georgette Carpentier, Maria Buffans (signature unclear) and Yvette Vervat in T.A.D., Jhb. Landdrost, Vol. 1852, Criminal Cases, State *vs* August(e) Roger, January 1898.

73 *Ibid*. See reports filed by Detectives E. H. Maher and P. J. van der Heever over the two-week period.

74 See 'The Morality Law', *S. & D.N.*, 16 July 1898.

75 See, for example, either 'Fordsburg Items' or 'Humbugged by a Harlot' in the *S. & D.N.* of 25 October 1895 or 28 January 1896 respectively. The classic dilemma of the brothel customer in these circumstances, however, is well illustrated in the anonymous letter of 'A.G.B.' to the Head of the Johannesburg Detective Force, 14 June 1896 in T.A.D., Jhb. Landdrost's Papers, Vol 502, Speurpolisie, Inkomende Stukke. See also, 'Rand Morality Law', *S. & D.N.*, 5 August 1898.

76 'Scene at the Station', *S. & D.N.*, 18 April 1898.

77 Krause felt that prostitution was 'a necessary evil which, while it could not be eliminated, could certainly be controlled'. See N. van den Berg, 'Die Polisiediens in die Zuid Afrikaansche Republiek', p. 661. Drs Coster and van Leeuwens' influence on Krause are clear from T.A.D., Z.A.R., State Attorney, Secret Minutes, Vol. 193, File 1197/98. In later years Krause apparently continued to hold strong opinions about prostitution. In 1908, for example, while a Member of Parliament, Krause chose to defend a notorious ex- 'American Club' pimp by the name of H. Epstein against charges laid under the Morality Act. His successful defence of Epstein drew stinging criticism to Krause's head and it seems unlikely that financial gain would have been his sole motive for accepting this brief. See 'The Pimp H. Epstein' in the *South African Pink' Un*, 27 June 1908; and 'What the Magistrate Said', *Transvaal Critic*, 24 July 1908.

78 See 'The Ontucht Law', *S. & D.N.*, 24 November 1898.

79 In his defence of some of the inhabitants of 'Sylvio Villa' in October 1895, for example, Attorney J. J. Raaf told the Magistrate that 'these people were a sort of safety valve, especially in a mining community such as Johannesburg', and that if

these activities were stopped entirely 'it would open the way to all manner of indecent assaults and bestial crimes'. 'Four Sinful Sisters', *S. & D.N.*, 2 October 1895.

80 This finding naturally produced considerable controversy. See the following central pieces in the *S. & D.N.*: 'Black and White', 20 October 1897; 'A Judge's Crusade', 20 October 1897; and 'The Kafir's Enemies', 21 October 1897.

81 On the operation of the Morality Law during this period see especially 'A Foul Tammany' and 'The Public Service' – editorials in the *S. & D.N.* on 8 October and 12 November 1898 respectively. For an overview of changes in the Morality Squad over this period see 'The Ontucht Law', *S. & D.N.*, 24 November 1898. On Donovan's accusations against Krause (allegations which in part involved Bertha Hermann), see T.A.D., Z.A.R., S.P., Gehieme Minutes, Vol. 193, File 1197/98, statements by Donovan, Krause and others.

82 Some of the more important editorials in the *S. & D.N.* during this campaign included: 'A Dead Letter', 29 April 1897; 'The Public Shame', 1 July 1897; 'A Reign of Terror', 13 July 1897; 'Police and Morals', 21 September 1897; 'Blackguard Syndicates', 30 September 1898; and 'The Social Evil', 1 October 1898.

83 'The Morality Law', *S. & D.N.*, 28 September 1898.

84 See 'The Morality Law', *S. & D.N.*, 14 October 1898; and *Der Locale Wetten der Zuid Afrikaansche Republiek (1899)*, pp. 304–6.

85 See especially 'The Morality Law', *S. & D.N.*, 15 October 1898.

86 Para. based on: 'The Public Shame', *S. & D.N.*, 15 October 1898; T.A.D., Z.A.R., S.P., Gehieme Minutes, Vol. 193, File 1197/98; and *A Young South African – A Memoir of Ferrar Reginald Mostyn Cleaver, Advocate and Veldcornet* (Johannesburg 1913), edited by 'His Mother'.

87 *A Young South African*, pp. 2–3, 19. For Krause's friendship with Broeksma see also, E. J. Potgieter (ed.), *Standard Encyclopaedia of Southern Africa*, Vol. 6 (Cape Town 1972), p. 457.

88 *A Young South African*, pp. 2–3, 19–22. For an example of Skirving's work see 'The Great Ontucht Plot', *S. & D.N.*, 15 February 1899. For Burchardt's contribution see, for example, the following items in the *S. & D.N.*: 'When Police Fall Out', 16 February 1899, and 'The Ontucht Plot', 17 February 1899.

89 This para. based on the following items drawn from the *S. & D.N.*: 'A Pimpsverein', 7 December 1898, and 'The Great Ontucht Plot', 2 February 1899. Note that in these cases Krakower usually appears under the name 'Dave Davis' – his underworld alias.

90 Para. based on a study of the following items in the *S. & D.N.*: 'A Pimpsverein', 7 December 1898, and 'The Morality Law', 30 December 1898. Also T.A.D., Z.A.R., Jhb. Landdrost's Collection, Vol. 1827, State *vs* Dave Davis, Henry Rosenchild and Morris Rosenberg. None of this, of course, escaped Cleaver who noted: 'Here was a pretty mess! Crime rampant, every source of reaching it closed; the very forces of the State assisting it!' *A Young South African*, p. 21.

91 *Ibid.* See also 'The Seamy Side – Shuttlecocked' and 'The Seamy Side' in the *S. & D.N.* of 9 and 14 December 1898 respectively.

92 Joseph Silver to the Editor, *S. & D.N.*, 10 December 1898.

93 See 'The Morality Law – Charge of Procuration', *S. & D.N.*, 30 December 1898. Cleaver's tactics are perhaps best described by himself: 'To make a long story short, there occurred a split in the ranks of the enemy. Of this I made such use that within a month of the day I started on the job I had packed the Head-centre of the New York pimps in gaol'. *A Young South African*. p. 22.

94 This para. based on a study of the following items in the *S. & D.N.*: 'The Seamy Side', 14 December 1898; 'Ontucht Raid', 10 January 1899; 'The Seamy Side', 11 January 1899; 'Brewing on Morality Intriguers', 25 January 1899; and 'When

Police Fall Out', 16 February 1899. See also, *A Young South African*. p. 23.

95 'Ontucht Raid – Sensational Arrests', *S. & D.N.*, 10 January 1899, and 'The Seamy Side', 11 January 1899. See also, T.A.D., Z.A.R., Criminal Cases, Z.T.P.D. 3/115, State *vs* Joe Silver and Sam Stein; and State *vs* Jenny Stein and others.

96 This picture of Cleaver's actions is built up from a series of telegrams sent by the Second Public Prosecutor to J. C. Smuts and contained in T.A.D., Z.A.R., S.P., Vol. 195, File 244/99, File 251/99, File 307/99 and File 313/99. See also, however, 'The Seamy Side', *S. & D.N.*, 11 January 1899, and *A Young South African*, p. 23.

97 See 'The Great Ontucht Plot' and 'The Morality Law' in *S. & D.N.* of 7 and 22 February 1899.

98 *Ibid.* See also, *A Young South African*, pp. 3–23.

99 For Silver's cleverly devised letter – which attempted to exploit the differences between Cleaver and Krause, see T.A.D., Z.A.R., Jhb. Landdrost's Collection, Vol. 1720, J. Silver and S. Stein to The Hon. Mr Dietzch. See also the following in the *S. & D.N.*: 'Great Ontucht Plot', 7 February 1899; and 'Great Ontucht Plot', 15 February 1899.

100 See the following items in the *S. & D.N.*: 'Great Ontucht Plot', 15 February 1899; 'When Police Fall Out', 16 February 1899; 'The Ontucht Plot', 17 February 1899; 'The Ontucht Scandal', 18 February 1899; and 'Perjury Epidemic', 23 March 1899. On Silver, Stein and Lizzie Josephs' attitudes see the letter cited in note 99 above, and 'A Dynasty Overthrown', *S. & D.N.*, 6 April 1899.

101 See T.A.D., Z.A.R., Criminal Cases, Z.T.P.D., 3/115, State *vs* Joe Silver, Sam Stein and others. See also, *A Young South African*. p. 23.

102 See T.A.D., Z.A.R., Johannesburg Landdrost's Archive, Vol. 1824, State *vs* Joe Silver, 13–20 September 1899. See also the small item reported in the *S. & D.N.*, 22 September 1899. The name given in certain black prison gangs to the officer responsible for procuring young African boys for homosexual relationships is 'MaSilver'. See Vol. 2, Chapter 4, 'The Regiment of the Hills', p. 187.

103 *S. & D.N.*, 27 September 1899; and allegations made by the Cape Town Public Prosecutor in 'Morality Law', *The Argus*, 23 September 1904.

104 *A Young South African*, p. 3, and 'The Second Raad', *S. & D.N.*, 24 August 1899.

105 *S. & D.N.*, 2 November 1899. See also T.A.D., Johannesburg Landdrost's Archive, Vol. 1940, Leon Lemaire to Messrs Schutte, van den Berg and Dr Krause, 5 October 1899.

106 For a brief summary see 'A Question of Health', *S. & D.N.*, 9 August 1899.

107 Some of this is reflected in Robin Hallett's 'Policemen, Pimps and Prostitutes – Public Morality and Police Corruption: Cape Town, 1902–1904'. Unpublished paper presented to the History Workshop Conference, University of the Witwatersrand, Johannesburg, 2–7 February 1978.

108 On H. J. Dempers see 'Social Purity League' and 'The Morality Act' in *The Star*, 18 July and 28 August 1903. Dempers and his partner in law, van Ryneveld, also had certain professional dealings with Joseph Silver in relation to the management of the latter's 'properties'. See Cape Archives Depot, A. G. 1531/12984, State *vs* Joe Lees alias Joe Silver, 30 August 1904, p. 20. On the other events recounted in this paragraph see Hallett, 'Policemen, Pimps and Prostitutes', and Cape Archives Depot, A.G. Vol. 1902, Acting Commissioner of Police, District 3, Annual Report for 1901.

109 Cited in Hallett, 'Policemen, Pimps and Prostitutes', p. 4.

110 Hallett, 'Policemen, Pimps and Prostitutes', p. 5. For a lengthy and detailed account of the passage of the 'Morality Act', however, see 'Social Reform' and 'Suppression of Vice', in the *Diamond Fields' Advertiser*, 13 and 22 October 1902.

111 Elements of the Silver saga are to be found in the following items reported in the *Bloemfontein Post*: 'The Burglary', 26 November 1902; 'The Morality Muddle', 19

January 1903; 'The Reign of Terror', 19 January 1903; and 'Joe Silver Convicted', 21 January 1903. See also, *Laws of the Orange River Colony 1900–1906*, Ordinance 11 of 1903, pp. 686–92. For movement to Johannesburg see, for example, the travels of Max Harris as recounted in Cape Archives Depot, Cape Supreme Court, Criminal Records, September–October 1904, evidence of M. Harris, p. 28.

112 On the 1897 influx see note 54 above. Alexander's evidence on this matter was given before the *South African Native Affairs Commission, 1903–05*, Vol. III, p. 647, para. 28,285. On Pietermaritzburg see *ibid.*, evidence of C. W. B. Scott (Solicitor), p. 292, para. 21,937; and various small items as reported in *Ipepa lo Hlanga*, 24 May 1901.

113 Natal Archives Depot, Pietermaritzburg, Durban Corporation Collection (uncatalogued), Police Report Book No. 6. See reports by R. C. Alexander dated 6 July 1900; 31 July 1900; 4 October 1900; 6 January 1902; 5 January 1903; and 6 April 1903. See also, 'The Immorality Act – Prosecution in Durban', *The Star*, 9 October 1903.

114 *South African Native Affairs Commission 1903–05*, Vol. III, evidence of J. L. Hulett (p. 164, para. 20,174); R. C. Alexander (p. 647, para. 28,285), and C. W. B. Scott (p. 292, para. 21,937). See especially, however, T.A.D., Colonial Secretary, Vol. 139, S. O. Samuelson, Under-Sec. for Native Affairs to Sec. for Native Affairs Natal, 13 June 1902.

115 On 'French' prostitutes catering for the troops see T.A.D., South African Constabulary (S.A.C.), Vol. 22, File 8/67, Major T. E. Mavrogordato to Commissioner of Police, 11 July 1908. Baden-Powell was sufficiently concerned about the men of the S.A.C.'s morals that he arranged for the British White Cross Society to forward them a special consignment of reading in the hope that it would help keep them chaste. See Bristow, *Vice and Vigilance*, p. 138.

116 On the 'Immorality Trust', see T.A.D., Law Dept., A.G. File 172/06, E. H. Showers, Commissioner of Police, to Sec. Law Dept., 2 May 1905; T.A.D., S.A.C., Vol. 22, File 8/62, Chief Det. Inspector to Commissioner of Police, 6 July 1908; and T.A.D., Law Dept., A.G. 172/06, 'Copy of Minute dated 8 May 1906 by Acting Chief Detective Inspector, C.I.D., to Commissioner of Police, Johannesburg'. On others named, see T.A.D., S.A.C., Vol. 23, File 8/96 (1908), 'C.I.D. – List of persons who habitually take houses for brothels'. Compare this 1908 C.I.D. list with the original membership of the 'American Club' as reproduced in '*Ontucht* Freemasonry', *S. & D.N.*, 7 February 1899.

117 See G. K. Turner, 'The Daughters of the Poor', pp. 45–61. See also, however, G. J. Kneeland, *Commercialised Prostitution in New York City* (New York 1913), p. 80.

118 For the origins of the N.Y. Independent Benevolent Association see G. K. Turner, 'The Daughters of the Poor', p. 48. For the connection of some of its members with the Johannesburg underworld – notably Max and Louis Souvina and P. Jacobs – see *New York World*, 22 December 1912. (I am indebted to Ed Bristow for this reference.) On the Souvina brothers' activities in Johannesburg, see T.A.D., Law Dept., A.G. File 172/06, Commissioner of Police to Sec., Law Dept., 25 January 1906. There is also an account of the Souvina brothers' prior and subsequent activities in G. J. Kneeland's *Commercialised Prostitution in New York City*, pp. 82–4.

119 For the more general background to Parisian prostitution and sexuality during this period, see T. Zeldin, *France, 1848–1945*, Vol. I, *Ambition, Love and Politics* (Oxford 1973), especially pp. 305–14. On Paris as a 'white slave' entrepôt, see G. K. Turner, 'The Daughters of the Poor', p. 46. On the different nationalities of women 'exported' to South Africa during this period see also A. Flexner, *Prostitution in Europe* (New York 1914), p. 93. For similar reports at the South African end during this post-war period, see L. Freed, *The Problem of European*

Prostitution in Johannesburg, p. 9.

120 National Archives of the United States of America (N.A. of U.S.A.), Washington, D.C., Dept. of Commerce and Labour, Bureau of Immigration and Naturalization, File 1-G, 52484, 'Braun European Reports', October 1909. (Once again I am indebted to Ed Bristow for drawing this source to my attention.)

121 On le Cuirassier in Cape Town, see Cape Archives Depot, Cape Supreme Court, Criminal Records, May–July 1904, Rex *vs* Thor Osberg, evidence of Max Harris, p. 16, and Valentine Dufis, pp. 23–24. Also Cape Archives Depot, Cape Supreme Court, Criminal Records, September–October 1904, Rex *vs* Charteris, evidence of Alexander Clark, p. 42.

122 In 1908 le Cuirassier was in Vladivostok. See N.A. of U.S.A., Dept. of Commerce and Labour, File 1-G, 52484, 'Braun European Reports', October 1909. One of Freed's informants on the early history of Johannesburg prostitution claimed that 'Japanese prostitutes were also imported in order to meet the requirements of the Chinese labourers who were employed on the mines'. L. Freed, *The Problem of European Prostitution in Johannesburg*, p. 9.

123 G. K. Turner, 'The Daughters of the Poor', p. 48. Even before the Russo-Japanese War, however, there were some pimps turning up in local circles who had Chinese experience – notably one 'James Lee', known in the local trade as 'Japanese Hersch'. For the sketch of 'Lee', and an account of an assault on him by Joe Silver, see 'Joe Silver Again', and 'Lee's Story – He comes from Pekin', in *Bloemfontein Post*, 23 January 1903. It seems possible that 'Lee' – like Silver – might have fled Kimberley when the Cape Morality Act came into force in late 1902. If so, there were certainly Japanese prostitutes left behind in Kimberley. See 'Japanese Interpreter Wanted', *The Star*, 20 March 1903.

124 On these earlier groups and the origin of the term *Karayuki-San*, see note 10 above. For the service which these Japanese ladies provided Chinese miners on the Rand, see T.A.D., Law Dept., A.G. Vol. 367, Enquiries and Inquests 1906–1909, 'Confidential Enquiry into alleged unnatural practices amongst Chinese Coolies', September 1906, evidence of C. D. Stewart given on 10 September 1906. (I am indebted to Peter Richardson for making this source available to me.)

125 Such as denying vice traffickers orthodox burial rights within the community. On this and other actions taken by Hertz, see unpublished manuscripts by G. Saron, entitled 'The Communal Scene, Pathology: The White Slave Trade and Liquor Offences', and '"The Morality Question" in South Africa'. These essays, which Mr Saron very kindly made available to me, will be incorporated in his forthcoming history of South African Jewry.

126 T.A.D., C.S., Vol. 595, Joseph H. Hertz to Private Secretary, Lord Milner, 25 January 1902, with appended petition.

127 T.A.D., C.S., Vol. 595, Assistant Private Secretary to J. T. Lloyd, 28 February 1902.

128 The C.I.D., of course, did not fail to point out this lack of cooperation during the subsequent months. See T.A.D., Law Dept., A.G. File 172/06, 'Extract from Annual Report, C.I.D., 1904/05'.

129 Para. based on: T.A.D., C.S., Vol. 139, Governor (Natal) to Acting Prime Minister (Natal), 24 May 1902; and Under-Secretary for Native Affairs (Natal) to Sec. for Native Affairs, 13 June 1902. Also T.A.D., C.S., Vol. 151, Attorney General to Lieutenant Governor, 25 September 1902.

130 T.A.D., C.S., Vol. 151, A.G. No. 12640, Attorney General to His Excellency, The Lieutenant Governor, 25 September 1902.

131 T.A.D., L.T.G., Vol. 1, File No. 2, Lieutenant Governor to His Excellency, The Governor of Natal, 24 October 1902. It is possible, however, that these agitations did produce some minor concessions from Milner and Solomon, since a few weeks later 'barmaids' were banned in Johannesburg. See 'The Banning of the Barmaid',

Diamond Fields' Advertiser, 10 November 1902 and the small item reported in *The Star*, 15 November 1902.

132 T.A.D., C.S., Vol. 595, Onslow to Governor, 7 February 1903.

133 This para. based on: T.A.D., L.T.G., Vol. 1, File No. 2, Will Gordon Sprigg (Y.M.C.A.), Secretary to the 'Morality Committee', to His Excellency, Hon. Sir Arthur Lawley, 16 March 1903; and *ibid.*, Will Gordon Sprigg to The Town Clerk, Johannesburg, 26 March 1903. See also, 'The Evening Sitting – Immorality Draft Ordinance', *The Star*, 23 June 1903; and *Ordinances of the Transvaal 1903*, pp. 315–24.

134 See especially T.A.D., L.T.G., Vol. 1, File No. 2, Will Gordon Sprigg to The Town Clerk, Johannesburg, 26 March 1903.

135 See *South African Native Affairs Commission 1903–05*, Vol. IV, Evidence of T. E. Mavrogordato (C.I.D.), p. 863, para. 44,514; and T.A.D., S.N.A., N.A. 776/06, J. S. Marwick to Secretary for Native Affairs, 28 February 1906.

136 G. J. Kneeland, *Commercialised Prostitution in New York City* (New York 1913), p. 80.

137 Showers' views are spelt out in some detail in T.A.D., Law Dept., A.G. File 172/06, Commissioner of Police to Sec. to the Law Dept., 2 May 1905.

138 Para. based on: T.A.D., Law Dept., A.G. File 172/06, E. H. Showers to Sec. to the Law Dept., 25 January 1906, appended 'Copy of Report from Mr Mavrogordato re. Immorality'; L. Freed, *The Problem of European Prostitution in Johannesburg* p. 10; G. K. Turner, 'The Daughters of the Poor', p. 48; and G. J. Kneeland, *Commercialised Prostitution in New York City*, pp. 80, 83.

139 Para. based on the following items drawn from *The Star*: 'Raising the Fallen', 25 July 1904; 'Raising the Fallen', 4 February 1905; 'Our Fallen Sisters', 19 October 1907; 'Immorality at Pretoria', 13 November 1908; 'House of Mercy', 7 April 1909; and 'Social Purity', 24 March 1914. On the background to such 'rescue homes' as they developed in Britain during the Victorian era see Bristow, *Vice and Vigilance*, pp. 66–78.

140 This para. based on the following letters in T.A.D., Law Dept., A.G. File 172/06: H. Ternant, Sec. to the Law Dept., to Commissioner of Police, 12 January 1906; Commissioner of Police to Sec. to the Law Dept., 25 January 1906; Commissioner of Police to Sir Richard Solomon, 27 January 1906; and Commissioner of Police to Sec. to the Law Dept., 12 June 1906.

141 See T.A.D., Law Dept., A.G. File 172/06, 'Copy of Minute dated 8 May 1906 addressed by the Acting Chief Detective Inspector, C.I.D., to the Commissioner of Police'. See also T.A.D., S.N.A., Vol. 63, File N.A. 776/06, J. S. Marwick, Native Commissioner, Central Division, to the Secretary for Native Affairs, 28 February 1906.

142 T.A.D., Law Dept., A.G. File 172/06, E. H. Showers to Sec. to the Law Dept., 12 June 1906.

143 T.A.D., S.A.C., Vol. 23, File 8/96, T. E. Mavrogordato to Commissioner of Police, 21 May 1907.

144 For these returns see T.A.D., Law Dept., A.G. File 172/06, Form 111 – 'Return of Brothels at Johannesburg and Pretoria as at 21 May 1907'. In general, Mavrogordato appears to have minimised police corruption in the post-war period by only allowing senior officers to conduct raids on brothels. See T.A.D., Law Dept., A.G. File 172/06, Acting Commissioner of Police to Sec. to the Law Dept., 22 May 1907. Mavrogordato, however, was fully aware that a certain amount of bribery persisted, and he also had clear ideas of the tariffs involved. See his evidence to the Select Committee on the Police Bill as reported in 'Detectives Pay', *The Star*, 20 March 1911. The list of these pimps' names is derived from a variety of sources, but particularly from the Transvaal Police 'Special Circular' Series of 'List of Persons deported from the Transvaal under the Immigrants Restriction

Act, 1907', copies of which are to be found in T.A.D., Justice Dept., Vol. 34, File 3/228/10, 1900–1910.

145 T.A.D., S.A.C., Vol. 23, File 8/96, T. E. Mavrogordato to Sec. to the Law Dept., 19 August 1908.

146 For Krause's views on the law and morality at this time see his contribution to the debate on the Criminal Law Amendment Bill in *Transvaal Legislative Assembly Debates 1908*, col. 1423–1425.

147 Para. based on T.A.D., S.A.C., Vol. 22, File 8/62, T. E. Mavrogordato to The Commissioner of Police, 6 July 1908; T.A.D., S.A.C., Vol. 23, File 8/96, T. E. Mavrogordato to Secretary, Transvaal Police, 18 August 1908; 'The Pimp, H. Epstein' in *The South African Pink'Un*, 27 June 1908; and 'What the Magistrate Said' in *The Transvaal Critic*, 24 July 1908.

148 *Ibid.*

149 T.A.D., S.A.C., Vol. 23, File 8/96, T. E. Mavrogordato, Deputy Commissioner of Police to Secretary, Transvaal Police, 19 August 1908.

150 T.A.D., S.A.C., Vol. 23, File 8/96, T. E. Mavrogordato to Secretary, Transvaal Police, 16 October 1908.

151 On deportations see T.A.D., Law Dept., A.G. File 172/06, T. E. Mavrogordato to The Commissioner of Police, 12 February 1906; *ibid.*, T. E. Mavrogordato to Secretary, Transvaal Police, 16 October 1908; and T.A.D., Justice Dept., Vol. 34, File 3/288/10, 'Special Circular' Series, 'Lists of Persons deported from the Transvaal under the Immigrants' Restriction Act 1907'. See also W. C. Scully, *The Ridge of the White Waters* (London 1911), p. 221. As early as late 1909 some of these deportees from the Transvaal started to reappear in important roles in the vice capitals of Europe. See, for example, the cases of Max Malitzky and Mrs Margarete Weiss as reported in N.A. of U.S.A., Washington, D.C., Bureau of Immigration and Naturalization, File 1-G, 52484, 'Braun European Reports', October 1909.

152 See T.A.D., Justice Dept., Vol. 34, File 3/288/10, 'Approximate Number of Prostitutes in Johannesburg and along the Reef on 18 July 1910'; and *ibid.*, 'List of Reputed Pimps still in Johannesburg', June 1910.

153 On employment possibilities and conditions of service, see the evidence of the following witnesses to the *Transvaal Indigency Commission 1906–1908*: Lieut-Col. O'Brien, paras 1497–1502; Sister Evelyn, paras 1743–1757 and paras 1882–1886; Rev. A. M. Kriel, paras 1948–1951; and Dr T. B. Gilchrist, para. 5635. See also, however, the particularly illuminating survey on 'Starvation' as reported in the *Transvaal Leader*, 4 June 1908. On prostitution in Fordsburg and Vrededorp see *Transvaal Indigency Commission 1906–1908*: Lieut-Col. O'Brien, paras 1449–1453; Sister Evelyn, para. 1708; Dr T. B. Gilchrist, para. 5648 and para. 5704. The possibility of sexual advantage being taken of female factory workers was, of course, not a new one. Law No. 11 of 1899, the Ontucht Law, in Section 9, made provision for the punishment of immoral acts committed, 'By managers or overseers in working institutions, work places or factories, with their minor servants or subordinates'. See *Laws of the Transvaal 1901*, p. 1060.

154 T.A.D., Law Dept., A.G. File 172/06, 'Return of Brothels at Johannesburg and Pretoria, 21 May 1907'; and T.A.D., S.A.C., Vol. 23, A.G. Circular Letter No. 49 of 1908 – appended undated letter from Inspector W. Cartlidge to the Deputy Commissioner of Police.

155 The case of Susan Broderick who was 'sold' to various Afrikaners in Vrededorp before being 'sold' to Ho King is recounted in T.A.D., Justice Dept., Vol. 109, File 3/153/11. See also, 'The Yellow Peril', *Transvaal Chronicle*, 13 February 1911.

156 Para. based on: T.A.D., Justice Dept., Vol. 34, File 3/288/10, 'Approximate Number of Prostitutes in Johannesburg and along the Reef on 18 July 1910'; 'List of Reputed Pimps still in the Transvaal, 1910'; and 'Summary of Work done under Ord. 46 of 1903 and Act 16 of 1908 from 1 July 1909 to 30 June 1910'.

157 U.G. 51–13, *Report of the Small Holdings Commission (Transvaal) 1913*, p. 12.
158 Para. based on: T.A.D., S.A.C., Vol. 23, File 8/96, Commissioner of Police to Secretary, Law Dept., 24 August 1908; and J.P.L., 'Minutes of Meetings of the Witwatersrand Church Council, 26 July 1909–2 June 1913.

CHAPTER FOUR

Johannesburg's Jehus 1890–1914

Cabs, cabbies and tramways during the transition from private to public transport in the principal industrial city of the Witwatersrand

> The town council will thus accept the duty of providing for the welfare of workers with moderate incomes, to whom a cheap, efficient and well-regulated tramway-system is practically a necessity, tending as it does to remove the disadvantages of residence at a distance from their work. . .
>
> Major O'Meara, Military Mayor of Johannesburg, April 1901

The mining capitalist revolution that occurred on the Witwatersrand between 1886 and 1914 created and transformed Johannesburg. From a diggers' camp of about 3,000 adventurers in 1887, there developed first a mining town with a population of over 100,000 people in 1896, and then, by 1914, an industrialising city with over a quarter of a million inhabitants. From the tented mining camp at the diggings in the 1880s, there grew the single-quarters and boarding-houses built of corrugated-iron that clustered around the deep-level mines and city centre in the 1890s, and then the more substantial brick-built homes of the working-class and other suburbs by 1914. This dramatic surge and spread of population also reflected itself in other ways, for example in the changing municipal boundaries of Johannesburg. In 1898 the Town Council held jurisdiction over an area of five square miles; when the nominated Town Council under the occupying British forces first took control in 1901 this was extended to nine square miles; and by the time that civilian local government was firmly re-established in 1903 this had yet again increased to an enormous 82 square miles.

But these developments, crammed as they were into a 25-year period, embraced changes of nature as well as of number. The move of Johannesburg from tent-town, through its intermediate stages to a city with suburban homes, thus also saw the shift from an economic system that was dependent on European immigrant miners for its skilled labour, to one characterised by a more socially stabilised proletariat in which the working class reproduced itself on the Rand through the agency of the nuclear family. The move to the suburbs, which accompanied this latter development, became particularly pronounced after 1901 and was consciously facilitated by the state, which saw in the geographical dispersal of the white working class a means of enhancing its social and political control in a rapidly maturing capitalist system.[1] While this working-class exodus from the high-rental areas of the city centre might have solved some difficulties, it also created at least one other significant problem – it tended, by an ever increasing margin, to separate the worker from his place of work. This in turn meant that a greater amount of time and effort had to be spent in the daily movement of the worker between his home and the point of production, and movement, like everything else, cost money. In Johannesburg, where this latter problem assumed increasingly urgent proportions between 1896 and 1906, the bourgeoisie and the working class alike drew at least some consolation from the fact that this obstacle was not without recent precedent in capitalist development.

In Europe, capital had at a much earlier date produced its own transformation of society which, by way of comparison, clearly dwarfed the economic unfolding of the Witwatersrand. Right from its inception, however, the industrial revolution had confined the bulk of its urban proletariat to within the immediate bounds of the 'walking city'. This meant that while the working class for the largest part lived in the sordid congested conditions that Engels and others described so well, it was not forced to spend a significant proportion of its income on daily transport to and from the manufacturing enterprises in which it laboured. Much of this changed from the mid-nineteenth century onwards when the working class, for a complex set of reasons, started to become more widely dispersed within European cities.

Starting in the 1870s many European cities attacked the problem of a more widely dispersed urban population through the implementation of a horse-drawn tram service within the inner city. It was the cheaper and more efficient technology that came with electricity, however, that revolutionised public transport during the following two decades. By the mid-1890s large industrial cities throughout the world, from Kiev to Kansas, were introducing the electric tram or 'trolley' to their inhabitants – both as a response to the dispersal of the working class, and as a means by which to facilitate that process further. So smooth was the transition from horse-car to trolley, and so efficient was the electric tram in its new function, that the cost of transport in metropolitan Europe and the United States fell consistently in the two decades before the First World War.[2] Above all else, it was to this strikingly successful contemporary European experience that the Witwatersrand capitalist class looked in its search for a solution to the developing urban transport problem in Johannesburg between 1890 and 1914. The solution, when it did come to the Rand, was neither swift nor painless.

The electric tram first ran in the streets of Johannesburg in 1906, a good ten years after the possibility of its use was first seriously mooted. Even then, the fact that it eventually ran at all was only due to the momentous upheavals that had occurred in the intervening decade. It took a war to replace a rural bourgeoisie with urban-based capitalists as the ruling class of the Transvaal, a searching commission of enquiry by the British government, a cash settlement of £150,000 with the earlier horse-drawn tram company, the sacrifice of a sizeable cab-owning class and the structural unemployment of hundreds of cab drivers, for the electric tram to establish itself in Johannesburg. This essay will seek to illustrate the process of class struggle as it developed in the field of urban transport during an era of revolutionary capitalism.

Urban transport under the dominance of a rural bourgeoisie, 1889–1899

Capitalist transport – the Johannesburg City & Suburban Tramway Company

It was A. H. Nellmapius, one of the Transvaal's wealthiest and most progressive farmers who, in late 1888, first approached the State President with a view to securing the exclusive right to operate a tramway system in Johannesburg. As a close confidant of Kruger, and as one of the architects of the Boer Republic's concessions policy, Nellmapius had already secured several such grants from the *Volksraad* in the past. At the centre of at least one of these previous concessions – the spectacularly successful *Eerste Fabrieken* or Hatherley Distillery – lay the idea that industrial enterprises in the new Republic should form a market for the produce of the Dutch farmers and, as such, should aid in the development of specific linkages between the urban and rural sectors of the economy. Nellmapius's idea for a Johannesburg transport system, which revolved around the exclusive use of animal power harnessed to a tramway, again proceeded from this premise. Kruger had little difficulty in persuading the members of his Volksraad that a concession which would result in the burghers being able to sell large quantities of horses, mules and forage was worthy of their support. Thus, in early 1889, A. H. Nellmapius secured a thirty-year concession to operate a horse-drawn tramway in Johannesburg, one of the conditions being that no alternative power source be utilised in the system without the prior consent of the government.[3]

But if the tramway concession initially only half-aroused the interest of the Volksraad and its farming constituency, then it certainly succeeded in fully capturing the imagination and enthusiasm of the local capitalists. In April 1889, almost as soon as he had acquired the concession, Nellmapius sold a three-quarter share in it to a Rand mining company owned by Sigmund Neumann and his then partners, Carl Hanau and H. J. King. At the same time the concessionaire sold a further five per cent of his venture to Messrs Mosenthal Sons & Co., of Port Elizabeth, 'one of the oldest and most prominent South African mercantile firms'. So swiftly did these events occur that Nellmapius requested that the Volksraad simply issue the original concession directly in the name of Sigmund Neumann.[4]

Neumann and his partners were well-respected entrepreneurs, and when they floated the Johannesburg City & Suburban Tramway Co. Ltd. with a capital of £125,000 on 19 September 1889, the £1 shares traded at a premium. The new issue immediately drew the support of other local capitalists and a man like Carl Meyer, for example, swiftly acquired 2,500 shares for himself. Mosenthal Sons showed their confidence in the venture by buying a further 7,500 shares to supplement the five per cent interest which they already held in

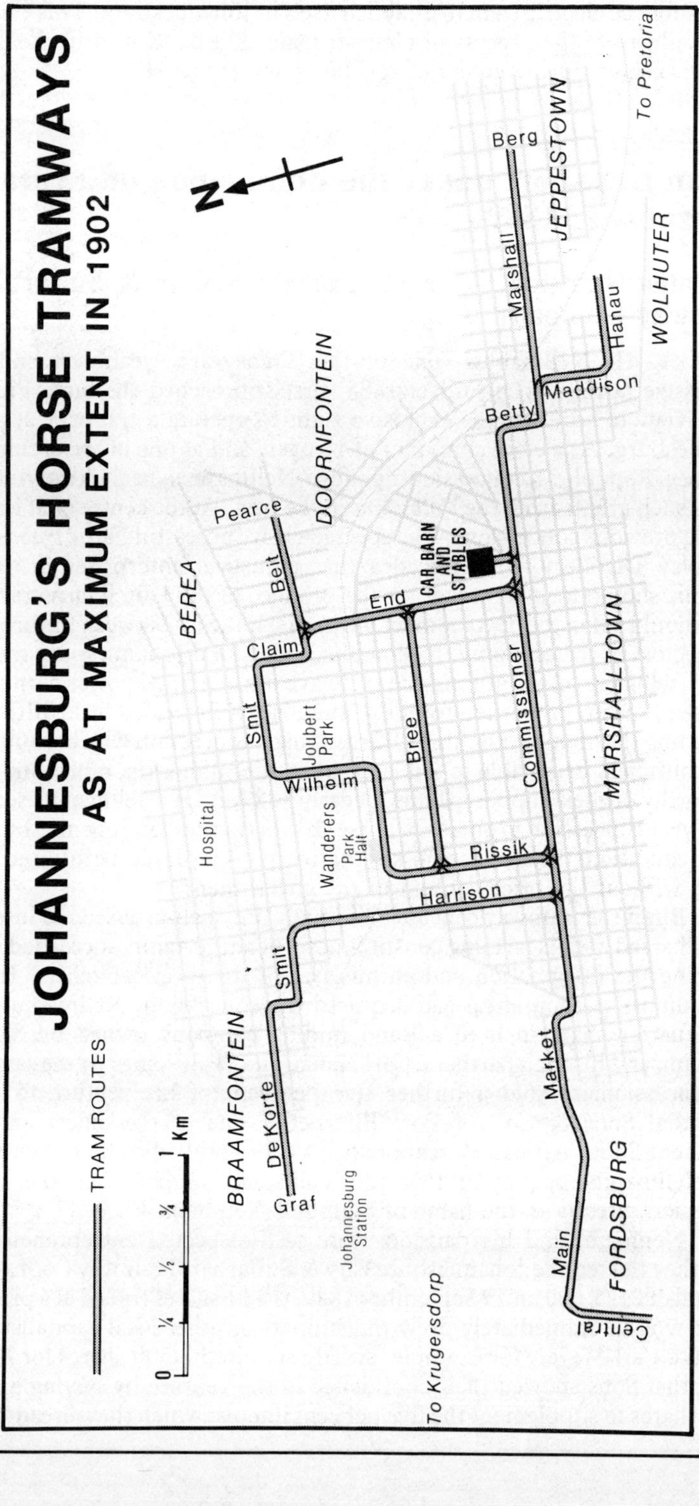
JOHANNESBURG'S HORSE TRAMWAYS
AS AT MAXIMUM EXTENT IN 1902
TRAM ROUTES
0 ¼ ½ ¾ 1 Km
N
BRAAMFONTEIN
BEREA
DOORNFONTEIN
JEPPESTOWN
WOLHUTER
MARSHALLTOWN
FORDSBURG
To Krugersdorp
To Pretoria
Johannesburg Station
Hospital
Wanderers
Park Halt
Joubert Park
CAR BARN AND STABLES
Graf
De Korte
Smit
Harrison
Wilhelm
Claim
Beit
Pearce
End
Bree
Rissik
Commissioner
Market
Main
Central
Betty
Maddison
Hanau
Marshall
Berg

the original concession. Elsewhere in the Cape, Natal and the Transvaal members of the public 'best acquainted with the conditions and prospects of the country' also purchased shares in the company 'long before it commenced active operations'.[5] These swirls and eddies in the local financial currents, however, were soon swamped by the huge tide of European capital that flowed into the Johannesburg City & Suburban Co.

Immediately after the company was floated some of the most prominent groups in international mining and finance capital bought their way into the new Transvaal transport business. Porges & Co. (later Wernher, Beit & Co.) acquired 15,000 shares, while A. Reimers & Co. purchased a massive block of 30,000 shares within four weeks of the project's public launching. Here then, a section of mining capital – as it was to do again shortly afterwards in the case of Hatherley Distillery – showed its willingness to invest in secondary enterprise on the Rand at least half a decade before the more secure developments that came with deep-level mining took place.[6]

In France, together with Belgium acknowledged to be the most developed continental centre for horse-drawn and electric tramway enterprise, the *Banque Internationale de Paris* promoted the Johannesburg company and, amongst many other prominent investors, Messrs N. M. Rothschild & Sons bought 15,000 shares. In Brussels, where investors were apparently slower off the mark, the bulk of the investment only came in 1895 when a group around M. Josse Allard, a prominent banker in the city and the Director of the Belgian Mint, acquired a large parcel of shares. By then, however, a twenty-shilling share in the Johannesburg City & Suburban Co. was trading at an all-time high level of 50 shillings.[7]

With its working capital requirements easily satisfied, the tramway company commenced its construction activities in July 1890, and by 2 February 1891, when the system opened, it could offer a service on a track that extended along Commissioner street for four and three-quarter miles, between Jeppe in the east and Fordsburg in the west. By mid-1896 the system had reached the apex of its development with a line of track some ten and three-quarter miles long, laid out in a series of loops designed to cover the inner city. In the same year, City & Suburban operated a fleet of about 35 trams, and employed a staff of over 200 workers – including 140 Cape coloured tram drivers dressed in the distinctive blue and gold uniform of the company. Thereafter, the company's scale of operation remained more or less constant and six years later, by 1902, only one more mile of track had been laid bringing the total track distance covered to eleven and three-quarter miles.[8]

This pattern of growth in the company's activities was also to be seen in other areas of its operation. The basic fare of 3d per mile proved popular in Johannesburg, and right from the outset the service was well patronised. By 1896 the City & Suburban's fleet of trams was covering 1,000 miles per day through the town, and transporting a good two and a half million passengers during the course of a year. This volume of business showed itself in the company's turnover, and up to the mid-1890s in growing profits and dividends – see Table 5.[9]

Whilst this financial statement revealed a modest growth in the income of the company over an eight-year trading period, it also pointed to a high cost structure that tended to keep pace with any expansion in gross receipts. The

Table 5. Johannesburg City & Suburban Tramway Co. Ltd., Financial Statement, 1891–98

Year	Gross income	Costs	Gross profit	Dividend
1891	£14,511	£12,262	£ 2,488	–
1892	21,617	16,780	4,836	–
1893	27,162	20,507	6,655	4%
1894	29,484	22,780	6,703	4%
1895	41,374	27,490	13,883	6%
1896	–	–	–	10%
1897	–	–	–	7½%
1898	–	–	–	nil

large majority of these costs derived directly from the fact that the tramway system was animal-powered. The working life of a tram-horse, relegated as it was to a strenuous round of endless stopping and starting, was about four years. From the mid-1890s the City & Suburban Co. required a stable of over 200 horses to operate its trams, and new animals were constantly having to be purchased in order to keep the system up to strength. While this would have been an expensive business in the normal course of events, the situation was exacerbated through most of the 1890s by endemic horse-sickness which forced prices to remain at a high level.[10] To make matters worse, the local price of forage also remained high during the same period – not only because demand constantly outstripped supply, but because a series of severe droughts aggravated the situation. The company attempted to cope with this latter problem through a policy of bulk purchasing, its Doornfontein silo being built to hold a four-month supply of forage. But not even this solved the problem fully – the cost of forage consistently accounted for two-thirds of the company's expenses, and in 1896 the annual bill for that item alone ran to £18,000.[11]

These high costs did not cause the Transvaal farmers any concern. On the contrary, a market for burgher produce on this scale must have gone some way towards vindicating the Volksraad's decision to grant Nellmapius the concession in the first place. From the City & Suburban's point of view, however, the problem was that the concession no longer belonged simply to Nellmapius. Once the concession had passed into the hands of the international capitalists, much of the unstated *raison d'être* for its existence also disappeared. Whereas a national capitalist like Nellmapius might live with a high cost structure which saw himself and his fellow burghers benefit from the prices for horses and forage, the same was not true for an international capitalist like Rothschild. While Nellmapius could look forward to reaping profits at both the rural and urban ends of an integrated economic enterprise, the Rothschilds were confined to the dividends that could be directly extracted from the tramway company. It was largely because of this latter reason that the international shareholders who dominated the company were deeply disturbed by a high cost structure that ate directly into profit margins.

The City & Suburban Co.'s profit margin between 1891 and 1898 was certainly worthy of concern. In three of those years it paid no dividend at all, while in the remaining period it declared a dividend which averaged out at only a little above five per cent. While such profits might arguably have been suited to a public utility, they were less than satisfactory for a private company in search of profit – especially one that had increased its capital from £125,000 to £210,000 in 1894. That City & Suburban was then still able to raise more capital on the strength of such a mediocre business performance, revealed the extent to which there was a large speculative component in dealings in the company's shares before 1896. Especially during the early 1890s, shareholders in Europe had repeatedly seen modestly successful horse-drawn tramways profitably converted into electric systems based on the 'trolley'. The wonder of electricity not only cut costs by between 30 and 40 per cent, it helped expand gross receipts for tramway companies by enabling them to provide a faster, more efficient, and more frequent service for the travelling public.[12] It was largely this – the belief that the Volksraad would soon sanction the conversion from animal power to electricity – that continued to ensure European support for City & Suburban shares during the early 1890s.

In Johannesburg, the directors of the company were forced to nurture this belief, at first simply to maintain the short-term speculative buoyancy of the share market but later, and more urgently, out of a genuine desire to reduce costs and increase profits, and by so doing secure the long-term value of its appreciating shares. It was this set of overlapping reasons that twice within five years prompted the City & Suburban directors to approach Kruger's government for permission to electrify their tramway system. In 1891 their request was quickly dismissed, but in 1895 the State President, while again turning down their application, took time to explain that he was most reluctant to sacrifice a valued Boer produce market to electricity and higher company profit margins.[13] Neither of these refusals did the company much harm on the stock market, the shareholders choosing to interpret these dismissals from Pretoria as evidence of ambition being delayed rather than denied. Under these circumstances the level of City & Suburban shares remained high – right up to 1896.

Early in 1896 a group of four speculators – J. P. B. Lombard, P. J. Botha, F. G. de Beer, and a Californian named William G. Keller – first saw their own vision of an electric tramway and the profits which it could produce. Since central Johannesburg was already served by a horse-drawn tram, however, the Lombard quartet was forced into composing an imaginative variation on a theme of urban transport. The group thus devised a scheme for an electric tramway which, while basically serving the ten-mile area *surrounding* Johannesburg, would also be linked to the city centre through two lines of access. The logic behind this seemingly strange idea only became slightly more apparent when it was understood that the system was to carry goods as well as passengers. But once it was further explained that the tramway was also to be linked to a system of low rates and free storage in the city centre for farmers conveying their produce to market, the whole idea seemed to assume a rounder and more rational form.

A scheme such as that proposed by Lombard and his colleagues would have held obvious attractions for the burghers of the South African Republic. As one contemporary observer noted:

> The gain to them would have been great, for it would have enabled their ox waggons to discharge their load ten miles outside the town and return

> homewards, instead of having to complete the journey and keep the oxen outspanned without food and water twenty-four hours on the market square.[14]

Armed with the nucleus of an idea that would have a clear appeal to the farmers, the speculators now turned their attention to Pretoria.

When the Lombard proposal was first put to the State President and his Executive Committee early in July 1896, Kruger was at once enthusiastic. 'The feature in the project that appealed to him most strongly', wrote someone who was closely involved in the negotiations, was 'the provision for the opening up of the Johannesburg market to the farmers.'[15] The State President was thus perfectly willing to envisage an elaborate two-tier transport system in the mining town – an inner core served by horse-drawn trams for the exclusive use of passengers, and a surrounding electric system which, while it would also carry passengers, would be largely devoted to carrying Boer produce to the market.[16] Both sections of such a system would have the merit of being of direct benefit to burgher agricultural production, and for this reason Kruger and his closest colleagues believed that they would have little difficulty in persuading the Volksraad to endorse the granting of such a concession. While giving the scheme his blessing, however, the State President also took the precaution of asking Lombard and his colleagues to deposit a sum of £5,000 in the National Bank as an indication of their good faith. It was in the course of their search for this money that the speculators, not surprisingly, found their way to the Johannesburg offices of the Banque Française d l'Afrique du Sud.

The French Bank, which had been founded in the early 1890s at the instigation of the local French Consul, Georges Aubert, had a reputation for being well connected and willing to look beyond mining for profit. Besides modest interests in local secondary enterprise, the Banque Française had also had the past good fortune of having made a highly profitable investment in one of Kruger's concessions – indeed, its local manager, Henri Duval, served on the board of Hatherley Distillery.[17] Furthermore, one of the most powerful principals in the French Bank, Baron de Gunzburg of Paris, had more than a passing interest in tramways during the mid 1890s.[18] For these and other reasons the Banque Française, on the strength of the promised concession, granted Lombard and his partners the necessary £5,000 which was duly deposited in the National Bank.[19]

With these preliminaries behind them, Lombard and his colleagues now proceeded to float a company through which they raised the capital which would ultimately turn the scheme into a reality. Nearly all the shares in this new enterprise were bought by a thirty-strong syndicate in the United States of America. It was probably William Keller who succeeded in getting much of this financial support from his native state of California, but other shareholders also subscribed from as far apart as New York, Massachusetts, Kansas, Nevada and Montana.[20] At least £17,000 of this capital was soon spent in having routes surveyed for the electric tram in Johannesburg, and in orders for plant and equipment from the United States.

The first rumours of all this activity centred around the possibility of a new electric tram system for Johannesburg shook the directors of the City & Suburban Co. rigid. They immediately realised that if the Lombard concession were granted and ratified, then the value of their own concession would be dramatically reduced, and that they would instantly forfeit the speculative support of the European shareholders which they had so long enjoyed. The chairman of the company, Julius Berlein, at once brought these considerations to the attention of Kruger's Executive Committee. On 18 July 1896 he wrote a lengthy letter to the State Secretary, F. W. Reitz, pleading that if any party had a moral right to the use of electricity then it was the City & Suburban Co., and further pointing out that if the Lombard concession were granted, then it would have the most serious repercussions for his European shareholders.[21] Berlein's approach to Pretoria proved ineffectual, and within weeks he was made to pay for his lack of success with his job. In August 1896 the City & Suburban Co., in a desperate attempt to shore up its position, appointed C. S. Goldmann as its new chairman.

Charles Goldmann personally went to Pretoria in order to impress on the State Secretary the large amount of foreign capital at stake in the company which now owned the first government tramway concession. Reitz, as befitted a cautious and correct bureaucrat, responded by calling for a list detailing all the names and holdings of European investors in the company. This information Goldmann handed to the State Secretary as soon as he was able to.[22] By then, however, it was already too late. Rumour of the Lombard concession had become public knowledge, and in two weeks' trading, between 12 and 23 September 1896, £125,000 was written off the stock exchange value of City & Suburban shares.[23]

This was a blow from which the Johannesburg tramway company never fully recovered, although Goldmann and his colleagues continued to make strenuous efforts to salvage the situation. A deluge of letters and telegrams from the French and Belgium governments now poured onto the State Secretary's desk, all urging that the Lombard concession be refused, and that the City & Suburban Co. be given the right to electrify its lines.[24] In October Goldmann again asked the government for permission to convert his company's system from horse-drawn tram to trolley – this time attempting to coax compliance out of Kruger and his colleagues by offering the state a share in the company's subsequent profits.[25] But neither the stick of foreign pressure, nor the carrot of financial incentive, would make the State President and his Executive Committee budge. On 4 November 1896 a contract for the Johannesburg electric tram system was entered into by the Z.A.R. government with the Lombard group representing the American syndicate.

But if Goldmann's appeals did not catch the attention of those higher up in the government, then they were certainly heard by those lower down in the echelon with their ears closer to the ground. The Volksraad had for some time been disturbed by the State President's concessions policy, and in 1895 had gone so far as to appoint a commission to enquire into the matter.[26] Members of the Raad now became concerned lest the besieged position of the City & Suburban Co. culminate in the loss of a substantial market for burgher agricultural producers. Moreover, they felt constrained by the fact that the Lombard concession would operate in damaging opposition to the horse-drawn tramway company which they had fully examined and exonerated in the previous year. Thus, when the Volksraad met in December 1896, it narrowly passed a resolution denying Kruger's right to issue the electric tram concession independently. This political impasse heralded the advent of a new and protracted round of lobbying by all the parties concerned.[27] When the Lombard concession finally came up for ratification in July 1897 the members of the Volksraad – led by Messrs Labuschagne and van Niekerk – again defeated the Executive Committee's proposal for an electric tramway system by twelve votes to eleven.[28]

This defeat in the South African Republic's debating chambers left the American syndicate thoroughly stranded amidst its substantial preliminary capital outlay. Over a year later – in October 1898 – William Keller and his Californian cohorts were still unsuccessfully attempting to recover their £5,000 deposit in the National Bank through the offices of the United States Consul in Pretoria.[29] The City & Suburban Co., although still in business, was in bad shape. Not only had it already lost a chairman, but in 1897 continental investors, unhappy with the way that earlier events in the Transvaal had tended to pass them by, had insisted on the company opening offices in Brussels and Paris to keep the shareholders more informed.[30] Some of the first new information which those shareholders received was not good. In the wake of the rinderpest epidemic and a pronounced increase in the price of forage, the company issued no dividend at all in 1898. By the following year Belgian investors were so concerned about the value of the shares that they had acquired four years earlier, at 50 shillings each, that they sent a European tramways expert out to Johannesburg to investigate fully the operations of the City & Suburban Co.[31] This commission exonerated the company, and pointed out that within the limitations imposed by the horse-drawn tram, it was functioning as well as could be expected. It was by this and other means in the late 1890s that shareholders in Brussels and Boston alike made an elementary but painful financial discovery. In the Boer Republic urban transport was under the control of a rural bourgeoisie.

Petty-bourgeois transport – cab owners and cab drivers under Pretoria's protection

From the late 1880s onwards at least part of Johannesburg's growing transport needs were met through the initiative of small-scale private enterprise. Most prominent of all in this sector of the urban economy were the owner-drivers of horse-drawn cabs. These men, who plyed their small hooded 'Cape carts' through the dusty streets in search of fares, formed an easily identifiable group with common class interests. In 1891, over eighty of them cooperated to establish a Cab Owners' Association when they petitioned the local Sanitary Board for better roads and the setting aside of cab ranks.[32] The Association continued to serve its members in this form until 1896, when the organisation was reconstituted. By then, private transport and its linked activities had grown to form an important part of the local economy.

When the Sanitary Board conducted a census in 1896 it revealed that there were 80 cab owners and 700 cab drivers resident within a three-mile radius of the Market square. In practice this figure was likely to be substantially higher since most cab owners tended to keep their stables further out of town, and a closer appreciation of the actual numbers directly involved in the business can be gauged from the fact that, in the same year, the Sanitary Board dealt with over 1,200 applications for cab-driving licences.[33] On its own, however, even the latter figure gives a misleading idea of the size and importance of the cab trade in Johannesburg. In order to get a more complete picture of the petty-bourgeois transport sector it would be necessary to include at least some of the 8 stable keepers, 16 farriers, 16 horse traders, 18 carriage trimmers, 26 coach builders, 43 harness makers, 70 produce merchants, 165 grooms, 325 stable boys and 504 blacksmiths who, in 1896, served cabbies in the city centre.[34]

Throughout the 1890s, but more especially so before 1896, the ranks of the Johannesburg cabbies contained within them men drawn from several different national, cultural and racial backgrounds. From scattered fragments it is known that a small number of these, perhaps between six and twelve, were black. Simon Untembu, for example, left Weenen in Natal in 1889 in order to take up cab driving in the city, and in the course of so doing deserted his wife and children. Untembu might have been alone in his attempt to get away from his family commitments, but he was certainly not alone in his desire to lead an independent economic existence. By 1894 there were sufficient black cabbies plying between the location and the town for them to ask the Sanitary Board to set aside a special rank for them. Although the large majority of their customers were fellow blacks, these cabbies – except when they were legally prevented from doing so during the smallpox outbreak of 1893 – also took fares from whites as and when they could find them. It was this practice of also touting for white customers that led a section of the local press, in the depression year of 1897, to demand that they be refused licences – a rather misguided way of trying to force them out of business, since the Sanitary Board had in any case always declined to lend them legal recognition in this manner. Despite a continuing measure of white hostility and some ambiguity surrounding their legal status, these black cabbies remained in business right up to the advent of British rule in the Transvaal.[35]

More prominent, more legally protected, and certainly more acceptable to the racist white community, were the numerous coloured cabbies of Johannesburg with their allegedly 'inborn knowledge of horses, and their civility to superiors'.[36] These coloured muslims, so-called 'Malays', had made their way from Kimberley and Cape Town in increasing numbers after the discovery of gold, and by the mid-1890s there must have been between 200 and 300 of them at work as cabbies in the city. Although some of these immigrants may have been drawn to the unsympathetic South African Republic by the opening up of new opportunities in the horse-drawn tram service or cab driving, it seems at least as possible that others were forced out of the Cape by increasing talk and implementation of a policy of tramway electrification in the 1890s.[37] But whatever their initial motivation, cabbies from the Abdulla, Dollie, Domingo, Kamalaer and Salie families were amongst those who continued to play an important, albeit declining role, in Johannesburg's urban transport over the succeeding 25 years.[38]

In addition to these black and coloured drivers, the city was also largely served by a cosmopolitan collection of white cabbies in the years before the South African War. Although generally more socially secure than their fellow-drivers in the European-dominated community, these white cabbies were nevertheless also susceptible to a measure of the prevailing prejudices – in their case dependent on their ethnic origins, and their ability to communicate fluently with their passengers. Most acceptable were those English speakers drawn from Britain or the Cape Colony who, in the early 1890s, appear to have dominated the ranks of the white cabbies. Less acceptable were the growing number of Afrikaners who took to cab driving in the mid-1890s, and least acceptable were the first small number of Polish or Russian Jews – 'Peruvians' – who started to become cabbies between 1897 and 1899.[39]

Some of these white drivers, as in the case of their coloured predecessors, were possibly drawn into petty-bourgeois enterprise by new economic possibilities during the early years of Johannesburg. From the mid-1890s, however, cab driving – for reasons that will transpire later – offered fewer rewards, and from then on it was likely to be hardship in a former occupation, rather than financial opportunity as a cabby, that forced new entrants into the profession. The arrival of the Natal railway on the Witwatersrand in 1895, as well as the locust, drought and rinderpest plagues of 1896–7, combined to attack the livelihood of transport drivers and poor farmers, and assisted in pushing them off the land and into the towns. For some of these destitute Afrikaners, equipped as they were with rural skills in the use of horse and cart, cab driving must have presented itself as one of the few ways of leading an independent economic existence in an otherwise hostile urban environment.[40] Similarly, it was a combination of skills previously acquired in the villages of Eastern Europe, and the necessity of finding a new way of earning a living after the Rand illicit liquor trade started to decline, that forced the poorest Jewish immigrants to turn to cab driving after 1897.[41]

Despite their very diverse origins and the distinctive paths that they had followed in their entry into the transport business, the Johannesburg cabbies displayed a significant degree of class solidarity during most of the pre-war period. While it is true that the black and coloured cabbies never played a part in the formal proceedings of the Cab Owners' Association, they were nevertheless fully incorporated into all the organised approaches that were made to the authorities. When the cabbies combined to approach the Sanitary Board in 1891, British, Dutch and coloured drivers did not hesitate to sign a joint petition – at least one of the latter group signing in Arabic. Even after the Jameson Raid, when it would be reasonable to expect a certain amount of hostility between Boer and Briton, there was every sign of substantial cooperation, and in December 1896 African, Afrikaner, English and coloured cabbies again combined to direct a common appeal to the State President and his colleagues as 'protectors of the working classes'. On the eve of the South African War, in February 1899, class interest was still strong enough for most of the prominent British, Dutch and Jewish cab owners to unite in an appeal to the town council.[42]

While some of this class solidarity undoubtedly derived simply from the pragmatic sharing of common economic interests in periods of stress, the bonds between the cab drivers were also strengthened by community ties throughout the 1890s. Most of those involved in the cab-driving business chose to keep their stables and equipment in Fordsburg, from where they had easy access to the city centre and the forage supplies of Market square. This meant that cabbies not only spent a considerable amount of time on the rank together, but they also tended to live in the same working-class suburb and to frequent the same recreational haunts. Thus, when their professional association was reconstituted in its new form in 1896 it was formally known as the 'Fordsburg Vigilance and Cab Owners' Association', and its meetings were frequently held in the Avenue Beer Hall of J. Zeeman, a local publican who also operated a fleet of cabs.[43]

Although Fordsburg clearly formed the heart of cabby-country, the constituency also merged and extended into the adjacent areas of the 'Malay Camp', Brickfields and Vrededorp, where many of the poorer coloured and Afrikaner cab drivers lived.[44] The Fordsburg Vigilance and Cab Owners' Association recognised this, and through appointing prominent local Afrikaners such as S. Venter, F. W. Axsel and J. W. Stegmann as office-bearers, allowed Dutch-speaking cabbies to identify with their professional association.[45] The fact that as burghers these latter members enjoyed the franchise, and that as a class cabbies were large and conspicuous consumers of Boer produce, combined to give the Cab Association considerable political muscle which the cab drivers used to defend themselves within the changing economic climate of the 1890s.

The early 1890s, marked as they were by the rapid growth of population in the mining town and the increased call for intra-city transport after the arrival of the railway in 1892 and 1895, were largely good years for Johannesburg's cabbies.[46] This relatively prosperous era, however, came to a rather prompt halt in 1896. While the general recession that followed on the Raid partly accounted for this, it was a series of more specifically aimed blows that did most to hurt the cab trade. Talk of introducing the electric trolley to the Rand simply alarmed the cabbies, but the actual extension of the horse-drawn tram line by 25 per cent in 1896, and the growing popularity of the bicycle amongst the working class in the same year, did immediate and lasting damage to their business.[47] Then, as if these new structural demands were somehow not enough, the cabbies were also asked to withstand the higher prices for horses and forage that came after the rinderpest. The cumulative effect of these blows was almost to halve the ranks of the cabbies. Whereas there were 1,200 licensed cab drivers in the town at the beginning of 1896, by the end of the following year there were only 700 cabbies left in the profession. This, as one local newspaper put it, was 'staggering shrinkage'.[48]

The Cab Owners' Association remained passive throughout much of this assault since the large and powerful economic forces that lay behind it were clearly beyond the sway of small-scale transport operators. The Association was, however, more inclined to accept and resist any additional challenges that might come its way during such troubled times. The most notable of such challenges in the mid-1890s came from a body that was well within the fighting weight of the organised cab drivers – the Johannesburg Sanitary Board.

In the period of prosperity that immediately preceded the Jameson Raid, the local authorities were put under considerable pressure by citizens who felt that cabbies were extracting extortionate fares from the travelling public. It was largely in response to these complaints that the Sanitary Board drafted a new set of regulations to govern the cab trade in late 1895. The draft regulations, which were referred to Pretoria for government approval in the

Johannesburg's horse-drawn tramway service – a Kruger concession

normal manner, reduced the full fare for any second passenger on a journey by 50 per cent, but attempted partially to redress the balance by allowing cabbies to make a seasonal surcharge of 50 per cent on night fares between April and October.[49] The full significance of these proposed fare changes did not immediately strike the cab drivers in the balmy and prosperous summer days of 1895. When they made their appearance in the *Government Gazette* in the cooler and changed economic conditions of autumn 1896, however, they immediately concentrated the cab drivers' minds. Early in May – some two months before the regulations were due to be enforced – several of the more far-sighted cab owners met in central Johannesburg and decided to send a deputation to the local authorities in an attempt to get the proposed tariffs amended.[50] This manoeuvre bought the cabbies time, but it did not bring them success. The Sanitary Board, more anxious than ever to deliver some relief to its constituency during the recession, was in no mood to listen to cabby complaints and dismissed the deputation's pleas.

By the time that the regulations appeared for a second time in the *Gazette* in early September 1896, the recession had deepened and there was more widespread concern amongst the cabbies. This time a meeting of between 200 and 300 cab owners, held at the Mynpacht Hotel in Fordsburg, decided to by-pass the local authorities and appeal directly to the State President and his Executive Committee.[51] The Sanitary Board immediately countered this move with its own representations, and found an unexpected ally in the pro-government *Standard and Diggers' News* which now also made an editorial call for the removal of the 50 per cent night surcharge.[52] Kruger and his colleagues, already beset with the more urgent problems surrounding the Lombard concession and the City & Suburban Tramway Co., nevertheless listened attentively to the cab drivers' submissions and promised to reconsider the Johannesburg tariffs.

From this point on the cab drivers never let the initiative slip from their grasp. They followed up the first deputation to Pretoria with a second, and kept up the pressure in the interim by sending Kruger and his colleagues a telegram. When neither of these supplementary measures produced a speedy decision, they set about organising a further petition that was signed by drivers of all colours and religious persuasions. This latter document they chose to present to the State President and the Executive Committee in December 1896 – that is, at exactly the time that the Volksraad was delivering its rebuke to Kruger over the Lombard concession, and expressing its fears about the possibility of a declining forage market on the Witwatersrand. By January of the following year the triumph of the cab drivers was assured, and in March 1897 the Sanitary Board was forced to revert to the schedule of tariffs that had operated in the city before the Jameson Raid.[53] To add insult to local authority injury, Kruger not only restored the full fare for second passengers, but also allowed the cabbies to continue to make the 50 per cent surcharge on night fares.[54] Thus, in the mid-1890s Johannesburg's citizens discovered, as did others elsewhere, that in the Boer Republic urban transport was ultimately under the control of a rural bourgeoisie.

The cab drivers, through the tacit development of a class alliance with agricultural producers in the countryside, had unquestionably managed to score a notable victory over the local Sanitary Board and its constituents.[55]

While this success largely derived from the exercise of orthodox political skills, it also owed much to the degree of unity which the cab-owning petty bourgeoisie had been able to display during a period of economic crisis. It was the presence of this overriding element of class solidarity amongst the cabbies that made their struggle of 1896–7 unique. For, at the very moment when the cabbies succeeded in uniting in common cause, the logic of capital set to work within their trade – ever increasing the division between owner and driver, and relentlessly fragmenting the petty bourgeoisie along more fundamental class cleavages. Especially after 1896, the basic differences that divide employer from employee could be detected in the cab trade.

Cab owners – as distinct from owner-drivers – had formed part of Johannesburg's transport business since its very earliest days. In 1890 there were already five operators who owned sufficient cabs to make it worth their while to pay for individual entries in the local trade directory. Although it is difficult to estimate how many cabs such early owners kept on the streets, it is known that one of them, J. de Vries, operated nine such vehicles in 1891. By the middle of the decade there were still only a half-dozen cab proprietors in the city and the largest of these, the American, Samuel Thornton, ran a sufficiently complex cab and livery stable business to necessitate employing a full-time manager.[56] However, despite the presence of these features, the cab trade still remained overwhelmingly dominated by owner-drivers throughout this period, and for this the Cape cart was largely responsible.

The small, two-wheeled Cape cart, drawn by a single horse, was in many respects ideally suited to the requirements of the hundreds of independently operating cabbies in early Johannesburg. Its outstanding virtue, of course, was its cheapness, and it was this factor, as much as any other, that lay behind the initial expansion of the private transport sector. For a capital outlay of £35–50 any prospective cabby could acquire a Cape cart, as well as the necessary equipment and team of two horses that were required alternatively to service any hard-working cab. The simple design and modest size of the cart facilitated the rapid and easy harnessing of the horse, and by so doing reduced stable delays for the versatile man who wished to be a cabby. In addition, the vehicle had the added attraction of being relatively easy to clean and maintain. From the passenger's point of view, however, the Cape cart had less to commend its use as a cab. The cart was not particularly comfortable, it was fairly open and therefore exposed to the elements, and both ascent and descent from it were made difficult by its high body.[57] But while Johannesburg remained a largely male-dominated mining town not even these disadvantages could detract from the Cape cart's overriding utility as a cab.

The problem for the cart cabbies was, however, that the rough mining community of early Johannesburg started to give way to a more diversified and stabilised society in the mid-1890s, and that as this happened so their clientele changed. The arrival of the railways brought more women to the town, just as the workers started to desert the cabs for the bicycle or the City & Suburban tram. At about the same time, sizeable pockets of mercantile, trading and other groups started to congeal as a middle class in the society, and so came to supplement the small but ever-present stratum of truly wealthy families in the city. For the majority of people in these new categories, etiquette and class snobbery dictated that a 'proper' cab rather than a mere cart be called for when town transport was required.[58] It was this greater demand for comfort, style and elegance that ultimately proved to be the undoing of the old Cape cart.

By the mid-1890s coach builders and carriage trimmers in the city were already producing – in considerable numbers – the two vehicles that increasingly met the new demands of the cab trade. Of these, the most sought-after and expensive model was the Landau, which sported a fully enclosed carriage with glass windows, blinds and curtains. More widely used, however, was the cheaper Victoria with its well-sprung low body that could, if necessary, be completely covered by a retractable hood.[59] While both of these four-wheelers had the advantage of being able to carry more passengers, they had the disadvantage of having to be drawn by two animals – something which necessitated the acquisition and maintenance of *two* pairs of cab horses. This in turn meant that by 1898 the cost of a complete new turn-out was of the order of £200 – that is, about four times the previous price that had to be paid for entry into the cab trade.[60] Moreover, the cost of maintenance of a Victoria or Landau was higher than for a Cape cart, and it was said that such cabs required two to three hours of labour each morning before they were ready to be put on the rank.[61]

Capital costs and recurrent expenditure on this scale were probably beyond the financial reach of most independent cabbies in 'normal' times, let alone in the distinctly adverse economic conditions that generally prevailed after the Jameson Raid. Thus, although under some public pressure to convert to the fashionable new four-wheelers, many of the small operators desperately clung to their old economic life-line of the Cape cart, and by 1899 the unsympathetic *Standard and Diggers' News* was complaining loudly, and calling for the 'removal of the weird procession of monstrosities that disgrace many parts of the town'.[62] Others, while they still had access to limited savings, sold their carts and proceeded to hire fully-equipped Victorias from Thornton's or Stegmann's at £14 per week – a precarious way of earning a living that was said to yield a 'profit' of between £2 and £3 per week. For a small but growing number of cabbies, however, the loss of the Cape cart heralded an unceremonious entry into the ranks of the working class. In return for 'board and lodging' and cash wages of between 40 and 60 shillings per week, these men sold their services as cab drivers to those proprietors who had survived the economic crisis of the mid-1890s.[63] As the South African War approached the Johannesburg cab trade was steadily splitting into its component parts of capital and labour – a process that was to reach its fullest, and perhaps most appropriate manifestation, in the years after 1900.

Urban transport under the hegemony of mining capitalism, 1900–1914

Johannesburg's tramways – from private company to public utility

When British armed forces occupied Johannesburg in 1900 the city and its government were not – for the first time since the discovery of gold – ultimately subject to the approval of a rural bourgeoisie located in the Transvaal capital.

Under the new dispensation the British government, in alliance with the Rand mining capitalists, came to exercise authority over the city and its inhabitants, and nowhere was the impact of the emerging industrial state more clearly visible than in the fields of urban planning and public transport. Any full appreciation of the changing role, function and ownership of Johannesburg's tramways, therefore, has to be firmly located in an understanding of the capitalist vision of the Witwatersrand that developed during the period of reconstruction.

Within a month of the occupation of the town, on 31 May 1900, a member of the Royal Engineers – Major W. O'Meara – was appointed Acting Mayor of Johannesburg. A military man, in what was for some months essentially a military town, O'Meara was at first not unduly concerned about the fate of the city's former transport system. As a former intelligence officer, however, the Mayor would not have failed to notice that there was at least one 'war correspondent' around who *did* have a lively interest in the future role of trams in the town. As early as July 1900 C. S. Goldmann, in his interim guise as journalist, was hard at work representing the interests of the City & Suburban Co. and attempting to pave 'the way for reviving electric tramway rights'.[64] But the chairman of the horse-drawn tram company was not the only one quick off the mark, since elsewhere others too were already at work. In Cape Town, Lord Milner and Percy FitzPatrick – with no direct interest in tramways *per se* – were busy discussing the need for a full-scale investigation into all the concessions which had been granted by the Kruger government.[65] The resulting commission, which amongst others investigated the Johannesburg Tramway Co., sat down to its initial deliberations in the closing months of 1900.

The swift preliminary planning and manoeuvring by the incoming administration and its allies was further accelerated when the first British residents were allowed to return to the Transvaal in the early months of the following year. Milner, anxious that the path to civilian rule on the Witwatersrand should be made as smooth as possible, now looked around for an assistant who could help O'Meara in his role as Mayor of Johannesburg. It was in the course of this search that the Oxford old-boy network put forward the name of a promising candidate named Lionel Curtis, and it was this young man who did much to determine what the future role of tramways in the city would be.[66]

In several respects Curtis was an obvious choice for the position of Acting Town Clerk in the largest city of the newly conquered territory. Curtis had seen service as a despatch rider in the early months of the South African War, and was thus already familiar with some aspects of what was a complex society. He also possessed a series of more pertinent qualifications, however, which could be directly harnessed to the job in hand. In the late 1890s he had gained insight into the problems of working-class housing and social engineering in Britain by serving on one of Octavia Hill's famous committees in London. This experience had left Curtis with a clear understanding of the importance of the geography of class, and its related aspect of social control.[67] Moreover, as former Private Secretary to Lord Welby, Chairman of the London County Council, he had also had the opportunity to study carefully the official planning of local administration in a great city – and that in a country which in the late nineteenth century prided itself on the fact that it led the world in municipal government.

Thus in March and April 1901, Curtis and O'Meara – acting as complementary social and civil engineers – set about drafting detailed proposals about the future nature and government of Johannesburg.[68] The central consideration that underpinned these early discussions was most explicit. There was a clearly expressed need to avoid the emergence of a sharply demarcated central working-class area with its frequently associated problems of markedly different rating values, high rentals, and the development of an aggressive class consciousness. Curtis had seen the difficulties which the absence of such a policy had produced in the East and West Ends of London, and was most anxious to avoid the potential for conflict which it carried within it. As the Acting Town Clerk later put it in an official version:

> What we have to fear and avoid is the creation of a similar state of things in Johannesburg – where the area north of the reef would be covered by the residences of the well-to-do, and by streets of shops supplying their wants – while the area south of the reef would be inhabited solely by the poorer employees of the mines and by an inferior class of local shopkeepers. There are, therefore, strong reasons based upon the broadest political ground for securing now and for ever that the various townships shall radiate from their economic centres, that each class shall bear the political and social burdens which should fall to their lot as members of an economic whole, and that one class should not be allowed to separate its life from another class with which it is bound up by an inseparable economic tie.[69]

In order to achieve this objective, Curtis and O'Meara proposed that Johannesburg's boundaries be substantially extended, that the population be more widely scattered within the new area, and that the design be made practical through the integrating linkages which a comprehensive tramway system would provide for.[70]

The principles involved in this grand design were approved by Milner, and within weeks of its formulation the two original planners had the opportunity to implement a small part of their blueprint when they drafted a proclamation extending the city's boundaries from five to nine square miles. For the Acting Town Clerk, more accustomed to the measured political pace of a constitutional democracy, the speed and power of this form of government proved exhilarating. 'Just at present', Curtis wrote in his diary on 25 April 1901, 'one gets things done with a stroke of the pen that in England would entail an act of Parliament and an exhaustive parliamentary enquiry.'[71] The full scheme, however, called for a municipal area embracing 82 square miles, and this could not – without raising serious political and economic problems – simply be achieved 'with a stroke of the pen'. This latter extension called for a more subtle and flexible approach.

As soon as the first nominated Town Council was appointed in May, Curtis and Mayor O'Meara immediately set about educating its members and soliciting their support for the proposals which the two had earlier drafted. The Acting Town Clerk, in particular, impressed upon his council members the need to include the mining property that lay to the south of the reef in any plans for a greater consolidated Johannesburg. Curtis's success in these efforts was only briefly interrupted by the *Report of the Concessions Commission* in June 1901. The commissioners, aware of the large amounts of European capital tied up in the City & Suburban Co., were unwilling to deny the validity of the original concession and recommended that the horse-drawn tramway enterprise be recognised and come to terms with.[72] The town councillors took this potential hurdle in their stride, and in September officially endorsed the 'Memorandum on the Present and Future Boundaries of Johannesburg' and had Curtis send a copy to the Chamber of Mines for its 'comment'.[73]

The Chamber of Mines was at first deeply suspicious about the memorandum and the purpose of its authors. Harold Strange and most of his fellow capitalists were opposed to any southward extension of the city's boundaries which would include mining property, and thereby make the companies liable to pay rates and incur other financial obligations. The Chamber thus reacted negatively and with some hostility when it responded to the Town Council in October. Curtis and O'Meara, eager for any fray in which they enjoyed such powerful covert support, immediately issued a sharp rejoinder on behalf of the Council. Then, just when the stage seemed set for a long and acrimonious intra-ruling class battle, Milner intervened. Somewhat irritated by the mine owners' penny-pinching attitude, Milner now called on Percy FitzPatrick to persuade his colleagues in the industry of the long-term advantages contained in the proposal. This he proceeded to do, and late in 1901, the Chamber of Mines withdrew its objections to the scheme.[74]

With this major obstacle out of the way, the Town Council now felt that it could confidently set to work on developing the necessary infrastructure for the Mayor and the Acting Town Clerk's scheme. In January 1902 it called for plans and tenders to be submitted for a new system of tramways in the city, and awarded the contract to Messrs Mordey & Dawburn of England.[75] This time, however, the speed and swagger of the reconstruction momentum caused the Council to stumble since it failed to take sufficient cognisance of one unresolved issue – the fate of the City & Suburban Co.

C. S. Goldmann and his colleagues in the established tramways enterprise had been much heartened by the *Report of the Concessions Commission* in the previous year, and they now used its favourable recommendations as a base from which to fight a tenacious struggle against the new masters of the Transvaal. They constantly pressured the British administration for a decision on the fate of their company, and in June 1902 Milner, unable to avoid the issue any longer, conceded the legality of the original concession and acknowledged the right of City & Suburban to continue running horse-drawn trams in Johannesburg. The nominated Town Council, alarmed by this development, now rushed to its mentor and requested that it be granted the exclusive right to electric or mechanically worked tramways in the city. This Milner promptly did by issuing Proclamation No. 39 which became law in the same month – June 1902.[76] The net effect of these decisions was simply to legalise a stalemate situation that had been developing for some time.

Both parties – the City & Suburban Co. and the Town Council – now proceeded to use their respective rights as bargaining counters in an attempt to acquire the holdings of the rival since there was obviously no long-term future in *two* competing tramway systems within the city. When suitable terms could not be swiftly agreed upon, however, the opponents made unashamed use of the only other weapon available to them – time. The company, aware that its own operations hampered the city's planning and construction activities, hoped that any delay would increase public pressure on the Town Council and so facilitate a settlement.[77] The Council, for its part, was equally aware that the value of the horse-drawn tramway declined with each week that brought the electric trams closer, and thus looked to a sudden collapse by the company's principals. But, as so often happens in such evenly matched bouts, each contestant underestimated the other's capacity for resistance. In the end, it was only on 30 June 1904 that the Council acquired the undertaking and assets of the City & Suburban Tramway Co. at a cost of £150,000.[78]

In practice, however, the price that the public were made to pay for the horse-drawn trams far exceeded the cash transaction which the Town Council negotiated. While the lengthy dealings between the Council and the company dragged on, the City & Suburban directors were understandably loath to spend any additional amounts on the maintenance or extension of the old tramway system. This meant that while the city was experiencing a rapid expansion and spread of population, its only available 'public' transport system was actually declining, and between 1903 and 1905 there was a steady decrease in the number of passengers which the horse-drawn trams carried each year. As a direct consequence of this inadequate service, many urban commuters were forced to turn to alternative forms of transport during this period. It was thus with a sense of some relief that the travelling public finally witnessed the running of the first municipal electric tram on 14 February 1906. But, although the number of passengers using the trams jumped from three and a half million per year in 1904–5 to fourteen and a half million in 1906–7, the tramways offered an intermittent and restricted service for much of the period between 1906 and early 1908. Thereafter, there was a steady increase in the number of citizens making use of the electric trams and by 1914 the system was carrying over 30 million passengers annually.[79]

As soon as the Council had the nucleus of the new system established, however, it proceeded to pursue its declared policy of 'scattering' the white working population with some vigour. Aided by capital and land grants from the Malvern, Kensington and Braamfontein Estate Companies (at least one of which was wholly owned by mining capital), the Council extended the tramways to several new suburbs. Any additional capital costs which it incurred through such line extensions the Council recouped by imposing a special levy on ratepayers living in the newly connected working-class residential areas. These measures, when supplemented with a conscious policy of keeping fares relatively high until such time as the initial capital loan had been repaid, placed Johannesburg's electric tramways on a firm financial footing. In the first fourteen years of its operation the new public transport system yielded a profit of over half a million pounds, and this sum was accordingly credited to the city's general funds.[80]

In summary then, it may be suggested that Johannesburg's transition from a privately owned horse-drawn tramway to an electrically operated public utility was far from smooth. It took a war, three years of hard negotiating, and a substantial cash payment to the City & Suburban Co. for the reconstruction overlords to shake themselves free from a public transport system that had previously been designed to serve the needs of a rural bourgeoisie and its European capitalist partners. Once the British administration and its industrial allies had become hegemonic, however, they made use of the urban transport system as part of a strategy of social control which was ultimately intended to reduce conflict between capital and labour. But it was during the transition between these systems that the tramways left most to be desired, and thus it was that between 1902 and 1908 there were still opportunities for a petty bourgeoisie looking to urban transport for its living.

Johannesburg's cab trade in the post-war period – re-emergence, fragmentation and decline

As soon as significant numbers of refugees started to return to the Witwatersrand under the permit system, Johannesburg's dormant cab trade started to revive. Indeed, so swiftly and securely did the private transport sector re-establish itself, that it is possible that by the end of 1902 there were more cabbies at work in the city than there had been in 1896. At least part of this early vitality in the post-war cab business derived from the fact that the horse-drawn tramway did not operate at all until Milner's decision in principle on the City & Suburban Co. in June 1902. Thereafter, the cabbies simply reaped their share of the profits that became available during a period when the reconstruction government implemented its policy of 'scattering' the white working class whilst the public only had access to a declining horse-drawn tram service. Between 1902 and 1906, when the electric trams were introduced, there were always close on 800 licensed cab drivers in service in Johannesburg – see Table 6.[81]

But if the immediate post-war years brought the cabbies a period of great promise, then it also taxed them with its measure of problems. As might be expected in the wake of a war, forage and horses were in markedly short supply for some time, and throughout 1902–3 prices remained at record levels. In addition, the cost of repairs and maintenance both increased significantly after the war. The cost of having a horse shod, for example, rose from 6/- in 1899 to 8/- in 1903, and it was also in the latter year that it was estimated that the overhead costs for maintaining a four-wheeler cab and its horses ran to 40/- per day. As always, these costs pressed hardest on those who lacked capital, and under these conditions there was further consolidation in the trade as several large proprietors bought out many of the smaller and more vulnerable cabbies. By early 1903 the luxurious Victorias cruised the streets of Johannesburg, virtually in total command of the cab trade, and hopelessly outnumbering the three small Cape carts that somehow still survived on the ranks.[82]

Not all the independent cabbies fell meekly before the economic onslaught, however; many simply passed on these higher costs to their customers and by so doing attempted to keep their profit margins intact. In the six months before the horse-drawn tramway resumed service, but also for a considerable time thereafter, there were consistent public complaints about

Table 6. Number of licensed cab drivers and cabs in Johannesburg, 1904–14

Six-month period ending	Number of cabbies licensed	Number of cabs licensed	Number of cabbies per licensed cab
31.12.04	945	575	1.64
30.6.05	–	587	–
31.12.05	799	618	1.29
30.6.06	853	530	1.61
31.12.06	606	406	1.64
30.6.07	623	417	1.49
31.12.07	558	368	1.51
30.6.08	523	373	1.40
31.12.08	490	367	1.34
30.6.09	476	363	1.31
31.12.09	389	337	1.15
30.6.10	437	328	1.33
31.12.10	424	344	1.23
30.6.11	485	368	1.32
31.12.11	483	378	1.28
30.6.12	477	367	1.30
31.12.12	401	336	1.19
30.6.13	400	384	1.04
31.12.13	349	277	1.26
30.6.14	343	298	1.15
31.12.14	302	297	1.02

cabbies refusing to accept engagements which they did not consider to be lucrative enough, or of drivers demanding excess fares. These practices frequently brought the cabbies into conflict with their clients, and during nine days in early 1902 no fewer than ten such complaints were lodged with the police. It was also in this same period that the most notorious case of such conflict was deliberately drawn to the public's attention by a local evening newspaper. On 13 January 1902 a leading Johannesburg socialite and member of the nominated Town Council, Colonel J. Dale Lace, first assaulted an Afrikaner cabby named Theron for what he construed to be wilful disobedience, and then drove off with the man's cab. When Lace subsequently appeared in court and was found guilty of assault, *The Star* – through a series of provocative articles and editorials – attempted to justify the Colonel's characteristic bullying behaviour by pointing to public grievances against the cab trade.[83]

It was partly because of such cases of conflict, but more particularly for the fundamental reason that the cab trade assumed an enhanced importance and power in the years before the introduction of the electric tram, that the reconstruction engineers regularly and vigorously intervened in the private transport sector. In the early months of 1902 Milner personally corresponded with members of the Refugee Committees at the coastal cities in an attempt to facilitate the prompt return of 'genuine cab proprietors'. But this benign and accommodating Imperial involvement was not typical, and most of the state's intervention during this early period was directed towards 'tidying up' and controlling the cab trade. On two occasions within twelve months the Town

Council debated elaborate draft regulations to govern the cabbies and their business, while the state obligingly turned these recommendations into law through the proclamation of Government Notice No. 685 of 1902. Indeed, so extensive were these new by-laws, that the *Transvaal Leader* was moved to complain that 'the poor cabby has been legislated out of his business'.[84] What the *Leader* considered as ironic comment, however, was less than funny. For the most vulnerable cabbies in a racist state there was no humour in such a statement, only a chilling reality.

In the second week of January 1902 the reconstruction authorities arbitrarily withdrew the licences of all black cabbies operating in the city. When their documents were reissued a little later the cab drivers were informed that in future they would no longer be allowed to transport European passengers. 'At the stroke of a pen', Curtis and his colleagues created the 'second class cab' – a classification which, in the case of black cabbies, rested on the colour of the driver rather than on the quality of the vehicle or the service provided. Thus, after surviving more than a decade of legal twilight in Kruger's Republic, Johannesburg's black cabbies emerged into the unequivocal glare of formalised segregation under the Milner administration. Thereafter, the city's black cab drivers were restricted by law to accepting fares from only the poorest section of the urban population – their fellow Africans.[85]

It was this same device – the new classification system – that Milner and his men employed to divide the ranks of the Malay cabbies. The 75 to 100 coloured cabbies who owned vehicles that were considered to meet the required standard had their cabs rated 'first class', and were thus allowed to convey European passengers at the minimum rate of 2/6d per mile. The remaining cabbies, whose vehicles failed to meet the test set by the municipality's inspector, had their cabs classified as 'second class', and were thus restricted to transporting non-white passengers at the rate of 6d per mile. While the classification in this case did not derive simply from colour, since it was the cab rather than the driver that was supposedly under scrutiny, it nevertheless had the effect of penalising the poorest and most vulnerable Malays – those who had struggled hardest to make the transition from the old Cape cart to the new four-wheeled Victoria.[86] Moreover, since 'second class' cabs were again restricted to conveying lower-income groups, it was difficult for these less fortunate coloured drivers to accumulate sufficient capital with which to extricate themselves from their economic predicament.

In addition to these measures directed against the black and Malay cabbies, the new government also moved – in more subtle fashion – against the European drivers in its effort to rationalise and reorganise the city's cab service. Making use of the 'permit system' operating at the coastal towns, it sought to screen out unqualified or 'undesirable' white cabbies and prevent them from reaching the Rand. Its conspicuous failure in this regard, however, derived not so much from a lack of administrative zeal or skill, as from a series of complex problems that were clearly beyond its immediate influence. The manpower demands of the British army, the pace of demobilisation and the slow release of prisoners of war, all combined to place experienced cabbies with a knowledge of Johannesburg in short supply. This, together with the pattern of European immigration to South Africa at the turn of the century, meant that most of those white cabbies who did find their way to the city after 1902 differed sharply in religious, cultural and class background from their predecessors in the trade.[87]

Poor East European Jews were no newcomers to South Africa. From the mid-1880s onwards oppressive Russian legislation, pogroms, demands by the Tsar's army and economic stagnation in the Pale of Settlement, all had contributed to a steady flow of emigrants from Lithuania. The majority of these emigrants who made their way to the Witwatersrand were drawn from the small commercial centres situated in the agricultural areas that surrounded the larger towns of Kovno and Wilna. It was in their native Lithuania that most of these Jews acquired experience of petty trading, but a significant number of them had also been involved in the transport business – including cab driving.[88] This European background also came to reflect itself in the way in which these Lithuanians inserted themselves into the economic fabric of Johannesburg in the pre-war period – most turned to hawking and trading for a living, but a small number also took to cab driving.

After the recession of 1897 and the decline of the liquor trade, however, the poorest and most vulnerable of these Jewish immigrants were forced out of commerce and onto the Rand labour market. Shortly thereafter they were turned into wartime refugees, and it was while they were at the Cape between 1899 and 1902 that they were joined by new arrivals from Lithuania.[89] It was also during this period that most of these unskilled East European immigrants came to appreciate that their best chance of obtaining a permit for work in the Transvaal lay in presenting themselves as cab drivers. With the support and assistance of a small number of Jewish cab proprietors many of these immigrants succeeded in obtaining the necessary clearance certificates, and made their way to the Witwatersrand. In Johannesburg it was this influx of new cabbies that was considered to be 'undesirable' by many of the local whites, and that was greeted with ill-concealed prejudice and contempt by the English press.

What these cabbies perhaps lacked in cash, they more than compensated for through close cooperation with their colleagues, and by demonstrating a genuine concern for the well-being of their countrymen. Drawing from a rich Jewish cultural tradition in which the notion of *tsedaka* – social justice – played an important part, they were soon active in the many *chevras* or charitable associations on the Rand.[90] The Lithuanians rapidly discovered, however, that an enlightened social conscience alone did not provide sufficient professional protection in reconstruction Johannesburg. Anti-semitism, the Dale Lace assault, a barrage of local government legislation and a growing tendency for a few large proprietors to dominate the cab trade, all persuaded the cab drivers to draw on another strand of their East European experience – that of the *Yiddisher Arbeiter Bund*, the union. Thus, when a Cab Drivers' Union (C.D.U.) was formed in April 1902, the Jewish cabbies were amongst its most active and enthusiastic members.[91]

This move towards co-ordinated action by the drivers, together with a measure of shared apprehension about the Milner administration's moves to regulate the cab trade strictly, prodded the cab owners into action as well. In October 1902 the older and more established Cab Owners' Association was resuscitated and J. Zeeman was elected as its first post-war chairman.[92] By the end of that year then, the Johannesburg cab trade had two professional associations which – amongst other things – represented divisions between older and newer immigrants, conservative and more radical elements, and capital and labour. In theory these divisions held considerable potential for conflict, but in practice they seldom produced major rifts.

One reason that lay behind the usually amicable relationship between the two associations was the fact that class differences within the trade were still not fully crystallised. A good number of owner-drivers chose to belong not to the C.D.U., but to the Cab Owners' Association. While such small self-employed operators had interests that differed in certain respects from those of the drivers, they were also not at one with the large cab proprietors, and this ambiguous situation tended to produce cross-cutting loyalties. At least as important a factor in reducing tension between the rival associations within the trade, however, was the fact that bonds of kinship, culture and religion tended to draw the two bodies together. Indeed, so strong were these ties by late 1904 when the C.D.U. acquired the old Austrian Imperial Hotel premises for a social club, that in its application for a liquor licence the C.D.U. committee made a point of stating that the building would be used by the 'Jewish Cab-owners *and* Drivers of Johannesburg'.[93]

It was largely this underlying unity between the C.D.U. and the proprietors that enabled the trade to challenge Milner's nominated Town Council when it introduced Government Notice No. 685 of 1902. This contentious legislation, amongst other things, made provision for the introduction of half-fares for the second and subsequent passengers on a cab journey – an old idea which the cabbies had resisted when the Sanitary Board first tried to implement it in 1896–7. On this occasion the small independent operators opposed the provision for exactly the same reason they had done six years earlier – namely, that it reduced their income. The large cab proprietors, however, had an additional reason for objecting to the clause, since its introduction came at precisely the same time that they were put under great pressure from the C.D.U. to increase the £2 per week cash wage which they paid their drivers. This meant that the big cab owners were caught between the economic scissors of rising costs and falling revenue, and this was an argument which they successfully pressed home on the Union negotiators. Thus, when a joint meeting of the two professional associations was called to discuss the Milner proclamation on 15 January 1903, it drew more than 1,500 interested people to the Fordsburg Market square.[94]

Partly as a consequence of this large gathering, a deputation was sent to the Town Council in order to put the cab trade's grievances. This delegation, led by C.D.U. President W. N. Kingsley, put its case so forcefully and effectively that the Council agreed to withdraw virtually all those provisions in the legislation which the cabbies found objectionable. In March, Government Notice No. 241 of 1903 came to replace the earlier proclamation, and for the second time within a decade the organised cab trade had defeated the local authorities on the issue of tariffs. Needless to say this reversal of policy by Milner's nominees was greeted with derision and displeasure by many of the cab-users in Johannesburg.[95]

But despite the cooperation which brought about a victory on the half-fare issue, and despite the fraternity that lay behind the idea of the social club in Fox street, there were also ongoing conflicts and tensions within the cab trade. Predictably perhaps, the most noteworthy of these differences lay between the two parties with the most divergent interests – the cab owners and their drivers. The drivers were deeply resentful of the small cash wage which they received in exchange for a working day which often averaged between twelve and eighteen hours in length. As unskilled immigrants, however, they were also reluctant to confront their employers openly about this grievance. Instead, exploiting the absence of meters on their horse-drawn vehicles, the drivers made their own 'adjustments' to their wages by manipulating the amount of the takings which they handed over to the cab owner at the end of the day.[96]

The cab owners, aware of this growing practice, increased their vigilance and demanded that returning drivers hand over *all* the cash in their possession at the end of a shift. This in turn meant that drivers were often forced into handing over their 'tips' to their employers, as well as their takings. The whole cash extraction ritual therefore produced great tension and resulted in heated arguments which frequently culminated in the dismissal of the cab driver. The drivers, ever resourceful, responded to this by forging themselves new licences and documents which they promptly presented to other cab proprietors in their search for alternative employment.[97] It was this smouldering post-war conflict which finally caught alight in full-scale class confrontation in 1905.

As early as January 1905 there were signs of substantial discontent in sections of the cab trade. In particular, cab drivers complained about being arrested for 'loitering' while attempting to secure a full complement of passengers for the journey to the race course at Auckland Park. At a series of mass meetings, attended by both owners and drivers, resolutions were passed requesting that the Town Council provide more cab stands, and that it provide more protection for cabbies by defining 'loitering' more precisely in the local statutes. Over the next five months, however, nothing happened and the police continued to harass the drivers on race day – a most unpopular action since it disrupted the cabbies' work during a particularly busy shift on a day when they could normally look forward to a sizeable haul in 'tips'. In June 1905, the frustrated drivers again raised these grievances at a meeting, but the cab owners cautioned them about the need for patience and on the importance of maintaining a united front in any further approaches that might be made to the authorities. Four weeks later – and with their grievances still unattended to – the drivers learned that the Town Council intended to introduce a new form of licence for cabbies modelled on that which was in use in London. This document, and a copy which had to be lodged with the municipal Inspcctor of Vehicles, had to indicate both when a driver had completed his period of employment and the reason for the termination of the contract. For many drivers, but especially for the Lithuanian cabbies, this action constituted the proverbial last straw.[98]

On 12 July the cabbies and a significant number of independent owner-drivers of cabs held an emergency meeting at Fordsburg at which the Lithuanians at once pressed for an official C.D.U. strike until such time as all their grievances had been met. Although the Union leaders refused to give their official sanction to strike action, they and the small independent cab owners did agree to consolidate their alliance by electing a 36-man 'General Executive Committee' of cabmen. It was this committee, under the chairmanship of the 'Quiet little Napoleon of the Jehus', L. Joffe, that decided that a strike should commence on the very day that the new licences were to be first issued – Saturday, 15 July 1905. Delighted with this decision, at least 300 drivers at once handed in their old licences to the Committee as an indication of their support for the strike.[99]

The strike started on a promising note for the drivers when, on the Saturday morning, a somewhat bemused Johannesburg awoke to find only six cabs plying for hire in the city. While members of the public searched for rickshaw-pullers to meet their transport needs, bands of strikers combed the city streets 'persuading' scabs about the folly of their ways, and distributing handbills which outlined the cabbies' grievances and actions. At eleven o'clock hundreds of cab drivers, decked out in the distinctive colours of organised labour, met in the Fordsburg 'Dip' to take part in a procession to Von Brandis square where they planned to hold a meeting. The strikers then marched behind the Red Flag and sang the Marseillaise as they made their way towards the city centre. But, at Von Brandis square, the cab drivers met with an initial setback when they were dispersed by a contingent of mounted police even before they could commence their rally.

On the same afternoon, however, the strikers regrouped and held their meeting on the more familiar and secure ground of Avenue road, Fordsburg. Here, the cabbies were given the cheering news that the drivers of horse-drawn buses – partly out of solidarity, and partly out of fear of reprisals – had refused to convey large numbers of race-goers to Auckland Park. At the same time the strikers also listened to a warning from their leaders about the need to avoid violence – hardly inappropriate advice, since W. N. Kingsley of the C.D.U. and one Mr Goldberg of the Cab Owners' Association had already been arrested for exchanging blows in a public place. That others too feared a breach of the peace by the strikers became clear later that evening when the police promptly arrested a prominent Town Councillor – J. W. Quinn – for loudly hailing a cab in Commissioner street.[100]

Early on the following morning – Sunday – bands of strikers again roamed the city centre looking for any of the thirty drivers who had been bold enough to venture out and offer their vehicles for hire. Numerous arrests were made, as, for example, when Solly Levy, Harris Sollar and Harry Spencer stopped a 'non-Union man's cab' in Rissik street and used knives to slash the cushions and leather hood of the Victoria. It was in the afternoon, however, that the strikers once more gathered for a rally – this time near their base at the Moonlight Hotel in Commissioner street. Here, a crowd of between 500 and 1,000 cab drivers and their sympathisers succeeded in blocking all traffic for several hours. But, as on the previous day, the strikers were again to be denied the right of a public meeting. No sooner did the Lithuanian founder of the short-lived Social Democratic Workers' Party – Yeshaya Israelstam – start his address to the crowd, than he was stopped by the police who asked him to produce his official authorisation to hold such a meeting.[101] By the time that Israelstam had solved this problem the crowd had dispersed, and that night the C.D.U. instead held a meeting in the Trades Hall which was attended by about 400 drivers. At this meeting the cabbies discussed their campaign strategy, and elected a deputation to wait upon representatives of the Town Council on the following day.[102]

On Monday morning, 17 July, when most of the white workers in Johannesburg again set out for their places of employment after the weekend, the cabbies were still out on strike. With transport still continuing to be seriously disrupted at the start of a working week, the attitude of both the press and public started to change significantly. Whereas the cab drivers' action had been received with some humour and amusement over the previous two days, there was now a more strident, aggressive and prejudiced tone to newspaper reports. The *Rand Daily Mail*, for example, published a list of 'Suggestions to the Municipality' which included recommendations that cabbies be made to wash and shave regularly, and that they be required 'to know some English beyond "Nitchevo"'. There was also evidently some satisfaction at the fact that about two dozen strikers – most of whom were 'not of British nationality' – had been made to appear in the magistrate's court on the grounds of 'malicious damage to property' and other charges.[103]

Sensing this new mood of hostility towards the drivers, about twenty of the largest and most powerful proprietors in the Cab Owners' Association now took it upon themselves to put pressure on the city authorities to resist the strikers' demands. With a former cab proprietor and lawyer, B. Alexander, acting as their spokesman, the owners sent a deputation to the Works Committee of the Town Council which strongly urged the retention of the London-style licence for cabbies. No sooner had the cab owners' delegation been dismissed, however, than the Works Committee received and granted a request to hear the cab drivers' case. L. Joffe and W. N. Kingsley outlined what the cabbies' grievances were in general, and then proceeded to argue particularly strongly that the new licences were 'on the lines of the native pass' and that they allowed 'employers who might be spiteful, the power to injure a man's character when the man did not deserve it'.[104] As far as the C.D.U., and the Lithuanian drivers in particular were concerned, the new licence forms had to be abandoned completely.

Caught in the cross-fire of open class conflict, the Works Committee proceeded to attempt the impossible – it tried to satisfy both parties to the dispute. In order to get urban transport back to normal it immediately made full concessions to the drivers on the question of 'loitering' and on the issue of the need for more cab stands. In addition, it sought to appease the militant Lithuanians by agreeing to a change in the wording of the new licence and by assuring them that proprietors would not be allowed to enter prejudicial comments about drivers or 'secret marks' on the document. But in order to save some face and accommodate the cab owners, the Committee refused to entertain the C.D.U. demand that the new licence be scrapped entirely.[105]

Since the Works Committee had gone so far towards meeting the cab drivers' demands, Joffe and Kingsley agreed to put the proposed concessions to the cabbies. At this point a rumour to the effect that the strike was over swept through the city, and this misinformation was given further credence by the publication of an incorrect press report. When the strikers met that night, however, they quickly dispelled such wishful thinking by voting overwhelmingly to continue their action until such time as the Council was willing to abandon the new licence entirely.[106]

On the following morning, Tuesday 18 July, between 60 and 70 owner-driven cabs appeared on the ranks, many as a result of the rumour that the strike was supposedly over. The large cab proprietors – I. Moyes, N. Kramer and B. Davidson – immediately capitalised on this development by persuading the police to increase the number of men on duty at the cab stands. This act, which threatened to increase conflict, aroused great bitterness within the cab trade as a whole. The strikers, however, responded to it by sending out bands of roving pickets and by mid-morning they had succeeded in reducing the number of cabs plying for hire to about twenty.[107]

With this successful counter-thrust behind them, and the strike entering its fourth day, Joffe and his General Executive Committee now decided to apply further pressure to the local authorities by sending a delegation of six representatives to the Inspector of Vehicles, Mr Jefferson. The Inspector, after listening to the cabbies' arguments, agreed to suspend the introduction of the new licences and proposed that the C.D.U. again put their grievance to the full Town Council which was due to meet on the following afternoon. From Jefferson's words and actions it became clear to the drivers that the local authorities were about to accede to their major demand – and that the new licence be abandoned. But, as had happened once before, the story got afoot that the strike had been called off. This time the response in the trade was instant and by late afternoon close on 200 cabs were out on the streets plying for hire. For the second time that day it was left to the pickets to get the cabs and their drivers off the streets – a clear indication that sections of the trade were becoming impatient with the strike.[108]

That night, when a joint meeting of the 'small owners' and the cab drivers was held at the Moonlight Hotel, however, the Lithuanians again demonstrated that they were foremost among the ranks of the militants. In a lengthy speech delivered in Yiddish, B. Slavin berated the large proprietors for their treachery in approaching the Town Council and the police in the name of the Cab Owners' Association. He was followed by yet another speaker who proposed that the owner-drivers 'leave the big cab-owners and do without them' – a development which did in fact materialise to some extent as several independent cabbies switched their affiliations to the C.D.U. At the end of the meeting resolutions condemning the large cab proprietors, and supporting the strikers, were carried 'with enthusiasm'.[109]

On Wednesday morning, 19 July – the fifth and final day of the strike – the cab drivers awoke to find themselves the subject of a vicious attack in the *Rand Daily Mail.* In an editorial the newspaper suggested that the Town Council adopt a firm stance against the strikers, and that 'no licences be granted to men who are palpably little better in their appearance than the most filthy Kaffir'.[110] The effect that this verbal venom would have on members of the public and the Town Council undoubtedly worried the strike leaders. In addition, Joffe and Kingsley were becoming deeply concerned about the lack of strike funds and the difficulty they were experiencing in keeping non-Union cabs off the streets. All of these problems contributed to making Wednesday a long and tense day for the General Executive Committee and their hardcore of Lithuanian supporters.

When the Town Council met in the afternoon its members at once retreated into a series of prolonged procedural manoeuvres. This intentional or unintentional filibustering took several hours, and it was late in the day before the Rand trade unionist, Peter Whiteside, managed to put the C.D.U.'s case to his fellow councillors. As evening fell, the cab drivers were still without a decision from the Council and, at this point, Joffe and his colleagues again conferred at their strike headquarters. Members of the General Executive Committee were of the opinion that the drivers were too poverty-stricken to continue the struggle, and that the effect of the strike was already starting to seriously undermine the condition of those horses that belonged to the sympathetic owner-drivers. Under the circumstances Joffe and Kingsley felt duty-bound to recommend a return to work, and to this end summoned a meeting of the strikers. In the courtyard of the Moonlight Hotel the cab drivers and the 'small owners' had already decided to return to work on the following morning when the news arrived that the Town Council had agreed to suspend the introduction of the new licenses for a period of three months. This 'concession' was immediately interpreted as a victory by the strikers, and the celebrations in Commissioner street lasted into the small hours of the morning.[111]

On the following day the Cab Owners' Association issued a sour 'official statement' to the press through its Secretary, J. Harcourt-Stuart. The large proprietors felt that the drivers, in endeavouring 'to act without the sanction and cooperation of their masters, had made a mess of things, and had alienated the sympathy of the public'.[112] But despite the Owners' opinion to the contrary, the men who came 'for the most part from down-trodden Russia' had succeeded in defending their economically precarious position with some skill and determination. The London-style licences were never re-introduced, which in effect meant that cabbies could continue to supplement their low wages by manipulating the amount of cash takings which they handed over to the proprietors. Moreover, since the Lithuanians had convincingly demonstrated their collective strength, large proprietors tended to exercise more caution in dismissing cabbies, and one consequence of the strike was the establishment of an 'Arbitration Board' which sought to settle all disputes arising between owners and drivers.[113]

Important and impressive as the strike of 1905 may have been, it also came in the twilight of the cab trade's powerful position within the local transport system. In the midst of a capitalist revolution, and without the protection which the old pre-war rural bourgeoisie afforded them, the bargaining power of those involved in horse-drawn transport was rapidly ebbing away. After 1905 the cab trade never again succeeded in halting or defeating the municipal government on any issue of substance. Indeed, thereafter – and especially between 1906 and 1909 – the cab trade declined steadily as the modern industrial city which Curtis and Milner had planned started to take shape

In February 1906 the first electric tram ran through the streets of central Johannesburg. In the months that followed, it was swiftly extended to the most populous suburbs, and by December of that year – much to the cabbies' distress – it had already reached the Auckland Park race course. Despite its early lack of reliability and efficiency, the new system nevertheless succeeded in immediately carving off an enormous slice of the cab trade's business in what was already an economically depressed year. In six months,

The electric tram introduced to Johannesburg in February 1906

between June and December 1906, no fewer than 247 cab drivers were thrown out of work as close on 150 horse-drawn vehicles were permanently withdrawn from the ranks.[114]

Over the next two years the cab trade continued to contract, and a further 166 drivers lost their jobs as tramline extensions were made to yet more suburbs. But, despite the slow market erosion caused by the expansion of the electric system, the horse-drawn vehicles continued to serve a need by providing a flexible service which, free of a dependence on rails, could reach inaccessible parts of the city or take cross-town routes. The cab drivers must have known, however, that even this sector of their market was under threat from yet another post-war competitor – the motorised taxi.[115]

In December 1908 the cabbies' worst fears were realised when the Town Council announced that it had received its first application for permission to run a taxi service in the city. In a vain attempt to head off this competition, over 500 cabmen put their signatures to a petition protesting against this new development but, in February 1909, the first taxi duly made its appearance in Johannesburg. The fact that an ex-cab proprietor – B. Golub of Terrace road, Fordsburg – was a major shareholder in the Transvaal Taxi-cab Co. Ltd. did nothing to make this venture more acceptable to the Jehus, and neither did the competitive table of tariffs which the municipality announced shortly thereafter. In the latter half of 1909 it was the taxi, at least as much as the tram, that pushed a further 168 drivers into the ranks of the unemployed.[116]

This series of savage blows to the cab trade left ugly scars in several places. As the horse-drawn vehicles grew progressively less competitive, so the declining number of proprietors worked their drivers harder and longer for lower wages. Never an easy way of earning a living, by 1907 'cab driving was looked upon as the last resort of the destitute'. Poor, and confronted with the prospect of joblessness, at least some of the cabbies sought a way out of their predicament by supplementing their meagre incomes through developing links with prostitutes or illicit liquor sellers.[117] But, as the Transvaal Indigency Commission of 1906–8 revealed all too clearly, it was in Fordsburg and adjacent Vrededorp that the collapse of the cab trade took its heaviest toll. Much of the old bustle, vitality and social cohesion of these communities was lost, and replaced by the open unemployment and tell-tale apathy that accompanies urban decay in capitalist societies. In 1913 the remaining active cabbies in Fordsburg – a suburb where the C.D.U. eight years earlier had marched behind the Red Flag, and where before that the Vigilance and Cab Owners' Association had once been a single indivisible body – were sufficiently vulnerable for their fellow citizens to challenge their right to keep 'stables and kaffirs'.[118]

Within the cab trade itself the professional associations too went into a predictable decline after the introduction of the electric tram. By 1908 the separate owners' and drivers' organisations had been amalgamated into a single Cabmen's Association of Johannesburg (C.A.J.). To some extent this latter body continued to interest itself in the activities of organised labour on the Witwatersrand – as when, for example, it supported the strike of Krugersdorp cabbies against the introduction of a new municipal table of tariffs in 1908.[119] But, largely shorn of its Lithuanian component, the C.A.J. offered but a faint echo of the more vibrant and socially conscious voice of labour that had earlier been heard within the trade.

Already defeated by a combination of capitalist development and modern technology, the Cabmen's Association had no easily identifiable focus for its anger or despair. Instead, the C.A.J. made use of the dominant 'white labour policy' to turn on those sixty or more coloured drivers who continued to operate 'first class' cabs in the city. Between 1911 and 1913 the Cabmen's Association continually demanded that the local authorities take action against these remaining 'Malay' cabbies. Early in 1914 this racist agitation finally bore fruit when the Town Council duly legislated against coloured cabbies accepting 'first class' fares.[120] By then there were all of 300 drivers of horse-drawn cabs left in Johannesburg.

Conclusion

It is commonplace to suggest that the Witwatersrand experienced a capitalist revolution between 1886 and 1914. A number of scholars, through detailed and rigorous studies, have thrown light on that transformation, and through their efforts we now have valuable insights into the changing 'forces and relations of production', and the role of the state. Using the light shed by these enquiries, social historians are well placed to search for additional questions and answers that can further enhance our understanding of those formative years in the evolution of modern industrial South Africa. A detailed examination of the development of urban transport in Johannesburg can perhaps go some way towards illustrating the process of class struggle in one arena during that capitalist revolution.

It is possible that when Kruger and the Volksraad first gave A. H. Nallmapius a concession to run a horse-drawn tram service in Johannesburg they did not fully appreciate the size of the market which it would create for burgher agricultural produce. What is clear is that once the State President and his advisers did realise the value of the transport concession to their class constituents – the rural bourgeoisie and a section of the urban petty bourgeoisie – they defended it with the utmost determination. Kruger, contrary to the criticisms implicit in the writings of mining capitalists such as J. P. FitzPatrick and others, was no living anachronism opposed to modern technology *per se*. The State President was, however, fully aware of the fact that technology was not 'neutral', and that in a developing capitalist society it could be made to serve different class interests. Thus, Kruger was only willing to countenance the introduction of an electric tramway in the principal industrial city of his Republic if it could supplement or enhance the interests of his country-based ruling class. The longevity of the horse-drawn tram in Johannesburg offers evidence of burgher economic penetration into the new system, rather than of the supposedly stubborn opposition of Boers to 'progress'.

The British imperialists, having smashed the old landed ruling class in the Transvaal, were equally aware that technology was not in any way 'neutral' in the class struggle. For Milner and his colleagues, however, Johannesburg was first and foremost an industrial capitalist city, and only thereafter an outlet for agricultural produce. It was thus in accordance with this new priority that Lionel Curtis and others planned the geography of class distribution within the modern city. Within this scheme the town planners made provision to 'scatter' the white working class over a wider area so that social control might be enhanced, and that the risks of class conflict might be reduced. Again, it was within the parameters of this design that the city required an electric tramway system which could provide for the cheap and efficient transport of workers to and from their places of residence. But, as Curtis and his colleagues discovered, the *ancien régime* did not end with the Peace of Vereeniging. In the boardrooms of Brussels, and in the backstreets of Fordsburg and Vrededorp, some of Kruger's oldest allies fought on until well after 1902. The class struggle moves at its own pace. In Johannesburg the electric trolley only came to town in 1906.

Notes

1 This intention is expressed clearly, and at some length, in 'Memorandum on the Present and Future Boundaries of Johannesburg' in L. Curtis, *With Milner in Africa* (Oxford 1951), p. 260.

2 See J. P. McKay, *Tramways and Trolleys* (Princeton 1976), especially pp. 5–6, 51–2, 71 and 80. Also S. B. Warner, *Streetcar Suburbs* (Cambridge, Mass. 1962).

3 H.M.S.O., *Report of the Transvaal Concessions Commission*, Part 1 (Command 623 of 1901), para. 4. Also, Transvaal Archives Depot (T.A.D.), Gov. Vol. 463, 'Johannesburg City & Suburban Tramway Concession', Statement signed by S. Neumann, London, 22 October 1901.

4 T.A.D., Gov. Vol. 463, 'Johannesburg City & Suburban Tramway Concession', 22 October 1901.

5 *Ibid.*

6 See also Chapter 2 above, 'Randlords and Rotgut', p. 52.

7 See T.A.D., S.S. Vol. 5085 (1895), 'List of Continental Shareholders'; Gov. Vol. 463, 'Jhb. City & Suburban Tramway Concession', 22 October 1901; and J. P. McKay, *Tramways and Trolleys*, p. 145.

8 Paragraph based on the following sources: T.A.D., S.S. Vol. 5084 (1895), Directors, Jhb. City & Suburban Tramway Co. Ltd., to His Honour, The State President and Executive Council, 9 October 1896; 'Tramway Company – General Meeting', *Standard and Diggers' News* (hereafter: *S. & D.N.*), 26 February 1897; Johannesburg Public Library (J.P.L.), W. P. Howarth, 'Tramway Systems of Southern Africa: Historic Notes and Extracts' (Mimeo. 1971), p. 19 (hereafter: 'Tramway Systems of Southern Africa'); and H.M.S.O., *Command 623 of 1901*, para. 7.

9 Table constructed from: T.A.D., S.S. Vol. 5084 (1895), Directors, Jhb. City & Suburban Tramway Co. Ltd. to H.H. The State President and Executive Council, 9 October 1896, and H.M.S.O., *Command 623 of 1901*, para. 7.

10 See J. P. McKay, *Tramways and Trolleys*, pp. 25–6; T.A.D., S.S. Vol. 5084 (1895), Directors, Jhb. City & Suburban Tramway Co. Ltd. to H.H. The State President and Executive Council, 9 October 1896; and T.A.D., Gov. Vol. 463, 'Jhb. City & Suburban Tramway Concession', 22 October 1901.

11 *Ibid.*

12 See J. P. McKay, *Tramways and Trolleys*, pp. 51–83.

13 Howarth, 'Tramway Systems of Southern Africa', p. 19, and T.A.D., S.S. Vol. 5083, Chairman, Jhb. City & Suburban Tramway Co. Ltd to State Secretary, 18 July 1896.
14 D. M. Wilson, *Behind the Scenes in the Transvaal* (London 1901), p. 141.
15 *Ibid.*, pp. 141–2.
16 In this regard it should be noted that while the City & Suburban Co. nominally held a right to carry goods on their trams, the Kruger government never allowed it to exercise this right – probably in an attempt to protect Afrikaner transport riders. See T.A.D., Gov. Vol. 463, 'Jhb. City & Suburban Tramway Concession', 22 October 1901.
17 See above, Chapter 2, 'Randlords and Rotgut', pp. 52, 70.
18 J. P. McKay, *Tramways and Trolleys*, p. 145. The Baron also held a watching brief over the City & Suburban Co. through a nominal one-share holding in the horse-drawn tram company – see T.A.D., S.S. Vol. 5085 (1895), 'List of Continental Shareholders', p. 18.
19 D. M. Wilson, *Behind the Scenes in the Transvaal*, p. 42. Wilson incorrectly puts this figure at £500 instead of £5,000.
20 National Archives of the United States of America, Washington, Despatches from United States Consuls in Pretoria 1898–1906, Vol. 1; Petition from W. Keller and others to C. E. Macrum, 17 October, 1898.
21 T.A.D., S.S. Vol. 5083 (1895), J. Berlein to State Secretary, 18 July 1896.
22 T.A.D., S.S. Vol. 5085 (1895), C. S. Goldmann to State Secretary, 12 September 1896.
23 T.A.D., S.S. Vol. 5084 (1895), C. S. Goldmann to State Secretary, 23 September 1896.
24 For a selection of such letters see T.A.D., S.S. Vols 5083–5085.
25 T.A.D., S.S. Vol. 5084 (1895), Chairman and Directors, City & Suburban Tramway Co. Ltd. to H.H. The State President and Executive Committee, 9 October 1896.
26 For the general background to this see C. T. Gordon, *The Growth of Boer Opposition to Kruger 1890–5* (London 1970), pp. 35–57.
27 See the rather flamboyant account of D. M. Wilson, *Behind the Scenes in the Transvaal*, pp. 142–5.
28 See the following editorials in the *S. & D.N.*: 'Tifts and Trams', 1 July 1897, and 'Those Terrible Trams', 9 July 1897.
29 National Archives of the United States of America, Washington, 'Despatches from United States Consuls in Pretoria, 1898–1906', C. E. Macrum to State Secretary, 19 October 1898.
30 See 'Tramway Company – General Meeting', *S. & D.N.*, 26 February 1897.
31 'The Tramway Company – The Annual Meeting', *S. & D.N.*, 5 March 1898. See also T.A.D., Gov. 463, 'Jhb. City & Suburban Tramway Concession', 22 October 1901.
32 J.P.L., Johannesburg City Archive (J.C.A.), Box 213, Cab Owners to Chairman and Members of the Sanitary Committee, 10 January 1891.
33 See *Johannesburg Census 1896*, Order VI, p. 39. See also 'Johannesburg Jehus', *The Star*, 19 February 1898.
34 *Johannesburg Census 1896*, pp. 44–7. For the names and addresses of the majority of businessmen involved see *Longland's Johannesburg and District Directory 1896*, entries on the following pages: 185, 207, 240, 263, 267 and 277.
35 Para. based on: T.A.D., Jhb. Landdrost Collection, Spesiale Landdrost Vol. 93, Sophia Untembu to Chief Landdrost, 30 May 1891; J.P.L., J.C.A., Box 217, S. van As to Sanitary Superintendent, 2 October 1894; J.P.L., J.C.A. Box 218, S. van As to Chairman and Members Central Smallpox Committee, 27 October 1894; and items in *S. & D.N.*, 5 September 1895, and *Johannesburg Times* of 8 and

10 June 1897.

36 'Johannesburg Jehus', *The Star*, 19 February 1898. See also – on the earlier period – W. H. Somerset Bell, *Bygone Days* (London 1933), p. 137.

37 As early as 1890 a battery-powered tram ran at Beaconsfield on the diamond fields, and a full electric tram service was introduced to Kimberley and Cape Town. See Howarth, 'Tramway Systems of Southern Africa', pp. 2, 37 and 47. In Kimberley, however, much of the structural unemployment of coloured cabbies derived from the closing down of mining companies during the depression. Between 1888 and 1890 the number of cab licences issued in Kimberley fell from 631 to 489. See Cape of Good Hope, *A7–91*, Office of Issuer of Licences, Appendix E, p. XI. I am indebted to Rob Turrell for drawing these statistics to my attention.

38 These names are not meant to be fully representative of the 'Malay' community on the Rand. In fact, they simply include the names of the most visible literate cabbies of the 1890s. See, for example, J.P.L., J.C.A. Box 213, Petition to Chairman and Members of the Sanitary Board, 10 January 1891; or T.A.D., S.S. Vol. 4934, Petition to H.H. The State President and Executive Committee, 8 December 1896.

39 *Ibid*. See also 'Cab Proprietors' in *S. & D.N.*, 27 February 1897; 'Johannesburg Jehus', *The Star*, 19 February 1898; and 'Incompetent Cab Drivers' in *The Sportsman and Dramatic News*, 15 August 1899.

40 There is clear evidence of the increasingly important role of Afrikaners after this date. Note, for example, the address in Dutch to the meeting of 'Cab Proprietors' in *S. & D.N.*, 27 February 1897, and the fact that a 'Dutch Representative' was included in the delegation sent to see the State President. See also 'Johannesburg Jehus', *The Star*, 19 February 1898.

41 On Jewish involvement in cab driving see G. Simonovitz, 'The Background to Jewish Immigration to South Africa and the Development of the Jewish Community in the South African Republic between 1890 and 1902', University of the Witwatersrand, B.A. Hons dissertation 1960, p. 16. (Hereafter: Simonovitz, 'The Jewish Community in the South African Republic, 1890–1902'.) On the liquor trade see above, Chapter 2, 'Randlords and Rotgut', pp. 73–4.

42 Para. based on: J.P.L., J.C.A. Box 213, Petition to Chairman and Members of the Sanitary Board, 10 January 1891; 'Meeting of Cab Owners', *S. & D.N.*, 7 May 1896; T.A.D., S.S. Vol. 4934, Petition to H.H. The State President and Executive Committee, 8 December 1896; and J.P.L., J.C.A. Box 232, Petition to Chief Inspector of Vehicles, 23 February 1899.

43 See items in the *S. & D.N.* of 7 and 8 May 1896; T.A.D., S.S. Vol. 4934, Petition to H.H. The State President and Executive Committee, 8 December 1896; 'Cab Proprietors' in *S. &D.N.*, 27 February 1897; and *Johannesburg Times*, 4 August 1897.

44 Collectively these areas formed the western working-class complex of early Johannesburg. However, some of these patterns managed to survive Milner's era of reconstruction. See, for example, *Longland's Transvaal Directories of 1903 and 1908*, p. 552 and 491 respectively.

45 'Meeting of Cab Owners', *S. & D.N.*, 7 May 1896, and 'Cab Proprietors', *S. & D.N.*, 27 February 1897.

46 For the tendency of railways to expand the need for horse-drawn cabs see F. M. L. Thompson, 'Nineteenth Century Horse Sense', *Economic History Review*, 29, 1, p. 65. I am grateful to Ian Phimister for drawing this source to my attention.

47 See 'Tramway Company', *S. & D.N.*, 26 February 1897, and 'Johannesburg Jehus', *The Star*, 19 February 1898.

48 'Tramway Company', *S. & D.N.*, 26 February 1897, and 'Johannesburg Jehus', *The Star*, 19 February 1898.

49 'Cab Fares', *S. & D.N.*, 2 March 1897.

50 'Meeting of Cab Owners', *S. & D.N.*, 2 May 1896.
51 *S. & D.N.*, 5 September 1896.
52 'The Town is inclined to be very grateful to the Sanitary Board if the war it is waging against exorbitant cab-fares results in the confusion of the Jehu' – 'The Cab Question', *S. & D.N.*, 23 September 1896.
53 See 'Cab Proprietors', *S. & D.N.*, 27 February 1897, and 'Cab Fares', *S. & D.N.*, 2 March 1897.
54 For an example of continued complaints see 'How We are Bled', *S. & D.N.*, 2 July 1897.
55 As late as August 1897 the cab drivers were still operating the alliance by circulating a petition against the introduction of the electric tram in both the town and the countryside. See report in the *Johannesburg Times*, 4 August 1897.
56 Para. based on: *Longland's Johannesburg and District Directory 1890*, p. 101; J.P.L., J.C.A. Box 213, Cab Owners to Chairman and Members, Sanitary Board, 10 January 1891; *Longland's Johannesburg and District Directory 1896*, p. 277; 'Cab Proprietors', *S. & D.N.*, 27 February 1897; 'Johannesburg Jehus', *The Star*, 19 February 1898; and the advert for 'Thornton's Trolley and Cab', *S. & D.N.*, 2 December 1898.
57 This para. based on: 'Johannesburg Jehus', *The Star*, 19 February 1898; 'Johannesburg Cabmen', *The Star*, 7 January 1907; and an interview with Mr Isadore Sagorin at Turffontein, Johannesburg, on 15 August 1978. (Interview conducted by C. van Onselen and Mr S. Kahn, and hereafter referred to as 'Sagorin Interview'.)
58 As one local journalist put it; 'The "Cape cart" is dropping into disfavour, and the winter of its existence is already autumned'. 'Johannesburg Jehus', *The Star*, 19 February 1898.
59 *Ibid.*, and Sagorin Interview, 15 August 1978.
60 'Johannesburg Jehus', *The Star*, 19 February 1898.
61 *Ibid.* See also 'Discontented Drivers', *Transvaal Leader*, 14 January 1903; E. Humphrey to Editor, *Transvaal Leader*, 17 April 1902; and Sagorin Interview, 15 August 1978.
62 'Our Cabs and "Cabbies"', *S. & D.N.*, 25 February 1899.
63 'Johannesburg Jehus', *The Star*, 19 February 1898.
64 J. P. FitzPatrick to J. Wernher, 25 July 1900, in A. H. Duminy and W. R. Guest (eds.) *FitzPatrick* (Johannesburg 1976), p. 274.
65 *Ibid.*
66 Curtis, *With Milner in South Africa*, p. vii.
67 For Curtis's most explicit statement about this see *With Milner in South Africa*, p. 256. For further background to the work and context of the Octavia Hill schemes see Gareth Stedman-Jones, *Outcast London* (London 1971), pp. 193–6.
68 See the Curtis diary entries for March and April in *With Milner in South Africa*, pp. 203–18. See also Major O'Meara's 'Note on Proposed Reconstruction, Johannesburg Municipality', 15 April 1901, cited in Sir John Maud's *City Government* (Oxford 1938), p. 119.
69 Extract from 'Johannesburg Municipality – Memorandum on the Present and Future Boundaries of Johannesburg'. Reprinted in full in Curtis, *With Milner in South Africa*, p. 260.
70 *Ibid.*, pp. 257–73.
71 Curtis, *With Milner in South Africa*, p. 217.
72 See *Command 623 of 1901*, and T.A.D., Gov. Vol. 463, 'Jhb. City & Suburban Tramway Concession', 22 October 1901.
73 Curtis, *With Milner in South Africa*, pp. 258–73.
74 *Ibid.*, in C. Headlam (ed.) *The Milner Papers*, Vol. 2 (London 1933), pp. 276–7.
75 Johannesburg, *Mayor's Minute 1901–3*, p. 8.

76 *Ibid.* See also J. Maud, *City Government*, p. 119.
77 For some public responses to these delays see the following examples drawn from *The Star*: 'Trams at Last', 21 June 1902; 'The Tramways', 3 September 1902; and 'An Elector' to Editor, on 'Electric Tramway Silence', 7 March 1904.
78 Johannesburg, *Mayor's Minute 1905*, p. 9. Also J. Maud, *City Government*, p. 119.
79 Para. based on: S. Court, 'The Progress of Johannesburg', *Addresses and Papers read at the Joint Meeting of the British and South African Associations for the Advancement of Science 1905*, Vol. 4, Appendix 9, p. 186; Johannesburg, *Mayor's Minute 1913–15*, p. 93; and J. Maud, *City Government*, p. 120.
80 Para. based on: Johannesburg, *Mayor's Minute 1905*, p. 8; S. Court, 'The Progress of Johannesburg', p. 171; J. Maud, *City Government*, p. 120; and 'Notes and Comments', *The Star*, 27 July 1909.
81 Data derived from Johannesburg, *Mayor's Minute*, covering the period from 1904 to 1914.
82 Para. based on: 'Work for the Council', *The Star*, 17 January 1902; 'Cab Drivers' Union', *Transvaal Leader*, 24 April 1902; 'Discontented Drivers', *Transvaal Leader*, 14 January 1903; and Johannesburg, *Minutes of the Town Council Meeting*, 28 January 1903, pp. 1276–7.
83 Para. based on the following reports in *The Star* of 17 January 1902: 'The Cab Service', 'Work for the Council', and 'Assault on a Cab Driver'. See also, however, Johannesburg, *Mayor's Minute 1907*, p. 99, 'Comparative Statement of Convictions against Cab Drivers from 1 January 1905 to 30 June 1907'.
84 Para. based on: 'Transvaal Refugee Committee – Monthly Report', *The Star*, 13 March 1902; Johannesburg, *Minutes of the Town Council Meetings* 1902, p. 378 and p. 951; and 'Discontented Drivers', *Transvaal Leader*, 14 January 1903.
85 See: 'The Cab Service', *The Star*, 17 January 1902; 'Cab Drivers' Union', *Transvaal Leader*, 24 April 1902; and Johannesburg, *Minutes of Town Council Meetings*, 28 January 1903, p. 1277. By 1905 at least one black cab owner remained in business – one William Beukes. See T.A.D., SNA Vol. 60, NA 3681/05, 'List of Letters of Exemption Granted'.
86 *Ibid.*
87 See, 'Work for the Council', *The Star*, 17 January 1902.
88 Simonovitz, 'The Jewish Community in the South African Republic, 1890–1902', pp. 16, 63–6.
89 Afroim Sagorin who arrived in Cape Town in 1902 was one example of such an immigrant. Born at Wilna, in 1885, Sagorin was conscripted into the Russian army in the mid-1890s and spent the duration of his military service attending to the horse of a Colonel in the Cossack Regiment. At the end of his military service the young Afroim made his way to South Africa where he already had two elder brothers. After trying unsuccessfully to get work as a cab driver in Cape Town, where proficiency in English was a requirement for a licence, Afroim made his way to Johannesburg late in 1902. Here he learnt English, as well as the cab and horse trade, through Jimmy Green, who later became a Mayor of Johannesburg. Green accompanied the young Lithuanian immigrant on the 'box' of the Victoria and translated the customers instructions into Yiddish until such time as Sagorin had sufficient mastery of the new language. With the example of an older brother already making a living as a produce merchant, Afroim eventually also accumulated sufficient capital to enter the related business of buying and selling horses. In later years Afroim Sagorin and his sons came to run one of Johannesburg's most successful saddlery and harness businesses. Sagorin Interview, 15 August 1978.
90 Simonovitz, 'The Jewish Community in the South African Republic, 1890–1902', p. 15.
91 In addition to the customary objectives of any union, the association sought to

'establish harmony and good fellowship, and to provide legal and monetary assistance to deserving members'. See 'Cab Drivers' Union', *Transvaal Leader*, 24 April 1902.

92 'Cabmen's Grievances', *Rand Daily Mail*, 14 October 1902.

93 Para. based on: 'Cabmen's Grievances', *Rand Daily Mail*, 14 October 1902, and T.A.D., Lt. Gov. 68/75/82, William Kingsley to the Lieutenant Governor of the Transvaal, 22 November 1904.

94 This para. based on: 'Discontented Drivers', *Transvaal Leader*, 14 January 1903, and 'Cabby's Grievances', *Rand Daily Mail*, 16 January 1903.

95 Para. based on: Johannesburg, *Minutes of the Town Council Meetings*, 28 January 1903, pp. 1276–7; 'The New Cab Tariff', *Transvaal Leader*, 17 April 1903; W. N. Kingsley to the Editor, *The Star*, 20 April 1903; and 'Cab Drivers and their Methods', *The Star*, 27 May 1903.

96 Sagorin Interview, 15 August 1978. Also, interview with Mr Ben Gaddie at Greenside, Johannesburg, on 10 April 1977. From these interviews and other material it is also clear that cab owners frequently set 'traps' for their drivers. See, for example, 'Cabby and his Fare', *S. & D.N.*, 24 September 1897.

97 Sagorin Interview, 15 August 1978. The cab drivers also had a long history of bribing the police and municipal officials. For a selection of examples see: 'The Cab Question', *S. & D.N.*, 23 September 1896; 'The New Cab Tariff', *Transvaal Leader*, 17 April 1903; 'Cab Drivers and their Methods', *The Star*, 27 May 1903; and 'Bribing an Official', *Transvaal Leader*, 7 December 1905.

98 For this background information see: 'Johannesburg Jehus', *Rand Daily Mail*, 15 July 1905; 'The Cabmen's Strike', *The Star*, 17 July 1905; 'Jehus on Strike', *Rand Daily Mail*, 17 July 1905; and 'The Owners' Point of View', *Rand Daily Mail*, 20 July 1905.

99 See 'Cabmen on Strike', *Transvaal Leader*, 17 July 1905; 'Jehus on Strike', *Rand Daily Mail*, 17 July 1905; and 'The Cab Strike Ends', *Transvaal Leader*, 18 July 1905.

100 The two preceding paras. based on: 'The Cabmen's Strike', *The Star*, 15 July 1905; 'Cabmen on Strike', *Transvaal Leader*, 17 July 1905; 'Jehus on Strike', *Rand Daily Mail*, 17 July 1905; and 'Cab Strike Sequel', *Transvaal Leader*, 18 July 1905.

101 See Leibel Feldman's Yiddish work, *The Jews of Johannesburg* (South African Yiddish Cultural Federation, Johannesburg 1956), pp. 137–41. I am most grateful to Mr G. Saron for drawing this work to my attention and generously providing me with a translation.

102 Para. based on: 'The Cabmen's Strike', *The Star*, 17 July 1905; 'Cabmen on Strike', *Transvaal Leader*, 17 July 1905; and 'Jehus on Strike', *Rand Daily Mail*, 17 July 1905.

103 Para. based on: 'Without Prejudice' and 'Jehus on Strike', in *Rand Daily Mail*, 17 July 1905; 'The Cabmen's Strike', *The Star*, 17 July 1905; and 'The Cab Strike Ends', *Transvaal Leader*, 18 July 1905.

104 'The Cabmen's Strike', *The Star*, 17 July 1905. See also, 'The Cab Strike', *Daily Express*, 18 July 1905.

105 *Ibid.* See also W. N. Kingsley to the Editor, *The Star*, 22 July 1905.

106 See 'The Cab Strike', *Daily Express*, 18 July 1905, and 'The Cab Strike', *Rand Daily Mail*, 19 July 1905.

107 'The Cab Strike', *Rand Daily Mail*, 19 July 1905, and 'The Cab Strike', *Transvaal Leader*, 19 July 1905.

108 *Ibid.*

109 See especially, 'Owners support Drivers' in *The Star*, 19 July 1905, and 'Cabmen's Union', *The Star*, 24 July 1905.

110 'The Cabmen's Strike', *Rand Daily Mail*, 19 July 1905.

111 'Cab Strike Ends', *Transvaal Leader*, 20 July 1905.

112 'The Owners' Point of View – An Official Statement', *Rand Daily Mail*, 20 July 1905.
113 'Cabmen's Union', *The Star*, 24 July 1905.
114 See the following items drawn from *The Star*: 'The Electric Trams', 14 February 1906; 'The Trams', 3 April 1907; 'The Tramways', 5 April 1907; and 'Johannesburg Cabmen', 7 January 1907. Statistics derived from Table 4.2.
115 The first attempt at introducing a form of taxi service in Johannesburg dated back to immediately after the war. See 'Prospectus of the Johannesburg Motor Car Company', *The Star*, 19 August 1902.
116 Para. based on the following: 'Motor Taxi-Cabs', *The Star*, 17 December 1908; 'The First Taxicab', *The Star*, 5 February 1909; 'Taxi Please!', *Transvaal Leader*, 9 February 1909; 'The Taxi in Johannesburg', *The Star*, 8 April 1909; 'Taxi-Cab Owners', *The Star*, 15 September 1909; and 'How we Travel', *The Star*, 17 August 1909.
117 Para. based on: 'Johannesburg Cabmen', *The Star*, 7 January 1907, and '"Cab Sir"', *The Star*, 4 January 1913.
118 See *Report of the Transvaal Indigency Commission 1906–1908*, evidence of S. J. Halford, p. 9; Acting Commissioner of Police, paras 1508–13, and Dr T. B. Gilchrist, paras 5638–9. Given his experiences in charity work in London it is perhaps predictable that Lionel Curtis was a member of this commission. Curtis was thus in the position of introducing the electric tram to the city and then having to investigate at least some of its structural consequences.
119 See the following items in *The Star*: 'Jehus on Strike', 7 October 1908; 'Cabmen's Strike', 8 October 1908; and 'Cabdrivers' Strike', 19 October 1908.
120 See especially: 'Cab Owners and Drivers – Complaint against the Council', *The Star*, 21 December 1911; '"Cab Sir"', *The Star*, 4 January 1913, and 'Notes and Comments', *The Star*, 19 February 1914.

Index

accommodation, institutional (*see also* boarding-houses; compounds)
  effects of, 5–8, 18
Afrikaners
  men, 174, 175
  politics, 36, 65, 67
  unskilled
    employment, *see* brickmakers; cab drivers
    unemployment, 20, 22, 35–6
  women, and prostitution, 145–6
agricultural surplus
  role in development of capitalism, 45–7, 94
agriculturalists
  advantages of electric tram to, 169–70
  alliance with cab drivers, 177–8
  Kruger's protection of, 9–10, 37, 165, 196
  relationship with mine owners, 15, 23
alcohol (*see also* Hatherley Distillery; liquor syndicates), 44–102
  analysis of, 55–7
  as health hazard, 55, 62
  distillation from agricultural surplus, 45–7, 94
  European trade in, 45–6
  illicit trade in (*see also* liquor syndicates), 16, 33
    control of, 64–6, 85–6
    effects of war on, 89, 96
  persistence of despite prohibition, 72, 78
  petitions against, 86–7
  Sammy Marks' involvement in, 70–72
  Transvaal Leader's campaign against, 82–5
  importance in working-class culture, 5–6
  imported, 46, 53–5, 67, 70–72
  link with recruitment and control of black mineworkers, 51–2, 59–60, 94–5
  manufacture of
    concession granted for, 6, 48
    increase in, 49, 51
    prohibition on, 32, 88
  mine owners' attitude to, 6, 15–16, 52, 59–60, 62–7, 79–81, 82, 90–92, 94–5
  processing by wholesalers, 55–7
  public opinion concerning, 58–9, 65, 67, 82–4
  quality control for, 69
  rapid expansion in market for, 51, 52
  restrictions on, 15–16, 58–9, 63–7
    difficulties of enforcing, 61–2, 72, 78
    lifting of, 87
    opposition to, 59–60, 68–9, 95–6
  resumption of trade in during reconstruction period, 91–2
  state monopoly in advocated, 79, 91
Alcohol Trust, 68, 70, 71
Alexander, R. C., 136
AmaWasha, 8, 18–19, 34–5
American Club, 119–20, 127, 135, 136, 138, 143
  exposure of workings of, 129–31
  re-establishment as 'Immorality Trust', 137
anti-semitism, 73, 74, 84, 187
Applebe, Mrs, assault on, 83, 85

Babylon, Johannesburg compared to, 2
Banque Française de l'Afrique du Sud, 52, 70, 115, 170
Banque Internationale de Paris, 167
Beit, Otto, 12, 14
Belford, S. F., 71
Berg, Landdrost N. J. van den, 108, 115
Berlein, Julius, 171
Bertha, Mathilda, 122
Betting Houses, Gaming Houses and Brothels Suppression Bill, 136
black cab drivers, 173, 186
black pimps, 114–15
black prostitutes, 146
black workers
  accommodation in mine compounds, 5, 18
  alcohol consumption (*see also* liquor

syndicates)
effects of, 62–3, 95
link with recruitment and control, 51–2, 59–60, 94–5
restrictions on, 15–16, 32–3, 58, 61–2, 63–7, 87, 92
control over, 13, 33
'houseboys', 18, 33–4
prohibition supported by, 83
sex ratio, imbalance in, 104
social distance from whites, 39–40
unemployment, 22–3, 36–7
wages, 24, 25
Bleksley, A. H., 116, 117
census of brothels, 111–12, 115
Bloemfontein, prostitution in, 136
boarding-houses, 5, 6, 18, 27, 31, 49, 120
Boer Republics, alcohol distillation in, 46–7
Boksburg, S. Nathanson's control of, 76–7
Bowery Boys
Cleaver's offensive against, 130–35
intimidation of witnesses, 132
Krakower's challenge to, 129
organisation, 118–22
bribery and corruption
by organised gangsters, 76–7, 119, 120, 126
of police, 62, 81, 105, 110
Brickfields, 8
brickmakers, 8, 19–20, 35
British administration
development of public transport under, 179–84, 197
impact on mining industry, 24
intervention in cab trade, 185–6, 188, 189
legislation against prostitution, 105, 139–43, 149
liquor trade resumed by, 91–2
negotiation with over compensation for Hatherley shareholders, 93–4
prohibition on alcohol, 88–9, 96
social control, 26, 27–36, 38–9, 181–4
British government, intervention by, 14
Broeksma, Cornelis, 85, 128, 130
brothels
censuses of, 111–12, 143, 146
closure of, 142
location of, 112, 146–7, 150
post-war operation of, 141
Sylvio Villa, 123–4, 141
Brown, Rev. Andrew, 90
Brussels, 167, 172, 197
Budner, Salus, 119
building, 8, 19–20
Burchardt, Arendt, 129

cab drivers, 9
Afrikaner, 174
black, segregation of, 186
class solidarity, 174, 178
classification, 186, 196
conflict with clients, 185
diverse origins of, 173–4, 187
opposition to Johannesburg Sanitary Board regulations, 175–8
strike by, 189–93
Cab Drivers' Union, 187, 188
conflict with cab owners, 189–93
Cab Owners' Association, 9, 172, 174, 188
conflict with drivers, 189–93
cab trade
costs, 179, 184
decline in, 20, 35, 175, 193–5
fares, 177, 188–9
official intervention in, 185–6, 188, 189, 191–3
owner-drivers, 172–9
post-war, 184–96
professional associations, 172, 174, 175, 187–8, 195–6
conflict between, 189–93
size and importance, 172–3, 185
vehicles used, 178–9
Cabmen's Association of Johannesburg, 195–6
canteen keepers (*see also* Witwatersrand Licensed Victuallers' Association)
'Peruvians' employed by, 74
reaction to prohibition, 72
weakness of law enforcement exploited by, 61–2
canteens
licences for, 58, 64
mine managers involvement in, 60
prostitution associated with, 7, 17, 107–8
rapid increase in number of, 6, 57
Cape cart, 178–9
Cape Colony
prostitutes from, 106–7, 120
prostitution in, 135–6
Cape Town, 69, 135, 136, 173

capital, international
investment in City & Suburban Tramway Co., 167
investment in Hatherley Distillery, 52
capital accumulation
through distillation of agricultural surplus, 45–7
capitalism
development of prostitution under, 148
sensitivity of Milner administration to needs of, 26, 27–31, 38–9
census (1896), 104
Chamberlain, Joseph, 91
Chinese mineworkers, 26
Christian feminists, 115
City & Suburban Tramway Co. Ltd., 9, 20, 165–72
assets acquired by Town Council, 30–31, 182–3
costs and profits, 167–9
effect of Lombard concession on, 170–72
investment in, 165, 167, 169
proposal to electrify, 9, 20, 169, 171
class, social, *see* ruling class; working class
class conflict, 2
avoidance of, 28, 29–30, 181, 197
between mine owners and petty bourgeoisie, 82
Cleaver, F. R. M., 16, 85, 149
Morals Act implemented by, 128–35
clergymen
involvement in reclamation of prostitutes, 141
prostitution condemned by, 17, 116–17, 127–8, 138–9, 147
reform of liquor trade advocated by, 83, 86–7, 90–91
Cohn, William, 82, 84
Companhia do Assucar de Moçambique, 53–4
compounds, 5, 6, 18, 27, 31–2, 39
illegal drinking dens described as, 78
concessions, 37–8, 48, 61
alcohol manufacture, 6, 48
enquiries into, 30, 93, 171–2, 180, 182
tramway, 9, 165, 196
Consolidated Gold Fields of South Africa Ltd., 11, 12, 28
construction industry, 8, 19–20
Contagious Diseases Act (1885), 106–7, 135
Coster, Dr Herman, 66, 115–16, 125
Crawford, Hugh, 48
crime, organised, *see* gangsters; liquor syndicates; Ninevites; prostitution; vice, organised
Crimes Prevention Ordinance (1905), 105, 145
Critic, The, 114–5
Cuirassier, George le, 138
culture, working-class (*see also* alcohol; prostitution), 5–7, 39–40
Curle, J. H., 52
Curtis, Lionel, 29–30, 35, 180–82, 197

Dale Lace, Col. J., 185
Dam, G. M. J. van, 125
Darragh, Rev. J. T., 90, 91
De Eerste Fabrieken in de Zuid Afrikaansche Republiek Ltd (*see also* Hatherley Distillery), 6, 48–9
Delagoa Bay, see Lourenço Marques
Dempers, J. H., 135
depression, economic (*see also* mining industry, boom and depression in)
of 1890–1, 4, 5, 11
of 1896–7, 25, 26, 32, 34, 36, 143–4, 146, 195
De Volkstem, 116
Diggelen, L. E. van, 129–30, 131
diggers, 3–4
distilleries, *see* Hatherley Distillery
disturbances, 118, 124, 190
domestic servants
demand for, 7, 18
female
relationships with 'houseboys', 34
supply of, 28, 33–4
Donovan, Detective, J. J., 66, 81, 117, 125, 126, 128, 131
drunkenness, 62–3, 95
Ducoin, George, 141, 142
Durban, prostitution in, 136–7
Dutch Reformed Church, 83, 86, 116
Duval, Henri, 52, 70, 170
Dyball's Distillery, 71

East Rand Proprietary Mines, 28
Eckstein, H. & Co., 4, 16, 22, 28, 35, 52, 82
economy, depression in, *see* depression
Ehrlich, Ludwig, 52
Employers' Domestic Native Labour Association, 34
Epler, Adolf, 52

Epstein, Harry, 143–4
Esselen, Ewald, 65, 66, 115
Europe
  agricultural surpluses and capital accumulation in, 45–5
  immigrants from, *see* immigrants
  investment in City & Suburban Tramway Co., 167
  urban public transport, 164
Evans, Samuel, 82

family life
  absence of, 5, 27
  increase in, 31, 39
fares, cab, 177, 188–9
Feirerstein, Beile, 121
Finestone syndicate, 75
FitzPatrick, J. P., 30, 34, 182, 196
forage costs, 168
Fordsburg
  concentration of cab drivers in, 174–5
  effect in of decline in cab trade, 195
  prostitution in, 146
Fordsburg Vigilance and Cab Owners' Association, 175
Franco-American gangsters, prostitution organised by, 122–4
'Frenchfontein', 112–13, 114–15, 147
Friedman, Nathan, 86
fusel oil, 55

gangsters
  organised vice controlled by, 104–5, 118–25
  post-war control of, 140–43
  success of Cleaver's attack on, 130–35
Germany
  liquor trade, 45–6, 54–5
  prostitutes from, 109
Goch, George, 64
gold (*see also* mining industry)
  discovery of, 1, 3
  low grade of, 3
  yields of, 11
Gold, Joe, 131–2
Goldmann, Charles S., 171, 180, 182
Gothenburg system, 79
government (*see also* British administration; Kruger, S. J. P.)
  legislation, *see* alcohol, restrictions on; prostitution, legislation against
  monopoly of liquor trade advocated, 79, 91
  unemployment alleviation, 22
government officials (*see also* police force)
  corruption, 76–7
Graham, T. L., 136
Gunzburg, Baron de, 170

Hamburg, 46, 54, 57, 109, 138
Hatherley Distillery (*De Eerste Fabrieken in de Zuid Afrikaansche Republiek Ltd*)
  acquisition of *Societé Française de Distillerie*, 70
  attempt by mine owners to reach settlement with, 80
  board of directors, 52
  capital investment in, 51, 52
  closure, 88–9
  compensation for shareholders, 93–4
  competition from cheaper spirits, 53–5, 67
    strategy to combat, 70–72
  development and expansion, 49–51, 53, 94
  increase in production of quality liquor, 69–70
  opposition to prohibition, 15, 68–9
  profitability, 67–8, 88
Hermann, Mrs Bertha, 122
Hertz, Dr. Joseph, 84, 138–9, 159
Heymann, Samuel, 66, 69, 100
horse tramways, *see* tramway, horse-drawn
Hoskin, William, 59
'houseboys', 18, 33–4
housing, working-class (*see also* boarding-houses; compounds), 28–9, 31, 114, 137, 153, 164
Hovent, Theodore, 141
Hunt and Auerbach, 70, 71

immigrants (*see also* gangsters; Jews; Peruvians; prostitutes, sources of)
  undesirable, deportation of, 80, 145, 149–50
Immigrants' Restriction Act (1907), 105, 145
Immorality Act (Ordinance 46, 1903), 31, 105, 140–41
'Immorality Trust', 137, 141, 143, 144
Industrial Commission of Enquiry, mining industry investigated by, 13
industrial revolution, 2
industrialisation
  as cause of prostitution, 103

contribution to success of alcohol trade, 47, 49, 51
Kruger's strategy for, 6, 9, 37–8, 61, 165
institutional accommodation, effects of, 5–8, 18
investment, *see* capital investment *and under* mining industry
Israelstam, Yeshaya, 190

Jameson Raid, 12, 13, 64, 125, 174, 177, 179
Japanese prostitutes, 138
Jews (*see also* liquor syndicates; Marks, Sammy; Nathanson, Sam; Nellmapius, A. H.; 'Peruvians'; Silver, Joe, etc.)
cab driving, 174, 187, 192, 193
economic opportunities for, 73–4
involvement in prostitution (*see also* American Club; Bowery Boys), 109–11, 137, 138
role in liquor trade (*see also* Liquor syndicates; 'Peruvians'), 45, 73, 74–8, 82, 84, 85–6, 87, 89, 96
Joffe, L., 190, 191, 192, 193
Johannesburg
economic development, 2–3, 163–4
local government powers, 14
size, 2, 30, 163, 181–2
Johannesburg Brick & Potteries Co., 20, 28
Johannesburg City & Suburban Tramway Co. Ltd., *see* City & Suburban Tramway Co. Ltd.
Johannesburg Insanitary Area Improvement Scheme (1902), 27–8
Johannesburg Protestant Ministers' Association, 115, 116, 117
Johannesburg Sanitary Board
census conducted by, 104
conflict with cab drivers, 175–8
draft regulations on prostitution, 1895, 115, 117
Joost and Gubler, 70
Josephs, Lizzie, 129
Joubert, General Piet, 65

'Kaffir Boom' (1895), 12, 16, 18, 19, 108
Karayuki-San (*see also* Japanese prostitutes), 138
Keller, William G., 169, 170, 172
Kimberley, 4, 60, 69, 106–7, 134, 173, 199
King, Mrs Ho, 146, 147
Kingsley, W. N., 188, 190, 191, 192, 193
korchma keepers (*see also* canteens), 45, 73
Krakower, David, 129–31, 132
Krause, Dr Frederick E. T., 85, 125
attitude towards prostitution, 125–6
defence of Epstein, 144
resentment of Cleaver, 128–9
Kreslo, Fanny, 121
Kruger, Tjaart, 85
Kruger, President S. J. P.
agriculturalists protected by, 9–10, 37, 165, 170, 196
appointment of liquor commission, 78
attitude towards alcohol prohibition, 15–16, 87
attitude towards mining industry, 13–14
attitude towards prostitution, 17, 106, 116–17, 128
attitude towards unemployment, 22
concessions, 37–8, 48, 61
alcohol manufacture, 6, 48
enquiries into, 30, 93, 171–2, 180, 182
tramway, 9, 165, 196
effects of Jameson Raid on, 13–14
enthusiasm for electric tramway, 170
friendship with Nellmapius, 48
friendship with Sammy Marks, 61
industrialisation strategy, 6, 9, 37–8, 61, 165
Joe Silver's unsuccessful appeal to, 134
opposition of Afrikaner progressives to, 65, 67
support for cab drivers, 177

Labour Union, 59
Landau, 179
landlords, advantages of prostitution to, 114–15
laundry, *see AmaWasha*; steam laundries
Lawley, Sir Arthur, 139, 140
Leeuwen, Dr Schagen van, 78, 80, 81, 116
Levin, Bessie, 121
Levinsohn, David, 121
Lewis, Isaac, 93, 94
Lexow Commission (1894), 110
Leyds, Dr, 117
Liquor commissions, 78–80, 87
Liquor crusade, 82–5
Liquor Licensing Boards, 58, 64

Liquor Licensing Commission, 91–2
liquor syndicates
  effect of war on, 89, 96
  lobbying by against prohibition, 87
  operation of, 74–8
  police offensive against, 85–6
  Transvaal Leader's campaign against, 82–5
Lisbon, 54, 57, 71
Lithuania
  cab drivers from, 187, 192, 193
  recruitment of prostitutes in, 121
Lombard, J. P. B.
  electric tram scheme, 169–72
London, 70, 88, 93, 102, 110–11, 119, 134, 189
  prostitute recruitment in, 121
Lourenço Marques, 20, 53, 54, 67, 70–1, 93, 108, 109, 148
  potato spirit recruited through, 55
Louw, Rev., 86, 87
lumpenproletariat, 74

MacArthur-Forrest process, 11
McCulloch, Norman, 116, 117, 127
McCullum, Sir Henry, 139
Macdonald, James Ramsey, 27
macquereaux, see pimps
Malays, 173
Marks, Sammy, 48, 49, 51, 52, 64, 73, 88, 93
  friendship with Kruger, 61
  reaction to competition and prohibition, 68–72
Martial law
  effect on liquor trade, 88–9
Mavrogordato, Major T. E., 141–2, 143, 144, 145
Meiring, Rev. P. J., 116, 117, 127
Mendelsohn, Emmanuel, 82, 83, 126
Meyer, Lukas, 65
Milner, Sir Alfred (*see also* British administration), 90, 91, 139, 141, 149, 180, 185
mine compounds, 5, 18
mine locations, 146
mine managers
  involvement in liquor trade, 60
mine owners
  attitudes towards alcohol, 6, 15–16, 52, 59–60, 62–7, 79–81, 82, 90–92, 94–5
  attitudes towards extension of Johannesburg's boundaries, 182
  attitudes towards prostitution, 7, 17
  conflict with Afrikaner ruling class, 64
  conflict with petty bourgeoisie, 82
  investment in tramway, 167
  involvement in liquor industry, 52, 80
  relationship with agriculturalists, 15, 23
  relationship with British administration, 89–92, 96
  Special Liquor Commission (1898), 80–81
  Transvaal Leader as voice of, 82–5
  unemployed Afrikaners taken on by, 22
  working-class housing provided by, 28–9
mineworkers
  accommodation, 5–8, 18, 28–9, 31, 39
  alcohol consumption, *see* alcohol
  strike, 36
mineworkers, black
  recruitment and control link with alcohol consumption, 51–2, 59–60, 94–5
  social distance from whites, 39–40
mineworkers, immigrant
  vulnerability to unemployment, 10
mining industry
  boom and depression in (*see also* depression), 3–4, 10–15, 22, 24–6
  capital investment, 3–4, 11
  confidence in restored after war, 24
  costs, 12, 24–6
    contribution of drunkenness to, 62–3, 95
  deep-level, 11, 12
  dramatic development of, 1–2
  financial crises, 10–11, 24–6
  government attitudes towards, 13–14
  group system, 11, 12
  Industrial Commission of Enquiry (1897) into, 13
  labour shortage, 33
  rationalisation, 11, 12
  technological innovations, 24–5
  technological problems, 4, 11
Morality Act (1902), 136
Morality Squad, 117–18
  bribery and corruption in, 119, 120, 126, 129
Mosenthal Sons & Co., 165
Mozambique, 5, 22, 91, 145

alcohol consumption, 46, 51, 52, 94–5
alcohol production, 53–4
alcohol trade, Sammy Marks' capture of, 70–72
Alcohol Trust, 68, 70, 71
Msane, Saul, 83
Muller, Alice, 123

Natal, prostitution in, 136–7, 139
Nathanson, George, 85–6
Nathanson, Sam, 76–7, 85, 86, 100
Nellmapius, Alois Hugho, 48
concession to manufacture alcohol granted to (*see also* Hatherley Distillery), 6, 48
concession to run tramway granted to, 9, 145
Neumann, Sigmund, 9, 52, 165
New York, 16, 109, 111, 118, 119, 122, 129, 132, 137, 141, 148
organised vice in, 110
New York Independent Benevolent Association, 137
Nineveh, Johannesburg compared to, 2
Ninevites, 23, 37
Note, Jan, 23

O'Meara, Major W., 30, 163, 180, 181, 182
Onslow, Lord, 140

Paris, 70, 122, 178
prostitutes from, 138
Parkhurst, Dr Charles, 110
Pass Regulations (1896), 13
'Peruvians'
Liquor Crusade against, 82, 84
role in illicit liquor trade, 74, 76, 77
petitions, 69, 77, 79, 91, 174, 188, 195
Phillips, Lionel, 12, 29, 39–40, 64
Pilgrim's Rest, 48
pimps
absence from early Johannesburg, 108
arrest and deportation, 144–5, 149–50
cosmopolitan nature of, 113–14
enforcement of legislation against, 128–35
harassing tactics, 124
numbers of, 143, 145
organisation of, 118–25
war with prostitutes, 143–5
police force (*see also* Morality Squad)
attempts to reform, 14, 16, 65–6, 81, 128
bribery and corruption in, 62, 81, 105, 110
ineffectiveness, 61
offensive against liquor syndicates, 85–6
'Policy of Grab', 47
Portuguese capitalists
involvement in wine trade, 71–2
Portuguese government
approval of alcohol manufacture in Mozambique, 54
potato spirits, 46, 54–5
'progressives', 65, 78
prohibition, *see* alcohol, restrictions on
proletarianisation
facilitated through alcohol consumption, 52, 95
struggle against, 7
property ownership, 29
property rentals
influence of prostitution on, 114–15, 137
prostitutes
censuses of, 104, 111–12, 145
demand for, 120, 137
deportation of, 145, 149–50
indigenous (black and Afrikaner), 146–7, 150
reclamation of, 141
recruitment of, 120–22, 137–8
sources of, 16–17, 106–7, 108–11, 112, 120–21, 137–8, 145, 148
war with pimps, 143–5
prostitution, 103–62
control by professional gangsters, 104–5, 108, 118–25
overthrow by prostitutes, 143–5
decline in, 147
development under capitalism, 148
importance in working-class culture, 5, 6–7, 16–17
in Cape Colony, 106–7, 135–6
in Natal, 136–7, 139
income from, 123–4
increase in, 32
influence on house rents, 114–15, 137
legislation against, 17–18, 31, 106–7, 115–18, 136, 137, 139–41, 149
implementation, 128–35, 142–3
ineffectiveness, 105, 118, 141
planning and organisation to circumvent, 118–25
links with liquor trade, 7, 17, 107–8

official attitudes to, 6–7, 17, 31–2, 115–18, 125–8, 148–9
post-war resurgence of, 137–8
public concern over, 104, 112, 116–17, 127, 135–6, 137, 138–9, 147
relationship to urban growth, 103
sources of information about, 113
venereal disease spread by, 114
working-class unemployment as cause of, 109, 146–7
protest march, 87, 190
public transport, *see* transport
public works programme, 22

railways
effect of improvements in on prostitution, 16, 108–9
transport riders' unemployment caused by, 20, 22
Rand Aid Association, 35
Rand Daily Mail
attack on cab drivers, 192
Rand Mines Ltd., 11, 28, 29
Rand Relief Fund, 22
Rand Unemployment Investigation Committee, 36
Rathbone, E. P., 34
reconstruction administration, *see* British administration
Regiment of the Hills (Ninevites), 23, 37
resistance (*see also* class conflict)
cultural influences on, 7
formal
anti-social gangs, 23, 37
demonstrations and meetings, 83, 188, 190–91, 192
deputations, 86–7, 177, 188
strikes, 36, 189–93
informal, *see* gangsters; liquor syndicates; vice, organised
Reitz, F. W., 171
Rhodes, Cecil, 11, 13
Roger, Auguste, 123
Rosenberg, Morris, 129, 130
Rosenchild, Henry, 129, 130
Rothschild, N. M. & Sons
investment in City & Suburban Tramway Co., 167, 168
ruling class, Afrikaner
divisions within over liquor question, 78, 79–80, 86
rum production, 53–4

Rumania, spirit distillation in, 45
Russia, 73, 74, 187
liquor trade in, 45
prostitutes from, 109–11
Russian Jews, *see* 'Peruvians'

Schumacher, R. W., 29
Schutte, D. E., 61
segregation, 173, 186
Selborne, Lord, 36, 39, 149
concern over housing shortage, 29
concern over prostitution, 142
servants, *see* domestic servants/'houseboys'
service sector employment (*see also AmaWasha*; cab trade; domestic servants)
structural changes in, 19–23, 34
sex, commercialised, *see* prostitution
sex ratio, imbalance in, 104
decline of, 31
effects of, 5, 18, 137
Shivinsky, Louis, 137, 142
Showers, E. H., 141, 142
Shrednicki, Jacob, 134
Shreiner, W. P., 135
Silver, Joe, 119, 121, 122, 127, 129, 136
arrest and trial, 131, 132–4
exposure of at Krakower's trial, 129–30
release from prison, 134
Skirving, L. B., 129
Slavin, B., 192
Smuts, Jan Christian, 14, 16, 77, 83, 126, 131,
deportation of 'undesirables', 145, 149–50
efforts to reform police force, 14, 16, 81, 128
support for Liquor Crusade, 84–5
social control
efforts of Milner administration in, 27–36, 38–9
through separation of labouring and dangerous classes, 29
through tolerance of alcohol and prostitution, 6, 32
through town planning, 29–31, 181–4, 197
Social Democratic Workers' Party, 190
Societé Française de Distillerie, 54, 70
Society for the Prevention of Crime, 110
Solomon, Richard, 139–40, 142

South African Alliance for the Reform of the Liquor Traffic, 90–91
South African Colonisation Society, 34
Special Liquor Committee, 80–81
spirits, raw
  processing of by wholesalers, 55–7
Sprigg, Sir Gordon, 118
Standard and Diggers' News, 82, 126–7, 179
  editorial on analysis of alcohol, 56–7
  opposition to night surcharge on cab fares, 177
Star, The, 185
State Attorney
  separation from post of Head of Police, 65
steam laundries, 19
Steenkamp, J. P., 67, 86
Stein, Sam, 119, 131, 132–4
Strachan, Thomas, 51
Strange, Harold, 182
strikes
  cab drivers (1905), 189–93
  white miners (1907), 36
Sylvio Villa, 123–4, 141

Tammany Society, 110, 122
taxi, motorised, 195
technology, uneven impact of, 196–7
Thornton, Samuel, 178
town planning, social control through, 29–31, 181–4, 197
Township Owners' Association, 29
tramway
  electric, 31, 164–5, 169–72, 182–4, 193–5
  horse-drawn (*see also* City & Suburban), *176*
    assets acquired by Town Council, 30–31, 182–3
    capital investment in, 165, 167, 169
    concession granted for, 9, 165
    costs and profits, 167–9
    effect of Lombard concession on, 170–72
    proposals to electrify, 9, 20, 169, 171
transport (*see also* cab trade; railways; tramway; transport riders), 9–10, 163–203
transport, public
  development under British administration, 30–31, 179–84, 197
transport riders, 10, *21*
  unemployment, 20, 22
Transvaal Concessions Commission (1901), 30, 93, 180, 182
Transvaal Indigency Commission (1906–8), 36
Transvaal Leader, 186
  Liquor Crusade by, 16, 82–5
Transvaal Medical Association, 116
Transvaal Taxi-cab Co. Ltd., 195
Transvaal Temperance Alliance, failure of, 59
Transvaal White Cross Purity League, 117
Treaty of Commerce (1875), 53
Trimble, Andrew, 66
Turner, G. K., 138

USA, 109, 170, 172
  organised vice in, 110
  prostitutes from, 137
unemployment, 195
  Afrikaners, 20, 22, 35–6, 146
  black workers, 22–3, 36–7
  contribution to prostitution, 109, 146
  official attempts to alleviate, 22
  vulnerability of miners to, 10
  white, 35–6
urban transport, *see* transport

Van den Berg, N. J., 65, 99, 108, 115
Van Leeuwen, 5, 78, 79, 80, 81, 116, 125
venereal disease, 114
vice, organised (*see also* gangsters; prostitution), 118–25
  attempts to control, 17–18, 128–35, 136, 139–43, 144–5, 149–50
  decline in, 32
  in New York, 110
  interest of capitalists in, 114–15
  public concern over, 112
  re-emergence after war, 32, 137–9
  replacement by prostitution in working-class areas, 147, 150
Victoria (cab), 179
violence
  against liquor syndicates, 82–3, 84
Vrededorp
  poverty and unemployment in, 145–6, 195
  prostitution in, 146
Vries, J. de, 178
washermen, 8, 18–19, 34–5
washing (clothes)

prohibition of within residential areas, 7–8
Wernher, Beit & Co., 4, 9, 11, 12, 29, 115, 167
'white slave' trade, *see* prostitutes, recruitment of,
wine trade, 71–2
Witwatersrand Boarding-House Keepers' Protection Association, 18
Witwatersrand Licensed Victuallers' Association, 57
opposition to prohibition, 15
prostitutes encouraged by, 7, 107
Witwatersrand Native Labour Association, 25
women
absence from early Johannesburg, 5, 18, 104, 137
proletarianisation of, 145–7
white, relationship between 'houseboys' and, 34
Woolf, Sadie, 131–2
working class
concentration of, 5, 27
culture (*see also* alcohol; prostitution), 5–7, 39–40
dispersal of, 30, 164, 181, 183, 197
family life, 5–6, 8, 27, 31, 39, 40, 114, 147
housing, 28–9
institutional accommodation, 5–8, 18
politics, turbulence of, 36
prostitution amongst, 146–7, 150
return to Johannesburg after war, 26–7

'Yellow Peril', 146–7
Yiddisher Arbeiter Bund, 187
Young Men's Christian Association, 116, 117, 127

Z.A.R., *see* S. J. P. Kruger
Zarps, *see* police force
Zulus, *see AmaWasha*; black workers; houseboys